FOR Dummies™

BESTSELLING
BOOK SERIES

Maui For Dummies
4th Edition

D0291482

Haleakala National Park

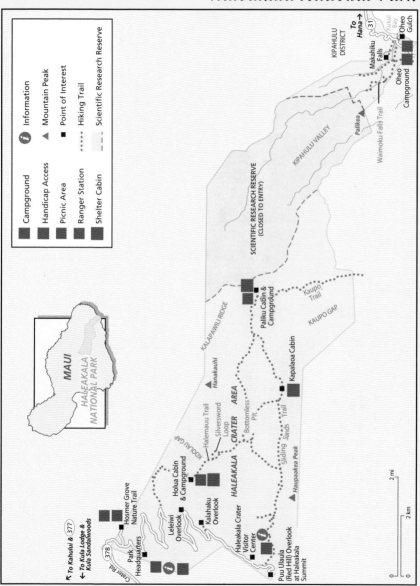

Legend:
- Campground
- Handicap Access
- Picnic Area
- Ranger Station
- Shelter Cabin
- (i) Information
- ▲ Mountain Peak
- ■ Point of Interest
- ····· Hiking Trail
- Scientific Research Reserve

To Kahului & 377
← To Kula Lodge & Kula Sandalwoods

MAUI
HALEAKALA NATIONAL PARK

Crater Rd.
378
Park Headquarters
Hosmer Grove Nature Trail
Leleiwi Overlook
Holua Cabin & Campground
Kalahaku Overlook
KOOLAU GAP
Halemauu Trail
Silversword Loop
Bottomless Pit
HALEAKALA CRATER AREA
KALAPAWILI RIDGE
Hanakauhi ▲
Sliding Sands Trail
Haupaakea Peak ▲
Haleakala Crater Visitor Center
Puu Ulaula (Red Hill) Overlook at Haleakala Summit
Kapalaoa Cabin
Paliku Cabin & Campground
Kaupo Trail
KAUPO GAP
SCIENTIFIC RESEARCH RESERVE (CLOSED TO ENTRY)
KIPAHULU VALLEY
Palikea ▲
Waimoku Falls Trail
KIPAHULU DISTRICT
To Hana → 31
Kukui Bay
Oheo Gulch
Makahiku Falls
Oheo Campground

0   2 mi
0   2 km

Central Maui

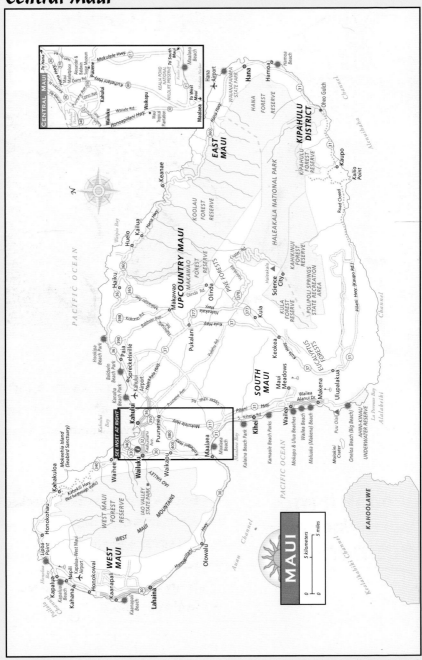

FOR DUMMIES

The fun and easy way™ to travel!

U.S.A.

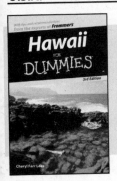

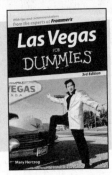

Also available:

Alaska For Dummies
Arizona For Dummies
Boston For Dummies
California For Dummies
Chicago For Dummies
Colorado & the Rockies For Dummies
Florida For Dummies
Los Angeles & Disneyland For Dummies
Maui For Dummies
National Parks of the American West For Dummies

New Orleans For Dummies
New York City For Dummies
San Francisco For Dummies
Seattle & the Olympic Peninsula For Dummies
Washington, D.C. For Dummies
RV Vacations For Dummies
Walt Disney World & Orlando For Dummies

EUROPE

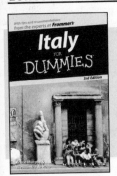

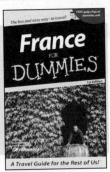

Also available:

England For Dummies
Europe For Dummies
Germany For Dummies
Ireland For Dummies
London For Dummies

Paris For Dummies
Scotland For Dummies
Spain For Dummies

OTHER DESTINATIONS

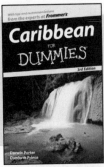

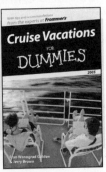

Also available:

Bahamas For Dummies
Cancun & the Yucatan For Dummies
Costa Rica For Dummies
Mexico's Beach Resorts For Dummies
Montreal & Quebec City For Dummies
Vancouver & Victoria For Dummies

WILEY

Maui
FOR
DUMMIES®
4TH EDITION

by Cheryl Farr Leas

WILEY

Wiley Publishing, Inc.

Maui For Dummies® 4th Edition

Published by
Wiley Publishing, Inc.
111 River St.
Hoboken, NJ 07030-5774
www.wiley.com

For general information on our other products and services, please contact our Customer Care Department within the U.S. at 800-762-2974, outside the U.S. at 317-572-3993, or fax 317-572-4002.

For technical support, please visit www.wiley.com/techsupport.

Wiley also publishes its books in a variety of electronic formats. Some content that appears in print may not be available in electronic books.

ISBN: 978-0-470-39321-5

Manufactured in the United States of America

10 9 8 7 6 5 4 3 2 1

WILEY

About the Author

Cheryl Farr Leas may live on the mainland, but she's a Hawaii girl at heart. She fell in love with Diamond Head, aloha wear, and mai tais in 1994 and has had trouble staying away ever since. Whenever she's not on the islands, she and her husband, Rob, make their home in Phoenix, Arizona, where they love to hike the desert mountains with their German Shepherd, Caleb.

Before embarking on a writing career, Cheryl served as senior editor at Macmillan Travel (now Wiley), where she edited the *Frommer's Hawaii* travel guides for the better part of the 1990s. Now happy to be a globetrotting branding consultant and writer, Cheryl also writes *Hawaii For Dummies.*

Dedication

This book is for Rob, for loving Maui as much as I do.

Author's Acknowledgments

Thanks to Lisa Renaud for her encouragement and assistance throughout the years, and to Tiffany Ewing for her diligent assistance. Also, thanks to the many Maui-based partners who made this book possible with their kind assistance, generous support, and genuine warmth.

Publisher's Acknowledgments

We're proud of this book; please send us your comments through our Dummies online registration form located at www.dummies.com/register/.

Some of the people who helped bring this book to market include the following:

Editorial

Editors: Christina Summers,
   Development Editor;
   Heather Wilcox, Production Editor

Copy Editor: Elizabeth Kuball

Cartographer: Andrew Murphy

Editorial Assistant:
   Jessica Langan-Peck

Senior Photo Editor: Richard Fox

Cover Photos:
   Front: © Ron Dahlquist/
      Getty Images
   Back: © Photo Resource Hawaii/
      DanitaDelimont.com

Cartoons: Rich Tennant
   (www.the5thwave.com)

Composition Services

Project Coordinator:
   Patrick Redmond

Layout and Graphics: Carl Byers,
   Christine Williams

Proofreaders: Cara Buitron,
   John Greenough

Indexer: Potomac Indexing LLC

Special Help: Christine Ryan

Publishing and Editorial for Consumer Dummies

Diane Graves Steele, Vice President and Publisher, Consumer Dummies

Kristin Ferguson-Wagstaffe, Product Development Director, Consumer Dummies

Kelly Regan, Editorial Director, Travel

Publishing for Technology Dummies

Andy Cummings, Vice President and Publisher, Dummies Technology/General User

Composition Services

Debbie Stailey, Director of Composition Services

Contents at a Glance

Maps at a Glance

Table of Contents

Part V: The Part of Tens 311

Chapter 18: Ten Steps to Incredible Island Dining ...313

Chapter 19: Ten Ways to Lose the Tourist Trappings and Look Like a Local................324

Introduction

1 have excellent news if you're planning a trip to Hawaii: Maui really does live up to the hype. Considered to be among the finest beach vacation destinations in the world, Maui can fulfill everyone's unique island dream, whether you're 6 or 60, single or with family in tow, the *Survivor* type or a newly minted millionaire. Enjoyment is just a matter of knowing what you want from your Maui vacation and how to make it happen.

Planning a trip to Maui is easy — too easy, in fact. Far too many people head off blindly, without bothering to tailor a one-size-fits-all vacation to their own needs, tastes, and desires. So just knowing that you want to look before you leap puts you well ahead of the pack.

And picking up this guidebook shows that you have the right instincts about your vacation planning.

About This Book

Maui For Dummies, 4th Edition, separates the wheat from the chaff — or the husk from the pineapple. An island vacation, after all, is supposed to be relaxing and fun. Your trip planning should be easy and fun, too.

I've done all the legwork for you, and your vacation will benefit accordingly. I'm not afraid to share my honest opinions, so you can make easy, informed decisions about what to include in your island vacation — and, even more important, what *not* to include. You work hard to set aside a few precious weeks of vacation time, and I don't want you wasting it. Chances are good that you don't want to waste it either.

Everyone's tastes and needs differ, of course. In the following pages, I give you the tools — just what you need, not too much — so that you can make smart decisions about where to spend your hard-earned time and money. I try to give you the clearest picture of your choices and options so you can make informed decisions easily and efficiently.

Because this book is a reference guide, you don't need to read it from cover to cover — unless you want to, of course. Instead, start at any point and flip to the parts that specifically address how you want to spend your vacation time and money. This way, you can concentrate on finding exactly what you want to know at any given time.

Think of building your Maui vacation like assembling a jigsaw puzzle. This book helps you find just the right puzzle pieces so that they interlock smoothly. The finished product will reflect the vacation you and your family want, not somebody else's image of what your island paradise should be.

Conventions Used in This Book

The structure of this book is nonlinear: Feel free to dig in anywhere. I list hotels and restaurants alphabetically, with actual prices and frank evaluations to make your search easy and well-informed.

I also include general pricing information to help you decide where to unpack your bags, where to dine, and what activities to enjoy, although keep in mind that those prices are subject to change. Still, even if prices do change during the lifetime of this edition, the information you have at your fingertips gives you a good idea of what to expect.

In order to help you find accommodations, restaurants, and activities within your budget, I use a system of dollar signs that you can quickly scan. These symbols show a general range of costs for one night in a hotel or one meal at a restaurant (including appetizer, entree, dessert, one drink, taxes, and tip). Use the following table as your guide to deciphering the dollar signs:

Cost	Hotel	Restaurant
$	Less than $150	Less than $20
$$	$150–$224	$20–$34
$$$	$225–$324	$35–$49
$$$$	$325–$449	$50–$74
$$$$$	$450 or more	$75 or more

In addition, I use these abbreviations for credit cards:

AE: American Express

DC: Diners Club

DISC: Discover

MC: MasterCard

V: Visa

To make pertinent information — such as attractions and main telephone numbers — stand out, I put them in bold typeface.

Foolish Assumptions

As I wrote this book, I made some assumptions about you and your needs as a traveler:

✔ You may be an inexperienced traveler looking for guidance when determining whether to take a trip to Maui and how to plan for it.

✔ You may be an experienced traveler who hasn't had much time to explore Maui or its beaches. You want expert advice when you finally do get a chance to enjoy them.

✔ You're not looking for a book that overwhelms you with all the information available about Maui. You don't have time to wade through a gigantic list of every single hotel, restaurant, or attraction out there. Instead, you want to zero in on the very best places or most unique experiences on Maui.

If you fit any of these criteria, then *Maui For Dummies,* 4th Edition, is the book you've been waiting for!

How This Book Is Organized

Maui For Dummies, 4th Edition, is divided into five parts, plus an information-packed appendix called the Quick Concierge. You can read each chapter or part without reading the preceding chapter, but as you read, I may refer you to other chapters for more information on certain subjects.

Part 1: Introducing Maui

This first part gives you an overview of what Maui is like, so you can start getting excited about all the fun that lies ahead. It includes

✔ An easy-to-scan list of the very best of the best — my personal picks of Maui's top hotels, restaurants, beaches, golf courses, and more

✔ A quick overview of Hawaiian history and culture

✔ An introduction to Hawaiian foods and traditions (How else do you know whether you want the saimin, the *poke,* or the *opakapaka* — and whether you want to save room for a little *haupia* for dessert?)

✔ Time-tested advice on how to divide your time so that you see the best of Maui without sacrificing that all-important beach and relaxation time

✔ The details on when to go: A complete calendar of events, tips on avoiding the crowds, and the lowdown on Maui's weather patterns

Part 11: Planning Your Trip to Maui

In this part, I get down to serious trip preparation, including

✔ How much you can expect your trip to cost and how to find great deals

✔ The pros and cons of planning your trip on your own, using a travel agent, and buying an all-inclusive package deal

- The ins and outs of flying to Maui

- Special considerations for families, seniors, travelers with disabilities, and gay and lesbian travelers

- A how-to guide for couples who want to tie the knot in the Aloha State

- Tips for getting ready to go, from the pluses and minuses of buying travel insurance to renting cars to making advance luau reservations to *akamai* (smart) packing tips

Part III: Settling Into Maui

This part covers everything you need for your trip, including

- Navigating Maui's airport

- Driving around Maui and figuring out the island's geographical layout

- The very best places to stay: hotels, resorts, B&Bs, and condos in all price ranges

- No-holds-barred reviews of Maui's best restaurants, whether you want a gorgeous oceanfront setting or a funky local joint, Maui's best burger or sophisticated Hawaiian regional cuisine

Part IV: Exploring Maui

You came to Maui for this part, didn't you? Here, I show you the most beautiful places on Maui and tell you all about the island's best adventures and activities, including

- An array of beautiful beaches

- Watersports galore, including fabulous snorkel cruises

- Amazing whale-watching

- Otherworldly Haleakala National Park

- The scenic drive along the Heavenly Road to Hana

- A complete shopper's guide

- The lowdown on where to party when the sun goes down

Maui has an incredible array of attractions, but some curious travelers may want to venture off the beaten path to explore two destinations that are among Hawaii's best-kept secrets:

- Molokai, where your own trusty mule carries you on an unforgettable journey down lush sea cliffs to discover a hidden leper colony

- Lanai, where two world-class luxury hotels offer you the chance to truly get away from it all

Part V: The Part of Tens

Every *For Dummies* book has a Part of Tens. If Parts I through IV are the meat of a travel meal, think of these fun top-ten-list chapters as dessert.

Chapter 18 gives you the lowdown on Maui's fabulous dining scene. You find a menu guide to Hawaii's incredible seafood, tips on what to expect at a luau, and hints on how to enjoy authentic local foods and traditions.

Chapter 19 tells you how to ditch the tourists in order to look and act like a local, with tips on everything from how to pronounce those tongue-twisting place names to getting to know a few points of island-style etiquette.

Chapter 20 focuses on everybody's favorite topic — romance! I provide some tips to make your romantic getaway unforgettable.

Quick Concierge

The Quick Concierge puts facts about Maui at your fingertips, from the lowdown on taxes to Web sites with accurate online weather forecasts and everything in between. You also get toll-free numbers and Web addresses for major airlines, car-rental agencies, and hotel chains for easy reference. And, in case you want more information, I give you the contact numbers for all the local visitor bureaus you may want to consult.

Icons Used in This Book

Think of the following icons as signposts. I use them to highlight especially helpful advice and to draw your attention to features you don't want to miss.

This icon points out useful advice on things to do and ways to schedule your time.

Watch for this icon to identify annoying or potentially dangerous situations, such as tourist traps, rip-offs, time-wasters, and other things to avoid.

This icon highlights attractions, hotels, restaurants, or activities that are particularly hospitable to children or people traveling with kids.

This icon highlights money-saving tips or particularly great values.

Money is no object with this icon, which indicates the absolute finest places and experiences that Maui has to offer.

This icon indicates well-guarded *kamaaina* (local) advice that will give you the edge over *malihini* (newcomers) who don't know better.

Where to Go from Here

As you read through this book and start to formulate your vacation, remember: The planning really *is* half the fun. Don't think of choosing your accommodations and solidifying the details as a chore. Make the homebound part of the process a voyage of discovery, and you'll end up with an experience that's rewarding, enriching, and relaxing — *really.* Have a blast with it. Happy planning!

Part I
Introducing Maui

In this part . . .

This part of the book introduces you to the wonders of Maui. You'll discover why so many people are drawn to the magical Valley Isle, and you'll begin to shape the basic outlines of your trip. I'll help you figure out when to go, with information on Maui's climate, its least crowded (and least expensive) seasons, and a full calendar of special events.

Chapter 1

Discovering the Best of Maui

· ·

· ·

*I*n Maui, every day can be a slice of paradise. Here, everybody can feel like royalty: A simple beach apartment can be your castle; a fresh papaya and a cup of robust Maui-grown joe, your princely breakfast; a joyous aloha shirt, your royal robe.

Each of the places and experiences listed in this chapter are bound to have you exclaiming, *"No ka oi!"* ("It's the best!"). This chapter gives you a sneak peek at the absolute best that Maui has to offer — the cream of the crop. Skim them all and whet your appetite. And keep your eyes out for the Best of the Best icons throughout this book.

The Best Luxury Accommodations

Even if you want a different type of accommodations, such as a luxury condo or bed-and-breakfast, Maui's luxury scene can accommodate you. The following are a few of my favorite luxury accommodations:

✔ **Fairmont Kea Lani:** Not only is this fanciful Moorish palace on the sand one of the finest, most romantic, and most relaxing hotels in the islands, but it gives you much more for your money than Maui's other luxury resorts do. For the same price as a standard hotel room at other places — and sometimes less — here you'll enjoy a large one-bedroom suite with a luxurious living room, a complete entertainment system (including stereo and DVD player), and a huge marble bathroom. And there's hardly a better place to unwind. See Chapter 10.

✔ **Four Seasons Resort Maui:** This resort isn't my favorite on Maui — the Grand Wailea is grander and the Fairmont Kea Lani is a better value in the luxury category — but there's no arguing with the star power of this ultradeluxe hotel. The guestrooms are oversized, service is exceptional, and don't be surprised if you recognize a famous face or two lounging by the pool. However, beware of those "oceanview" rooms that overlook the driveway — they can put the kibosh on your island-perfect mood. See Chapter 10.

✔ **Grand Wailea Resort & Spa:** Many tout the reserved understatement of the neighboring Four Seasons, but I'm underwhelmed. Instead, I prefer this grand beach palace, with its exclusive, tropical, theme-park vibe; playtime ambience; and over-the-top treats at every turn. Hawaii's best pool complex awaits your (very lucky) kids, and you can indulge in the islands' finest spa. The ultradeluxe Napua Tower offers extra amenities, such as personalized concierge service. See Chapter 10.

✔ **Hooilo House:** Perched on a breezy hill above the West Maui coast is this elegant Balinese-style bed-and-breakfast, with six custom-designed suites and graceful open-air public spaces for romance-seeking couples who can afford to enjoy them. I have a few quibbles — why no hot tub? — but there's no denying the tranquility of this intimate, romantic retreat. See Chapter 10.

✔ **Hotel Hana-Maui:** Rejoice, for the Hotel Hana-Maui is glorious once again. After years in the doldrums, this breathtaking resort at the end of the heavenly Hana Highway has been reborn as a luxurious haven of genuine Hawaiiana, thanks to the folks behind Big Sur's Post Ranch Inn. This easygoing yet elegant hideaway on 62 expansive oceanfront acres is reason enough to cruise to the remotest end of the island. Book a Sea Ranch Cottage for a few days if you really want to slow down and recharge. The intimate Honua Spa only adds to the ecstasy. See Chapter 10.

✔ **Kaanapali Alii:** Luxury condo living hardly gets better than this high-rise beachfront condo complex — and with princely sizes between 1,500 and 1,900 square feet, the whole family can make themselves at home. Prices are high, but so is quality; and you'll get far more luxury for your money than you would if you and the kids are shoehorned into a pricey hotel room or two. An excellent choice for families and couples alike. See Chapter 10.

The Best Good-Value Beachfront Accommodations

Maui is full of wonderful expensive hotels on the sand. However, you can also find plenty of good-value beachfront accommodations on this diverse island:

✔ **Kaanapali Beach Hotel:** This charming, older, beachfront hotel is the last hotel left in Hawaii that gives you a real resort experience at a moderate price. The resort brims with genuine aloha spirit and good value — and the on-the-beach location can't be beat. See Chapter 10.

✔ **Koa Lagoon:** This delightful condo complex just may be the top bargain of the Kihei coast. This midrise building has 42 units — all with a breathtaking oceanfront setting, with views that most visitors have to pay much more to enjoy. See Chapter 10.

✔ **Mauian Napili Beach Hotel:** This family-run hotel may not be fancy, but it sure is a great deal for the money. And there's no arguing the quality of the location — on a fabulous half-mile-long stretch of white-sand beach with great swimming and snorkeling. See Chapter 10.

✔ **Napili Bay:** These petite studios on the sand are among Hawaii's best beachfront bargains — and they're an even better deal considering their prime location. The beach is gorgeous; the snorkeling, prime; the units, thoughtfully outfitted; and the value, even better. See Chapter 10.

✔ **Noelani Condominium Resort:** This top-notch, oceanfront condo complex is both an excellent value and a really enjoyable place to stay. Every unit boasts an ocean view and all the comforts of home. See Chapter 10.

✔ **The Whaler on Kaanapali Beach:** This well-maintained, 1970s luxury condo complex sits front and center on golden Kaanapali Beach, making it the ideal island home for travelers who want home-style comforts. The individually owned condos are comfortable, quiet, and wonderfully located, and a much better value than your average oceanfront hotel room. See Chapter 10.

The Best Restaurants

The increasingly sophisticated Valley Isle rivals Oahu as the fine-dining island of choice for vacationing gourmands. Whether you want a casual burger or a lavish meal with fine wine, Maui's got just the ticket.

The island's waters are so pristine that the wealth of fabulous seafood on Maui's menus should come as no surprise. What you may not have expected is the degree to which Maui's chefs celebrate the bounty of this fertile island, showcasing its fresh produce and tropical fruits.

Maui's location at the crossroads of the Pacific also guarantees that you can enjoy an incredible culinary adventure, sampling an authentic taste of Japan, China, Vietnam, Thailand, and Malaysia.

Whether you're looking to celebrate a special occasion or mapping out a culinary calendar for the length of your stay, don't overlook these fabulous restaurants:

✔ **Haiilimaile General Store:** Star chef Bev Gannon, the queen of Hawaii Regional Cuisine, continues to deliver one of Hawaii's finest all-around dining experiences — top-quality, island-style cooking joyfully presented in a refreshingly casual and pretension-free setting. A delight from start to finish and well worth the drive Upcountry. See Chapter 12.

✔ **Lahaina Grill:** This Lahaina mainstay still shines as one of most glorious dining experiences in the Hawaiian Islands. Lahaina Grill gets it all just right, from the pretty sophistication of the dining room to the beautifully prepared, generously portioned dishes to the first-rate service that perfectly fuses personal warmth and professionalism. Special-occasion restaurants hardly come finer than this. See Chapter 11.

✔ **Mama's Fish House:** My absolute favorite choice on Maui is this delightful seafood house, which offers a magical combination of food, ambience, and service. Sure, prices are high — but the tiki-room setting is an archetype of timeless Hawaii cool, the beach-front setting is glorious, and fresh island fish simply doesn't get any better than this. See Chapter 11.

✔ **Roy's Kahana Bar & Grill/Roy's Kihei:** Nobody should miss the opportunity to eat at one of the restaurants of Roy Yamaguchi, king of Hawaii Regional Cuisine. This liege is still at the top of the heap in the Pacific culinary world, and his food still shines. No matter which dining room you choose, you'll find a casual ambience, friendly service, and an oversized menu of dim sum, appetizers, *imu*-baked (underground luau-style) pizzas, and creative main courses that allow you to eat as special-occasion or affordably as you want. See Chapter 11.

✔ **Sansei Seafood Restaurant & Sushi Bar:** Maui chef D. K. Kodama's two superstar sushi bars offer some of the finest dining in the islands. Choose from an adventurous sushi menu, or opt for family-style dining on a slate of D. K.'s palate-stimulating, Euro-Asian, signature creations. Best of all, the restaurants are casually comfortable, service is always a delight, and it's easy to keep the bill within reason. You can't go wrong with Sansei. See Chapter 11.

The Best Beaches

Maui boasts an array of wide, breathtaking beaches — more than 80 in all. Luxurious, golden sands stretch beside calm, turquoise waters, while palm trees sway in the wind. These settings are what make great vacations. Even in the most crowded months, you can easily stake out your own little slice of paradise.

And not that you need any more incentive, but Maui's best resort coasts face west, so you can mosey over to a beachfront bar right on the sands and conclude your day by toasting a Technicolor sunset.

✔ **Baldwin Beach Park:** This off-the-beaten-path beach is the perfect place to spend the day away from the crowds. Pick up a picnic lunch, bring a blanket, and stretch out on the sand — you've found the perfect place to bask in the Maui sun. Heed the lifeguard warnings, though — the surf can get rough here, especially in the winter. See Chapter 12.

✔ **Hamoa Beach:** This remote, half-moon-shaped beach near the end of the Hana Road is one of the most breathtakingly lovely in all of Hawaii. The beach is generally good for swimming and wave-riding in the gentle seasons, but stick close to the shore because you're in open, unprotected ocean. Stay out of the water entirely in the winter. See Chapter 12.

✔ **Hookipa Beach Park:** Come to watch the world's best windsurfers pirouette over white-capped waves at this glorious North Shore beach. Surfers have eminent domain in the mornings; the colorful windsurfers take over in the afternoons. The action is equally breathtaking at any time of day, especially when the winter waves are in top form. See Chapter 12.

✔ **Kaanapali Beach:** This fabulous, crescent-shaped beach is reminiscent of the Waikiki of yesteryear, before the entire world made it their destination of choice. There's something for everyone here: crystal-clear snorkeling, thrilling wave-jumping, golden sands inviting hours of sunbathing, even beachfront bars for that perfect, middle-of-the-day mai tai. See Chapter 12.

✔ **Oneloa (Big) Beach:** *Oneloa* means "long sand" in Hawaiian, and locals call it Big Beach. It comes by both names honestly, for this gorgeous crescent of white sand is 3,300 feet long, more than 100 feet wide, and is a beautiful spot for swimming, sunbathing, surfing, body-boarding, or just hanging out and strolling along the picture-perfect shoreline. See Chapter 12.

The Best Activities and Attractions

The sheer variety of watersports available — diving, surfing, body-boarding, kayaking — is astounding. What are you waiting for? Go on, get out and explore the great blue ocean.

✔ **Diving Molokini:** This sunken volcanic crater is one of Hawaii's top dive spots thanks to calm, clear, protected waters; an abundance of marine life — from reef dwellers to manta rays — and exciting viewing opportunities for every level of diver, even first-timers. You don't dive, and you're not ready to learn? No worries — Molokini offers excellent viewing for snorkelers, too. Molokini is only reachable by boat, so see Chapter 12 for recommended outfitters.

✔ **Driving the Heavenly Road to Hana:** Hawaii's most spectacular drive is well worth a day of your vacation. For 52 winding miles, this blissful highway takes you past flowering gardens, spectacular waterfalls, and magnificent ocean vistas. Start early and keep in mind that it's all about the drive, not about getting to the end of the road. Rent a convertible for maximum effect. See Chapter 13.

✔ **Exploring otherworldly Haleakala on horseback:** The best way to experience this desolate, otherworldly canyon — painted in hues of blue and green and red — is to delve deep into the crater with **Pony Express Tours,** which leads excellent and informative trail rides along Sliding Sands Trail into the heart of the volcano on well-trained and well-cared-for horses. See Chapter 13.

✔ **Exploring Upcountry Maui:** Discover the Valley Isle's bucolic side on the slopes of Haleakala, where beaches, condos, and tourists give way to verdant fields dotted with purple-flowering jacarandas and grazing cattle; rambling, plantation-style ranches; rural towns; and friendly, local-style warmth. You can experience the inner workings of Maui's agricultural heartland at such Upcountry attractions as Alii Kula Lavender Farm and Surfing Goat Dairy. See Chapter 13.

✔ **Getting a bird's-eye view:** Touring Maui by helicopter gives you a whole new perspective as you swoop over the island's otherwise inaccessible heartland, where nature has been unspoiled by modern man. You'll scale the desolate peak of Haleakala National Park and enjoy a breathtaking view of the road to Hana that takes an hour instead of a day. It's expensive but worth it. See Chapter 13.

✔ **Hitting the links:** If you love golf, don't miss the opportunity to play at least one of Maui's premier courses. Glorious Kapalua is the best, but you have a bounty of quality courses to choose from, duffers. See Chapter 13.

✔ **Learning to surf:** Believe it or not, surfing is easier than it looks — and there's hardly a feeling finer than conquering a wave. A number of good surfing schools guarantee that you'll be hanging ten in a single two-hour lesson. My Maui favorite is the **Nancy C. Emerson School of Surfing.** See Chapter 12.

✔ **Saying "aahh . . ." at the spa:** What's the icing on the cake of any vacation? A pampering spa day, of course. On Maui, nobody does it bigger and better than **Spa Grande,** a temple to the good life, where the hydrotherapy circuit is reason enough to come. For something different, try the petite but magical **Maui Spa Retreat,** a hidden Upcountry gem that made me finally understand the magic of aromatherapy. See Chapter 13.

✔ **Shopping the Valley Isle:** Maui has become a premier shopping destination, especially for those who eschew traditional chains for boutiques that are artful, offbeat, or unique. The charming, funky surf town of Paia and sophisticated, cowboy-infused Makawao are best for creative spirits, while Kaanapali's Whaler's Village and the Shops at Wailea offer creative choices and art-filled galleries in elegant, open-air environments. See Chapter 14.

✔ **Snorkeling:** Even if you're not usually the sporting type, you don't want to miss the chance to try snorkeling on Maui. The waters offshore are so clear that snorkelers are guaranteed to see clouds of tropical fish in every color of the rainbow, and possibly even a green turtle or two. You can see a stunningly beautiful underwater world. See Chapter 12.

✔ **Visiting Haleakala National Park:** The massive, 10,023-foot-high dormant volcano that sits at the heart of the Valley Isle is Maui's biggest natural attraction. Its crater looks like a barren moonscape; no wonder NASA's astronauts have used it for space-exploration training. Haleakala is best known for its mystical sunrise vistas, as crowds of visitors arrive in the dark at predawn hours to watch the spectacle of dawn breaking over the crater. But take heed, early-morning-phobes: You can enjoy this wondrous park at any time of day. See Chapter 13 for details.

✔ **Whale-watching with the Pacific Whale Foundation:** Whale-watching is a premier activity in the islands from mid-December to mid-March; in some lucky years, the great humpbacks remain in Hawaii's warm waters into April. Boats are available to take you whale-watching, but I love the Pacific Whale Foundation for its excellent naturalist guides and its commitment to protecting these gentle giants. The foundation also operates a **Whale Information Station** on the road to Lahaina, where you can spot humpbacks from shore, with an expert, for absolutely free. The Pacific Whale Foundation can also take you out on terrific snorkel cruises year-round, even when the whales aren't in town. See Chapter 12.

The Best Luaus

The best luaus are in high demand, so book your spots before you leave home to ensure access:

✔ **The Feast at Lele:** The folks behind the Old Lahaina Luau (see the following bullet) also operate this interesting twist on a traditional luau. The Feast at Lele is an excellent alternative for romance-seeking couples or anyone who would prefer a luau with a more upscale demeanor, a more intimate setting, and/or a fine-dining twist. The multicourse meal and thrilling performance troupe reach beyond the Hawaii tradition to celebrate the food and culture of the South Seas as well, and the beachfront setting can't be beat. See Chapter 11.

✔ **Old Lahaina Luau:** Hawaii's most authentic and acclaimed luau is justifiably celebrated and a real treat to experience. Come early to watch craftspeople at work in the lovely oceanfront setting; you can also watch as the luau pig is unearthed from its underground oven, where it's been slow-cooking all day. The live hula show is dazzling. You simply can't do better than this. See Chapter 11.

Chapter 2

Digging Deeper into Maui

- -

In This Chapter

▶ Discovering the fascinating story of Hawaii's past
▶ Experiencing the joys of island-style dining
▶ Mastering a few key Hawaiian words and phrases

- -

*Y*ou've had a stressful day at the office. The kids have been driving you crazy, and you realize that everybody in the family needs a break. Or maybe you've just had it with gray skies and gloomy weather.

Then the idea comes, and it's a gem: *Maui*. Ah, Maui.

Just thinking about a Maui vacation warms the soul, doesn't it? Turquoise ocean, white sand, toasty sun. Surfers riding crested waves as emerald-green cliffs rise up to meet a sweet, blue sky. Palm trees swaying in the breeze as the strum of a slack-key guitar carries you into tropical reverie. . . .

Vacation is the ultimate antidote to the stresses and strains of daily life — and no destination is more relaxing and restorative than Maui. On this exquisite and exciting island, days of soaking up the sun are interwoven with adventure and plenty of friendly *aloha* (an all-purpose greeting meaning "hello," "welcome," or "goodbye").

Introducing the Valley Isle

The Hawaiian Islands are just a hair's breadth larger, in total landmass, than the state of Connecticut — but oh, what glorious square miles they are. The islands are actually the summits of underwater volcanoes that have grown tall enough, in geologic time, to peek above the waves. (All the volcanoes are dormant except for two on the Big Island.) A volcanic core gives each island a breathtakingly rugged, mountainous heart.

Most of the island development is at sea level, along the sunny coastal fringe of each island. Thanks to Hawaii's proximity to the equator, those coastal areas experience near-perfect weather year-round: temperatures in the low 80s, clear skies, and gentle trade winds.

The eight main islands are Oahu (oh-*wa*-hoo), the hub of the Hawaii island chain, and the "neighbor" islands: Maui (*mow*-ee); Hawaii, or the Big Island, as it's commonly called; Kauai (ka-*wah*-ee); Molokai (mo-lok-*eye*); Lanai (la-*nah*-ee); Niihau (nee-*ee*-how); and Kahoolawe (ka-hoo-o-*la*-we). These islands make up more than 99 percent of the state's landmass.

Oahu is the most populous of the islands, but Maui is the most popular, hands down. When people think Hawaiian paradise, they usually think Maui. Almost everyone who comes to Maui falls in love with the island, and for good reason: The Valley Isle offers the ideal mix of unspoiled natural beauty and tropical sophistication, with action-packed fun and laid-back island style.

Here are just a few breathtaking facts about this wondrous isle: Maui has 81 accessible beaches — with more miles of swimmable beaches than any other Hawaiian island. At the island's heart sits a national park — featuring Haleakala, the world's largest dormant volcano. About 3,000 humpback whales visit Maui every winter — out of the 8,000 that populate the entire planet. It's no wonder that the readers of *Condé Nast Traveler* vote Maui "Best Island in the World," year after year after year — 13 out of the past 14 years. That same poll even crowned Maui as the "World's Best Travel Destination" in 2005.

Maui does have a few caveats, however. The Valley Isle is more like the mainland than any other place in Hawaii (yes, even Honolulu, Hawaii's capital and biggest city). There's even some L.A.-style traffic. (Because Maui generally has only one main road going in each direction, traffic can be worse at times in the Valley Isle's prime resort areas than it is on Oahu.) The highways and minimalls look comfortingly familiar, or annoyingly so — it all depends on your perspective.

Although hotels have a bit more breathing room on Maui than they do in Waikiki, the shoulder-to-shoulder resort development is far more urban than what you find on the Big Island or Kauai. Maui also has the highest-profile population of relocated mainlanders. A quicker pace of living prevails, which can make Maui feel more like Southern California than Hawaii, especially in the resort areas. Touristy cheesiness has invaded the old whaling town of Lahaina, and Kihei's dominant architectural style is high strip mall.

Still, nothing can dull the sheen on Maui, which oozes sex appeal. There's enough excitement and activity to keep even the most go-go-go travelers constantly on their toes. And the mainland-style development doesn't detract from the island's natural beauty.

Maui really is a tropical paradise, with golden beaches, misty tropical cliffs, and countless waterfalls along the Heavenly Road to Hana, one of the most spectacular drives in the United States. Offshore are two of Hawaii's finest snorkel and dive spots. Onshore, at the summit of one of the island's two great mountains (between which lies the valley for

Maui

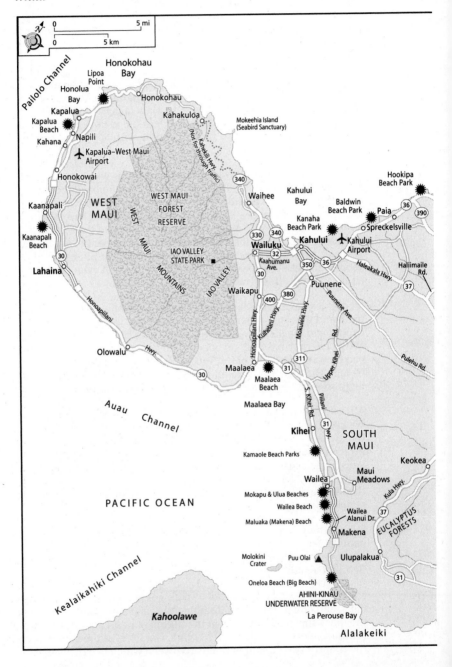

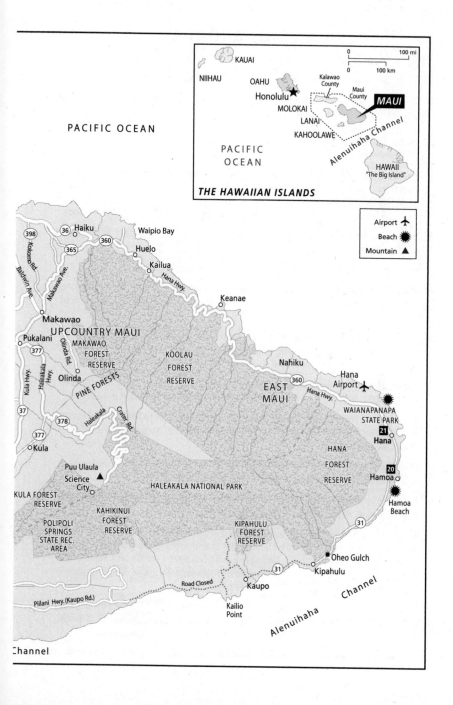

Maui pros and cons

Here are some of Maui's pros, with just a few cons that you should be aware of:

✔ **The Valley Isle boasts abundant, wide, breathtaking beaches.**

✔ **Maui wows with its sheer variety of great snorkel, dive, and learn-to-surf spots.** One caveat: Molokini, a sunken offshore crater that's world famous for snorkeling and diving, has lost a great deal of its appeal because of shoulder-to-shoulder snorkel boats and a worn-down reef. The Big Island's Kealakekua is a much better snorkel-cruise destination.

✔ **Despite its popularity and high resort rates, Maui has a decent number of beach-front bargains.** If you don't want to go condo, which is probably your best value-for-dollar bet, try the Kaanapali Beach Hotel, one of my midrange faves. Still, you're likely to pay more for accommodations here than you do on other islands.

✔ **Maui has enough world-class golf courses to keep club-wielders happy for a good, long time.**

✔ **The windsurfers at Maui's Hookipa Beach are a blast to watch.**

✔ **Maui is the humpbacks' favorite place to hang offshore.** If you show up during prime whale season (Jan–Mar), you're bound to see them, even if you don't head out to sea.

✔ **This action-packed island wins for its wealth of kid-friendly condos and beaches, plus family activities galore.** Your kids will wonder why you haven't come here before.

✔ **Outdoor fun is the name of the game here.** There's something new to do around every corner, from riding a bike down a volcano to taking a snorkel cruise.

✔ **If you have a yen to frolic among waterfalls, head straight to Maui.** The drive to Hana is chock-full of fabulous falls, and at the end of the road is the granddaddy of 'em all, Oheo Gulch.

✔ **Maui boasts an innovative dining scene, from casual to chic — and with a wealth of beautifully situated oceanfront restaurants to boot.**

✔ **Attention, shoppers: Maui has an increasingly excellent specialty boutique and gallery scene, especially in Paia and Upcountry.**

✔ **Maui has surpassed Oahu as the nightlife capital of Hawaii.** A party mood characterizes Lahaina town; the resorts offer lots of after-dark fun; and the Old Lahaina Luau is Hawaii's absolute best. This island even boasts the state's best live theater in the form of the Cirque du Soleil–goes-to-the-islands show *'Ulalena*, plus a couple of excellent ongoing magic revues.

✔ **Traffic can be a bear on occasion, especially in the prime resort areas.** But the other neighbor islands are catching up quickly, so it's increasingly difficult to single out Maui on this front.

which the island is nicknamed), is Haleakala National Park, a wild, other-worldly place that's hugely popular with hikers, bicyclers, and sunrise- and sunset-watchers.

Sixteen golf courses enthrall duffers, while a bounty of *Food & Wine*–worthy dining keeps sybarites satisfied. In fact, Maui is a close second to Oahu as a fine-dining destination. Hawaii's finest luau, some excellent theatrical entertainment, and an energetic party vibe in Lahaina make Maui the best choice for travelers who enjoy after-dark activities. With so much to do, you can easily fill a week or ten days — and you'll be ready to come back for more.

 Maui's attractions are no secret — so expect to battle a few crowds and pay for the privilege of visiting. I've heard an increasing number of complaints about overdevelopment in the last few years. And thanks to the rules of supply and demand, Maui's resorts tend to be more expensive than resorts on the other islands. Booked-to-capacity hotels can be less than willing to reduce rates; high demand for car rentals often push rates north of what you'll find on the other islands; restaurants are pricey, even at the casual end of the spectrum; and the high cost of all those available activities doesn't help matters either. You can drop a bundle if you choose to splurge.

But you can find good values, too; you just have to know where to look. And that's where this book comes in. It's your key to discovering Maui's best: the island's best values, its loveliest beaches, its most unforgettable experiences, and its authentic spirit of aloha. In the pages that follow, I steer you away from the overpriced and overcrowded and help you design the island getaway that's right for you.

Maui Nui: Molokai and Lanai

Geologists believe that, sometime around 1,000,000 B.C., the summit of Haleakala volcano broke the surface of the ocean. Flows from this volcano and adjoining ones joined to form a large prehistoric underwater land mass called *Maui Nui,* or "Big Maui." Encompassing Maui Nui was not only the island of Maui, but the neighboring islands of Molokai and Lanai, plus the unpopulated island of Kahoolawe.

Today, Maui County comprises Maui and its two sister islands, Molokai and Lanai. In prehistoric tradition, the tripartite island group is often called Maui Nui. Both Molokai and Lanai are covered in distinct chapters near the end of this book and can be visited on day trips from the Valley Isle or on extended stays. I recommend visiting one or both of these islands if you have the time and a yen to explore off the beaten path.

The most Hawaiian isle: Molokai

Sleepy Molokai is a rural island that's largely untouched by modern development (although, as residents like to boast, they do have KFC now). This lean, funky, unspoiled little island is often called the most Hawaiian of the Islands because it's the birthplace of the hula and it has a larger native Hawaiian population than any other in the chain. Although it offers some gorgeous, secluded beaches and a few adventure-style activities, don't expect any luxury hotels or dining. Now that the Molokai Ranch has shut down, taking the island's best hotel and best restaurant with it, facilities for visitors are minimal. Still, the vibe can be pure magic for travelers who want a genuine, off-the-beaten-path experience. The island's most famous site is Kalaupapa National Historical Park, a world-famous, 19th-century leper colony that can only be reached by mule, prop plane, or helicopter. (See Chapter 16 for complete coverage.)

The private island: Lanai

Staying on Lanai (population 3,500) is less a Hawaiian experience and more a generic, park-yourself-at-a-resort vacation. There's little to do here beyond what you can four-wheel-explore in a day, which is the entire idea of this getaway island. Just about everything that *is* here is completely handled through the two ultraposh, mega-expensive resorts that have taken over this humble little place: the English manor house–style **Four Seasons Resort Lanai** and **The Lodge** at Koele, which sits on the cool, misty peak of the island, while the **Four Seasons Resort Lanai** at Manele Bay sits on the beach, Hawaii-style. Lanai's fans love the total pampering and utter solitude. Bill Gates booked the entire island so that he could get married here, beyond the prying eyes of the media and public, a few years back. (See Chapter 17 for complete island coverage.)

History 101: The Main Events

Hawaii's historic tapestry is far richer than the story that can be shared in these few pages. If you'd like to immerse yourself in the whole story, pick up *Shoal of Time: A History of the Hawaiian Islands,* by Gavan Daws (University of Hawaii Press). Both definitive and delightful to read, *Shoal of Time* is the ideal, one-volume history of Hawaii. From the geologic formation of the islands through statehood, the Hawaii story is so well told that it reads like a novel. It's so rich with detail that the characters who shaped Hawaiian history come alive in its pages.

A.D. 700: The first Hawaiians arrive

The first Hawaiians arrived by canoe from Tahiti and the Marquesas Islands, some 2,500 miles to the south, as part of a greater Polynesian migration. They likely came ashore first at the southernmost Big Island, where they found a pristine and blessedly empty island, roiling with fire from the volcanoes at its heart.

An entire Hawaiian culture grew from these first settlers. As islanders migrated throughout the chain, each island became its own distinct kingdom. The inhabitants built temples, fish ponds, and aqueducts to irrigate taro plantations. Sailors became farmers and fishermen. The *alii* (high-ranking chiefs) created a caste system and established taboos. Ritual human sacrifices were common. Life was both vicious and blissful — just like the islands' breathtaking landscapes. Piilani was crowned as Maui's first king in the late 1300s.

1778: The "modern" world arrives

For more than a thousand years, no Hawaiian imagined that an outsider would ever appear in these remote "floating islands." But in 1778, Captain James Cook sailed into Waimea Bay on Kauai on his ship *Resolution,* where he was welcomed as the Hawaiian god Lono.

Cook stumbled upon the Hawaiian Islands quite by chance. He named them the Sandwich Islands, for the Earl of Sandwich, a great friend and first lord of the British admiralty, who had bankrolled the expedition. The Big Island would ultimately be the death of the world-famous explorer, but not before stone-age Hawaii entered the age of iron, and the West forged a permanent foothold in these virgin islands. Gifts were presented and objects traded: nails for fresh water, pigs, and the affections of Hawaiian women. The sailors brought syphilis, measles, and other diseases to which the Hawaiians had no natural immunity.

Cook never made it to Maui before his unfortunate demise. Captain Jean François de Galaup de La Perouse docked at Makena in 1787, becoming the first foreigner to set foot on Maui soil.

La Perouse ignored the King of France's orders to claim Maui for France, but Maui's days as an independent island were numbered anyway. In 1790, King Kamehameha I defeated the forces of Maui's last king, Kahekili, using guns seized from a British ship to establish his iron-fisted rule. By 1810, all the Hawaiian Islands were united as one kingdom, and the new Hawaiian monarchy welcomed the west with open arms. In 1819, the first whaler arrived from Massachusetts, establishing Lahaina's reputation as the whaling capital of the Pacific. The first New England missionaries were not far behind: They arrived on Maui in 1823. Victorian mores overtook island style, and eventually subsumed it; hula was abolished in favor of reading and writing, and neck-to-toe dress became the norm. The first sugar mill began operations in 1828, bringing industry to Maui. The same year, the first high school west of the Rocky Mountains, Maui's Lahainaluna High, opened, which firmly established Western-style education in the islands.

At the same time, missionaries also played a key role in preserving island culture. They created the 13-character Hawaiian alphabet and began recording the islands' history. Until this time, history was only passed down from generation to generation orally, in memorized chants.

The children of the missionaries became the islands' business and political leaders. They married Hawaiians and stayed on the islands, causing one astute observer to remark that the missionaries "came to do good and stayed to do well." More than 80 percent of all private land was owned by non-natives within two generations. Sugar cane became big business, and planters imported immigrants by the thousands to work the fields as contract laborers. The first Chinese came in 1852, followed by Portuguese in 1878, and Japanese beginning in 1885. These immigrants would have a lasting and influential impact on island culture that persists to the present day.

King David Kalakaua — known as the Merrie Monarch for the elaborate parties he threw — ascended to the throne in 1874, marking the beginning of the end of the short-lived Hawaiian monarchy. He performed a couple of acts of note, however: He built Iolani Palace in 1882, lifted the prohibitions on the hula and other native arts, and gave Pearl Harbor to the United States. In 1891, King Kalakaua visited chilly San Francisco, where he caught a cold and died. His sister, Queen Liliuokalani, assumed the throne.

1893: Paving the way for tourism and statehood

On January 17, 1893, a group of American sugar planters and missionary descendants, with the support of the U.S. Marines, imprisoned Queen Liliuokalani in her Honolulu palace, where she penned "Aloha Oe," the famous song of farewell. The monarchy was dead. Hawaii was now a U.S. territory ruled by the powerful sugar-cane planter Sanford Dole. He and his cohorts, known as the "Big Five," controlled the entire economic, social, and political life of the islands, including Maui. Sugar was king, and the native Hawaiians became a landless minority.

The first tourists to the islands were hard-core adventure travelers — among them Mark Twain — who came to the Big Island in the late 1800s to see the roiling Kilauea volcano. But the new industry didn't stick until transportation improved and the sugar industry became too expensive to support.

In 1901, W. C. Peacock built the elegant Moana Hotel (now the Sheraton Moana Surfrider) on Waikiki Beach. After a concentrated marketing effort in San Francisco, 2,000 tourists came to Waikiki in its first big tourism year, 1903. Tourists came by steamship; the sailing took four-and-a-half days. By 1936, visitors could fly to Honolulu from San Francisco on the *Hawaii Clipper,* a seven-passenger Pan Am plane; the flight took 21 hours, 33 minutes. Modern tourism was born and was doing brisk business — until the Japanese arrived, that is.

On December 7, 1941, a Japanese air raid wreaked havoc on the American warships parked at Pearl Harbor, drawing the heretofore reticent United States into World War II. Martial law was declared throughout Hawaii for the duration of the war.

1959: Setting the stage for today's Hawaii

The harsh realities of war gave way to the lighthearted culture of *Blue Hawaii*, Trader Vic's, and Arthur Godfrey. Hotels sprouted along the curvaceous beach at the foot of Diamond Head, known as Waikiki. Resorts finally arrived on Maui in 1946, when the Hotel Hana-Maui (now gloriously restored) opened its doors.

In 1959, this blossoming paradise became the 50th state of the United States. That year also saw the arrival of the first jet airliners. Postwar Americans had disposable cash, and now Hawaii was an easy flight away. Visitors began to arrive in droves, and tourism as we know it was off the ground, surpassing sugar as the premier industry of the islands. Kaanapali — Hawaii's first master-planned resort — debuted on Maui's curvaceous northwest shore in 1961.

Tired of the plastic aloha that had supplanted genuine island culture, Hawaiian elders started making a concerted effort to integrate traditional hula, chant, visual arts, and values into the experience of visitors. In 1976, the Hokulea, a replica of an ancient Polynesian voyaging canoe, set sail from Maui for Tahiti, reversing the ancestral journey and reestablishing ties to the ancient past. Tourism and hospitality employees are now educated in Hawaiian history, culture, and genuine aloha spirit. The culture that was once clipped at the roots has now come back in full bloom — and, thankfully, it's stronger than ever.

Building Blocks: Local Architecture and Design

Thanks to blessedly mild weather that includes cooling year-round trade winds and temperatures that don't vary by more than 15°F from January through July, Maui thrives on open-air living. A seamless blend of indoors and out is the prevailing architectural style. Why put up a wall when there's no reason to keep out the weather — or the dazzling view?

The local architectural style is called *kamaaina,* or "native born." *Kamaaina* is a style rich in beautiful simplicity and island tradition. True *kamaaina* architecture is generally open plan, in keeping with the importance of multigenerational family living and the strength of the community spirit — and to capitalize on those gentle ocean breezes. Decoration is simple but beautiful, generally focused on the shapes, materials, and hues of nature.

The finest homes are fitted with natural woods, such as *ohia* floors and gleaming koa furnishings. Koa is a gorgeous, slow-growth hardwood that has been a favorite of local artisans for centuries, thanks to its deep palette and rich grain. Crafts and furnishings made from the wood are increasingly expensive, simply because koa is a slow-growth wood that takes decades to replenish. If you can afford a piece to take home — perhaps a jewelry box or a hand-turned calabash — you'll likely treasure it as a family keepsake for generations to come, as island families do.

Not all native materials must necessarily be expensive, however. Some of the most beautiful and tropically evocative home furnishings are crafted of simple, light materials, such as bamboo and rattan. Most floor coverings are woven mats, soft and cool on bare feet. The finest are tightly woven *lauhala,* crafted from pandanus leaves by talented artisans.

The beautiful shapes and hues of Hawaii's bold fauna have woven their way into the island's favorite fabrics, too. Boldly hued tropical bark cloths — nubby cotton fabrics that wear well and say "Old Hawaii" with their large-leafed tropical and storytelling patterns — are famously suited to the islands. Fabric shops on Maui and throughout the islands can be located at www.thestateofhawaii.com/fabric.

Despite its glitz and glamour as a tourist destination, Hawaii is fundamentally a farming and fishing community — and the story is abundant in its streetscapes. Simple plantation cottages were built to house the workers brought in from all over the world to farm the islands' abundant sugar, pineapple, and taro fields; now, plantation style is the most pervasive architectural style in the islands, especially on the still-rural neighbor islands. With their single-story style, bright facades, and sloping roofs (many still crafted of corrugated aluminum), plantation cottages embody the simple beauty of island life. A more elaborate, multistoried style originated as the plantation manager's home. Lahaina's **Best Western Pioneer Inn** (see Chapter 10) offers a charming example of this design style, albeit with a seafaring bent. Ranch life predominates in the cool Upcountry of Maui, where plantation life gives way to *paniolo* (cowboy) style. *Paniolo* style is built for somewhat cooler weather; as a result, you're likely to find it to be a bit more familiar. Expect ranch-style homes with island touches such as brightly painted exteriors and broad porches, best evidenced in the Haleakala foothills in and around the town of Kula. Grander buildings take on Victorian details and the aura of the Old West. The storefronts of Makawao, in Upcountry Maui, have a distinct cowboy feel, as do the western-style storefronts of old Wailuku town and Paia, the funky cowboy-turned-surf town on the road to Hana.

The whaling town of Lahaina was a missionary bulkhead, as the town's architecture evidences. Wailuku's **Baldwin Home Museum** (see Chapter 13), built in 1831 and Maui's oldest surviving house, is the best example of imported Victorianism on the islands.

Maui is roughly halfway between Asia and the mainland United States, so the Asian influence is pervasive in island architecture and design. Pagoda-style influences are evident in residential and commercial architecture throughout the islands, especially in areas that absorbed the wealth of Chinese and Japanese immigrants who came to work in the fields generations ago, and stayed.

A Taste of Maui: Local Cuisine

About 15 or so years ago, Hawaii Regional Cuisine was born. Local chefs were tired of turning out a stodgy menu of continental fare that was unsuited to Hawaii living. So they began to celebrate the bounty of the islands, emphasizing the use of fresh, locally grown (often organic) produce; tropical fruits; the freshest seafood; and island-raised beef. Their light, creative combinations often feature Asian accents as a nod to Hawaii's multicultural heritage.

This type of cuisine is often disguised under other names — Euro-Asian, Pacific Rim, Indo-Pacific, Pacific Edge, Euro-Pacific, Island Fusion, and so on — but it all falls under the jurisdiction of Hawaii Regional Cuisine. Although there are variations, you can expect the following keynotes: lots of fresh, island fish; Asian flavorings (ginger, soy, wasabi, seaweed, and so on) and cooking styles (searing, grilling, *panko* crust, wok preparations) galore; and fresh tropical-fruit sauces (mango, papaya, and the like).

Maui has lured some of the world's finest chefs to its kitchens. Thanks to its proximity to the Pacific Rim and its large Asian population, the island boasts a wealth of Chinese, Thai, Vietnamese, and Japanese restaurants. And, if Asian fare isn't your thing, you'll find plenty of other options, from the French classics to good ol' ranch-raised, fire-grilled steaks. Maui's cooks have even managed to put their own spin on some of the world's most revered foods — pizzas, burgers, and burritos — with rousing success.

Seafood lovers, rejoice: Maui offers you an astounding array of fresh-caught fish. In fact, you may find yourself puzzling over lists of unfamiliar fish on island menus. (See Chapter 18 for a handy list of definitions that help you decide what to try.)

Lest all this unfamiliar food talk makes you think otherwise, remember that the majority of Hawaii islanders are red-blooded, flag-waving Americans — and they love a good burger just as much as your average mainlander.

Real local food is generally starchy and high in calories, so the Atkins crowd will want to skip the traditional plate lunch, which usually consists of a main dish (anything from fried fish to teriyaki beef), "two scoops rice," an ice-cream-scoop serving of macaroni salad, and brown gravy, all served on a paper plate. Plate lunches are cheap and available at casual restaurants and beachside stands throughout the islands.

Chapter 18 takes a more in-depth look at the diversity of wonderful taste sensations just waiting to be discovered on Maui.

A Word to the Wise: The Local Lingo

Everyone on Maui speaks English, of course. But a number of Hawaiian words and phrases regularly pop up in everyday conversation.

You probably already know the Hawaiian word *aloha* (a-*lo*-ha), which serves as an all-purpose greeting — hello, welcome, and goodbye. It's a warm and wonderful word that expresses the sense of peace and hospitality that epitomizes the islands.

You'll definitely need to learn the word *mahalo* (ma-*ha*-low), which means "thank you" and is used extensively throughout Hawaii. If you want to say "Thanks very much!" or "Thank you *so* much," say *mahalo nui loa* (ma-*ha*-low *noo*-ee *low*-ah). Not only will the locals be impressed with your efforts to learn, but they'll be flattered by your graciousness, too.

Islanders don't like "goodbye" to be so permanent. So to really sound like a local, part from others warmly with *a hui hou* (ah *hoo*-ee *ho*), which means "until we meet again."

Here's a handy list of other words you may encounter:

- ✔ *Hale* (*ha*-lay): House
- ✔ *Haole* (*how*-lee): Foreigner or Caucasian (literally "out of breath" — pale, or paleface); a common reference, not an insult (usually)
- ✔ *Hula* (*hoo*-lah): Native dance
- ✔ *Kamaaina* (ka-ma-*eye*-nah): Local person
- ✔ *Kapu* (*ka*-poo): Anything that's taboo, forbidden
- ✔ *Keiki* (*keh*-kee): Child
- ✔ *Lanai* (*lah*-nigh): Porch or veranda
- ✔ *Lei* (lay): Garland (usually of flowers, leaves, or shells)
- ✔ *Luau* (*loo*-ow): A celebratory feast
- ✔ *Mana* (*ma*-na): Spirit, or power
- ✔ *Muumuu* (moo-oo-*moo*-oo): A loose-fitting dress, usually in a tropical print
- ✔ *Ono* (*oh*-no): Delicious
- ✔ *Pau* (pow): Finished or done
- ✔ *Pupu* (*poo*-poo): Starter dish, appetizer

The Hawaiian language has only 12 characters to work with — the five vowels (*a, e, i, o,* and *u*) plus seven consonants (*h, k, l, m, n, p,* and *w*). Consequently, Hawaiian words and names tend to be long and difficult, with lots of repetitive syllables.

The vowels are pronounced like this:

a	*ah* (as in father) or *uh* (as in above)		**o**	*oh* (as in vote)
e	*eh* (as in bed) or *ay* (as in they)		**u**	*oo* (as in too)
i	*ee* (as in police)			

Almost all vowels are sounded separately, although some are pronounced together, as in the name of Maui's county seat, Wailuku, which is pronounced "Why-*loo*-koo."

The simplest way to pronounce a Hawaiian word or name is to approach long words or names as a collection of short syllables. Accents almost always fall on the second-to-last syllable. All syllables end with vowels, so a consonant will always indicate the start of a new syllable.

The Hawaiian language actually has a 13th character: the glottal stop, which looks exactly like a single opening quotation mark (') and is meant to indicate a pause. I've chosen not to use the glottal stop throughout this book; it's often left out in printed Hawaiian and on such things as store and street signs. Although serious Hawaiian-language students insist on using the glottal stop, you don't need to worry about it as a visitor; just ignore it when you see it.

Background Check: Recommended Books and Movies

Studying up on Hawaii can be one of the most fun bits of "research" you'll ever do. If you'd like to learn a bit more about the islands before you go — which I encourage — these books and movies are an enjoyable way to do it.

Books

In addition to *Shoal of Time* (see the "History 101: The Main Events" section, earlier in this chapter), one of my all-time favorites is *Hawaii*, by James Michener (Random House), the epic Pulitzer Prize–winning novelist who loved the island's heart and soul. Michener's novel charts a similar course as Daws' book, but this fictionalized account has the style — and the can't-put-it-down appeal — of a beach read. The missionary chapters are focused on Lahaina, so *Hawaii* is especially suited to a Maui visit.

Another intriguing work of fiction that tells the story of Hawaii, albeit on a smaller scale, is Kiana Davenport's *Shark Dialogues* (Plume).

Fortunately for us, one of Hawaii's first tourists was also one of literature's greatest and most insightful wits. *Mark Twain's Letters from Hawaii*

(University of Hawaii Press) chronicles Twain's four months in Hawaii in 1866 while on assignment as a journalist for the *Sacramento Union*. This entertaining collection captures truths about Hawaii's past that no third-party history could. The letters are also available on audio CD (Audio Partners Publishing Corporation).

The Colony: The Harrowing True Story of the Exiles of Molokai (Scribner) tells the fascinating, harrowing, and insightful history of Molokai's Kalaupapa leper colony. This 2006 title from John Tayman, a former *Outside* magazine editor, is so thrillingly written that it reads like a page-turning novel.

Want to learn the stories of Pele, Maui, and the other gods and supernatural creatures, both fiery and benevolent, that comprise Hawaii's mystical back story? Check out *Hawaiian Mythology*, by Martha Warren Beckwith and Katharine Luomala (University of Hawaii Press). Steven Goldberry's *Maui the Demigod* (University of Hawaii Press) is a well-regarded historic novel focused on the multifaceted character who slowed the sun in order to dry his mother's tapa cloth, as legend has it.

Hundreds of books tell the personal stories of the great figures of Hawaiian history. One of my favorites chronicles the life — and bloody Big Island death — of the great, devastating seafarer who introduced Hawaii to the western world: *Farther Than Any Man: The Rise and Fall of Captain James Cook,* by Martin Dugard (Simon & Schuster). Only a sliver of the book is about Hawaii, but it articulates the British colonial mind-set beautifully.

University of Hawaii Press's richly illustrated *Atlas of Hawaii* is a fascinating source for everything you ever wanted to know about Hawaii's physical geography, weather patterns, population, and the like. It's an ideal gift for natural-science buffs who want to delve deeper.

Albert J. Schutz's *All About Hawaiian* (University of Hawaii Press) is a great pocket-size reference for those who want to know just a bit more about the Hawaiian alphabet and language, including how to pronounce all those funky place names.

Want to bask in the glory of Hawaii as innocent vacationland, in the days of Matson Cruise Lines, Duke Kahanamoku, and Don Ho crooning "Tiny Bubbles," when Waikiki really was paradise? *Leis, Luaus and Alohas: The Lure of Hawaii in the Fifties,* by Fred E. Basten and Charles Phoenix (Island Heritage), is the book for you. This vibrant coffee-table book will really put you in the mood for a mai tai.

Some beautifully illustrated books tell the story of the aloha shirt in all its silky, full-color glory. Best of the bunch is *The Aloha Shirt: Spirit of the Islands,* by Dale Hope and Gregory Tozian (Beyond Words Publishing). Broader in its reach — but no less beautiful — is Linda B. Arthur's *Aloha Attire: Hawaiian Dress in the 20th Century* (Schiffer Publishing).

Both craft and horticulture fans will find Ronn Ronck's *A Pocket Guide to the Hawaiian Lei: A Tradition of Aloha* (Mutual Publishing) to be an easy-to-carry reference to Hawaii's most visible and popular creative ritual: lei making and wearing.

If you can manage to find it, no book exudes the genuine spirit of living in Hawaii like Jocelyn Fujii's *Under the Hula Moon* (Crown Publishing Group), a gorgeous blend of photos and text with an introduction by Paul Theroux.

Hawaii culture is predicated on the wisdom of its elders, passed down through the generations. *Voices of Wisdom: Hawaiian Elders Speak,* by M. J. Harden (Booklines Hawaii, Ltd.), features interviews with 24 respected island elders, gorgeously illustrated with black-and-white portraits by photographer Steve Brinkman. This beautiful and easy-to-read book is a perfect primer for anyone who wants to embrace Hawaii's rich heritage and the cultural renaissance that the islands have experienced over the last two decades.

Chicken Soup from the Soul of Hawaii, by Jack Canfield, Mark Victor Hansen, Sharon Linnea, and Robin Stephens Rohr (HCI), really captures the magic of the island in one slim volume featuring some of the islands' most beloved stories. This book is a delightful introduction to the spirit and substance of Hawaii life and culture for those who want to set the tone but don't care to dig too deep.

Rita Ariyoshi's *Maui on My Mind* (Mutual Publishing) is a gorgeously written and illustrated coffee-table book focused on the beauty and magic of the Valley Isle. If you have a reluctant traveler in your group, this enticing collection of text and photos will change his tune.

In 2004, *Honolulu Magazine* put together a panel of experts and named *The 50 Greatest Hawai'i Music Albums,* by Roana Bolante and Michael Keany (Watermark). This gorgeous full-color book is a must for music lovers who want to learn about the best island sounds, from the hip atomic-age sounds of Martin Denny to the finest songsters of today, such as the Brothers Cazimero and Keali'i Reichel.

If you have a hard time finding any of these books — or if you want additional suggestions from Hawaii's rich library — two Big Island bookstores serve as particularly good resources: **Basically Books** (☎ **800-903-MAPS** [6277] or 808-961-0144; www.basicallybooks.com) and the **Kohala Book Shop** (☎ **808-889**-6400; www.kohalabooks.com). Both offer online catalog browsing and ordering services.

Movies

Gorgeous Hawaii has served as a backdrop for countless TV shows and movies, from *Hawaii Five-O* ("book 'em, Dano") to *Pearl Harbor.* Here are just a few of my favorite movies starring the islands, all available on DVD. Unfortunately, few star Maui, but all the movies listed here will give you a good feel for the islands.

The epic Academy Award winner *From Here to Eternity* (1953), starring Montgomery Clift, Frank Sinatra, Burt Lancaster, and a bevy of other Hollywood big names, tells the story of the attack on Pearl Harbor with gravity and intimacy. The location shots are gorgeous, even in black-and-white.

Tora! Tora! Tora! (1970), is a fascinating, fictional-yet-documentary-style depiction of the attack on Pearl Harbor from both the U.S. and Japanese perspectives. It was filmed on location on both Oahu and Japan.

Blue Crush (2002) is a silly surf movie that nevertheless captures the genuine heart of Oahu's North Shore surf culture. The stunning photography alone is worth putting up with the plot — you'll feel like you're riding the waves yourself. (Note: Although the movie was filmed on Oahu, its original working title was *Surf Girls of Maui*.)

50 First Dates (2004), starring Drew Barrymore and Adam Sandler, is a real island gem. This funny and romantic movie was filmed on North Shore and Windward Oahu and exudes warm island spirit.

Breathtaking Kauai hosts the dinosaur-dotted jungle of *Jurassic Park* (1993). Of course, Spielberg didn't exactly discover Kauai; Hollywood had discovered the Garden Isle's silver-screen magic decades before. For the best retro views, check out *Blue Hawaii* (1961) starring Elvis and *South Pacific* (1958), filmed on the north shore of Kauai, whose stunning Bali Hai mountains shape the film's incredible backdrop. And even flying Elvises can't upstage the gorgeous scenery when *Honeymoon in Vegas* (1992), starring Nicolas Cage and Sarah Jessica Parker, moves to Kauai.

One of my absolute favorite movies about Hawaii is the little-seen *Picture Bride* (1994), which tells the story of a young Japanese girl who sails to Hawaii in 1918 to marry a man — a laborer in the sugar-cane fields — whom she has never met. This stirring and beautiful movie is well worth seeking out.

You and the kids may want to check out *George of the Jungle* (1997), starring Brendan Fraser, which was partially filmed on Maui. Maui is also featured in *Die Another Day* (2002), starring Pierce Brosnan as James Bond. Garry Marshall's movie version of the Anne Rice novel *Exit to Eden* (1994), starring Rosie O'Donnell and Dana Delaney, was filmed largely on Maui and Lanai, but I'm not sure that's a worthwhile reason to rent this unfortunate film.

Molokai: The Story of Father Damien (2000) is true story of Molokai's leper colony, now preserved as a national historical park. The star-studded supporting cast includes Derek Jacobi, Sam Neill, Peter O'Toole, and Kris Kristofferson.

Chapter 3

Deciding When to Go

In This Chapter

▶ Decoding the secrets of the travel seasons
▶ Understanding Maui's climate
▶ Avoiding the crowds
▶ Zeroing in on special events

*M*aui enjoys fabulous weather year-round. Winter is virtually nonexistent. Severe storms are a rarity. Even the off-season — spring and fall — is gorgeous, meaning you can save a bundle with the right travel dates.

Still, some times are better than others. This chapter reveals when everybody else comes to Maui so that you can either join the party or steer clear and avoid the crowds.

Revealing the Secrets of the Seasons

Maui's high season is during the winter months, from the second half of December through mid-April, when people flee the cold, snow, and gray skies of home for Hawaii's warm sun and bathing-suit temperatures. During this winter high season, prices go up, and resorts can be booked to capacity, particularly during the holiday season. Book far in advance for a trip during this period, and expect to pay sky-high prices. Although not nearly as bad as Christmastime, Easter week can also be crowded with West Coast families flocking to the islands for a few days of fun in the sun over spring break.

Summer (mid-June through Aug) is a secondary high season. You won't find the bargains of spring and fall, but you may still do better on accommodations, airfare, and packages than in the winter months.

Maui's slowest seasons have traditionally been spring (mid-Apr to mid-June) and fall (Labor Day to mid-Dec) — which, paradoxically, also happen to be the best seasons in Maui in terms of reliably great weather. Herein lies the secret of the seasons: In late spring and fall, hotel rates traditionally drop, package deals abound, airfares are often at their lowest rates of the year, and you can expect consistently clear days after you arrive.

Truth be told, the weather is relatively constant year-round. You can bet that no matter what time of year you arrive, you can enjoy prime conditions. Your decision really boils down to how much you want to spend, how important it is for you to escape winter back home, your willingness to deal with crowds, and what's available.

Understanding Maui's climate

Maui lies at the edge of the tropics, so it really has only two seasons: warm (winter) and warmer (summer). Temperatures generally don't vary much more than 15°F or so from season to season, depending on where you are on the island. The average high is 88°F at the height of summer, while the average winter high is 80°F at its coldest — not much difference. Nighttime lows drop about 15 degrees, give or take a couple of degrees, year-round. August and September are usually the warmest months; January is generally the coolest. Almost-constant trade winds bring a cooling breeze in even the hottest weather.

The island's *leeward* side (the west and south shores) tends to be hot and dry; the *windward* side (the east and north shores) is generally cooler and wetter. For desertlike weather, visit South Maui or West Maui. The driest and sunniest areas of Maui are the communities of Kihei and Wailea, on Maui's south coast. When you want lush, junglelike conditions, go windward toward Hana on the northeastern shore.

Locals say that if you don't like the weather, just get in the car and drive — you're bound to find something different. That's because the island has many *microclimates,* which are highly localized weather patterns based on a region's unique position and topography.

The mountain communities of Upcountry Maui are much cooler than the coastal areas, and the higher you go, the cooler it gets. If you visit Haleakala National Park, for example, you climb from sea level to 10,000 feet in just 37 miles. Don't be surprised if the temperature is 30 to 35 degrees cooler at the summit than at the beach.

In general, November through March or April (depending on the year) marks Maui's rainy season; rainfall averages between 2 and 3 inches during these months. Summer, when average rainfall generally drops below 1 inch per month, is considered the dry season. The weather can get gray during the rainy season — but, fortunately, it seldom rains for more than two or three days in a row. Winter isn't a bad time to go to Maui — the sun's just a little less reliable, that's all.

Good news about Maui's rainy season — it's almost never raining *everywhere,* even in winter. So if it's raining on your parade, just get in the car and drive — you'll likely reach a sunny spot in no time.

Charting sea changes

Maui's ocean waters stay warm year-round. The average water temperature is a warm 75°F, and reaches a jump-right-in 83°F or so in summer.

Wave action, though, varies greatly between winter and summer, and from coast to coast. Maui's beaches tend to be as placid as lakes in the summer and autumn months. In winter, swells hit the north-facing beaches and the surf goes wild (attracting daredevil surfers, who are fun to watch, even if you're not brave enough to face monster curls yourself). South-facing beaches generally remain calm and friendly to swimmers and snorkelers of all ages and abilities throughout winter, although spring and early summer bring south swells right about the time North Shore waves flatten out.

If the waves are too powerful for you, seek calmer conditions by taking a short drive to another beach that's more sheltered. In Chapter 12, I recommend the best local beaches, including the safest for inexperienced swimmers. When in doubt, ask at your hotel or call the local tourist office for recommendations — and watch for warning flags and posted conditions at the beach.

 A few important words about ocean safety: Never turn your back on the ocean when you're at the beach. A big wave can come out of nowhere before you can say "aloha." Always watch the surf, even if you're just taking a casual stroll along the shoreline. Also, ocean conditions can change dramatically in a matter of hours; surf that was safe for swimming one day can develop a dangerous undertow the next. Get out of the water when the big swells come. And red flags hoisted on the beach are your warning that unsafe conditions are present. And last, don't be shy about wearing floaties or a life jacket if it makes you feel more comfortable in the water.

Avoiding the crowds

Yes, coming to Maui during certain times is a bad idea if you're allergic to crowds. At the very least, you should know what you're getting into.

The entire nation of Japan basically shuts down over Golden Week, which falls annually in late April or early May. (Oahu is more crowded, but Maui fills up, too.) Book hotels, interisland air reservations, and car rentals well in advance.

Halloween in Lahaina is a major event; up to 20,000 people come for the festivities. Booking your Lahaina hotel room a year or more in advance isn't too early. You shouldn't have a problem elsewhere on the island, though.

And keep in mind that the islands are at maximum capacity during the Christmas holidays; spring break and Easter week can also be crowded.

Perusing Maui's Calendar of Events

Check out the following rundown of the top events that take place annually. For a complete listing, as well as the latest events information, go to www.visitmaui.com (click on Calendar of Events at the bottom of the page). Also check out www.calendarmaui.com, which is probably the most comprehensive source for island-wide events. The lively port town of Lahaina has its own event hot line; dial ☎ **888-310-1117** to find out what's going on while you're in the area. For events on the island of Molokai, visit www.visitmolokai.com; a current-events calendar for the island of Lanai is posted at www.visitlanai.net/lanaievents.html. Or visit the Hawaii state visitor site at www.calendar.gohawaii.com, where you can search a comprehensive list of special events by island.

Many of the following events absolutely require significant planning before you leave home. Call ahead before any event.

In addition to the following listings, I encourage you to check the active events calendar at the **Maui Arts & Cultural Center** in Kahului, where events run the gamut from art exhibits, local entertainers, and film screenings to international entertainers, such as David Sedaris and the Who. Go online at www.mauiarts.org, where you can also buy tickets, or call the box office at ☎ **808-242-7469.**

January

'Tis the season for world-championship golf in paradise. The season kicks off with the first PGA event of the year, the **Mercedes Championships** at Kapalua Resort (☎ **877-527-2582**; www.kapalua.com/hawaii-golf/pga-tournament), starring the previous year's tournament champs. Next up is the **Wendy's Champions Skins Game** at Kaanapali or Wailea, Maui, depending on the year and the deal struck. Expect top-ranked talent at both events. Check www.pgatour.com for complete details on each event, including how to purchase tickets. January and February.

January through April is Maui's prime **whale-watching season,** when humpback whales — the world's largest mammals — make their way from frigid Alaska to the balmy waters of Hawaii. Maui is the best spot in Hawaii for whale-watching because the giants love to frolic in the channel separating the Valley Isle from Molokai and Lanai. Because whales prefer water depths of less than 600 feet, these endangered gentle giants come in relatively close to shore. You can see them regularly from the beach in prime season, spouting and *spy-hopping* (peeking above the waterline to "spy" on what's going on). They often prefer the west, or leeward, sides of the islands. The best onshore vantage is West Maui's MacGregor Point, a large pullout on the ocean side of Highway 30, halfway between Maalaea and Lanai. The nonprofit Pacific Whale Foundation operates a **Whale Information Station** there that's staffed by friendly naturalists daily from 8:30 a.m. to 3:30 p.m. from December through April. Just stop by — they even have high-powered binoculars you can use — or call ☎ **800-942-5311** or 808-249-8811 for more details. If you happen to be in the islands during whale season, you don't want to miss seeing these remarkable behemoths. You can often spot them from land, but I also recommend the best whale-watching cruises in Chapter 12.

Ka Molokai Makahiki Festival brings the most Hawaiian Isle to full life with this annual one-day celebration of traditional hula, ancient island games, Hawaiian arts and crafts, and food. Call ☎ **808-553-3673** or visit www.visitmolokai.com/evnt.html for this year's schedule. Mid-January.

Help ring in the **Chinese New Year** in historic Lahaina. Events include a traditional lion dance in front of the historic Wo Hing Temple, plus food, music, fireworks, martial arts, Chinese crafts, and much more in a full-blown Technicolor street festival. Call ☎ **888-310-1117** or 808-667-9175, or visit www.visitlahaina.com. January 26, 2009, ushers in the Year of the Ox; February 10, 2010, inaugurates the Year of the Tiger.

February

The **Mercedes Championships** and **Wendy's Champions Skins Game** continue from January (see the preceding section).

The Pacific Whale Foundation honors the majestic humpback whale with the **Great Maui Whale Festival,** a full winter-long calendar of events that culminates in mid-February with a parade, a regatta, special whale-watching events, the annual Whale Day Celebration (usually held on the third Sat of the month), and much, much more. Call the foundation at ☎ **800-942-5311** or 808-244-8390 or go online to www.greatmauiwhale festival.org or www.pacificwhale.org for all the details. Check with the foundation for the date of the **Great Whale Count,** when you can help count the number of humpbacks visiting Maui's waters; it usually falls at the end of the month.

March

The second humpback-themed celebration of the season rules Maui during the **Ocean Arts Festival,** Lahaina's own two-day series of special events honoring the island's most high-profile visitors, including whale-watching, an outdoor arts festival, games, and a touch-pool exhibit for kids. Call ☎ **888-310-1117** or 808-667-9175 or check www.visitlahaina.com for this year's schedule. Mid-March.

Maui's annual **Ritz-Carlton Kapalua Celebration of the Arts** is the premier Hawaii arts and culture festival. Well-known artists give free, hands-on lessons in hula, chant, Niihau shell lei making, tapa cloth making, primitive clay firing, and more. Events include a traditional luau, kids' activities, and live entertainment of the highest order. Call ☎ **800-262-8440** or 808-669-6200 or visit www.celebrationofthearts.org for this year's schedule and reservations. Easter weekend.

Depending on the year and schedule, the **East Maui Taro Festival** may fall in March (see the next section).

April

If Easter falls in April, check out the **Ritz-Carlton Kapalua Celebration of the Arts** (see the preceding section).

Want to understand the appeal of that mysterious local food staple, the taro root? Attend the **East Maui Taro Festival,** at the Hana Ball Park in Hana, a two-day celebration that includes exhibits, lectures, food booths, live entertainment, and traditional arts and crafts. This is a homegrown local event rather than a touristy one. For this year's schedule, call ☎ 808-264-1533 or visit www.tarofestival.org. April 25 and 26, 2009; check the Web site or call for 2010 dates.

May

May Day is **Lei Day** in Hawaii — and cause for big-time rejoicing. Although the most extensive celebrations are held on Oahu, expect a festive atmosphere on Maui as well; a number of island resorts, including the Fairmont Kea Lani, host their own Lei Day celebrations. Contact the Maui Visitors Bureau (☎ 800-525-6284; www.visitmaui.com) for a list of Maui events. The day is also a special one on Lanai, where the Lei Day celebration is a joyfully local event hosted by the Lanai Culture and Heritage Center; call ☎ 808-565-7177 or go to www.visitlanai.net for this year's details. Or merely don a fragrant garland, smile, and greet everyone you see with a warm, festive "aloha!" May 1.

All-star golf returns to Kapalua for the **Verizon Hawaii Hall of Fame Pro-Am and Championship.** Call ☎ 800-527-2582 or 888-665-9160 or visit www.kapalua.com for details. Early May.

The most Hawaiian Isle celebrates the birth of hula annually with **Molokai Ka Hula Piko Hula Festival,** a music- and dance-filled one-day event held at Molokai's Papohaku Beach Park. Call ☎ 800-800-6367 or 808-553-3876 or visit www.visitmolokai.com/evnt.html for this year's schedule and details. Mid-May.

A major Maui cultural event, **International Festival of Canoes,** honors the voyaging canoe that united Polynesia for two weeks in May. Throughout the event, Cultural delegations from Pacific island nations come together with master carvers to create Polynesian canoes from wood logs. Hosts from Hawaii welcome each nation in a traditional 'awa ceremony at the beach. Lahaina hosts cultural arts demonstrations and performances, a parade, ancient warrior demonstrations, Polynesian crafts, and food. On the final day, a ceremony launches the carved canoes at sunset, with entertainment. Free admission to most events. Call ☎ 888-310-1117 or 808-667-9193 or go to www.mauifestivalof canoes.com for details. Mid- to late May.

June

In honor of the great chief who united the Hawaiian Islands, **King Kamehameha Day** — Hawaii's longest-running holiday, since 1871 — is celebrated as a statewide holiday, with massive floral parades, slack-key guitar concerts, Hawaiian crafts shows, and plenty of partying. Probably the best event is the celebratory floral parade through Maui's old Lahaina town, which concludes with a food-and-craft fair, demonstrations of ancient warrior skills, and other entertainment; call ☎ **888-310-1117** or 808-667-9175 or check www.visitlahaina.com for details. June 11 (or nearest weekend).

The **Maui Film Festival at Wailea** is Hawaii's very own version of Sundance, with five days and nights of premiere screenings, parties, and celebrity appearances, plus Hawaiian cultural events for island flavor. An increasing number of celebrities are in attendance, so this tends to be a star-studded time to be on the island. Call ☎ **808-579-9244** or 808-572-3456 or visit www.mauifilmfestival.com for complete program information. June 17 through 21, 2009. Call or go online for 2010 dates.

Hawaii's finest musicians — and those who appreciate them — gather annually at the Maui Arts & Cultural Center for the **Ki Hoalu Fe Slack Key Guitar Festival,** an all-day outdoor event for the entire family. Bring a picnic and settle in for a day of soothing sounds from an all-star lineup. Call ☎ **808-242-7469** or visit www.mauiarts.org. Late June.

July

Maui celebrates **Independence Day** with appropriate panache all over the island. Kaanapali celebrates with free activities focused on families from noon to 5 p.m. at Whalers Village. Lahaina offers old-fashioned Fourth of July fun, including a free fireworks show at 8 p.m. (Front Street is closed to traffic from sunset to 9 p.m.) Call ☎ **800-245-9229** or visit www.kaanapaliresort.com for the schedule of events in Kaanapali; call ☎ **888-310-1117** or 808-667-9175 or visit www.visitlahaina.com for Lahaina schedules. July 4.

The **Makawao Fourth of July Parade and Rodeo** lets Maui's Upcountry cowboy country shine. The parade starts around 9 a.m. at the lower end of Baldwin Avenue and leads to the Eddie Tam Center, where genuine rodeo events are the star of the show. Call ☎ **808-572-9565** or go to www.makawaotowncenter.com for details.

Lanai celebrates the precious pineapple with the daylong **Annual Pineapple Festival,** which takes place at Lanai's Dole Park on the Saturday closest to July 4. Themed events celebrating Lanai's plantation and *paniolo* (cowboy) history include pineapple-eating contests and live local entertainment, culminating in fireworks. It's a spirited, local-style celebration. Call ☎ **800-947-4774** or 808-565-7580 or go online to www.visitlanai.net. Early July.

World-famous winemakers and chefs gather (along with appreciative gourmands) on Maui annually for the highly acclaimed — and appropriately grand — **Kapalua Wine & Food Festival,** a bounteous four-day series of wine tastings, cooking demonstrations, and gourmet meals prepared by celebrity chefs. It's well worth attending if you fancy yourself a foodie. Make your arrangements well in advance, because this event is hugely popular. Call ☎ **866-669-2440** or 808-665-9160 or visit www.kapalua.com for details. July 26 through 29, 2009; call or go online to confirm dates for 2010 (some years this event may fall in June).

August

The **Maui Onion Festival,** held in Whalers Village, Kaanapali, showcases the sweetest onions in the world, through food vendors, entertainment, tastings, a farmers' market, and a Maui Onion Cook-Off. Call ☎ **808-661-4567** or go to www.whalersvillage.com. Mid-August.

Hawaii became the 50th state on August 21, 1959, which is now celebrated as **Admissions Day;** all state-related facilities are closed. Third Friday in August.

September

Running exactly 26.2 miles from Kahului to Kaanapali, the **Maui Marathon** is regularly named one of the ten most scenic marathons in North America. A half-marathon and a 5K are also offered for runners working their way up to the big kahuna. Upcoming dates are Sunday, September 20, 2009, and Sunday, September 19, 2010 (the marathon's 40th anniversary). Visit www.mauimarathon.com for entry details.

Taste of Lahaina and the Best of Island Music is Maui's biggest foodie event. Some 30,000 people flock to the Lahaina Recreation Park to sample the signature dishes of Maui's top cooks throughout this weekend festival, which also includes cooking demonstrations, wine tastings, and nonstop live entertainment. The weekend before the main event features Maui Chefs Present, an elegant $100-a-plate dinner and cocktail party featuring about a dozen of the island's best chefs. Call ☎ **888-310-1117** or 808-667-9175, or visit www.visitlahaina.com for details. Mid-September.

'Tis the season in Hawaii for statewide **Aloha Festivals.** Each week from mid-September through October is Aloha Week on a different island, with events running the gamut from parades and royal balls to ethnic days and street festivals. This week is serious celebration time. Call ☎ **808-589-1771,** or go online to www.alohafestivals.com for a complete schedule of Maui, Molokai, and Lanai events. Mid-September.

The **Maui County Fair** is Hawaii's oldest and largest county fair. Expect a parade, rides, games, exhibits, live entertainment — all with an island twist, of course. Held at the Wailuku War Memorial Complex for four fun-filled days. Call ☎ **808-242-2721,** or visit www.mauicountyfair.com for this year's details. Late September or early October.

October

Depending on the year, the **Maui County Fair** may fall in October; check this year's dates (see the preceding section).

The only statewide film festival in the United States, the **Louis Vuitton Hawaii International Film Festival** specializes in films from Asia, the Pacific Islands, and North America. Most screenings and related events take place on Oahu, but the final weekend finds events on all the islands, including Maui. Call ☎ **808-528-3456,** or point your browser to www. hiff.org for more information. Late October.

Approximately 30,000 people show up to celebrate **Halloween** in Lahaina, an event so festive and popular that some call it the "Mardi Gras of the Pacific." Front Street is closed off from 4 p.m. to midnight for the costumed revelers and accompanying festivities; a children's parade launches the day. The Great Halloween Costume Contest takes place in Banyan Tree Park at 7 p.m. Lahaina is so gung-ho on Halloween, in fact, that the party starts the week prior to October 31 with haunted houses and other events around town. Call ☎ **888-310-1117** or 808-667-9175, or visit www.visitlahaina.com for this year's events. October 31, plus the week preceding.

November

The **Aloha Classic World Windsurfing Championships,** the final event in the Pro Boardsailing World Tour, is held at Maui's Hookipa Beach, universally considered to be the best windsurfing beach on the planet. These daredevils and their colorful sails are quite a sight to see as they pirouette over the wild winter waves; spectating is absolutely free. Check www. alohaclassicwindsurfing.com for this year's dates. Early November.

The annual **Maui Invitational Basketball Tournament** is held at the Lahaina Civic Center. Top college teams from around the nation vie in this annual preseason tournament. Visit www.mauiinvitational.com for more information, including details on how to purchase tickets. Usually held around Thanksgiving. Late November.

December

Celebrating **Christmas** on Maui can be quite memorable. Santa arrives to say "Mele Kalikimaka" at the annual lighting of Lahaina's historic banyan tree, followed by Christmas caroling in Hawaiian. Schedules vary; call ☎ **800-525-6284** or 888-310-1117, or check www.visitmaui.com or www.visitlahaina.com. Expect the major resort areas to be decked out in holiday finery all month. Throughout December.

Maximizing Your Time

As you plan your itinerary, keep the following tips in mind:

- ✔ **Fly directly from the mainland to Maui.** Doing so can save you a two-hour layover in Honolulu and another plane ride on an inter-island carrier — a process that can add four or five hours to your total travel time. Multiple direct flights from the mainland serve Maui. Mainland flights to the neighboring islands may be more expensive, although they tend to be comparably priced these days; still, be sure to price-compare if money matters.

- ✔ **Spend a week or ten days vacationing on Maui.** A week or ten days allow you to explore the island at your leisure while still enjoying plenty of time just lazing on the beach. I wouldn't advise anything shorter than a week for folks traveling from farther away than California. If you want to hop to one or two other Hawaiian islands as well, you really need a full two-week vacation to make it enjoyable.

- ✔ **Don't overplan your itinerary or try to do everything.** If relaxation is number one on your agenda, work plenty of do-nothing time into your travel plans. Keep your days loose. A Maui vacation is about going with the island flow — and a big part of the experience is just taking things as they come. Don't feel guilty that you're not doing or seeing enough; you do enough the other 50 weeks of the year, don't you?

- ✔ **Leave at least one day to chance.** Don't book a big activity for every day of your vacation. Leave at least one day for whatever strikes your fancy, whether it's sightseeing or shopping or just sitting on your condo's oceanfront lanai, soaking up a beach read and the laid-back vibe. Make the most of this carefree week in your life.

- ✔ **Make mornings your ocean time, if you're dividing your day between land and sea activities.** Beaches tend to be less crowded and the surf and winds tend to be calmer in the morning hours — especially in winter. Always take the first snorkel and dive cruise of the day, when conditions are calmest and clearest; you'll understand why outfitters offer discounts on their afternoon sails should you choose to wait until later in the day.

- ✔ **Keep an eye on the weather and plan accordingly.** Don't be a slave to your schedule — watch the local weather reports and keep your plans flexible enough to make the most of great weather.

- ✔ Book extra-special activities before you leave home so that you don't miss out. Many of Maui's best activities can book up weeks in advance. Do some plan-ahead reading and call to reserve a few select adventures — such as the best luau or a snorkel trip to Lanai you just don't want to miss — before you leave home. After all, you don't get to Maui just every day, and I don't want you to miss out on the best it has to offer. (For tips on those activities you may want to book before you arrive, see Chapter 8.)

Part II
Planning Your Trip to Maui

The 5th Wave
By Rich Tennant

In this part . . .

In this part, I'll discuss all your travel options: finding the best airfare, working with a travel agent, deciding whether to go the package-tour route, renting a car, and packing smart. I'll help you work out a realistic budget and show you where you can save and where it makes sense to splurge. I'll also give you an overview of your options for lodgings so that you can decide whether you want a luxury resort, a beachfront condo, your own rental house, or an intimate B&B.

Chapter 4

Managing Your Money

. . . .

In This Chapter

▶ Thinking about your major expenses

▶ Zeroing in on cost-cutting tips

▶ Dealing with a lost or stolen wallet

. . . .

"**S**o, how much is this trip going to cost me, anyway?"

It's a reasonable question, regardless of your income. Vacation can be expensive — and, as destinations go, Maui is a relatively pricey one. Planning ahead keeps your budget on track. In this chapter, I tell you what to expect and offer tips that can save big bucks on major expenses.

Planning Your Budget

The good news is that you can easily structure a Maui trip to suit any budget. Airfare and hotels probably end up being your largest cash outlays. Other items, such as rental cars, are relatively affordable, although rentals tend to be pricier on Maui than they are on some of the other Hawaiian Islands.

Activities also affect the budget: Relaxing on the beach or taking in Maui's natural beauty generally doesn't cost a dime. But guided tours and organized activities, such as snorkel trips and helicopter rides, luaus and dinner cruises, can carry surprisingly heavy price tags.

Transportation

The cost of your flight to Maui will be one of your top two expenses (the other being your hotel). The key is to plan ahead and do your research before booking transpacific and interisland flights. (For details on flying to Maui and getting the best airfare, see Chapter 5.)

Transpacific flights

Airfares at any time of year are almost impossible to predict and can change at the drop of a hat, especially as oil prices continue to rise. Still, here's a rough idea of what to expect: If you're going to Maui in the off-season — say, May or maybe October — you may be able to snag a round-trip ticket for as little as $500 from San Francisco or Los Angeles, or $700 from the East Coast. If you're traveling in the high season (late Dec to Apr, or in summer), you'll pay more — probably in the $600 to $900 range from the West Coast and $800 to $1,400 from back East. Your best bet is to shop carefully at any time of year.

Expect to pay more if you're departing from a city without a major airline hub. If you're traveling over the holidays, expect to pay full fare.

You can score any number of money-saving deals, especially if you consider an all-inclusive package. (See Chapter 5 for more details on travel packages. I tell you more about how to save on airfares in that chapter, too.)

Interisland flights

If you plan to visit more than one island during your stay, you will likely need to take an interisland flight. Fares for one-way trips between the islands, which are operated by Hawaiian Airlines and recent market entry go! Airlines, average about $160 in the high season. However, you often don't need to pay full fare. Numerous sales and special Internet-only fares are frequently available; one-way fares were available for around $109 at press time, with sale fares as low as $53 per flight in the off season. (See Chapter 5 for details.)

Ferry service is also available from Maui's Lahaina Harbor to its sister islands of Molokai and Lanai. Fares to Molokai are generally $40 per adult, with fares to Lanai only about $25 at press time. However, with the current airfare wars going on, it's worth price-comparing with the airlines before you book. (See Chapter 5 for details.)

Car rentals

Rental cars are fairly affordable on Maui, especially if you avoid the holiday season. Weekly rates almost always save you a bundle. You can often get a compact for as little as $35 to $45 a day, less if you book a weekly rental. If you need a family-size car, expect to pay more like $45 to $65 per day. Of course, everybody wants a convertible in the islands, so expect to pay upwards of $75 a day in season for one, although weekly rentals can sometimes be scored for about $400. You can sometimes wheel and deal for one at the rental counter in the off season, when business is slower. (For more information, see Chapter 8.)

Do yourself a favor and book a rental car with unlimited mileage. You'll appreciate the freedom, and you don't want to end up paying for your rental on a per-mile basis. Trust me, you'll end up with the short end of this stick. Most of the major car-rental companies rent on an unlimited-miles basis — just be sure to confirm this policy when you book.

And because you'll probably cover a good deal of ground, don't forget to factor in gas, which is typically more expensive on Maui than it is on the mainland. Despite rising gas costs, the gap between mainland and Hawaii prices has closed; at press time, island gas was only about 40¢ more per gallon. However, gas has been known to be as high as a dollar more per gallon in Hawaii than it costs on the mainland.

Also remember to account for any additional insurance costs, which generally run an extra $15 to $21 a day, depending on the coverage you select. Parking, thankfully, is generally free (except at some luxury resorts, so be sure to check for daily parking fees when you book).

You seldom save by waiting to rent your car; generally, prices only go up as your pickup date approaches — especially in the busy travel seasons. Book as far in advance as possible for the best rate. Also see the section "Cutting Costs, But Not the Fun," later in this chapter, for additional money-saving tips.

You may not have to worry about shopping around or wrangling a lower rate on a car rental. Often, rental cars and interisland flights are part of a package deal. In many hotel and airline packages, they're thrown in for a nominal fee or for free. (See Chapter 5 for more details.)

Lodging

Maui has a wealth of luxury hotels and resorts, but it also offers plenty of affordable choices — especially in the condo market. Still, although you can find decent hotel rooms or budget condo rentals for $125 or so a night, you really shouldn't expect to pay much less than that. After you start adding on amenities, such as kitchenettes, room service, ocean views, and so on, you can expect room rates to climb.

You can score reasonable rates on a per-person basis if you're traveling in a group or with your family. Maui boasts plenty of apartment-style condos that sleep four or more at moderate prices — between $125 and $225 per night on the lower end, and $250 or more for quite luxurious digs. Of course, if you stay at a condo, you likely miss out on resort-style amenities and services, such as a concierge, room service, kids' programs, and the like. But it may be worth it to you if you want to have more room to spread out, enjoy the convenience of having a kitchen, and keep costs down, because dining is quite expensive on Maui — especially when you start feeding a family. (For more on rates, including details on how to get the best rate, see Chapter 6.)

I've taken care to recommend a range of lodging choices on Maui, so you'll have plenty to choose from, no matter what your needs or budget. And remember: Although I've listed standard rack rates for every hotel, these tend to be the maximum. You'll rarely have to pay full price; you can find numerous ways to save. (For one thing, booking a package deal can be a huge money saver when it comes to hotels; for more information on packages, see Chapter 5.) For additional cost-cutting measures, see "Cutting Costs, But Not the Fun," later in this chapter.

So that you don't encounter any unwanted surprises at payment time, be sure to account for the 11.42 percent tax that will be added to your final hotel bill when planning your budget.

Dining: How to save, when to splurge

Maui has become quite a culinary mecca in the last few years, boasting an increasing number of top-quality restaurants, often charging top-dollar prices. So think about your bottom line. Many people look forward to sampling the island's finest restaurants and don't mind paying for the privilege. But if you want to spend your vacation dollars on other activities, Maui offers opportunities to dine on the cheap: If you choose carefully, you can spend as little as $5 to $10 for breakfast (a continental breakfast may even be included in your hotel deal), grab a quick-and-easy lunch for $10 to $15, and enjoy a casual dinner for $15 to $30. Still, thanks to the high cost of transpacific transport, island real estate and labor, you're likely to pay more even for casual food here than you do at home. Of course, extra niceties, such as wine or cocktails, will drive up dinner costs quickly.

Restaurant bills can add up fast, so if you want to save in this category, I strongly suggest booking a room or condo with kitchen facilities. By preparing a few daytime meals yourself (breakfast, in particular, can be a big money saver, and it's often convenient to make sandwiches to take to the beach), you're in a better position to splurge on a great dinner. Kitchen facilities are a virtual must if you're traveling with kids.

Sightseeing and activities: See it all without going broke

With sightseeing and other activities, the bills can really start to pile up, especially for families. Ultimately, though, it depends on what you want to do. If you're coming to Maui to simply kick back at the beach and leave your mainland worries behind, you don't have to budget much in this category; going to the beach is free, and even snorkel gear rentals are cheap. (See Chapter 12 for more information.)

But if you're planning to schedule some organized activities and tours — which I strongly suggest you do, especially if it's your first visit to Hawaii — budget ahead because they can get pricey. Expect to pay $70 to $95 per person for your average snorkel cruise, and even more for your average luau. Helicopter rides can easily run more than $175 a head. Budget-minded golfers may want to think twice before they tee up, because tee times at Maui's top courses don't come cheap. Greens fees commonly run close to $200. However, wallet watchers can often take advantage of twilight rates, which generally hover around $100.

This book lists prices for activities, entertainment, tee times, admission fees, and the like so that you can budget your money realistically. If you can snag a bargain, I include that information, too.

Shopping and nightlife

These two areas are the most flexible parts of your budget. Shopping, in particular, is a huge temptation in Maui. But if money is an issue, do yourself a favor and bypass the souvenirs.

Maui is one of the liveliest islands in terms of after-dark diversions, but the islands aren't overloaded with nightlife options. You can easily avoid racking up the bills in these categories if shopping and/or evening entertainment isn't a high priority for you.

Table 4-1 breaks down typical costs, so you can plan ahead.

Table 4-1	What Things Cost in Maui
Item	*Price*
An average cup of coffee	$1.50
A Grande Mocha Latte at Starbucks	$4
Compact rental car (per day)	$39
Convertible rental car (per day)	$78
Admission to the Maui Ocean Center	$24
Admission to Haleakala National Park	$10 per car
Trilogy Excursions snorkel trip	$129–$219
Helicopter tour with Blue Hawaiian	$173–$518
Greens fees at Kapalua Golf Club	$215–$295
A day at the beach	Free!
Luxury room for two at the Grand Wailea	$625–$1,180
Moderate room for two at the Kaanapali Beach Hotel	$199–$355
Affordable room for two at the Koa Resort	$100–$140
Affordable lunch at Cilantro Fresh Mexican Grill	$14
Oceanfront dinner for two at Hula Grill Kaanapali	$120
Adult ticket to 'Ulalena show	$60–$100
Adult admission to Old Lahaina Luau	$92

Cutting Costs, But Not the Fun

I don't care how much money you have — I know you don't want to spend more than necessary. In this section, I give you tips that can help you save your hard-earned money.

Getting the best airfares

Landing the best airfare is so huge that I dedicate the better part of a chapter to it. Before you even start scanning for fares, see Chapter 5, which also discusses how to find money-saving package deals.

How to avoid paying full price for your hotel room

There's often a huge gap between hotels' official "published" (full-price, or rack) rates and what you actually pay, so don't be scared off at first glance. What's more, savvy travelers can further widen the margin.

More often than not, the best way to score a cheap hotel room is to buy an all-inclusive travel package that includes airfare, hotel, and car, and sometimes other extras, in one low price. (For details on scoring a good-value package, see Chapter 5.)

 The second-best way to avoid paying the full rack rate when booking your hotel is stunningly simple: Just ask the reservation agent for a cheaper or discounted rate. You may be pleasantly surprised — I've been, many times. But you have to take the initiative and ask because no one is going to volunteer to save you money.

Here are a few more potential money-saving tips:

- ✔ **Rates are generally lowest in spring and fall.** The time of year you visit may affect your bargaining power more than anything else. During the peak seasons — basically mid-December through mid-April and summer — when a hotel is booked up, management is less likely to offer discounts or package deals. In the slower seasons — generally mid-April through mid-June and September through mid-December — when capacity is down, they're often willing to negotiate. In fact, many places drop rates by 10 percent to 30 percent automatically in the less busy times of year. (If you haven't decided when you want to visit Maui yet, see Chapter 3.)

- ✔ **Membership in AAA, AARP, or frequent-flier/traveler programs often qualifies you for discounted rates.** You may also qualify for corporate or student discounts. Attention, seniors: You may qualify for discounts even if you're *not* an AARP member (although I highly recommend joining; see Chapter 7 for details). Members of the military or trade unions or those with government jobs may also qualify for price breaks. Be sure to mention membership in these organizations and in any corporate rewards programs you can think of — or your Uncle Joe's Elks lodge in which you're an honorary inductee, for that matter — when you call to book. Even

Costco membership has been known to pay off. You never know when an affiliation may be worth a few dollars off your room rate.

✔ **Inquire about the hotel's own package deals.** Even if you're not traveling on an all-inclusive package (see Chapter 5), you may be able to take advantage of value-added packages offered directly by hotels, resorts, and condos, which includes such extras as free rental car, champagne and in-room breakfast for honeymooners, free dinners, discounted tee times or spa treatments, room upgrades, an extra night free (sometimes the fifth, sometimes the seventh), or some other freebie. I note what kinds of discounts are typically available in my hotel reviews. Properties often list these deals on their Web sites, but not always, so it never hurts to ask.

✔ **If you're booking a hotel that belongs to a chain, call the hotel directly in addition to going through central reservations.** See which one gives you the better deal. Sometimes the local reservationists know about packages or special rates, but the hotel may neglect to tell the central booking line.

✔ **Surf the Web to save.** A surprising number of hotels advertise great packages via their Web sites, and some even offer Internet-only special rates.

In addition to surfing the hotel's own sites, you may want to try using general travel booking sites, such as **Expedia** (www.expedia.com), **Travelocity** (www.travelocity.com), **Hotels.com** (www.hotels.com), **Kayak.com** (www.kayak.com), or **Orbitz.com** (www.orbitz.com) to book your hotel, or a pay-one-price package that also includes airfare. Acting much like airline consolidators, these sites can sometimes offer big discounts on rooms as well. However, always price-compare against the hotel's own Web site; these days, virtually every major hotel chain offers price parity with the online distributors through their own Web sites. Often, you'll save a few bucks through the hotel's own site and/or end up with a better room for the same money, because the hotel doesn't have to pay high distribution fees if you book direct. (See Chapter 6 for a more complete discussion of how to use the Web to find a great hotel bargain.)

✔ **Ask innkeepers for a break.** B&Bs are generally nonnegotiable on price. Sometimes, however, you can negotiate a discount for longer stays, such as a week or more. You may also score a price break if you're visiting off-season. And some do offer AAA and senior discounts. Remember: It never hurts to ask, politely.

✔ **Look for price breaks and value-added extras when booking condos.** Condos can sometimes be pretty flexible on rates. They tend to offer discounts on multinight stays, and many throw in a free rental car to sweeten the deal. Some condo properties have units handled by multiple management companies; if that's the case, inquire through both companies and see where you get the better deal. You may also want to check with **Hawaii Condo**

Exchange (☎ 800-442-0404 or 323-436-0300; www.hawaiicondo exchange.com), which acts as a consolidator for condo properties throughout the islands.

✔ **Reserve a hotel room with a kitchenette or a condo with a full kitchen and do your own cooking.** You may miss the pampering that room service provides, but you can save plenty of money because restaurant prices are high on Maui, even for casual eats. Even if you prepare only breakfast and an occasional picnic lunch in the kitchen, you still save significantly in the long run. (I've had some memorable island meals by simply buying fabulous fresh fish in the local supermarket and throwing it on the barbecue grill at an oceanfront condo.) Plus, if the beach is right outside your door, you don't ever have to leave it to go on restaurant runs.

✔ **Skip the ocean views, or stay away from the ocean altogether.** Being steps away from the surf is wonderful, but you pay through the nose for the privilege: Oceanview rooms are the most expensive rooms in any hotel, especially those on the upper floors. Mountain or garden views are usually much cheaper, and you probably don't plan on hanging out in your room much anyway. A stay in a hotel that is located slightly inland from the beach can be even cheaper. (For more on this subject, see Chapter 6.)

✔ **Ask whether the kids can stay in your room.** Or, better yet, book a condo with a sleeper sofa in the living room or a separate bedroom. A room with two double beds usually doesn't cost any more than one with a king-size bed, and most hotels don't charge an extra-person rate if the additional person is a child.

If that's a bit too much togetherness for you, book one of the many one-, two-, or three-bedroom condos that are available on Maui. These full apartments are often no more expensive than your standard hotel room, and they're always cheaper than having to book two or more hotel rooms. Furthermore, they solve the expensive eating-out-at-every-meal problem, too.

✔ **And remember, you don't need much luxury to make Maui feel like paradise.** To find true Hawaii happiness, the rule is always this: the simpler, the better. You won't need a 27-inch TV, 24-hour butler service, or a telephone in the bathroom to be happy. So when reserving your accommodations, don't overdo it by booking a place that taxes your budget too much. Save that extra dough for having fun!

Tips for cutting other costs

Here are a few more useful tips to help you enjoy your Maui vacation without breaking the bank:

✔ **Consult a reliable travel agent.** A travel agent can sometimes negotiate a better price with certain hotels and assemble a better valued complete travel package than you can get on your own. In fact, in a recent *Condé Nast Traveler* investigation, travel agents could always price out Hawaii resort vacations more cheaply than any other outlet (including airline packagers). Even if you book your own airfare, you may want to contact a travel agent to price out your hotel.

On the other hand, hotels, condos, and even B&Bs are sometimes willing to discount your rate as much as 30 percent — the amount they'd otherwise pay an agent in commissions — if you book direct.

✔ **Surf the Web to save on your rental car.** In addition to surfing rental-car agencies' own sites, try comparing rates through general travel booking sites, such as Expedia, Travelocity, Orbitz, Kayak. com, or Priceline. This one-stop-shopping method can save you more than money — it can save you time, too. However, always price-compare against the car company's own site, because most companies are now combating online booking agencies with on-par (or lower) pricing. (See Chapter 8 for more money-saving tips to keep in mind while booking your island wheels.)

✔ **Don't rent a gas guzzler.** Renting a smaller car is cheaper, and you save on gas to boot (an especially important point, because gas prices are always higher in Hawaii than on the mainland). Unless you're traveling with a large group, don't go beyond the economy size.

✔ **Skip the souvenirs.** I've heard it more than once: "That whale print that looked so right in the art gallery was all wrong back in my living room in Cincinnati." Spend your money on memories, not tchotchkes.

Handling Money

You're the best judge of how much cash you feel comfortable carrying or what alternative form of currency is your favorite. That's not going to change much on your vacation. True, you'll probably be moving around more and incurring more expenses than you generally do, and you may let your mind slip into vacation gear and not be as vigilant about your safety as when you're in work mode. But those factors aside, the only type of payment that won't be quite as available to you away from home is your personal checkbook.

Using ATMs and carrying cash

The easiest and best way to get cash while away from home is from an ATM. The **MasterCard, Maestro,** or **Cirrus** (☎ **800-424-7787;** www. mastercard.com) networks and **Visa PLUS** (☎ **800-843-7587;** www. visa.com) network span the globe; look at the back of your bank card to see which network you're on and then call or check online for ATM locations at your destination. Be sure you know your personal identification number (PIN) before you leave home and don't forget to find out your daily withdrawal limit before you depart.

Also, keep in mind that many banks impose a fee every time your card is used at a different bank's ATM. On top of this fee, the bank from which you withdraw cash may charge its own fee. (To compare banks' ATM fees within the United States, use www.bankrate.com.) To beat these fees (and to avoid wasting precious vacation time running errands), it makes sense to withdraw larger sums instead of relying on lots of smaller withdrawals.

Charging ahead with credit cards

Credit cards are a safe way to carry money: They also provide a convenient record of all your expenses, and for foreign visitors, they generally offer relatively good exchange rates.

You can also withdraw cash advances from your credit cards at banks or ATMs, provided you know your PIN. If you've forgotten yours, or didn't even know you had one, call the number on the back of your credit card and ask the bank to send it to you. It usually takes five to seven business days, though some banks will provide the number over the phone if you tell them your mother's maiden name or some other personal information. But keep in mind that cash advances are a bad idea, only to be used in case of emergency. Your issuing bank will start charging interest from the day you make the withdrawal, usually at significantly higher rates than you're charged on regular purchases.

 Some credit card companies recommend that you notify them of any impending trip so that they don't become suspicious when the card is used numerous times in a new destination and block your charges. Even if you don't call your credit card company in advance, you can always call the card's toll-free emergency number if a charge is refused — a good reason to carry the phone number with you.

Carrying more than one card with you on your trip is a good idea; a card may not work for any number of reasons, so having a backup is the smart way to go.

Toting traveler's checks

These days, it's so easy to find a 24-hour ATM that traveler's checks are becoming obsolete. Furthermore, the popularity of credit cards means that businesses are less and less interested in accepting them. Still, if you like the security of traveler's checks, and you don't mind locating a bank and/or showing identification every time you want to cash one, you may prefer to stick with the tried-and-true.

You can get traveler's checks at almost any bank. American Express offers denominations of $20, $50, $100, $500, and (for cardholders only) $1,000. You'll pay a service charge ranging from 1 percent to 4 percent (which negates any money you may have saved by avoiding ATM fees while you're on the road). You can also get American Express Travelers Cheques over the phone by calling ☎ **800-221-7282;** Amex gold and platinum cardholders who use this number are exempt from the fee. Travelers Cheques can also be ordered online at www.american express.com.

Visa offers traveler's checks at Citibank locations nationwide, as well as at several other banks. The service charge ranges between 1.5 percent and 2 percent; checks come in denominations of $20, $50, $100, $500, and $1,000. Call ☎ **800-732-1322** for information. AAA members can pick up Visa checks without a fee at most AAA offices or by calling ☎ **866-339-3378.** MasterCard also offers traveler's checks. Call ☎ **800-223-9920** for a location near you.

 If you choose to carry traveler's checks, be sure to keep a record of their serial numbers separate from your checks — safely, with a relative or friend back home. If the checks are stolen or lost, you'll get a refund faster if you know the numbers.

Dealing with a lost or stolen wallet

Be sure to contact all your credit card companies the minute you discover that your wallet has been lost or stolen and file a report at the nearest police precinct. Your credit card company or insurer may require a police report number or record of the loss. Most credit card companies have an emergency toll-free number to call if your card is lost or stolen; they may be able to wire you a cash advance immediately or deliver an emergency credit card in a day or two. Call the following emergency numbers in the United States:

- ✔ **American Express:** ☎ **800-268-9824** or 800-528-4800 (for card-holders) and ☎ **800-221-7282** (for Travelers Cheque holders)
- ✔ **MasterCard:** ☎ **800-307-7309** or 800-627-8372
- ✔ **Visa:** ☎ **800-847-2911** or 410-581-9994

For other credit cards, call the toll-free number directory at ☎ **800-555-1212.**

If you need emergency cash over the weekend, when all banks and American Express offices are closed, you can have money wired to you via **Western Union** (☎ **800-325-6000;** www.westernunion.com).

Identity theft or fraud is a potential complication of losing your wallet, especially if you've lost your driver's license along with your cash and credit cards. Notify the major credit-reporting bureaus immediately; placing a fraud alert on your records may protect you against liability for criminal activity. The three major U.S. credit-reporting agencies are **Equifax** (☎ **800-685-1111;** www.equifax.com), **Experian** (☎ **888-397-3742;** www.experian.com), and **TransUnion** (☎ **800-680-**7289; www.transunion.com).

Finally, if you've lost all forms of photo ID, call your airline and explain the situation. You may be allowed to board the plane if you have a copy of your passport or birth certificate and a copy of the police report you've filed.

Chapter 5

Getting to Maui

. . . .

In This Chapter

▶ Getting the best airfares to and around Maui
▶ Taking advantage of all-inclusive package deals
▶ Stretching your accommodations dollars

. . . .

G etting to Maui may not *really* be half the fun, but it's a necessary step — and a big part of the planning process. How can you beat the high cost of transpacific airfares? Should you reserve a package deal or book the elements of your vacation separately?

In this chapter, I give you the information to make the decisions that are right for you.

Flying to Maui

These days, nearly as many transpacific flights arrive at Maui's Kahului Airport as arrive at Oahu's Honolulu International Airport.

The following major airlines fly between mainland North America and one or more of Hawaii's major airports, including Maui's Kahului Airport:

- ✔ **Air Canada** (☎ 888-247-2262; www.aircanada.com).

- ✔ **Alaska Airlines** (☎ 800-252-7522; www.alaskaair.com).

- ✔ **American Airlines** (☎ 800-433-7300; www.aa.com).

- ✔ **Continental Airlines** (☎ 800-523-3273; www.continental.com), which offers nonstop flights from Newark to Honolulu, among many other options; all flights to Maui connect with an interisland flight at Honolulu's airport.

- ✔ **Delta Airlines** (☎ 800-221-1212; www.delta.com).

- ✔ **Hawaiian Airlines** (☎ 800-367-5320; www.hawaiianair.com), which offers interisland flights in addition to transpacific service from the mainland and international destinations.

- ✔ **Northwest Airlines** (☎ 800-225-2525; www.nwa.com).

- ✔ **United Airlines** (☎ 800-864-8331; www.united.com).

- **US Airways** (☎ 800-428-4322; www.usairways.com).
- **WestJet** (☎ 888-937-8538; www.westjet.com), which offers direct flights to Maui from Vancouver, Canada.

These days, an increasing number of airlines are charging all travelers except their elite customers $15 to $25 per bag to check luggage. Therefore, I recommend checking with your airline to understand its checked-baggage policy so you can prepare accordingly and avoid any unwanted surprises when you arrive at the airport.

No matter where you're coming from, it's bound to be a long haul to Maui. So help yourself choose the best seat available to you with **SeatGuru** (www.seatguru.com), which features cabin diagrams for just about every carrier, with individual seat ratings, details on ergonomics, entertainment options, power outlet accessibility, and more.

Getting the best airfare

Competition among the major U.S. airlines is unlike that of any other industry. Every airline offers virtually the same product, yet prices can vary by hundreds of dollars.

Business travelers who need to purchase their tickets at the last minute, change their itinerary at a moment's notice, or get home before the weekend pay the premium rate, known as the *full fare*. Passengers whose travel agenda is more flexible — who can book their tickets far in advance; who don't mind staying over Saturday night; or who are willing to travel on a Tuesday, Wednesday, or Thursday — pay the least, usually a fraction of the full fare. On most flights to Hawaii, even the shortest hops, the full fare is more than $1,000, but an advance-purchase ticket from the West Coast can sometimes be had for as low as $400. Obviously, I can't guarantee what the fares will be when you book — especially as oil prices continue to reach record highs and competition has tightened after two transpacific carriers (Aloha Airlines and ATA) folded their wings for good in early 2008 — but you can almost always save big by planning ahead.

Keep an eye out for newspaper, Internet, and TV airfare sales. Sale fares carry advance-purchase requirements and date-of-travel restrictions, but the price is usually worth the restrictions. The sales tend to take place in seasons of low travel volume (usually spring and fall). You'll almost never see a sale around the peak summer vacation months or in the winter high season.

Here are a few tips that can help you save on airfares:

- **Travel on off days of the week.** Airfares vary depending on the day of the week. Everybody wants to travel on the weekend. If you can travel on a Tuesday, Wednesday, or Thursday, you may find cheaper flights to Maui. When you inquire about airfares, check to see whether you can get a cheaper rate by flying on a different day.

Remember, too, that staying over on a Saturday night can lower your airfare.

✔ **Reserve your flight well in advance.** Take advantage of advance-purchase fares. Sometimes you can snag a last-minute bargain, but I wouldn't count on it. Airfares only get higher as the planes fill up. More often than not, the farther ahead you book, the lower your airfare is likely to be.

✔ **Fly direct to Maui to save on interisland airfares.** Although it all depends on the transpacific carrier you choose and your origination point, it's increasingly easy to fly across the Pacific directly to Maui. Maui is served by direct flights from the mainland, usually for comparable prices to flying to Honolulu. (See the list of carriers in the preceding section.) Compare the cost of flying to Honolulu plus an interisland fare with the cost of flying directly to Maui. Flying direct also saves you a few hours on each end, and time can be a more valuable commodity than money when your vacation time is limited.

✔ **Book online.** In an effort to encourage you to book on their Web sites, most of the major air carriers will charge you a fee — anywhere from $5 to $20 per ticket — to buy your tickets over the phone or in person at ticket offices. Therefore, booking your ticket online at the airline's Web site is usually going to be the cheapest way to buy direct.

Booking your flight online

The big one-stop online travel agencies — **Expedia** (www.expedia.com), **Travelocity** (www.travelocity.com), **Orbitz** (www.orbitz.com), **Hotwire** (www.hotwire.com), and **Yahoo! Travel** (http://travel.yahoo.com) — are excellent sources for one-stop price comparing across all the major airlines. (Canadian travelers should try www.expedia.ca and www.travelocity.ca; U.K. residents can go for www.expedia.co.uk, www.travelocity.co.uk, and www.opodo.co.uk.) Each has different business deals with the airlines and may offer different fares on the same flights, so shopping around is wise. Expedia and Travelocity will also send you **e-mail notifications** when a cheap fare becomes available to your favorite destination. All these online travel agencies also purport to save you money with pay-one-price packaging, but I suggest comparing the prices of each piece before you assume that you're saving.

Kayak.com (www.kayak.com) is also gaining popularity; it uses a sophisticated search engine, developed at MIT, to search the widest breadth of online resources available to find the best available fare. Kayak.com is a search engine, not an online travel agency, so after you identify the best fare, it links you directly to the source to book it. It also has a Fare Alert tool that will allow you to track fare prices through an e-mail notification system. **SideStep** (www.sidestep.com) works in a similar fashion and gets good reviews from users.

Newest on the scene is **Farecast** (www.farecast.com), an online travel agency designed to help you buy your tickets with confidence, knowing that you're getting the best deal available. Farecast's airfare prediction tool tracks whether fares are rising or dropping; based on these predictions, the site will let you know whether to buy now or wait. It also compares its prices to those available on such sites as Expedia and Hotwire. With these valuable features, it's no wonder that *Time* magazine has named Farecast one of its "50 Coolest Sites."

Attention, spontaneous travelers: Great last-minute deals are sometimes available through **Smarter Travel** (www.smartertravel.com), which compiles a comprehensive list of bargain-basement fares available from the airlines and the online agencies looking to fill those final empty seats.

Of course, some of the best fares are available through **Priceline** (www.priceline.com) especially if you're willing to play its "Name Your Own Price" game in which you "bid" for a rock-bottom price — and it's yours if an airline accepts it. You won't know who the carrier is until after you buy, and you may have an out-of-the-way connection (or two). However, the mystery airlines are all major, well-known carriers, and the possibility of being sent from Phoenix to Honolulu via Tampa is remote. Still, the inconveniences can be minimal compared to the savings. Priceline now offers standard online airfare shopping services as well.

Although third-party sites, such as Expedia and Travelocity, sometimes offer the best airfares, never assume. Also remember to check the airlines' own Web sites. These days, many major carriers are offering similar — or even cheaper — airfares through their own Web sites in order to avoid paying costly commissions to the online agencies. Even if you find a good fare from one of the services listed in this section, you can often shave off a few bucks by booking directly through the airline. Many airlines have special Internet-only fares that their phone agents don't even know about.

Attention **Upromise** members: If you use this online rewards service to save for your kids' college education (or to pay your own bills), you can earn cash back (usually 1 percent to 2 percent of the purchase price) by booking airfares and other travel reservations via Expedia, Travelocity, and a wealth of other travel partners when accessed through the Upromise portal (www.upromise.com). If you're not a member but there's someone in your life paying for college, visit the site to sign up.

Consolidators, also known as bucket shops, can be a good place to find low fares, sometimes below even the airlines' discounted rates. Basically, these companies are just big travel agencies that get discounts for buying in bulk and pass some of the savings on to you. These days, however, it's a rare day to get a fare through a consolidator that you can't get through mainstream sources, such as Expedia — or even the airlines themselves — so be sure to compare prices. Bucket-shop tickets are usually nonrefundable or rigged with stiff cancellation penalties, and some put you on charter airlines you've never heard of; be sure you know all the ins and outs before you buy.

Some of the most reliable consolidators include the following:

- ✔ **AirSaver** (☎ 800-325-2175; www.airsaver.com): AirSaver is an online consolidator that sometimes offers very good deals on transpacific round-trips.

- ✔ **Cheap Tickets** (☎ 800-504-3249; www.cheaptickets.com): I usually do better by calling than I do by pricing out fares on its Web site.

- ✔ **STA Travel** (☎ 800-781-4040; www.statravel.com): STA Travel is the world's leader in student travel, but it offers good fares for travelers of all ages.

Flying between the Hawaiian Islands

With the exception of limited ferry service between Maui and the islands of Molokai and Lanai (see the following section), the only real way to travel from island to island today is by airplane.

An interisland high-speed catamaran ferry service called **Hawaii Superferry** (☎ 877-443-3779; www.hawaiisuperferry.com) was introduced between Maui and Oahu in 2007. In theory, the service is a great idea, allowing locals and visitors alike to ferry between the islands with their cars and luggage. However, service has been intermittent at best since launching, and it was temporarily suspended as of this writing. Even when it resumes, only one ferry a day is slated each way between Oahu and Maui. For now, until service can get on a steady track, I recommend sticking with the airlines.

Despite the fact that it's a short and easy shuttle hop between islands — even the longest island-to-island flight clocks in around 45 minutes — booking in advance is vital. The airlines request that you show up at least 90 minutes before your flight to allow for security inspections, and I've found that to be good advice.

Three interisland carriers serve the islands: Hawaiian Airlines and go!, the upstart carrier operated by Mesa Airlines, carry the bulk of travelers between the islands, while Island Air offers supplemental service, usually between Hawaii's smaller airports. (Aloha Airlines filed for bankruptcy and halted all service in early 2008, citing skyrocketing fuel and predatory pricing by go! as the pressures that forced its hand.) Both Hawaiian and go! offer similar schedules — flights between the major islands every hour or so — at competitive prices.

Hawaiian Airlines (☎ 800-367-5320; www.hawaiianair.com) offers interisland jet service aboard Boeing 717-200s; the entire fleet was replaced with brand-new aircraft in 2001, making this the youngest fleet in the Pacific.

Hawaiian is mileage partners with American Airlines, US Airways, Continental, Delta, Northwest, and Virgin Atlantic airlines, which gives you plenty of mileage earning potential. They don't make it easy to enter another airline's frequent flier number online, however, so you may need to call to get the appropriate credit.

An upstart airline called **go!** (☎ **888-IFLYGO2** [888-435-9462]; www. iflygo.com), a subsidiary of Mesa Air Group, entered the market for interisland flights in June 2006 and has caused quite a ruckus since. They have fueled an ongoing price war by offering flights for as little as $49 per segment, forcing Hawaiian to also offer competitive sale fares in the face of increased competition. At the end of the day, we consumers are benefiting from fares that are staying low (for now, anyway) even as oil prices rise.

Island Air (☎ **800-652-6541** or 808-484-2222; www.islandair.com) operates deHavilland DASH-8 and DASH-6 aircraft and serves Hawaii's smaller interisland airports on Maui (Kapalua Airport), Molokai, and Lanai, as well as both Hilo and Kona on the Big Island. You may find yourself on a code-share flight operated by Island Air if you head to Molokai or Lanai, even if you buy through Hawaiian.

At press time, the full interisland fare was about $109 per one-way segment, depending on the dates and routes you want to fly. (At this writing, experts were forecasting price increases in the wake of lightened competition resulting from Aloha's disappearance, so don't be surprised if you see higher fares.) Booking more than 14 days in advance gives you the best shot at a bargain fare. I recommend comparing prices for the best deal.

If you're traveling on a package, you probably don't have to worry about any of this — your interisland flights are most likely included in your package deal, on whichever interisland carrier the packager is affiliated with. (For more on all-inclusive travel packages, see "Choosing a Pay-One-Price Package," later in this chapter.)

Ferrying between Maui and the Other Maui Nui Islands

If you're traveling between Maui and its sister islands of Molokai and Lanai, you might consider the ferry. Ferry service is available from Maui's Lahaina Harbor to Molokai and Lanai, which can really minimize interisland transport costs.

Molokai Ferry (☎ **866-307-6524**; www.molokaiferry.com) offers ferry service twice a day, Monday through Saturday, in each direction, between Lahaina and Molokai on the *Maui Princess* and the *Molokai Princess.* Travel time is approximately 90 minutes, and the one-way fare is $40 for adults, $20 for kids 4 to 12. One-day golf and guided sightseeing tours of Molokai are also available.

Expeditions Lahaina (☎ **800-695-2624;** www.go-lanai.com) offers service between Lahaina and Lanai's Manele Harbor five times daily; there's also twice-daily service from Maui's Ma'alaea Harbor, north of Kihei on Maui's neck. The one-way fare is $25 for adults, $20 for kids 2 to 11. The ferry is extremely popular with golfers who choose to spend the day playing Lanai's two spectacular championship courses. A variety of golf and sightseeing packages are also available.

Choosing a Pay-One-Price Package

Comprehensive, pay-one-price travel packages can be the smart way to go when booking your Hawaii vacation. Besides the convenience of having all your travel needs taken care of at once, a package can often save you lots of money. In many cases, a package that includes airfare, hotel, and transportation to and from the airport costs less than the hotel alone if you book it yourself.

One reason for this savings is that components of the packages are sold in bulk to tour operators, travel agents, and resellers, who bundle and sell them to the public. Even after the packager takes its cut, you may still realize substantial savings.

Package trips can vary widely. Some offer a better class of hotels than others; others provide the same hotels for lower prices. Some book flights on scheduled airlines; others sell charters.

Every destination, including Maui, usually has a few packagers that are better than the rest because they buy in even bigger bulk. The time you spend shopping around is likely to be well rewarded.

Finding a package deal

Online is probably your best source for package deals. Check out **Expedia** (www.expedia.com), **Travelocity** (www.travelocity.com), **Yahoo! Travel** (http://travel.yahoo.com), **Hotwire** (www.hotwire.com), and **Orbitz** (www.orbitz.com), which have become some of the most sophisticated and easy-to-access pay-one-price packagers in the market.

Liberty Travel (☎ **888-271-1584;** www.libertytravel.com) is one of the biggest packagers in the Northeast. Liberty frequently offers excellent-value packages, with or without air, to all the Hawaiian islands — and its agents are willing to help you construct a multi-island trip. Calling the toll-free number immediately connects you to the Liberty Travel store nearest your home.

Pleasant Holidays (☎ 800-742-9244; www.pleasantholidays.com), the biggest and most comprehensive packager to Hawaii, has more than 40 years of experience and offers tons of package options. Pleasant can arrange just about any kind of vacation you want, including fly/drive packages and land-only deals. And because it buys airfares and hotel-room blocks in such bulk, its deals are often excellent (although it offers better bargains on some properties than others). Another plus is that Pleasant maintains service desks on all the major islands; its employees can help you book activities and answer any questions you may have. These guys can even finance your vacation for you — but be sure to check the interest rates.

If you want to work with a travel agency that specializes in booking packaged Maui vacations, offers a more personalized shopping experience, and really knows its stuff, contact Melissa McCoy's Valley Isle–based **Aloha Destinations Vacations** (☎ 800-256-4280 or 213-784-6143; www.alohadestinations.com).

The big online travel agencies — including **Expedia** (www.expedia.com), **Travelocity** (www.travelocity.com), **Orbitz** (www.orbitz.com), **Hotwire** (www.hotwire.com), and **Yahoo! Travel** (http://travel.yahoo.com) — specialize in pay-one-price vacation packages these days. As with any packager, the best way to cover yourself — to insure that you're really getting the best price — is to price each piece individually and compare against the pay-one-price tag that any online or three-dimensional packager is offering.

Some travel packagers, such as Pleasant Hawaiian Holidays, are likely to book you on their own charter flights rather than on commercial flights on major airlines. Flying on a charter doesn't really make a difference, unless you have a particular allegiance to a specific airline (or to collecting miles in a frequent-flier program). Be sure you know what airline you're flying when you book. And if you really do want to fly with a specific airline, that doesn't rule out a packager. In fact, Pleasant has established relationships with major carriers, such as Delta, United, and Hawaiian — and just about any packager will be happy to book you a land-only vacation that lets you book your own airfare separately (even the airline packagers will do this; see the following section).

Uncovering an airline package

Many major airlines also offer travel packages to Maui, either directly or through a trusted package partner. I always recommend comparison shopping, but you may want to choose the airline that has frequent service to your hometown or the one on which you accumulate frequent-flier miles; you may even be able to pay for your entire package using miles. The following airlines offer travel packages to Maui as part of their services:

- ✔ **Air Canada Vacations** (☎ 866-529-2079;
  www.aircanadavacations.com)

- ✔ **American Airlines Vacations** (☎ 800-321-2121;
  www.aavacations.com)

- ✔ **Continental Airlines Vacations** (☎ 800-301-3800;
  www.covacations.com)

- ✔ **Delta Vacations** (☎ 800-654-6559;
  www.deltavacations.com)

- ✔ **Hawaiian Airlines** (☎ 800-236-5451 or 808-356-8040;
  www.hawaiianair.com; click on Vacation Packages)

- ✔ **NWA WorldVacations** (☎ 800-800-1504;
  www.nwaworldvacations.com)

- ✔ **United Vacations** (☎ 888-854-3899;
  www.unitedvacations.com)

- ✔ **US Airways Vacations** (☎ 800-455-0123;
  www.usairwaysvacations.com)

Choosing between a travel agent and a packager isn't an either/or proposition; in fact, your travel agent can be your best source in sorting through the various deals that are available. If you're an Amex customer, you may consider going through **American Express Travel Service,** which can book a full variety of travel packages for you. To locate the office (or official travel agent representative) nearest you, call ☎ 800-335-3342 or go online to www.americanexpress.com and select Travel; you can also book your vacation completely online, and even pay with Membership Rewards.

Ditto for members of the American Automobile Association, who have access to the **AAA Travel Agency,** which can also book good-value package deals. Visit www.aaa.com, or call ☎ 877-934-6222 to book your reservations or to find the regional office nearest you.

Weighing your options

With the multitude of packages on the market, you may need some help weighing the various merits of each one. Follow these tips as you sift through the options:

- ✔ **Read up on Maui.** Read through the hotel listings in this book (see Chapter 10) and select the places that sound interesting. Compare the rates that I list with the packagers' prices to gauge which operators are really offering a good deal and which have simply gussied up the rack rates to make their full-fare offer sound like a smart buy. Remember: Most packagers can offer bigger savings on some properties than on others. For example, Liberty Travel may give you a better rate on the Grand Wailea than Pleasant Holidays can, but Pleasant may offer you a substantial savings on the condo you want.

✔ **Compare apples to apples.** When comparing packages, make sure that you know exactly what's included in the quoted price and what's not. Don't assume anything: Some packagers include everything — including value-added extras, such as lei greetings, free continental breakfast, and dining discounts — while others may not even include airfare. Additionally, when considering package prices, factor in add-in costs if you're flying from somewhere other than Los Angeles or San Francisco; some operators price packages directly from your hometown, and some require additional premiums for airfares from your hometown to their Los Angeles or San Francisco gateway.

✔ **Before you commit to a package, make sure you know how much flexibility you have.** Some packagers require iron-clad commitments, while others charge only minimal fees for changes or cancellations. Consider the possibility that your travel plans may change, and select a packager with the degree of flexibility that suits your needs. And if you pay up front for a complete vacation package that carries stiff cancellation penalties, consider buying travel insurance that will reimburse you in case an unforeseen emergency prevents you from traveling. (See Chapter 8 for more on this topic.)

✔ **Don't believe in fairy tales.** Unfortunately, shady dealers and fly-by-night operations are out there. If a package appears too good to be true, it probably is. Any knowledgeable travel agent can help you determine whether a specific packager is reputable.

Chapter 6

Booking Your Accommodations

. . . .

In This Chapter

▶ Figuring out which type of lodging is right for you

▶ Finding luxury accommodations for less

▶ Getting your room at the best rate

. . . .

Maui's resort hotels are notoriously expensive. So prepare yourself for the fact that accommodations may take up a larger portion of your total travel budget than you might expect. That said, don't forsake Kaanapali for the Jersey Shore just yet. Maui boasts plenty of excellent values for every budget if you just know where to look, and I've included lots of reasonably priced options in Chapter 10.

Before you book your accommodations, you need to figure out what kind of place you want. You find five types of accommodations on Maui: resorts, hotels, condos, bed-and-breakfasts, and vacation rentals.

Getting to Know Your Options

In Maui, your accommodations options range from ultraposh luxury resorts to no-frills vacation rentals. Your choice depends on your travel needs and your budget. Though an expensive resort may be a great option for that romantic getaway, you may prefer to rent a condo if you have the kids in tow. Table 6-1 gives you an idea of what you can expect to pay in each price category.

Table 6-1	Key to Hotel Dollar Signs*	
Dollar Sign(s)	*Price Range*	*What to Expect*
$	Less than $150	Cheap — a basic hotel room a distance from the beach
$$	$150–$224	Still affordable — a midrange hotel room or condo, possibly near the beach
$$$	$225–$324	Moderate — a good-quality hotel room or condo on or near the beach, or a luxury bed-and-breakfast
$$$$	$325–$449	Expensive but not ridiculous — a high-quality room in a full-service hotel, or a multibedroom condo, on or near the beach
$$$$$	$450 or more	Ultraluxurious — the ultimate in deluxe resort living, generally on the beach

* Each range of dollar signs, from one ($) to five ($$$$$), represents the median rack-rate price range for a double room per night. This system applies to each resort, hotel, condo, B&B, or vacation rental.

Relaxing at a resort

Most resorts (or resort hotels) are multi-acre, multibuilding complexes located directly on the beach. Some are sophisticated (sometimes too sophisticated for laid-back Maui, if you ask me), ultraluxury affairs geared to monied adults; others are theme park–like spreads that cater largely to families with kids. More than a few fall somewhere in between.

A resort (or resort hotel) offers everything that your average hotel offers, plus much more. Each one is different, of course, but you can expect such amenities as direct beach access with beach cabanas and chairs, and often beach-toy rentals and ocean activities as well; pools (often more than one) and a Jacuzzi, often with poolside bar service; an activities desk; a fitness center and often a full-service spa; a variety of restaurants, bars, and lounges; a 24-hour front desk; concierge, valet, and bell services; twice-daily maid service (which can come in handy after you've dragged sand in your room and used all your towels by 4 p.m.); room service; tennis and golf (including some world-class courses); a business center; extensive kids' programs; and more.

Rooms may be in high-rise towers, but they're often scattered throughout the property in low-rise buildings or clustered cottages. They tend to be done in the same safe, mass-market style throughout the resort — generally, room no. 101 is going to look exactly like room no. 1901. As travelers increasingly demand more, however, many newer properties (and savvy new renovations) feature smart, high-style concepts that are intended to heighten the resort's unique setting, concept, or personality. Standards tend to be high, and rooms are usually outfitted with top-quality furnishings and linens. Many luxury resorts also boast an increasing slate of in-room extras, such as flat-screen TVs with Nintendo or other gaming systems, iPod docking units for in-suite music, and DVD players. Internet access is usually present throughout the property, but often you'll find wireless only in the public areas; expect to pay a charge more often than not.

Being the best outfitted, and usually the best located, of Maui's accommodations options, resorts are also the priciest choices on the market, although you can find a few midrange resorts. That said, you can sometimes score attractive rates, even at some of the island's most luxurious resorts. You may hit pay dirt by booking through a packager (see Chapter 5), or by just calling or checking a resort's Web site at the right moment, because many resorts host special offers and package deals on their own sites.

Hanging at a hotel

Hotels tend to be smaller and have fewer facilities than resorts — you may get a swimming pool, but don't expect a golf course or tennis courts, more than one or two restaurants and/or bars, and everything else that comes with a full-fledged resort.

Hotels are often a short walk from the beach rather than actually on the sands. Generally, a hotel offers daily maid service and has a restaurant and/or coffee shop, a bar or lounge, on-site laundry facilities, a swimming pool, and a sundries- or convenience-type shop (rather than designer shopping arcades). Top hotels also have activities desks, concierge and valet services, limited room service, a business center, and in-room Internet access (more often than not for a daily charge).

Boutique hotels are smaller — maybe 40 or 50 rooms rather than 200 or more — and more intimate than your average Doubletree or Hilton. The rooms are often more stylish, less cookie-cutter, and usually have more amenities. They tend to cater to adults rather than families.

Hotels run the gamut from very expensive to downright cheap. But even the priciest ones (usually boutique hotels) tend to be less expensive than fully outfitted resorts.

Staying in a condo

Condominium apartments make up a large percentage of Maui's accommodations. They're a great option for everyone because they're outfitted like a fully operational home and can accommodate anywhere from two to eight vacationers in one, two, or three bedrooms. You can't pick a better way to travel as a family or in a group, but even couples enjoy the extra space and home-style amenities.

Condos are usually apartments in either a single high-rise or a cluster of low-rise buildings, often on the beach, though sometimes not. Because they're real apartments, condos almost always come complete with a fully outfitted kitchen, a living room with pullout sofa (which usually means that one-bedroom condos can easily accommodate four guests; two-bedroom condos can accommodate six), a private phone line, and a washer/dryer (usually), as well as other home-style amenities, such as a TV and DVD player in the living room (and usually an extra in the master bedroom). Two-bedroom condos often (but not always) have a second bathroom; in fact, a good number of one-bedroom condos in Maui also have a second bathroom. Internet access, either wireless or wired, is often available, but not always; usually, there's a daily charge, just as at a hotel. (Never assume anything; always ask when you book.)

On-site you usually find a swimming pool, laundry facilities (if units aren't in the apartments), tennis courts (sometimes), a front desk or property manager to deal with any questions you may have, and sometimes an activities desk to book snorkel cruises, luaus, and the like.

Don't expect the kind of service in a condo complex that you'd get at a hotel. If you prefer room service to your own kitchen, or you want somebody else to schlep your bags or wash your laundry, go with a hotel or resort instead.

More often than not, rental condos are individually owned vacation apartments that the owners use maybe a month or two out of the year. When the apartments aren't owner occupied (which is most of the time), a management company or agent manages and cares for the units and rents them out. You may book a condo through any number of individuals: an on-site agent or manager, an off-site agent or manager, or an off-site individual owner. At some condo complexes, more than one manager may represent units at any one time. In this book, I recommend units that are all managed by reputable companies with good track records. (In the cases where more than one agent represents a property, I list the one I feel will give you the best deal and the best service.)

Because they're privately owned homes, condo apartments are almost always individually decorated. However, the management company always requires a certain standard of décor and certain amenities, so the rental agent you use should be able to tell you exactly what to expect. Be sure to ask the specifics on your unit when you book, including the last time it was renovated or refurnished. If you're not happy with the answers you get, inquire about more recently refurbished units in the same complex; sometimes they may be more expensive, but not always.

Condos range in price from bargain basement to ultraluxury, with the majority falling on the affordable end of the continuum. I find that condos are the best values on Maui, hands down, no matter what your price range. You almost always get more for your money than at a comparable resort. Also, because competition between condo properties is so tight, many good properties offer extras, such as a free rental car and the seventh night free, to lure you in. Packagers are a great source for bargain rates on condos (see Chapter 5).

Most condos offer some kind of maid service. Some have the kind of full daily service that you get in a hotel; others merely offer a basic weekly linen change. During my own stays, I've found minimal maid service to be just fine, even pleasant — I like not having the daily intrusion, and I don't mind rinsing my own breakfast dishes. But it can be an entirely different story if you're traveling with a big brood. Also, most properties that offer daily or midweek maid service include it in the rate, but a few charge extra for it. Be sure to ask for specifics when inquiring about a condo.

I list some great condo choices in Chapter 10, but many more options exist. For additional choices, contact the **Hawaii Condo Exchange** (☎ **800-442-0404** or 323-436-0300; www.hawaiicondoexchange.com), a Southern California–based agency that acts as a consolidator for condo properties throughout the islands, including a number of excellent choices on Maui. The Exchange works to match you up with the place that's right for you and tries to get you a good deal. In addition, most companies that offer all-inclusive travel packages to Maui can book you into any number of condos, as can your travel agent.

For a complete selection of upscale condos throughout sunny, luxury-minded Wailea, reach out to **Destination Resorts Hawaii** (☎ **866-384-1365** or 808-891-6249; www.destinationresortshi.com). Destination Resorts generally handles first-class properties boasting plenty of deluxe amenities. Prices start as low as $225 per night for a one-bedroom unit and go up for a spacious oceanfront four-bedroom. Value-added packages, such as fifth-night-free and car-condo deals, are regularly available.

Though all of their condos make pleasing choices, Destination Resorts' **Wailea Beach Villas** (☎ **866-901-5207** or 808-891-4500; www.wailea beachvillas.com) has set a brand-new standard for condominium luxury on Maui. New to the market in June 2006, these 98 glorious villas and penthouses blend luxe, home-style comforts with first-class resort services (even fully stocked kitchens and personal-chef services, should you wish) and a wonderful Wailea Beach location. Rates run $880 to $3,000 nightly for the 1,900- to 3,100-square-foot residences, with a five-night minimum.

If you like the sound of the tranquil Kapalua resort (see Chapter 10), but the luxury hotel rates are out of your league — or you simply prefer home-style amenities and privacy — consider renting an elegant condo or vacation home at **Kapalua Villas** (☎ **800-545-0018**, 800-227-6054, or 808-665-5400; www.kapaluavillas.com). Nightly rates range from $279 for a one-bedroom apartment with a fairway view to $759 for an ocean-front three-bedroom apartment — not bad, considering you enjoy the same delicious perks and spectacular views of your much-higher-paying neighbors (including Kelsey Grammer, who owns his own Kapalua spread). Three- to five-bedroom freestanding luxury vacation homes are also available, as are golf, tennis, rental-car, and romance packages. Whether you go large or small, you're sure to be pleased with your first-class accommodations.

If you're looking for affordable sleeps on the South Maui coast, contact **Bello Realty** (☎ **800-541-3060** or 808-879-3328; www.bellomaui vacations.com). Bello represents affordable condos throughout the Kihei/Wailea area, with prices starting as low as $99 in the low season, $115 in the high season. Be sure to check out **Koa Resort** and **Koa Lagoon,** two of Maui's best bargains (see Chapter 10). I've received plenty of good feedback from vacationers who've used Bello and come away with an excellent beachfront bargain and good service results, so I'm quite confident about the quality and values that Bello offers.

Condominium Rentals Hawaii (☎ **800-367-5242** or 808-879-2778; www. crhmaui.com) also books condos throughout Maui, with a concentration in Kihei. The car-and-condo packages and other regular specials can really add to the value of these units.

Maui Beachfront Rentals (☎ **888-661-7200** or 808-661-3500; www.maui beachfront.com) can book you into a range of good-value apartments along West Maui's condo coast. The studios at the **Napili Bay,** which start as low as $145 to $167, are an excellent value for budget-minded couples. You may even be able to save a few dollars at two of my favorite Kaanapali Beach condo complexes: **The Whaler** and **Kaanapali Alii.** (See Chapter 10 for more on these three properties.)

You can cut out the middleman and rent directly from the owner at a number of quality condo resorts throughout the islands by visiting **Aloha Condos Hawaii** (www.alohacondos.com), an online cooperative of owner-managed units; links on the site will connect you directly to the owner.

Also check out the resources listed under "Making yourself at home in a vacation rental," later in this chapter, many of which also offer a variety of condo rental options.

Enjoying the comforts of a B&B

Staying in a bed-and-breakfast is a very nice way to discover Maui's genuine aloha spirit. More often than not, B&Bs offer a more intimate, and often more romantic, setting than your average impersonal resort, and a host who's more than happy to help you get to know Hawaii as it really is. If you want to experience a real slice of island life, B&Bs are the way to go.

B&Bs vary widely in size, style, and services. Generally speaking, they're usually comprised of several bedrooms in a home or several cottages or suites scattered about a property, each of which may or may not have a private bathroom. (All the B&Bs that I recommend in Chapter 10 have units with private bathrooms.) Most offer Internet access to laptop toters, but I've found that their networks are not as reliable as those at the big hotels, so book with a name brand if you *must* be online.

When you book a B&B, be sure that you fully understand its policies regarding deposits, cancellations, and method of payment. Because a B&B is a small business and has a harder time filling last-minute cancellations than a big hotel does, it may have more rigid policies. Despite the name, B&Bs also vary in whether breakfast is actually included in the rates, so ask ahead of time. And inquire about any other quirks or policies that may matter to you, such as whether smoking is allowed (it usually isn't) or whether the owners like to have guests take off their shoes when they enter (they usually do).

You may want to contact one or more of the following agencies if you're considering a stay at a B&B:

✔ Tops in the state is **Hawaii's Best Bed & Breakfasts** (☎ 800-262-9912 or 808-263-3100; www.bestbnb.com). The owners and staff are committed to representing only quality B&Bs, inns, and vacation rentals, and they're not afraid to say "no" to any property that doesn't meet their standards. They represent only accommodations with private bathrooms, and all are nonsmoking. Some of their units are free-standing cottages that resemble vacation homes more than B&Bs; they even represent a few really nice condos. Note that their bed-and-breakfasts generally have a three-night minimum stay, and vacation rentals tend to require a seven-night minimum stay.

✔ **Bed & Breakfast Hawaii** (☎ 800-733-1632 or 808-822-7771; www.bandb-hawaii.com) can also book you into a range of vacation homes and B&Bs throughout the islands, with prices starting around $75 a night.

✔ You won't get the same personal service from the Web, but you can find lots of useful resources there. **InnSite** (www.innsite.com) features B&B listings in all 50 states, including Hawaii, and around the globe. Find an inn on the island of your choice, see pictures of the rooms, and check prices and availability; text is included only when the proprietor submits it. (It's free to have an inn listed.) The innkeepers write the descriptions, and many listings link to the inn's own Web sites. What's more, you may be able to score an additional discount by booking your reservation through InnSite. Other sites that are worth surfing for Hawaii B&Bs are **Bedand Breakfast.com** (www.bedandbreakfast.com) and **Bed & Breakfast Inns Online** (www.bbonline.com).

Making yourself at home in a vacation rental

Vacation rental usually means that you have a full cottage or house all to yourself. You may never even see an owner, agent, or manager after you pick up the keys. This option is great for families or people who like their space and privacy or don't want to eat every meal out at a restaurant — but if you prefer a full-service experience, it may not be for you.

The rental may be a studio cottage in a residential neighborhood, a condo, or a huge beachfront multibedroom house — or anything in between. They usually have some sort of kitchen facilities, laundry facilities, at least one TV, and at least one phone (ask when booking). Because vacation rentals are often privately owned homes, they also may come with such bonuses as extra TVs, DVD players, and stereos (never assume; always ask if it matters to you). Like condos, they usually come outfitted with the basics, such as sheets and towels.

Vacation rentals vary greatly in price, depending on their size, location, and amenities. They tend to be much better values than similarly priced resort or hotel accommodations, especially if you're trying to accommodate a group or you plan a long stay (a week or more). Just make sure that you get a 24-hour contact person for those times when the toilet won't flush or you can't figure out how to turn on the air-conditioning.

Hawaii's Best Bed & Breakfasts is useful for statewide vacation rentals. A statewide source that's also worth checking out is **Hawaii Beachfront Vacation Homes** (☎ 808-247-3637; www.hibeach.com).

Contact **Hawaii Condo Exchange** (☎ 800-442-0404 or 323-436-0300; www.hawaiicondoexchange.com), a Southern California–based agency that acts as a consolidator for condo properties on Maui and throughout the islands. They'll work to match you up with the place that's right for you and try to get you a good deal.

Also check with **Vacation-Maui.com** (☎ 800-676-4112 or 808-661-3484; www.vacation-maui.com) for vacation rentals of all styles and types, from affordable to luxury. **Kihei Maui Vacations** (☎ 888-568-6284; www.kmvmaui.com) offers affordable rentals on condos and homes in the sunny South Maui area.

If you'd like a rental house that's slightly off the beaten path — either in Upcountry Maui or in one of the charming communities along the road to Hana — contact **Hookipa Haven Vacation Services** (☎ 800-398-6284 or 808-579-8282; www.hookipa.com), which also offers West Maui beach houses for lease.

See **A Maui Vacation Rental Directory** (www.amauivacationrental.com) if you'd like a one-stop-shopping list of vacation rentals available direct from their owners. **Vacation Rentals by Owner** (www.vrbo.com) offers a similar service.

Landing the Best Room at the Best Rate

The *rack rate* is the maximum rate a hotel charges for a room. It's the rate you get if you walk in off the street and ask for a room for the night. You sometimes see these rates printed on the fire/emergency exit diagrams posted on the back of your door.

Hotels are happy to charge you the rack rate, but you can almost always do better. Perhaps the best way to avoid paying the rack rate is surprisingly simple: Just ask for a cheaper or discounted rate. You may be pleasantly surprised. But you have to take the initiative and ask, because many hotels bank on the fact that you'll just accept the first rate you're quoted. You should also chat with the reservations agent about which rooms are the best and which units match your needs. You never know what kind of insider advice or upgrade can be won just by asking a question and turning on the charm.

In all but the smallest accommodations, the rate you pay for a room depends on many factors — chief among them being how you make your reservation. A travel agent may be able to negotiate a better price with certain hotels than you can get by yourself. That's because the hotel may give the agent a discount in exchange for steering his or her business toward that hotel. However, these days, you can usually do just as well yourself as long as you're willing to spend some time online and investigate your options.

Reserving a room through the hotel's toll-free number or Web site may also result in a lower rate than calling the hotel directly. On the other hand, the central reservations number may not know about discount rates at specific locations. Your best bet is to call both the local number and the toll-free number and see which one gives you a better deal, and then check it against the rate available online.

Room rates (even rack rates) change with the season, as occupancy rates rise and fall. But even within a given season, room prices are subject to change without notice, so the rates quoted in this book may be different from the actual rate you receive when you make your reservation.

Don't automatically shy away if a hotel's rack rates seem out of your range at first glance. A hotel's official "published" (full-price, or rack) rates usually represent the upper end of what they charge when they're full to capacity, but most hotels routinely offer better prices. And special deals abound in Hawaii, so in each hotel listing throughout this book, I note what kind of bargains you can typically snag.

Often the best way to get a great deal on a hotel room is to book it as part of an all-inclusive travel package that includes airfare, hotel, and car, and sometimes other extras, in one low price. (For details on how to find the best package deals, see Chapter 5.)

You can find a big list of money-saving strategies in Chapter 4.

Surfing the Web for hotel deals

Shopping online for hotels is generally done one of two ways: by booking through the hotel's own Web site or by going through an independent booking agency.

Expedia (www.expedia.com) offers a long list of special deals, as well as "virtual tours" or photos of available rooms so that you can see what you're paying for. **Travelocity** (www.travelocity.com) posts unvarnished customer reviews and ranks its properties according to the AAA rating system. Also reliable are **Hotels.com** (a division of Expedia, so they often offer the same deals), **Orbitz** (www.orbitz.com), **Yahoo! Travel** (http://travel.yahoo.com), and **Quikbook** (www.quikbook.com).

Keep in mind that hotels at the top of a site's listing are usually there for no other reason than that they paid money to get the placement.

Always price-compare the rate you get through an online travel agency against the hotel's own Web site. These days, virtually every major hotel chain offers price parity with the online distributors through its own Web sites. Often, you'll save a few bucks through the hotel's own site and/or end up with a better room for the same money because the hotel doesn't have to pay high distribution fees (usually a whopping 25 percent of the rate you pay) if you book direct. If you do book through a third-party online agency, don't be surprised if you end up next to the ice machine or with a view of the parking lot. Hotels generally give their best rooms to guests that generate the most revenue for them. This practice shouldn't prevent you from using online agencies; it simply means that, unless you're saving money by booking through a third-party agency, you're likely to be better off booking your room direct with the hotel (or its parent hotel chain).

You may also want to check out **TripAdvisor** (www.tripadvisor.com) when you're considering a hotel. TripAdvisor isn't a booking site, per se (although it does offer links to sites that allow you to make bookings), but it does offer untainted, straight-from-the-customer's-keyboard reviews of hotels. Now, I don't recommend putting too much stock in a single review — most people have unrealistic expectations, or just plain-old, bad-luck experiences, now and again — but trends in positive or negative experiences can become apparent. Also, I love the candid travelers' photos, which show you what the hotel rooms *really* look like (and, often, how small they really are).

An excellent free program, **TravelAxe** (www.travelaxe.net), can help you search multiple hotel sites at once, even ones you may never have heard of — and conveniently lists the total price of the room, including the taxes and service charges.

It's always important to **get a confirmation number** and **make a print-out** of any online booking transaction to avoid any potential issues when you arrive at the hotel.

In the bidding Web site category, **Priceline** (www.priceline.com) and **Hotwire** (www.hotwire.com) are even better for hotels than for airfares; with both, you're allowed to pick the neighborhood and quality level of your hotel before offering up your money. On the downside, many hotels stick Priceline guests in their least desirable rooms. Be sure to go to **BiddingForTravel** (www.biddingfortravel.com) before bidding on a hotel room on Priceline; it features a fairly up-to-date list of hotels that

Priceline uses in major cities. For both Priceline and Hotwire, you pay upfront, and the fee is nonrefundable. Note: Some hotels don't provide loyalty program credits or points or other frequent-stay amenities when you book a room through opaque online services.

Reserving the Best Room

After you make your reservation, asking one or two more pointed questions can go a long way toward making sure that you get the best room in the house. Most Hawaii hoteliers are very friendly and willing to take the time with you, so don't be shy — try to find out which units are the nicest. If the reservations agent doesn't have any specific recommendations, try asking for a corner room. In some (but not all) cases, they may be larger and quieter, with more windows and light than standard rooms, and they don't always cost more.

Also ask whether the hotel is renovating, or if any construction is taking place nearby; this is especially important in Hawaii, where rampant renovation has taken hotels by storm in recent years (and will continue to do so for a few more). If it is, request a room away from the renovation work. Inquire, too, about traffic and the location of the restaurants, bars, and discos in the hotel — all sources of annoying noise.

And if you aren't happy with your room when you arrive, talk to the front desk firmly but nicely. (Don't get emotional — your mom's old saying about attracting more flies with honey than with vinegar really was good advice.) If another room is available, the front desk should be happy to accommodate you, within reason.

Choosing a room with a view

If you want to see the ocean from your room or condo, expect to pay for the privilege. Oceanview rooms usually cost substantially more than rooms with no view or only a partial view, to the tune of $100, $200, or even $300 more per night than the rate for a similar room without the view.

Deciding whether to pay for a view isn't a clear-cut issue. In fact, what constitutes *oceanview* is far from an agreed-upon industry standard. Witness these variations on the theme:

✔ **Oceanfront rooms:** Only hotels or condo complexes that sit squarely on the beach can have oceanfront rooms or apartments. Positioned directly over the sand and a stone's throw from the waves, these units are the best in the house and usually the most expensive. You may still have to walk through the lobby to get to the water, but you have an unblocked view of the beach. Keep in mind, however, that you hear the waves only from lower-floor rooms; these rooms are often my favorites.

✔ **Oceanview rooms:** Watch out — some hotels and resorts don't distinguish between oceanfront rooms and oceanview rooms, which also have a full view of the ocean. Oceanview rooms, however, don't have to be directly over the sand. They may sit farther back — or even across the street — from the beach, or they may look over the rooftops of other buildings. These units are still fabulous, and generally still expensive.

✔ **Partial oceanview rooms:** *Partial oceanview* is subject to a whole host of interpretations, depending on who's doing the offering. It can be almost as good as full oceanview, or it may mean that you see a razor-thin slice of blue between two high-rise mountains of concrete. Ask plenty of questions about any unit offered as "partial oceanview" and know exactly what you're paying for before you book.

✔ **Mountain or gardenview rooms:** Most non-oceanview rooms are called *mountainview,* meaning that they face the island's inland mountains, or *gardenview,* which means they face an inner courtyard or grounds. The view can be good or bad, depending on the location and the layout of the grounds; again, your best bet is to ask plenty of questions when you reserve. These rooms are usually the least expensive in a hotel or condo complex. They're not usually of poorer quality — they just don't have the million-dollar views that those guests on the other side of the building or grounds have (and are paying for!).

The big question, then, is, "Is it worth it to pay for an oceanview room?" Before my first visit to Maui, I was convinced that the answer was cut and dried: no way — too expensive. I'm not going to Maui to hang out in my room, so why should I pay through the nose for the privilege of seeing the water from it?

Then I stayed in an oceanfront room, and I was hooked. Letting the rhythmic sound of the waves and the caress of the ocean breeze lull you to sleep, and waking to gorgeous ocean views, are unforgettable experiences. You know you're in Maui — and that fabulous ocean is why you came all this way in the first place.

I highly recommend staying in an oceanfront (or oceanview) room if you can afford it. But don't blow your whole budget just to make it happen. First, choose the hotel or condo you want based on your needs. Make sure that the accommodations style suits you, that the space sleeps your travel companions comfortably, and that the property features all the amenities and services you need to be happy. To me, these considerations are much more important than the view. After you choose your property, see whether you can afford to book oceanfront, especially if the hotel or packager is offering you a nice deal on an upgrade. If you can, great! But if staying in an oceanfront room means you have to skip activities or skimp on meals, then go with a cheaper room with a lesser view. Having an oceanview room isn't worth compromising the rest of your trip.

Chapter 7

Catering to Special Travel Needs or Interests

. . . .

In This Chapter

▶ Taking the kids along

▶ Strategizing for senior travelers

▶ Navigating Maui with disabilities

▶ Getting tips for gays and lesbians

▶ Marrying on Maui

. . . .

*T*ravelers don't come in a standard package, of course — they come in all ages, sizes, and configurations. You may want to know: How welcoming will Maui be to my kids, my senior status, my disability, and/or my same-sex partner? If so, you've landed in the right chapter.

Plus, if you're looking to plan a dreamy tropical wedding, I tell you the ins and outs of tying the knot on the romantic island of Maui.

Traveling with the Brood: Advice for Families

If you have enough trouble getting your kids out of the house in the morning, dragging them thousands of miles away may seem insurmountable. But family travel can be immensely rewarding, giving you new ways of seeing the world through smaller pairs of eyes.

Maui is the perfect *ohana* (family) vacation destination. You and the *keiki* (kids) will love the beaches and the wealth of kid-friendly activities. Lots of families flock to the islands every summer, as well as at holiday time and during the spring-break season.

Most hotels and condo complexes, from luxury to budget, welcome the entire family. Virtually all the larger hotels and resorts have great supervised programs for kids 12 and under — which means that you can have plenty of relaxation time to yourself, as well as playtime with the kids. Most hotels can also refer you to reliable baby sitters if you want a night on the town sans youngsters.

By Hawaii state law, hotels can accept only kids between the ages of 5 and 12 into their supervised activity programs.

Condos are particularly suitable for families who want lots of living space in which to spread out. Parents also appreciate having a kitchen where they can prepare meals for fussy young eaters and save significantly on dining costs. One drawback of condo complexes is that they typically don't have the extensive facilities (like kids' activity programs) that you'd get in big resorts.

If you want to pack light, **Baby's Away** (www.babysaway.com) rents car seats, cribs, strollers (including jogging strollers), highchairs, playpens, room monitors, and even toys. It serves Maui (☎ **800-942-9030** or 808-875-9030), plus Honolulu (☎ **800-496-6386** or 808-685-4299) and the Big Island (☎ **800-996-9030** or 808-987-9236). Give Baby's Away a call, and it'll deliver whatever you need to wherever you're staying and pick it up when you're done. I suggest arranging your rentals before you leave home to ensure availability.

Any hotel or condo should be able to refer you to a reliable baby sitter with a proven track record. If yours can't, contact **Happy Kids** (☎ **888-669-1991** or 808-667-5437; www.happykidsmaui.com), **The Nanny Connection** (☎ **808-875-4777** or 808-667-5777; www.thenanny connection.com), or **Nana Enterprises** (☎ **888-584-6262** or 808-879-6262; www.nanaenterprises.com).

You can find good family-oriented vacation advice on the Internet from such sites as the **Family Travel Forum** (www.familytravelforum.com), a comprehensive site that offers customized trip planning; **Family Travel Network** (www.familytravelnetwork.com), an award-winning site that offers travel features, deals, and tips; **Travel with Your Kids** (www.travelwithyourkids.com), a comprehensive site that offers customized trip planning; and **Family Travel Files** (www.thefamilytravel files.com), which offers an online magazine and a directory of off-the-beaten-path tours and tour operators for families. **BabyCenter** (www.babycenter.com/travel) has terrific recommendations for planning baby's first trip, as well as advice on traveling while pregnant.

Here are a few tips for family travel planning:

- ✔ **Don't try to do too much.** I can't say it too strongly. You'll all consider it the trip from you-know-where if you spend too much time in the car or on interisland flights.

- ✔ **Take it slow at the start.** Give the entire family time to adjust to a new time zone, unfamiliar surroundings, and just being on the road. The best way to do so is to budget a few days in your initial destination without strict itineraries or lots of moving around.

- ✔ **Book some private time for yourself.** Most, if not all, hotels are prepared to hook you up with a reliable baby sitter who can entertain your kids while you enjoy a romantic dinner for two or another adults-only activity. To avoid disappointment, ask about baby-sitting when you reserve. Local visitor centers can also usually recommend licensed and bonded baby-sitting services in their areas; see the Quick Concierge for contact info.

✔ **Look for the Kid Friendly icon as you flip through this book.** I use it to highlight hotels, restaurants, and attractions that are particularly welcoming to families traveling with kids. Zeroing in on these listings can help you plan your trip more efficiently.

Making Age Work for You: Tips for Seniors

One of the many benefits of getting older is that travel often costs less. Many hotels and package-tour operators still offer deals for seniors. Senior discounts are also available at most major Hawaiian attractions, and occasionally at restaurants and luaus. So when you're making reservations or buying tickets, ask about senior discounts. Keep in mind, though, that the minimum age requirement can vary between 50 and 65. (It's usually between ages 55 and 65.) Always carry an ID card with you, especially if you've kept your youthful glow.

The statewide **Outrigger** (☎ **800-OUTRIGGER** [800-688-7444]; www. outrigger.com) and **Ohana** (☎ **800-462-6262**; www.ohanahotels.com) hotel chains offer all travelers over age 50 substantial discounts.

Members of **AARP** (☎ **888-687-2277** or 202-434-2277; www.aarp.org) get discounts on hotels, airfare, and car rentals. AARP offers members a wide range of benefits, including *AARP: The Magazine* and a monthly newsletter. Anyone 50 or over can join.

YMT Vacations (☎ **800-922-9000**; www.ymtvacations.com) and **Grand Circle Travel** (☎ **800-959-0405**; www.gct.com) are just two of the hundreds of travel agencies that specialize in vacations for seniors, including trips to Hawaii. But beware: Many of these outfits are of the tour-bus variety, with free trips thrown in for those who organize groups of 20 or more. If you're the independent type, a regular travel agent may be better for you.

Elderhostel (☎ **800-454-5768**;www.elderhostel.org), a nonprofit group that offers travel and study programs around the world, offers excellent low-cost trips to Hawaii for travelers ages 55 and older (plus a spouse or companion of any age). Trips usually include moderately priced accommodations and meals in one low-cost package.

U.S. citizens or permanent residents 62 or older who want to visit Hawaii's national parks — including Haleakala National Park on Maui — can save sightseeing dollars by picking up an **America the Beautiful National Parks and Federal Recreational Lands Pass for Seniors** from any national park, recreation area, or monument. This lifetime pass has a one-time fee of $10 and provides free admission to all the parks in the

National Parks system, plus 50 percent savings on camping and recreation fees, for the cardholder and all passengers (no more than four adults total). You can get one at any park entrance as long as you have a proof-of-age ID on hand. For details, visit www.nps.gov/fees_passes.htm.

Travel resources and discounts for seniors include the quarterly magazine *Travel 50 & Beyond* (www.travel50andbeyond.com); *Travel with a Challenge* online magazine (www.travelwithachallenge.com); *Travel Unlimited: Uncommon Adventures for the Mature Traveler,* by Alison Gardner (Avalon); and *Unbelievably Good Deals and Great Adventures That You Absolutely Can't Get Unless You're Over 50,* by Joann Rattner Heilman (McGraw-Hill).

Accessing Hawaii: Advice for Travelers with Disabilities

A disability shouldn't stop anyone from traveling. The Americans with Disabilities Act requires that all public buildings be wheelchair accessible and have accessible restrooms. Hawaii is very friendly to travelers with disabilities. Most hotels throughout the islands are on the newer side and boast wheelchair ramps, extra-wide doorways and halls, and rooms dedicated to accessibility with extra-large bathrooms, low-set fixtures, and/or fire-alarm systems adapted for deaf travelers.

Your best bet is to contact the local visitor bureaus. They can provide you with all the specifics on accessibility in the community; see the Quick Concierge at the back of this book for contact info.

Some excellent resources for information on accessible travel are:

✔ An excellent resource for trip planning assistance is **Access Aloha Travel** (☎ 800-480-1143 or 808-545-1143; www.accessaloha travel.com). This Hawaii-based travel agency has been planning accessible trips for travelers with disabilities for decades — and it donates half its profits to the disabled community. Inquire with these folks about renting an accessible van during your stay.

✔ **Moss Rehab ResourceNet** (☎ 800-CALL-MOSS [800-225-5667], 215-456-9900, or 215-663-6000; www.mossresourcenet.org) and **Access-Able Travel Source** (☎ 303-232-2979; www.access-able.com) are comprehensive resources for travelers with disabilities. Both sites feature links to travel agents who specialize in planning accessible trips to Hawaii. Access-Able's user-friendly site also features relay and voice numbers for hotels, airlines, and car-rental companies, plus links to accessible accommodations, attractions, transportation, tours, and local medical resources and equipment repairers throughout Hawaii, making this site an invaluable resource.

✔ You can join the **Society for Accessible Travel & Hospitality** (SATH; ☎ 212-447-7284 or 561-361-0017; www.sath.org) for $49 a year ($29 for seniors and students), to gain access to its vast network of travel connections. The organization provides information sheets on destinations and referrals to tour operators that specialize in accessible travel. Its quarterly magazine, *Open World,* is full of reliable information and resources.

✔ Vision-impaired travelers who use a Seeing Eye dog can usually bypass Hawaii's animal quarantine rules (which were dramatically loosened in 2004). You can arrange for your guide or service dog to be inspected in the terminal at Honolulu International Airport if you notify **Animal Quarantine (☎ 808-483-7151)** at least 24 hours in advance. Call or visit www.hawaii.gov/hdoa for specifics on rules and fees. Contact the **American Foundation for the Blind** (☎ 800-232-5463; www.afb.org) for further travel information.

✦ **Gammie HomeCare (☎ 888-540-4032** or 808-877-4032 on Maui, 808-632-2333 on Kauai; www.gammie.com) rents a wide variety of mobility aids, bathroom safety devices, and wheelchairs — including beach wheelchairs that can navigate sand. It'll deliver to any hotel on Maui or Kauai. You can reserve the equipment you need up to a year in advance.

Hawaii's **Disability and Communication Access Board** has a roundup of travel tips, with information on arriving, air travel, and where to find local support services. Visit its Web site at www.state.hi.us/health/dcab/home, and click on Community Resources in the scroll bar on the left. Before you book any hotel room, always ask lots of questions based on your needs. After you arrive, call restaurants, attractions, and theaters to make sure that they're fully accessible.

Avis has an "Avis Access" program that offers such services as a dedicated 24-hour toll-free number (☎ 888-331-2323; www.avis.com) for customers who are hearing impaired. Special car features, such as swivel seats, spinner knobs, and hand controls, and accessible bus service are available through the main customer service number (☎ 800-352-7900). Many of the big car-rental companies, including Avis, **Hertz** (☎ 800-654-3131 or 800-654-2280 for hearing-impaired travelers; www.hertz.com), and **National (☎ 800-227-7368,** 800-328-6323 for hearing-impaired travelers, 888-273-5262 for travelers with medical-related requests; www.nationalcar.com), rent hand-controlled cars for drivers with disabilities at Hawaii's major airports. At least 48 to 72 hours' advance notice is a must, but do yourself a favor and book further in advance to guarantee availability.

Following the Rainbow: Resources for Gay and Lesbian Travelers

Hawaii is extremely popular with same-sex couples due to its long-standing reputation for welcoming all groups.

The **International Gay & Lesbian Travel Association** (IGLTA; ☎ 954-630-1637; www.iglta.org) is the trade association for the gay and lesbian travel industry; they offer an online directory of gay- and lesbian-friendly travel businesses, structured trips, and occasional travel specials, including special discount codes for National and Alamo rental cars at press time.

The staff at **Pacific Ocean Holidays** (☎ 800-735-6600 or 808-545-5252; www.gayhawaiivacations.com) specializes in crafting Hawaii vacation packages for gay men and women. They can help you arrange a good-value trip that features either gay-friendly hotels serving the general public or hotels that serve a predominately gay clientele (your choice); you can even book your entire vacation online. Even if you don't want help planning your trip, the Web site is an invaluable resource. Its online island-by-island guide is a terrific community resource directory and guide to gay-owned and gay-friendly businesses throughout Hawaii.

Gay.com Travel (www.gay.com/travel) is an excellent online successor to the popular *Out & About* print magazine. Its OutTraveler page provides regularly updated information about gay-owned and gay-friendly lodging, dining, nightlife, and shopping in every important destination worldwide (including popular and emerging "gayborhoods" in cities worldwide), plus valuable trip-planning information.

Purple Roofs (www.purpleroofs.com) is a comprehensive online guide to gay-friendly B&Bs, guesthouses, vacation rentals, travel agencies, and tour operators worldwide, including extensive listings in Hawaii.

The **Gay and Lesbian Community Center,** 614 South St., Suite #105, in Honolulu (☎ 808-545-2848), offers referrals for nearly every kind of service that you might need. Also check out the **Gay Community Services Directory,** which you can find online at www.hawaiiscene.com/gsene/comsvc.htm.

1 Do! 1 Do! Planning a Hawaiian Wedding

No question about it: Maui is the perfect place to get married, which is why so many couples from around the country, and the world, tie the knot here every year. What better place to start your life together? And the members of your wedding party will most likely be delighted because you've given them the perfect excuse for their own island vacation.

For a rundown of the legalities, visit www.hawaii.gov/doh and click Getting a Marriage License. There you can find all the details, including a downloadable license application. You can also call ☎ 808-586-4545 for license information.

Using a wedding planner or coordinator

Wedding planning is a thriving industry in Hawaii. Whether your heart is set on a huge formal affair at a luxury resort or an informal beachside ceremony, you won't have any trouble finding assistance.

Many wedding planners are also marriage-licensing agents, which means that they can take care of the legalities for you, with only minimal effort on your part, and then arrange everything else — from providing an officiate to ordering flowers. A wedding planner can cost $500 or more, depending on how involved you want her to be and what kind of wedding you want.

Your best bet for finding a reputable wedding planner is to choose one endorsed by the **Hawaii Visitors and Convention Bureau,** whose Web site features a complete list of wedding planners to suit any budget; go to www.gohawaii.com and click Plan a Wedding or Honeymoon. You can also call the center for recommendations at ☎ **800-GO-HAWAII** [800-464-2924], or — even better — contact the **Maui Visitors Bureau** (☎ **800-525-6284** or 808-244-3530; www.visitmaui.com) for local recommendations.

In addition, virtually all the big resorts employ full-time wedding coordinators. Arranging your nuptials directly through a resort may be pricey, but it's a relatively worry-free option. The hotel coordinators are experts, they'll take all the pesky little details off your hands, and they'll usually offer the whole event to you as a pay-one-price wedding package, including accommodations. What's more, the hotels generally offer prime locations for both the ceremony and the reception, whether it's for 2 or 200 guests.

Great choices include the **Four Seasons Maui,** the **Grand Wailea,** the **Fairmont Kea Lani,** the **Ritz-Carlton Kapalua,** and the **Hotel Hana-Maui** (see Chapter 10).

Keep in mind that more affordable hotels and condos, and even some B&Bs, can often recommend wedding coordinators who have a proven track record with them. The **Kaanapali Beach Hotel,** for example, makes a great affordable option (see Chapter 10). The setting is magical, the hotel works with a very reliable local planner, and the on-site food-and-beverage director can arrange a pleasing reception. Don't hesitate to contact any property that strikes your fancy; most have wedding experience or can offer recommendations.

Do-it-yourself planning

When you arrive in Hawaii, you and your intended must appear together to a **marriage licensing agent** (basically, a local official who helps you wrap up the legalities) when applying for the license. A marriage license costs $60 (payable in cash) and is good for 30 days from the date of issue. Both parties must be at least 18 years of age (16- and 17-year-olds must have written consent of both parents, legal guardian, or family court) and can't be first cousins or more closely related. You'll need a photo ID, such as a driver's license; a birth certificate is necessary only if you're 18 or under. No blood tests, citizenship, or residency minimum is required.

To locate a marriage licensing agent on **Maui,** call ☎ **808-984-8210;** on **Molokai,** call ☎ **808-553-3663;** or on **Lanai,** call ☎ **808-565-6411.** Or contact the **Honolulu Marriage License Office,** State Department of Health Building, 1250 Punchbowl St., Honolulu (☎ **808-586-4545** or 808-586-4544), which can direct you to a marriage-licensing agent closest to where you'll be staying in the islands. The office is open weekdays from 8 a.m. to 4 p.m.

Local marriage-licensing agents are usually friendly, helpful people who can steer you to someone who's licensed by the state of Hawaii to perform the ceremony, whether you're looking for an officiate of a certain denomination or a plain ol' justice of the peace. These marriage performers are great sources of information; they usually know picturesque places to have the ceremony for free or at a nominal fee.

Some marriage-licensing agents are state employees, and, under law, they cannot recommend anyone with a religious affiliation; they can give you phone numbers only for local judges to perform the ceremony. Ask first what their limitations are, if it matters to you. If you're interested in arranging a church ceremony, inquire with the visitor center to locate an appropriate venue.

You can have a ceremony at any state or county beach or park for free, but keep in mind that you'll be sharing the site with the general public.

For a genuine Hawaiian experience, get married at **Keawali Congregational Church** (☎ **808-879-5557;** www.keawalai.org), a vintage 1831, oceanfront, coral-block church in picturesque Makena. The gorgeous grounds — with palm trees and exotic tropical flowers — make a perfect backdrop for your wedding photo.

Another great site is **D. T. Fleming Beach Park,** just north of Kapalua in West Maui. This crescent-shaped beach is generally empty on weekdays, so you can enjoy a quiet wedding on the beautiful beach as sailboats skim along offshore.

On Maui's North Shore is lovely, uncrowded Baldwin Beach Park, a long ribbon of powdery white sand backed by swaying palms and fringed by white-crested turquoise waves — perfect for an oceanfront ceremony.

Chapter 8

Taking Care of the Remaining Details

In This Chapter

▶ Renting a car
▶ Buying travel insurance
▶ Staying safe, healthy, and connected when you travel
▶ Dealing with airline security
▶ Making reservations before you leave home
▶ Packing what you really need

*T*his chapter helps you shore up the final details — from renting a car to packing the appropriate gear.

Renting a Car

Maui has so many fabulous things to see and do that it would be a real shame for you to miss out. The more you want to see, however, the more you'll be moving around. In order to maximize your time, you need to rent a car.

Unfortunately, traffic has increased on Maui in recent years, especially in the prime resort areas. This is a result of a number of factors — most notably, the increase in direct neighbor-island flights from the mainland and the return of cruise-ship traffic to the islands. Throughout this book, I tell you how to best avoid traffic hot spots whenever possible.

The following companies rent cars on all the major Hawaiian Islands, including Maui:

▶ **Alamo: ☎ 800-GO ALAMO** [800-462-5266]; www.alamo.com

▶ **Avis: ☎ 800-331-1212;** www.avis.com

▶ **Budget: ☎ 800-527-0700;** www.budget.com

▶ **Dollar: ☎ 800-800-4000;** www.dollar.com

✔ **Enterprise:** ☎ 800-261-7331; www.enterprise.com

✔ **Hertz:** ☎ 800-654-3131; www.hertz.com

✔ **National:** ☎ 800-CAR-RENT [800-227-7368]; www.nationalcar.com

✔ **Thrifty:** ☎ 800-THRIFTY [800-847-4389]; www.thrifty.com

Be sure to book your rental cars well ahead. They're almost always at a premium on Molokai and Lanai, and they may be sold out on all the islands on holiday weekends.

For tips on renting hand-controlled cars or vans equipped with wheel-chair lifts, see Chapter 7.

Getting the best deal

Rental cars are relatively affordable in Hawaii, although they do vary from island to island and from season to season. Because of its popularity, rental cars on Maui tend to be more expensive than the other islands. Of course, I can't guarantee what you'll pay when you book, but you can often get a compact car for between $160 and $250 a week. If you want a family-size car — or a convertible — expect to pay anywhere from $225 to $450 a week, which is pretty reasonable, especially if you can score a deal. Book ahead for the best rates, because cars tend to get more expensive as bookings increase.

Car-rental rates vary even more than airline fares. The price depends on the size of the car, how long you keep it, where and when you pick it up and drop it off, where you take it, and a host of other factors. Asking a few key questions may save you hundreds of dollars.

✔ **Book your rental car at weekly rates when possible.** Weekly rentals will almost always save you money over daily rates.

✔ **Mention membership in AAA, AARP, and frequent-flier programs when booking.** These memberships may qualify you for discounts ranging from 5 percent to 30 percent.

✔ **Ask the reservations agency that books your hotel or your inter-island air travel if it also books rental cars.** Many hotels, condo rental agents, and even B&B owners can book rental cars at seriously discounted rates; ditto for the interisland air carriers, Hawaiian and Aloha. Often, you can save as much as 30 percent off the standard rate. And many Maui hotels and condos offer excellent-value room-and-car packages that make your rental essentially free!

✔ **Shop online.** As with other aspects of planning your trip, using the Internet can make comparison-shopping for a car rental much easier. You can check rates at most of the major agencies' Web sites. Plus, all the major travel sites — **Travelocity** (www.travelocity.com), **Expedia** (www.expedia.com), **Orbitz** (www.orbitz.com), **Priceline** (www.priceline.com), **Hotwire** (www.hotwire.com), **Kayak.com** (www.kayak.com), and **Yahoo! Travel** (http://travel.yahoo.com), for example — have search engines that can dig up and book discounted car-rental rates for you.

✔ **If you see an advertised special, ask for that specific rate when booking.** The car-rental company may not offer this information voluntarily. Be sure to remind the staff; otherwise, you may be charged the standard (higher) rate.

✔ **Get some friendly help from the locals. AAA Aloha Cars-R-Us** (☎ 800-655-7989; www.hawaiicarrental.com) is a Hawaii-based travel agency that specializes exclusively in car rentals on all the islands. These folks are dedicated to the task of getting you the cheapest rate from the major car-rental firms — and making it one-stop-shopping easy to boot. They combine custom Internet searches using any available discounts you may be eligible for (including association and program memberships) with their exclusive wholesale contract rates to find you the best rate possible. Best of all, there's no fee for using their service.

✔ **Consider booking your car as part of a complete travel package.** Package deals save you money not only on airfare and accommodations but also on your rental cars, too. This one-stop shopping can help streamline the trip-planning process. For more on package deals, see Chapter 5.

✔ **Scrutinize your rental agreement when you pick up your car.** And check your receipt carefully when you return the vehicle. Make sure you got the rate you were originally quoted, and straighten out any discrepancies on the spot.

✔ **Don't forget to ask about frequent-flier mileage.** Most car rentals are worth at least 500 miles on your frequent-flier account. Be sure to find out which airlines the rental-car company is affiliated with so that you can earn mileage. Bring your card with you and make sure that your account is credited at pickup time.

✔ **Join the rental company's preferred customer program.** Most companies offer such promotions. You may be able to snag a bargain rate or have a better shot at an upgrade if you're a member. Some companies make the process of picking up your car more hassle-free for members, too. And membership can work just like the airlines' frequent-flier plans: Renting from the same company several times can land you a free day or other perks.

✔ **Make sure that you're getting free unlimited mileage.** Thankfully, most of the major car-rental companies rent on an unlimited-miles basis, but you should confirm this policy when you book. Even on an island, the miles you drive can really add up.

✔ **Find out whether age is an issue.** Many car-rental companies add on a fee for drivers under 25, while some don't rent to them at all.

In addition to the standard rental prices, other optional charges apply to most car rentals (and some not-so-optional charges, such as taxes). The *Collision Damage Waiver* (CDW), which requires you to pay for damage to the car in a collision, is automatically covered by many credit card companies. Check with your credit card company before you leave home so that you can avoid paying this hefty fee (as much as $20 or $25 a day). In any event, make sure that you're covered. (See "Following the rules of the road," later in this chapter; Hawaii is a no-fault state, which has important insurance implications.)

The car-rental companies also offer additional *liability insurance* (if you harm others in an accident), *personal accident insurance* (if you harm yourself or your passengers), and *personal effects insurance* (if your luggage is stolen from your car). Your car insurance policy back home probably covers most of these unlikely occurrences. However, don't assume — be sure to check before you leave home, and tote your insurance card with you.

If your own insurance doesn't cover you for rentals, or if you don't have auto insurance, definitely consider the additional coverage. (Ask your car-rental agent for more information.) Unless you're toting around the Hope diamond — and you don't want to leave that in your car trunk anyway — you can probably skip the personal effects insurance, but driving around without liability coverage is never a good idea. Note that credit cards don't cover you for liability, even if they cover you for collision.

Some companies also offer *refueling packages,* in which you pay for your initial full tank of gas up front and can return the car with an empty gas tank. The prices can be competitive with local gas prices, but you don't get credit for any gas remaining in the tank. If you reject this option, you pay only for the gas you use, but you have to return the car with a full tank or face charges of $6 or more per gallon for any shortfall. If you usually run late and a fueling stop may make you miss your plane, you're a perfect candidate for the fuel-purchase option, but for most people, it's not much of a hardship to top off your tank on the way to the airport.

Hawaii how-to: Renting convertibles

Renting a convertible is a lot like booking an oceanview room. It's a great idea if you can afford it, but not worth it if it's going to put a strain on your budget. The cost of going topless can be double or more than what you'd pay for a regular car. Expect to pay between $50 and $90 a day for a convertible, compared with $30 or $40 a day for a better-equipped midsize car (with such extras as power windows and power locks that don't usually come with convertibles).

If you really want to rent a convertible for your island driving but you're worried about cost, consider the following:

✔ **Rent a convertible for just part of your trip.** If you're going to be visiting two or three islands, book a convertible on just one of them. And Maui is the place to do it — cruising the road to Hana with the top down really is the ultimate Hawaii vacation dream.

✔ **Ask about upgrades when you pick up your rental car.** This question may prove especially beneficial if you're visiting in the off-season. Sometimes, if a rental-car branch has a few idle convertibles sitting around, you may be offered an on-the-spot upgrade for $15 to $25 more a day. If you negotiated a decent compact or midsize rate when you booked, the total should come out to substantially less than the convertible rate offered over the phone.

Following the rules of the road

Know these driving rules and common practices before you get behind the wheel on Maui:

✔ **Hawaii is a no-fault insurance state.** If you drive without collision-damage insurance, you're required to pay for all damages before you leave the state, regardless of who's at fault. Your personal auto policy may provide rental-car coverage; read your policy or check with your insurer before you leave home, and be sure to bring your insurance ID card if you decline the rental-car company's optional insurance. Some credit card companies also provide collision damage insurance; check with yours.

✔ **Seatbelts are mandatory for everyone in the car, all the time.** The law is strictly enforced, so be sure to buckle up. All children under age 4 must be strapped into car seats.

✔ **You can turn right on red unless a posted sign specifies otherwise.** Make sure that you make a full stop first — no rolling.

✔ **Pedestrians always have the right of way.** This is true even if they're not on a crosswalk.

✔ **Use your horn judiciously.** Honking your horn to express your anger at another driver is considered the height of rudeness in Hawaii. Don't do it unless you're alerting someone to immediate danger. Horns are used to greet friends in Hawaii.

Do *not* use your rental car as a safe in which to store valuables. Don't leave anything that you don't want to lose in the car or trunk, not even for a short time. Be especially careful when you park at beaches, where thieves know that you're going to leave your car for a while (and you're likely to leave goodies in the glove compartment).

Maui is very easy to negotiate, and all the rental-car companies hand out very good map booklets on each island. If all you have is what National or Hertz gives you, you'll do just fine.

Playing It Safe with Travel and Medical Insurance

Three kinds of travel insurance are available: trip-cancellation insurance, medical insurance, and lost-luggage insurance. Check your existing homeowner's and auto insurance policies and your credit card coverage before buying any additional insurance. You may already be covered.

The cost of travel insurance varies widely, depending on the cost and length of your trip, your age and health, and the type of trip you're taking, but expect to pay between 5 percent and 8 percent of the cost of the vacation itself. You can get estimates from various providers through **InsureMyTrip.com,** which compares more than a dozen companies.

Here are some tips on each of the three kinds of travel insurance and whether to buy:

✔ **Trip-cancellation insurance** may make sense if you're paying for your vacation up front — say, by purchasing a cruise, package deal, or escorted tour. Coverage will help you get your money back if you have to back out of a trip, if you have to go home early, or if your travel supplier goes bankrupt. Allowed reasons for cancellation can range from sickness to natural disasters to the Department of State declaring your destination unsafe for travel. (Insurers usually don't cover vague fears, though, as many travelers discovered who tried to cancel their trips in October 2001 because they were wary of flying.)

A good resource is **"Travel Guard Alerts,"** a list of companies considered high-risk by Travel Guard International (www.travel guard.com; click on Customer Service to find the alerts, which featured a fair number of in-trouble airlines in 2008). Protect yourself further by paying for the insurance with a credit card; by law, consumers can get their money back on goods and services not received if they report the loss within 60 days after the charge is listed on their credit card statement.

Note: Many tour operators include insurance in the cost of the trip or can arrange insurance policies through a partnering provider, a convenient and often cost-effective way for travelers to obtain insurance. Make sure that the tour company is a reputable one. Some experts suggest that you avoid buying insurance from the tour or cruise company you're traveling with, saying it's safer to buy from a third-party insurer than to put all your money in one place.

✔ For domestic travel, buying **medical insurance** for your trip doesn't make sense for most travelers. Most existing health policies cover you if you get sick away from home — but check before you go, particularly if you're insured by an HMO.

✔ **Lost-luggage insurance** is also not necessary for most travelers. On domestic flights, checked baggage is covered up to $2,500 per ticketed passenger. On international flights (including U.S. portions of international trips), baggage coverage is limited to approximately $9.07 per pound, up to approximately $635 per checked bag. If you plan to check items more valuable than the standard liability, see whether your valuables are covered by your homeowner's policy, get baggage insurance as part of your comprehensive travel-insurance package, or buy Travel Guard's BagTrak product. Don't buy insurance at the airport — it's usually overpriced.

The best advice is simple: Don't pack anything vital in your checked luggage. Be sure to take any expensive or irreplaceable items with you in your carry-on luggage, because many valuables (including books, money, and electronics) aren't covered by airline policies.

Always make sure you hold onto your luggage claim ticket until you reclaim your bags. If your luggage is lost, immediately file a lost-luggage claim at the airport, detailing the contents. For most airlines, you must report delayed, damaged, or lost baggage within four hours of arrival. The airlines are required to deliver luggage, once found, directly to your house or destination free of charge.

For more information, contact one of the following recommended insurers: **Access America** (☎ **800-284-8300;** www.accessamerica.com), **AIG Travel Guard** (☎ **800-826-4919;** www.travelguard.com), **Travel Insured International** (☎ **800-243-3174;** www.travelinsured.com), or **Travelex Insurance Services** (☎ **888-457-4602;** www.travelex-insurance.com).

Staying Healthy When You Travel

Getting sick will ruin your vacation, so I *strongly* advise against it. (Of course, last time I checked, germs weren't listening to me any more than they probably listen to you.)

Talk to your doctor before leaving on a trip if you have a serious and/or chronic illness. For conditions such as epilepsy, diabetes, or heart problems, wear a **MedicAlert identification tag** (☎ **888-633-4298;** www.medicalert.org), which immediately alerts doctors to your condition and gives them access to your records through MedicAlert's 24-hour hot line.

Be sure to consult Chapter 12, which contains lots of important advice on ocean safety and avoiding sunburn.

In the unlikely event that you do get sick in Hawaii, keep the following in mind:

✔ By law, all employers in Hawaii must provide health insurance for their employees, and almost all islanders have insurance. As a result, some doctors simply won't see patients who aren't insured. If you don't have insurance (or you don't have insurance that travels with you) and you need to see a doctor while you're in Hawaii, be sure to inform him when you call to make an appointment. Check the Quick Concierge at the back of this book to find a doctor or medical-care clinic that regularly caters to visitors.

✔ **Longs Drugs,** which has branches throughout the islands, accepts most national prescription cards, such as PCS — so if you have a card, bring it with you. If you get sick and need to fill a prescription during your trip, chances are good that you'll only have to pay a co-pay. To find a Longs near you, call ☎ **800-865-6647** or visit www.longsdrugs.com.

Staying Connected by Cellphone or E-mail

If you'd like to stay connected with your real life while you're in the islands, then the following sections are for you.

Using your cellphone across the United States

Most major cellphone networks have great coverage in Hawaii. However, don't just assume that because your **cellphone** works at home that it'll work in the islands. Take a look at your wireless company's coverage map on its Web site before getting on the plane. You should also check your cellphone contract, because coverage varies depending on the particular package you've purchased. If you need to stay in touch at a destination where you know your phone won't work, **rent** a phone that does from **InTouch USA** (☎ **800-872-7626;** www.intouchglobal.com).

If you're not from the United States, you'll be appalled at the poor reach of our **Global System for Mobiles (GSM) wireless network,** which is used by much of the rest of the world. Your phone will probably work in most major U.S. cities, but rural coverage tends to be haphazard; the good news is that Hawaii is well covered. (To see where GSM phones work in the United States, check out www.wireless.att.com/coverageviewer.) You may or may not be able to send text messages home. Assume nothing — call your wireless provider and get the full scoop. In a worst-case scenario, you can always rent a phone; InTouch USA delivers to hotels.

Accessing the Internet away from home

Travelers have any number of options to access the Internet on the road. Of course, using your own laptop — or even a PDA, pocket PC, or Web-compatible cellphone — gives you the most flexibility. But even if you don't have a computer, you can still access your e-mail and even your office computer from cybercafes and hotel business centers.

It's hard these days to find a destination that *doesn't* have a few cyber-cafes. Although there's no definitive directory for cybercafes, two places to start looking are at www.cybercaptive.com and www.cybercafe.com.

Almost all but the most budget-basic **hotels** offer wireless or wired Internet access that you can plug right into; the price of access can range from complimentary to $15 or $20 a day. Even most (but not all) bed-and-breakfasts offer Internet access these days. Check with your hotel in advance to see what your options are.

Most major airports now have **Internet kiosks** scattered throughout their gates, as well as wireless Internet access for laptop toters. Some airports charge, while others provide free service. Kiosks give you basic Web access for a per-minute fee that's usually higher than cybercafe prices. Most Hawaii airports offer limited access for a cost through **Boingo.com.**

To retrieve your e-mail, check with your **Internet service provider (ISP)** to see if it offers a Web-based interface tied to your existing e-mail account. Virtually all do these days. If your ISP doesn't have such an interface, you can use the free **mail2web** service (www.mail2web.com) to view and reply to your home e-mail. Or open a free, Web-based e-mail account with **Yahoo! Mail** (http://mail.yahoo.com). Microsoft's **Windows Live,** formerly known as Hotmail (http://mail.live.com), is another popular option.

If you need to access files on your office computer, look into a service called **GoToMyPC** (www.gotomypc.com). The service provides a Web-based interface for you to access and manipulate a distant PC from anywhere — even a cybercafe — provided your target PC is on and has an always-on connection to the Internet (such as with a Road Runner cable). The service offers top-quality security, but if you're worried about hackers, use your own laptop rather than a cybercafe computer to access the GoToMyPC system.

Keeping Up with Airline Security Measures

 Even after the federalization of airport security, security procedures at U.S. airports tend to be uneven. But generally you'll be fine if you arrive at the airport at least 90 minutes before a domestic flight (transpacific or interisland) and at least two hours before an international flight. Be sure to allow extra time if you're traveling on a high-volume holiday getaway day, or if the terrorism alert level has been raised.

Bring a **current, government-issued photo ID,** such as a driver's license or passport. Keep your ID at the ready to show at check-in, the security checkpoint, and sometimes even the gate. (Children under 18 don't need government-issued photo IDs for domestic flights, but they do for international flights to most countries.)

E-tickets have made paper tickets nearly obsolete. Passengers with E-tickets can beat the ticket-counter lines by using airport **electronic kiosks** or even **online check-in** from your home computer. Online check-in involves logging on to your airline's Web site, accessing your reservation, and printing your boarding pass; this is usually allowable 24 hours in advance of flight time. If you're using a kiosk at the airport, bring the credit card you used to book the ticket or your frequent-flier card. Print your boarding pass from the kiosk and simply proceed to the security checkpoint with your pass and a photo ID. If you're checking bags or looking to snag an exit-row seat, you'll be able to do so using most airline kiosks. **Curbside check-in** can also be a good way to avoid lines, if it's available.

Security checkpoint lines have become more efficient as the Transportation Security Administration (TSA) has staffed up and streamlined the process, but some doozies remain. If you have trouble standing for long periods of time, tell an airline employee; the airline will provide a wheelchair. Speed up security by not wearing metal objects such as big belt buckles. If you've got metallic body parts, a note from your doctor can prevent a long chat with the security screeners. Keep in mind that only ticketed passengers are allowed past security, except for folks escorting passengers with disabilities or children.

The TSA dictates **what you can carry on** and **what you can't.** The general rule is that sharp things are out, nail clippers are okay. Food and beverages are not allowed in containers larger than 3 ounces. Liquids or gels — that is, most toiletries — must be 3 ounces or smaller, and must be placed in a clear quart-size plastic, zip-top bag and screened separately from your other luggage. All other toiletries must be transported to your destination in your checked luggage.

Travelers in the United States are allowed one carry-on bag, plus a "personal item" such as a purse, briefcase, or laptop bag. Carry-on hoarders can stuff all sorts of things into a laptop bag; as long as it has a laptop in it, it's still considered a personal item. The TSA has issued a list of restricted items; I highly recommend checking its Web site (www.tsa.gov) for up-to-the-minute details.

Airport screeners may decide that your checked luggage needs to be searched by hand. You can now purchase luggage locks that allow screeners to open and relock a checked bag if hand-searching is necessary. Look for Travel Sentry–certified locks at luggage or travel shops and Brookstone and TravelSmith stores. (You can buy them online at www.brookstone.com or www.travelsmith.com.) These locks, approved by the TSA, can be opened by luggage inspectors with a special code or key. For more information on the locks, visit www.travel sentry.org. If you use something other than TSA-approved locks, your lock will be cut off your suitcase if a TSA agent needs to hand-search your luggage.

Making Reservations before You Leave Home

In addition to buying your airfare, booking your accommodations, and reserving a rental car, you may want to make a few plans before you leave home.

You don't have to call ahead to reserve most activities until you arrive on Maui. Most snorkel cruises, guided tours, and the like can be reserved a day or two in advance. Even high-profile restaurants can usually get you in within a few days of the day you call.

Still, planning is never a bad idea — especially if you're traveling over spring break or the holidays. I recommend booking anything you absolutely do not want to miss before you leave home to ensure that you're not disappointed. And it's an absolute necessity for certain special events and activities, including the following:

✔ **Luaus:** Maui's **Old Lahaina Luau** is the best luau in the islands; it always sells out at least a week in advance, often more, as does its sister luau, **The Feast at Lele.** It's never too early to reserve your seats; see Chapter 11 for contact information.

✔ **Snorkel cruises:** Maui's finest snorkel-cruise operator is **Trilogy Excursions.** These cruises are hugely popular, so you may want to book your trip to Molokai or Lanai, both red-hot snorkel spots, before you leave home (see Chapter 12).

✔ **Special guided tours:** I highly recommend making advance bookings for Maui's excellent **Pony Express** horseback rides into Haleakala National Park's crater to guard against disappointment (see Chapter 13).

✔ **Special events:** Certain special events require advance planning or arrangements, such as the **Kapalua Wine & Food Festival.** Check Chapter 3 to see what will be on while you're traveling, and whether it requires advance planning. You may also want to check www.visitmaui.com.

✔ **Special-occasion or holiday meals:** These should always be reserved in advance to avoid disappointment. This is especially true on holidays, when the nicer restaurants are overrun with locals and visitors alike. Take it from me on this one — I couldn't get a same-day table at a decent restaurant on Mother's Day to save my life.

✔ **Scuba classes:** First-time scuba divers may want to look into the various resort courses that are available, because they differ from outfitter to outfitter. See Chapter 12 for reputable local dive instructors.

Consider taking scuba certification classes before you leave home; that way, you don't waste time learning in some resort swimming pool and can dive right in as soon as you get to Maui. A great way

to find a local scuba instructor near your home is via the
Professional Association of Diving Instructors (PADI) Web site; go
online to www.padi.com and click on Dive Centers and Resorts.

✔ **Tee times:** If you've got your heart set on playing a particular
course, it's a good idea to call ahead to book your tee time. This
advice is especially true on Lanai, where the two resort courses
insist that you reserve *90 days* in advance.

✔ **Molokai mule ride to Kalaupapa National Historic Park:** Riding a
mule down Molokai's towering sea cliffs to visit this remote and
poignant site is a once-in-a-lifetime adventure. (Even if you're not
planning to stay on Molokai, you can do it on a day trip from Maui.)
Making reservations well in advance of your visit is important as
space is limited on these unique tours. See Chapter 16 for complete
details.

Planning a few of your activities in advance is often the best way to guarantee that you won't miss out on an event or a restaurant that you've
been counting on. That way, if a group suddenly decides that it's going
to take over a snorkel boat for a full day, or a restaurant is planning to
close down for a week to install a new stove in the kitchen, you have the
opportunity to amend your plans accordingly. Besides, you don't want
to spend your valuable Maui time on the phone in your hotel room,
do you?

Packing Smart

Now that airlines are charging for checked bags, it's more important
than ever to leave anything you really don't need at home. To start your
packing, set aside everything that you think you need to take. Then get
rid of half of it.

Even if the airlines will let you take it all (with some limits), carting loads
of stuff around Hawaii is a big fat drag. You really can do without that
sixth pair of sandals. Besides, suitcase and duffel-bag straps can be particularly painful on sunburned shoulders, and you'll probably spend all
day in your bathing suit anyway. What's more, almost all hotel and
condo complexes have on-site laundry facilities, lest you actually run
out of clothes or spill a mai tai on your favorite sundress.

Here are the essentials that you should pack:

✔ **More than one swimsuit:** Finding out that yesterday's swimsuit
isn't dry today is a real bummer. You'll use the extra, I swear.

✔ **Sunglasses, a sun hat, and high-SPF sunscreen:** Take SPF 15 at
minimum; 30 is better. The Hawaiian sun is *very* strong.

✔ **Beach sandals:** I don't want you to scorch your feet on the sand.
Inexpensive flip-flops do the trick.

✔ **A sweater or light jacket:** The evenings can get breezy. Windbreakers come in particularly handy for active travelers.

✔ **Good, comfortable walking shoes:** Bring sturdy tennis shoes or hiking boots if you plan to hike, especially if you're going to visit Haleakala National Park.

✔ **A warm jacket and long pants:** You really need these if you plan to visit Haleakala National Park or some other Upcountry location that gets cool even in summer. Basically, count on the temperature dropping 3½ degrees for every 1,000 feet you climb, which means that it can be 35 degrees cooler atop Haleakala's peak than it is at the beach.

✔ **Rain gear:** A waterproof jacket with a hood is always a good idea if you're visiting Maui between November and March.

✔ **Binoculars:** These come in handy during whale-watching season or to spot dolphins, birds, or other critters at any time of year.

✔ **Dramamine or nausea-prevention wristbands:** These can save the day on a snorkel or sunset cruise. (If you plan to rely on Dramamine to prevent car- or seasickness, be sure to take it *before* you set out — it's too late after you're already on the curving coastal road or rough open seas.)

✔ **A cellphone:** It can be an invaluable lifeline in the event that you get a flat or your rental car breaks down.

✔ **An extra pair of eyeglasses or contact lenses:** Always a good idea to prevent an inconvenient "Ack — I can't see!" emergency.

Maui is a very easygoing place, so leave the pantyhose and pumps and the jacket and tie at home. A casual dress or a polo shirt and khakis will get you by in most dining rooms in the islands — even the expensive ones. One or two ultrafancy resort restaurants may require a jacket, but that's all wrong for Maui, so I don't recommend them.

Hawaiian-print aloha wear is acceptable throughout the islands. I tell you where to buy Maui's best-quality and most beautiful aloha clothes in Chapter 14. You say that you'll never wear it again after you get home? You should — aloha wear looks great everywhere!

Bring all your prescription meds, of course, but don't bother hauling a half-dozen bottles of saline solution or 16 rolls of film from home. Maui has a fine collection of drugstores. If you forget anything, it's generally not a problem. You can buy everything you need, and lots of stuff you don't.

Part III
Settling into Maui

"We're going to Maui this year during the cliff diving, flame dancing, knife throwing festival just to, you know — relax."

In this part . . .

To help you orient yourself when you arrive on the Valley Isle, I'll explain what to do when you land, how to find your bearings, and how to get around. You also find a full listing of Maui's best hotels so that you can choose and book your ideal place to stay. Finally, I'll give you honest, accurate reviews of Maui's top restaurants in all price categories — from fine dining to down-home, local-style island fare.

Chapter 9

Arriving and Getting Around

In This Chapter

▶ Getting from the airport to your hotel without a hassle

▶ Finding your way around Maui and its major resort areas

▶ Getting around without a rental car

Maui is slightly more difficult to navigate than the other Hawaiian Islands. Instead of circling the island, all the major roads meet and crisscross on the flat land between the island's two volcanoes. Still, getting around isn't overly complicated. With a good map in hand, you're golden.

In this chapter, I give you a quick and easy overview of Maui's geography, with a thumbnail sketch of the island's major hotel districts. This information can help you decide where you want to base yourself.

Arriving at Kahului Airport

You'll most likely arrive at the island's centrally located main gateway, Kahului (ka-hoo-*loo*-ee) Airport, in Central Maui.

Kahului Airport (☎ 808-872-3893; www.state.hi.us/dot/airports/maui/ogg) is conveniently located 3 miles from the town of Kahului, Maui's main community, at the end of Keolani Place (just west of the intersection of Dairy Road and the Haleakala Highway).

Flying directly between the mainland and Maui is quite easy these days. **Hawaiian Airlines** provides interisland and direct mainland services to Kahului. **American, Air Canada, Continental, Delta, United,** and **US Airways** all serve Kahului directly from the mainland as well. And, in addition to Hawaiian, recent entry **go! Airlines** also connects Maui with Hawaii's other islands. (See Chapter 5 for complete details on contacting the airlines and scoring the best airfares.)

Maui Orientation

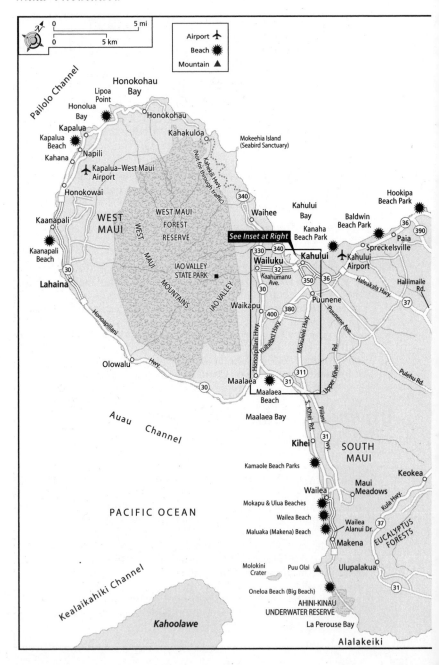

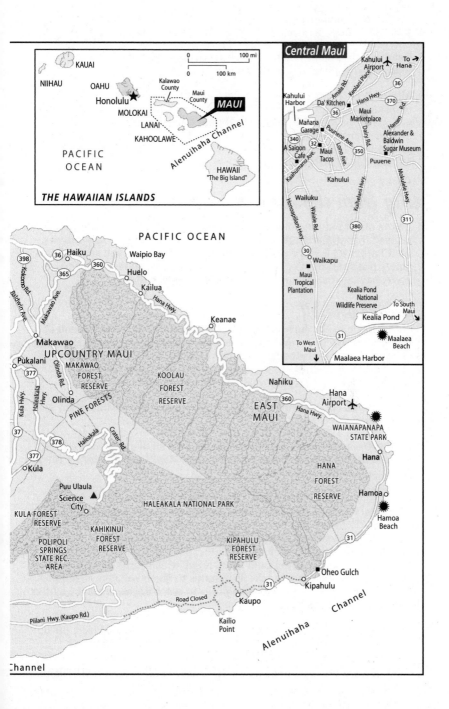

THE HAWAIIAN ISLANDS

KAUAI
NIIHAU
OAHU
Honolulu
MOLOKAI
Kalawao County
Maui County
LANAI
KAHOOLAWE
MAUI
Alenuihaha Channel
PACIFIC OCEAN
HAWAII "The Big Island"

0   100 mi
0   100 km

Central Maui

Kahului Airport   To Hana
Kahului Harbor   Amala Rd.   Keolani Place   36
Da' Kitchen   Hana Hwy.   370
Mañana Garage   Maui Marketplace   Hansen Rd.
340   Puunene Ave.   Alexander & Baldwin Sugar Museum
A Saigon Cafe   32   Maui Tacos   350   Puunene
Kaahumanu Ave.   Lono Ave.   Dairy Rd.   Mokulele Hwy.
Kahului
Wailuku   Kuihelani Hwy.
Waiale Rd.
Honoapiilani Hwy.   380   311
30   Waikapu
Maui Tropical Plantation
Kealia Pond National Wildlife Preserve   To South Maui
To West Maui   Kealia Pond
31   Maalaea Beach
Maalaea Harbor

PACIFIC OCEAN

398   36   Haiku   Waipio Bay
365   360   Huelo
Kailua   Hana Hwy.
Keanae

Kokomo Rd.   Makawao Ave.   Baldwin Ave.
Makawao
UPCOUNTRY MAUI
Pukalani   MAKAWAO FOREST RESERVE
377   Olinda Rd.   KOOLAU FOREST RESERVE   Nahiku
Olinda   PINE FORESTS   360   Hana Airport
37   Haleakala Hwy.   378   Haleakala   Crater Rd.   EAST MAUI   Hana Hwy.
Kula Hwy.   WAIANAPANAPA STATE PARK
377   Kula
Puu Ulaula   HANA FOREST RESERVE   Hana
Science City   Hamoa
KULA FOREST RESERVE   HALEAKALA NATIONAL PARK   Hamoa Beach
KAHIKINUI FOREST RESERVE
POLIPOLI SPRINGS STATE REC. AREA   KIPAHULU FOREST RESERVE   Oheo Gulch
31   Kipahulu
Road Closed   Kaupo   31
Piilani Hwy. (Kaupo Rd.)
Kailio Point   Alenuihaha Channel
Channel

Open-air Kahului Airport is easy to negotiate. The airport is relatively small, and the route from your gate to baggage claim is clearly marked.

Nearly all the island's highways are accessible just outside the airport, ready to whisk you to wherever you'll be staying.

Although nearly everyone arrives at Kahului Airport, Maui does have two single-strip airports served by commercial propeller carriers — one in Kapalua (in West Maui) and another in Hana. If you're interested in avoiding busy Kahului altogether, contact **Island Air** (☎ 800-652-6541 or 808-484-2222; www.islandair.com) or **Pacific Wings** (☎ 888-575-4546 or 808-873-0877; www.pacificwings.com).

Getting from the Airport to Your Hotel

All the major auto-rental agencies have cars available at Kahului, and I suggest that you arrange for one in advance. (For more on this subject, see Chapter 8.) If you'd rather not drive yourself, I give you some alternative transportation options in this section. But if you're willing to drive, having your own rental car is really the way to go.

Driving yourself

Step outside to the curbside rental-car pickup area at the ocean end of the terminal (to your right as you exit the building). Go over to the counter, if your rental company is represented, or wait for the appropriate shuttle van — they circle the pickup area at regular intervals — to take you a half-mile to your rental-car checkout desk.

All the rental-car agencies offer map booklets that are invaluable for getting around the island.

Getting from the airport to your hotel can be a bit of a trial because Kahului is Maui's main business district and Maui's main highways intersect just outside the airport.

If you're heading to **West Maui,** take the Kuihelani (koo-ee-hay-*la*-nee) Highway (Highway 380) to the Honoapiilani (ho-no-ah-pee-ee-*la*-nee) Highway (Highway 30). The Honoapiilani Highway curves around the knob that is West Maui, leading to Lahaina, Kaanapali, Kahana, Napili, and finally Kapalua. To pick up the Kuihelani Highway, exit the airport at Keolani Place and turn left onto Dairy Road, which turns into the highway you want. Expect it to take 30 minutes to reach Lahaina, 40 minutes to reach Kaanapali, and 50 to 60 minutes to reach Kapalua, maybe a little longer if the traffic's heavy.

If you're heading to **South Maui,** exit the airport at Keolani Place, turn left onto Dairy Road, and then left onto Puunene (poo-oo-*nay*-nay) Avenue (Highway 350), which takes you immediately to the Mokulele (mow-koo-*lay*-lay) Highway (Highway 311), leading directly south. Just north of Kihei, the Mokulele ends; you can choose to continue on the highway — now called Piilani (pee-ee-*la*-nee) Highway (Highway 31) — which takes you through Kihei and to Wailea along the speediest route, with frequent exits along the way. If you're staying at the north end of Kihei, though, exit the Mokulele Highway onto South Kihei Road, Kihei's main drag.

Taking a taxi

As long as you arrive before 10 p.m., you don't need to make arrangements before you leave home to have a taxi pick you up at the airport. Just go out to the well-marked curbside area and hop into the next available cab.

If you want to arrange for pickup ahead of time, call **Maui Airport Taxi** (☎ **808-281-9533;** www.nokaoitaxi.com), **Kihei Taxi** (☎ **808-879-3000**), **Wailea Taxi** (☎ **808-874-5000**), or **Maui Taxi Service** (☎ **808-276-9515;** www.mauipleasanttaxi.com).

The mandated fare on Maui is $3 per mile, accommodating one to six people. Expect to pay $65 to $105, depending on your West Maui destination, and about $42 to $55 to the Kihei/Wailea area. Don't forget to tack on a 10 percent to 15 percent tip, of course.

For limousine service, contact **Star Limousine** (☎ **877-875-6900** or 808-669-6900; www.limohawaii.com) or **Maui Executive Transportation** (☎ **800-833-2303;** www.mauishuttle.com).

Catching a shuttle ride

If you're not renting a car, the cheapest way to get to your hotel is via airport shuttle. **SpeediShuttle** (☎ **877-242-5777** or 808-242-7777; www.speedishuttle.com) can take you between Kahului Airport and any of the Maui resort areas between 6 a.m. and 11 p.m. daily. Rates vary depending on your destination, but figure on $38 to Wailea (one way) and $54 to Kaanapali. (Rates also vary depending on the number of people riding with you.) You can set up your airport pickup in advance (which allows you to snag a 10 percent online-booking discount on your return trip) or use the courtesy phone in baggage claim to summon a van (dial ☎ **65**).

When you're ready to leave Maui and fly home, call at least 24 hours before your departure flight to arrange pickup.

Choosing Your Location

The commercial hub of Maui is **Kahului** (ka-hoo-*loo*-ee). Just east of Kahului is **Wailuku,** Maui's appealingly funky county seat (and a burgeoning antiques center). These two Central Maui communities are Maui's largest, but despite their central-to-everything convenience, they aren't really vacation destinations.

Instead, most visitors stay on one of the two major resort coasts: West Maui and South Maui. Each one is made up of a series of smaller beach resorts and communities and offers its own distinct personality.

West Maui

Look at a map of Maui — the island faintly resembles the head and shoulders of a person in left profile. If you go with this geographical inkblot test, the West Maui coastline serves as the island's forehead (and Kahului is on Maui's "neck"). In winter, this coast is a little greener — and a little wetter — than the South Maui coast. Some of the best beaches on the island fringe West Maui; eastward, the beautifully jagged mountain peaks of the West Maui Mountains rise in the distance.

Of the coastal communities, only Lahaina is a real town; the others are really just collections of condos and hotels, each targeted to a different audience and anchored by a few fancy resorts or a high-end minimall. The following communities start at the southern end of West Maui and head northward along the Honoapiilani Highway (Highway 30):

- ✔ The port town of **Lahaina** still has a historic heart, but it equals Oahu's Waikiki as a tacky tourist center. The blocks are lined with bustling waterfront restaurants, touristy (but increasingly upscale) galleries and shops, and activities centers with employees that beg to book your activities (or, if they can, talk you into sitting through a timeshare presentation). The predominant vibe is that of one big surf-oriented street party. Many people love the freewheeling ambience, lively energy, and oceanfront setting; others, who prefer a quieter or more genuinely local vibe, don't. Lahaina also has three main advantages: some of Maui's best accommodations values, an extremely convenient location, and proximity to some very good restaurants and night spots. Lahaina boasts a couple of beaches that will do in a pinch, but if you stay here, you should expect to drive a bit to reach the best ones.

- ✔ Three miles north of Lahaina is **Kaanapali** (ka-ah-na-*pa*-lee), Hawaii's first master-planned family resort, and a real favorite of mine. Kaanapali's string of resort hotels and condos fronts a gorgeous golden beach and exudes a nice sense of continuity. A landscaped parkway and a walking path along the sand, with a very nice shopping and dining complex sitting at their midpoint, link them all together. Kaanapali is pricey, but not quite as expensive as Kapalua or Wailea. In fact, it's home to my favorite midrange resort, the **Kaanapali Beach Hotel,** and some of Maui's best midrange and upscale condos, including **Kaanapali Alii.** See Chapter 10 for more details.

- ✔ Two condo communities, **Kahana** and **Napili,** sit off the highway a few minutes north of Kaanapali, offering great deals for those travelers who want an affordable place to stay and a nice oceanfront setting. Apartment-style units offer a good value for families or anyone who wants homelike amenities that give you the freedom to cook a meal for yourself or wash your own socks. Some very good restaurants and supermarkets also are nearby. The only downside is a lack of personality — expect homogeneous, bulky, and bland condo complexes. (Who can complain, though, when the ocean is just a hop, skip, and a jump away?)

✔ North of Kahana is Hawaii's most beautiful master-planned community, **Kapalua,** the exclusive domain of a gracious Ritz-Carlton as well as some luxurious condos, fabulous gold-sand beaches, and world-class golf. Kapalua is a marvelous place to settle in and unwind, if you enjoy a gorgeously manicured resort setting and have the big bucks to do so. But because it's situated at the north end of the Honoapiilani Highway, Kapalua isn't the most convenient base; even Lahaina is a 20-minute drive to the south. Still, the glorious setting can be well worth the tradeoff. Kapalua also tends to get more rain than other Maui resorts, even those a few minutes south on the West Maui coast.

South Maui

South Maui is the island's hottest, driest, and most dependably sunny coast. Actually western-facing, but well-protected from the elements by peninsula-like West Maui, South Maui receives only about 15 inches of annual rainfall, and temperatures stay around 80°F year-round.

If you drive south from Central Maui along Piilani Highway (Highway 31) or Kihei Road (Highway 310), you first reach Kihei and then Wailea; which one you choose depends entirely on your budget.

✔ Centrally located **Kihei** (*key*-hay) is Maui's bargain coast. Its main drag is South Kihei Road, which is bordered by a continuous string of condos and minimalls on one side and a series of sandy beaches on the other. Kihei isn't charming or quaint — it feels more like Southern California than Hawaii at times, especially when Kihei Road has bumper-to-bumper traffic — but ongoing renovation is improving its appeal. And what Kihei lacks in physical appeal it more than makes up for in sunshine, affordability, and convenience.

✔ Just a few minutes south of Kihei, **Wailea** (why-*lay*-ah) is upscale all the way. This ritzy, well-manicured neighborhood is home to Maui's best luxury resort spreads, a host of championship golf courses, five outstanding beaches, the elegant Shops at Wailea for dining and shopping, and the Wailea Tennis Center (known as Wimbledon West). The strip is well developed and tightly packed, and my favorite Wailea resorts remain worlds unto themselves. Even though Kapalua is more beautiful, Wailea is no slouch — and I prefer its more accessible location and wider range of hotel choices. You even find some midrange and upscale condos in this appealing neck of the woods.

Upcountry Maui

Cool, agricultural, inland Upcountry Maui puts you away from the beaches (which are a 15- to 30-minute drive away) but closer to **Haleakala** (ha-lay-ah-*ka*-la) National Park. That proximity can save you hours of sleep if you want to see the sunrise over the crater. You also can visit the park from the beach resort areas, but you have to get up in the middle of the night to make the drive in time for the first rays of dawn.

Upcountry offers a beautiful glimpse into rural Maui. Most accommodations are quiet, intimate, isolated affairs (B&Bs or vacation rentals) that are perfect for those travelers who love solitude, wonderful views, and romance. Upcountry Maui is a little funkier and local-minded than the beach resorts, and more prone to cool weather and rain.

If you want easy access to sun and surf, plenty of action, and tons of services and facilities, Upcountry isn't for you. It is, however, reachable as a day trip from the West and South Maui resorts — and you may enjoy staying there for a couple of nights after you've had your fill of baking on the sands. Even if you decide not to stay there, I highly recommend that you at least take a drive Upcountry.

If you're considering a visit or a stay in Upcountry, check out Chapter 10.

East Maui and Hana

The gateway to east Maui is the funky-charming **Paia** (pa-*ee*-ah), a hip little surf town about ten minutes east of Kahului that has three main draws: some hip and artsy boutiquing, some of the island's best-value restaurants, and the best windsurfing beach in the world, Hookipa Beach Park, which I discuss in Chapter 12.

A few visitors like to stay way out in **Hana,** in easternmost Maui, for the ultimate escape. In Chapter 10, I review a handful of B&Bs and vacation rentals on the road to Hana or in this lovely town itself. In Hana, you can relax in a lush, green, rural setting with access to wonderful beaches. Hana tends to receive more rain than the dry South Maui coast, but as compensation, the vegetation is green, and it boasts a luxuriant rain forest — think giant ferns, vibrant tropical flowers, and swaying palms.

Hana is a sleepy area, where the accommodations tend to be intimate and exquisite, but not laden with facilities. If you want to get away, a stay in Hana is just the ticket; if you want to be in the thick of things, stay in West or South Maui.

You can see this beautiful area on a day's drive from the major resort coasts, but that tends to be a rushed experience. I highly recommend doing the drive at a leisurely pace and staying overnight in Hana if you can. If you have the time — and the wallet — I recommend doing the drive and staying overnight at the gloriously renovated **Hotel Hana-Maui** (reviewed in Chapter 10). More affordable, B&B-style options are also available if your pockets aren't quite so deep. Hana is a wonderful departure from the bustle of South and West Maui — a step back into Hawaii's simpler days before tourism spawned such intense development.

If you're contemplating a visit or a stay in Hana, check out Chapter 10.

Finding Information after You Arrive

After you land at Kahului Airport, stop over at the state-operated **Visitor Information Center** while you're waiting for your luggage. Pick up copies of *This Week Maui, 101 Things to Do on Maui,* and other free tourist publications, including ones on Maui dining and the arts scene. If you forget, don't worry — you can find these publications at malls and shopping centers around the island.

In addition, all the big resort hotels are overflowing with printed info. Even if your hotel or condo doesn't have a dedicated concierge, the staff can point you in the right direction, make recommendations, and give advice. They're usually happy to help — it's part of Maui's spirit of aloha.

The **Maui Visitors Bureau** is located in Central Maui at 1727 Wili Pa Loop, Wailuku (☎ **800-525-6284** or 808-244-3530; www.visitmaui.com), but it's not really designed as a walk-in office. Call before you leave home to order your free Maui travel planner or check the Web site for a wealth of useful information. The office can also offer visitor information on the islands of Molokai and Lanai.

The *Honolulu Advertiser* (www.honoluluadvertiser.com) and the *Honolulu Star-Bulletin* (www.starbulletin.com) are the two statewide dailies. Maui's own daily paper is the *Maui News* (www.mauinews.com). You can also check out *Maui Weekly* (www.mauiweekly.com) for news.

Getting Around Maui

To really see the Valley Isle, you have to drive it yourself. Maui has only a handful of major roads, but they all meet in a complicated web in the island's center, and untangling them can take some effort. Be sure to study a good island map and know exactly where you're going before you set out.

Maui is growing by leaps and bounds, with new housing developments going up in almost every direction. As a result, traffic can be challenging at times. Try to allow yourself extra time to get where you're going at rush hours, especially in Central Maui and the resort areas.

Navigating your rental car around the Valley Isle

If you get in trouble on Maui's highways and you don't have your cell-phone with you, look for the flashing blue strobe lights on 12-foot poles; at the base are emergency call boxes (programmed to dial 911 as soon as you pick up the handset).

Starting out in Central Maui

Kahului, in Central Maui, is where you'll land at the island's major airport. Kahului isn't a vacation destination, but a real town with Wal-Marts, parking lots, malls, and so on. Still, you may occasionally find yourself in Kahului as you head to other areas of the island because this is where all of Maui's highways intersect.

Kahului's main drag is **Kaahumanu** (ka-ah-hoo-*ma*-noo) **Avenue** (Highway 32). If you're heading to the town of Wailuku, either for some antiquing or to visit scenic Iao Valley (see Chapter 13), just follow Kaahumanu Avenue west for about ten minutes and — *voilà!* — you're there.

Reaching the West and South Maui resorts

If you're heading to any of Maui's beach resort areas, either in West Maui or South Maui, you first have to head south through the Central Maui corridor (often referred to as Maui's "neck").

To reach West Maui, you take the **Kuihelani Highway** (Highway 380) south from Kahului to the **Honoapiilani Highway** (Highway 30). The Honoapiilani Highway actually starts in Wailuku (it meets up with the end of Kaahumanu Avenue to make a neat inverted *L*) and runs directly south to Maalaea (ma-ah-*lay*-ah), a windy harborfront village at the south end of Central Maui — where you may be picking up a snorkel cruise to Molokini or visiting the state-of-the-art Maui Ocean Center aquarium (see Chapter 13 for details). Past Maalaea, the southbound Honoapiilani Highway begins to follow the curve of the land, turning abruptly west and north along the coast toward Lahaina.

West Maui's resort communities lie directly off the Honoapiilani Highway on the ocean side of the road. As you go from south to north, you first reach the old whaling town of Lahaina; then Kaanapali, Hawaii's first master-planned beach resort; then two quiet beachfront condo communities, Kahana and Napili; and, at the end of the road, the Kapalua Resort, a stunning manicured beauty. The road is about 30 minutes of easy highway driving from Lahaina to Kapalua.

Be extra careful as you drive the Honoapiilani Highway (Highway 30) because the road is rather winding, and drivers who spot whales in the channel between Maui and Lanai sometimes slam on the brakes in awe, precipitating tie-ups and accidents.

From Kahului, you basically drive a straight shot to South Maui, the island's hottest, driest, and sunniest resort coast. The **Mokulele Highway** (Highway 311) heads straight south across the Central Maui corridor from Kahului to the north end of Kihei, west of the Kuihelani Highway, Highway 380.

At the end of the Mokulele Highway, you have two choices. You can pick up South Kihei Road, Kihei's main drag, which is what you should take if you're heading to a destination in the northern portion of Kihei or if you're looking for a supermarket or gas station. If you're on your way to the southern portion of Kihei — to Wailea for a round of golf, or to Makena, farther south, to hang out on a quiet beach or go snorkeling — stick to the right, as the Mokulele ends, and pick up the **Piilani Highway** (Highway 31), which continues south to Wailea. Near the end of the Piilani Highway, veer right onto the coastal road to reach the Wailea resorts or Makena.

The Mokulele Highway (Highway 311) is often the scene of crashes involving intoxicated and speeding drivers, so be extra careful.

If you're traveling from South Maui to West Maui, or vice versa, you don't need to travel all the way back to Kahului to pick up the appropriate road. **Highway 310** (North Kihei Road) connects the Mokulele Highway (Highway 311, the road to South Maui) to the Honoapiilani Highway (Highway 30, the road to West Maui), running east–west at the south end of Maui's "neck."

Going Upcountry and to East Maui

The giant volcanic crater that dominates the main body of the island is Haleakala (ha-lay-ah-*ka*-la), officially preserved as Haleakala National Park. The road is only about 38 miles from Kahului to the summit of Haleakala, but the drive takes about 90 minutes because of its curving nature and steep ascent (to about 10,000 ft.). The drive, naturally, is called the **Haleakala Highway,** which is Highway 37 as it passes through open flatlands, past turnoffs for groovy rural towns, such as Haliimaile (home to **Haliimaile General Store,** one of Maui's finest restaurants; see Chapter 11) and Makawao (a charming shopping stop). Then, just past Makawao Avenue, the Haleakala Highway becomes Highway 377 — so don't miss the turn for it. After you pass through the little town of Kula, turn onto **Haleakala Crater Road** (Highway 378), which delivers you to the summit.

If you don't take the Haleakala Crater Road turnoff, you continue south on Highway 377, which soon connects up with Highway 37 again, called the **Kula Highway.** If you stay on this road, it eventually takes you all the way to Hana, the small, isolated town at the east end of the island.

But the more popular route to Hana is the **Hana Highway** (Highway 360), which hugs the north cliffs of Maui for about 52 miles east of Kahului. The Heavenly Road to Hana, as it's often called, is a winding

Central Maui and the Road to Haleakala

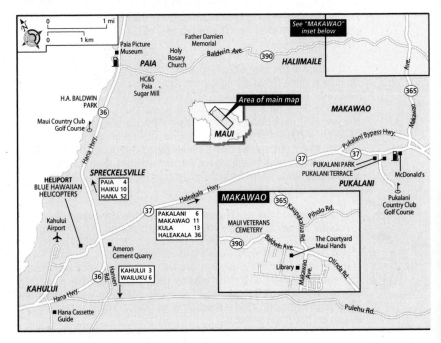

drive that borders on treacherous in each direction, crossing more than 50 one-lane bridges in the process. Still, the drive is one of the most spectacular scenic drives you'll ever take in your life. I guide you through it, mile by mile, in Chapter 13. Even if you don't head all the way to Hana, consider making a visit to charming Paia (pa-*ee*-ah), a hip little surf town about ten minutes east of Kahului that has two main draws: some hip and artsy boutiques, and the best windsurfing beach in the world, Hookipa Beach Park, which I cover in Chapter 12.

The south route to Hana — which is officially Highway 31, but most folks call it the **Kaupo** (*cow*-po) **Road** — was closed at press time due to 2006 earthquake damage. If you're interested in checking it out, check with your hotel or rental-car company regarding potential reopening and current road conditions. It's usually fine if the weather has been clear, but stay away if it's been raining, because unpaved sections of the road can wash out. And check with your rental-car company before you set out; many rental contracts actually *forbid* customers from driving their cars on Kaupo Road, so if you get stuck, the cost for the tow will be your responsibility.

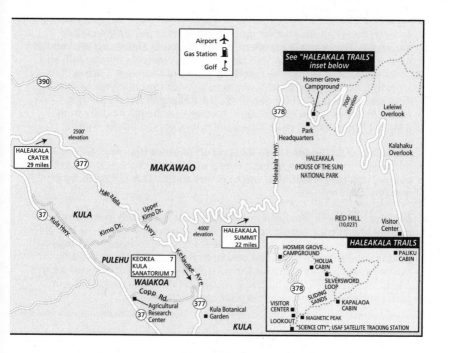

Getting around without wheels

Your options are limited if you're not going to rent a car, because the island has a limited public transportation system.

Operated by Roberts Hawaii, the **Maui Bus** public transit service (☎ **808-871-**4838; www.co.maui.hi.us/bus) runs 11 bus routes among Kahului, West Maui, South Maui, Paia, Haiku, and Upcountry Maui. Both the Upcountry and Paia/Haiku routes stop at the Kahului Airport; however, keep in mind that only one medium-size suitcase is allowed per passenger. The fare is $1 per boarding. Routes run generally from 5 a.m. to 10 p.m., but you should call or check the online route map to figure out your most suitable route and schedule.

Maui does have island-wide taxi service. The meter can run up fast, but a taxi will get you where you need to go if you don't have your own wheels. (See "Taking a Taxi" earlier in the chapter for more information.) Taxis also cruise Lahaina in the evening — good to know, in case you have an extra tipple or two and require a sober driver to take you back to the condo.

If you're going to skip renting a car on Maui, a good bet is to base yourself in Lahaina, where restaurants, shops, and attractions are right at hand. Your beach enjoyment will be limited, though, because even though Lahaina has a beach, it's not the greatest.

An even better alternative for auto-free visitors is basing yourself in Kaanapali. The beach is excellent, and restaurants and shops are right at hand in Whaler's Village. A free resort shuttle connects hotels, golf, and other attractions within the resort, but most of Kaanapali's attractions are within walking distance of one another. Ask the concierge or front desk staff at your hotel for details on the Kaanapali Resort Shuttle, which provides free transportation throughout the resort daily from 9 a.m. to 11 p.m.; everyone in Kaanapali is well-versed on the shuttle.

Kapalua and Wailea also have local resort shuttles that you can rely on to transport you between destinations within the resort — to the golf course, to local restaurants, and to resort shops. This option is, however, very limited.

If you're coming to Maui and not renting a car, ultimately your best bet may be to call your hotel's concierge before you leave home. He can give you a clear heads-up on how convenient the hotel or resort is to nearby restaurants, shopping, and the beach, as well as what kinds of transportation are readily available for you to get to other destinations on the island. See Chapter 13, which fills you in on taking bus tours that can pick you up and drop you off at your hotel.

Chapter 10

Checking In at Maui's Best Hotels

. . . .

In This Chapter

▶ Deciding where to stay

▶ Discovering a fabulous romantic getaway

▶ Uncovering the best family-friendly options

▶ Finding an affordable choice

. . . .

Maui boasts a terrific crop of resorts. But it's such a popular destination that resort hotels and condos both can — and often do — garner ridiculously high rack rates.

But take heart: You can find some good bargains, especially in the condo market. I reviewed some of the best values in this chapter. You can find additional condo options by going through one of the rental agencies listed in Chapter 6.

In fact, Chapter 6 has lots of advice geared to help you book the hotel of your dreams on Maui. It includes a handy overview of the various types of lodging available on the island that can help you choose the option that's right for you. It also features the best money-saving strategies and a discussion about whether to splurge on a room with a view.

You may save a bundle on Maui by purchasing an all-inclusive package deal, especially if you're looking for an upscale vacation. In this case, Maui's popularity may work in your favor: Packagers scoop up huge numbers of Maui hotel rooms, and because they're buying in bulk, they can negotiate substantial price breaks — passing the savings on to you. Of course, I can't guarantee what the prices will be when you book, but checking out what's available is worth the extra effort, even if you're booking the rest of your vacation on your own. (Some packagers can arrange land-only vacations if you already have your plane tickets covered.) See Chapter 5 for tips on finding the package deal that's right for you. An all-inclusive package can save you big bucks on accommodations and airfare alike, and sometimes car rentals and activities, too.

Maui's Best Accommodations

In the following listings, each resort hotel, condo, or B&B name is followed by a number of dollar signs, ranging from one ($) to five ($$$$$). Each represents the median rack-rate price range for a double room per night, as outlined in Table 10-1. (The *rack rate* is the listed full price for a hotel room.)

Table 10-1	Key to Hotel Dollar Signs
Symbol	**Meaning**
$	Cheap — less than $150
$$	Still affordable — $150–$224
$$$	Moderate — $225–$324
$$$$	Expensive but not ridiculous — $325–$449
$$$$$	Ultraluxurious — $450 or more

Don't be scared off by the rack rates listed in these hotel reviews. You almost never *need* to pay the asking price for a hotel room. Check out Chapter 6 for tips on how to avoid paying the rack rate.

Don't forget that the state adds 11.42 percent in taxes to your hotel bill.

Aloha Cottage
$$–$$$ Upcountry Maui

Ron and Ranjana Serle, refugees from Philadelphia who made Upcountry Maui their permanent home some years ago, have crafted a jungle oasis on the slopes of Haleakala for romance-seeking couples in search of a one-of-a-kind place to stay. They've built two gorgeous, studio-style vacation cottages on their lush Upcountry acreage, which is dense with eucalyptus, bamboo, banana trees, and fragrant tropical blooms. Ron and Ranjana have transported their love of Thai and Southeast Asian architecture to the cottages — literally. The Thai Tree House is a copy of a Chiang Mai river house, reinvented for jungle living. The spacious vaulted-ceiling cottage is outfitted with imported furniture and materials. Authentic Thai details are everywhere, from the teak floors to the kitchen cabinetry to the carpets. The luxuriant king-size bed, with its leaded glass headboard, is steps away from a small but comfortable sunken living room.

Your other option is the Bali Bungalow, an octagonal cottage with a rich Balinese-detailed interior. There are some lovely details in this newer cottage, including a silk bedspread, overhead skylight perfect for bedtime stargazing, a marble shower with a dual-head shower system, and Asian-style dining on sofas with a low table. Both beautiful cottages feature full, well-outfitted kitchens that stock everything you need to prepare and serve romantic meals (the Bali Bungalow's is the larger kitchen of the two); a large lanai with a soaking tub for two; TV with VCR; and plenty of privacy (each cottage is a comfortable distance from the main house and the other cottages). Really, it's hard to get more romantic than this — perfect for honeymooners. In fact, Ranjana can host small weddings on the idyllic grounds, cater romantic meals for two in the Lotus House meditation cottage, arrange for an in-cottage massage, or teach a private yoga session for two (with a certified instructor); ask about these and other add-on in-house services, if you're interested in exploring the exotic possibilities.

See map p. 120. 1879 Olinda Rd., Makawao (5 minutes uphill from town). ☎ *888-328-3330 or 808-573-8500 Fax: 808-573-2551.* www.alohacottage.com. *Parking: Free. Rack rates: $260–$295; $215–$230 for stays of 7 nights or more. Additional maid service charge for stays of less than 7 nights. MC, V.*

Best Western Maui Oceanfront Inn
$$–$$$$ South Maui (Kihei)

Want to stay on the beach without paying the exorbitant prices that usually tag oceanfront hotels? This well-maintained small hotel is a fine option. Like the neighboring Mana Kai Maui (see review later in this chapter), the Oceanfront Inn is located at the quietest south end of Kihei, just north of ritzy Wailea, on the golden sands of Keawakapu Beach, which offers excellent snorkeling and swimming. The Oceanfront Inn offers smaller rooms and suites than the Mana Kai's roomy apartments — making this a better choice for couples than families — but it compensates with fresh furnishings. Each smallish standard hotel room offers a queen-size Tempur-Pedic bed, minifridge, coffeemaker, and individually controlled air-conditioning; ceramic tile floors, plantation shutters, and ceiling fans add gentle island flair. Each of the two-room suites has a pleasing tropical-style sitting room and a microwave; the extra space is well worth the cost if you can afford it. On-site Sarento's on the Beach offers a splurge-worthy dining experience, especially for romance-seeking couples. Blue Hawaii Water Sports offers all the water toys and dive equipment you need — including PADI-certified instruction and boat dives — making this an excellent choice for wallet-watching divers and snorkelers. On-site laundry adds to the convenience. Not fancy or spacious — don't stay here if you're planning to hang out in your room — but a reasonable on-the-beach bargain.

See map p. 120. 2575 S. Kihei Rd., Kihei. ☎ *800-263-3387 or 808-879-7744. Fax: 808-874-0145.* www.mauioceanfrontinn.com *or* www.bestwestern.com. *Parking: Free. Rack rates: $159–$169 double; from $395 2-room suite. Deals: Excellent opportunities for discounts, including BestRates, AAA, military discounts, and senior rates; from $118 at press time. AE, DC, DISC, MC, V.*

Best Western Pioneer Inn
$$ West Maui (Lahaina)

This nicely restored 1901 whaler's inn overlooking Lahaina Harbor blends a genuine old-time ambience with proven Best Western comforts, and it's

Maui's Best Accommodations

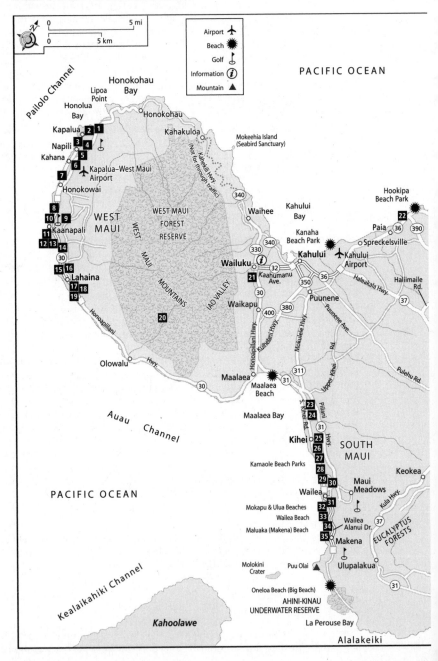

Aloha Cottage **37**
Best Western Maui
    Oceanfront Inn **29**
Best Western Pioneer Inn **17**
Fairmont Kea Lani Maui **35**
Four Seasons Resort
    Maui at Wailea **34**
Grand Wailea Resort & Spa **33**
Hana Oceanfront Cottages **40**
Heavenly Hana Inn **38**
Hooilo House **20**
Hotel Hana-Maui **39**

Hyatt Regency Maui
    Resort & Spa **14**
The Inn at Mama's
    Fish House **22**
Kaanapali Alii **13**
Kaanapali Beach Hotel **11**
Kahana Sunset **6**
Kapalua Villas **2**
Koa Resort **24**
Koa Lagoon **23**
Lahaina Shores
    Beach Resort **15**
Mana Kai Maui **28**
Mauian Napili
    Beach Hotel **5**

Maui Coast Hotel **27**
Maui Guest House **18**
Maui Spa Retreat **36**
Napili Bay **4**
Napili Kai Beach Resort **3**
Noelani Condominium Resort **7**
The Old Wailuku Inn
    at Ulupono **21**
Outrigger Aina Nalu **19**
Outrigger Maui Eldorado Resort **9**
Outrigger Palms at Wailea **30**
Plantation Inn **16**
Punahoa Beach Apartments **25**
ResortQuest at the
    Maui Banyan **26**
Ritz-Carton Kapalua **1**
Sheraton Maui **8**
Wailea Beach Villas **31**
Wailea Beach Marriott
    Resort & Spa **32**
Westin Maui Resort & Spa **10**
The Whaler at
    Kaanapali Beach **12**

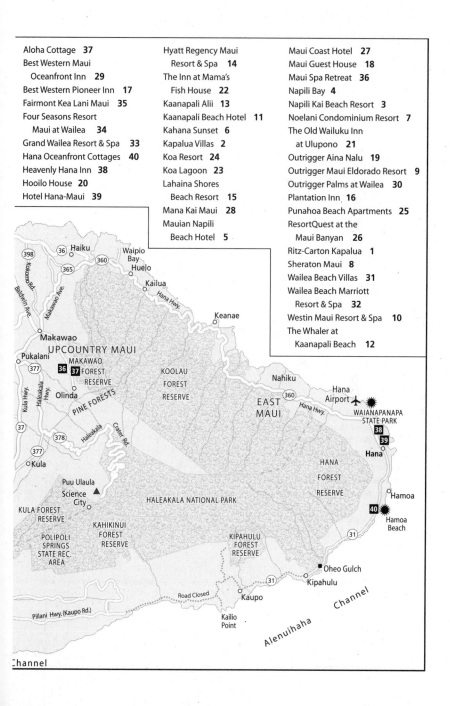

Accommodations and Dining in West Maui:
Kapalua, Napili, and Kahana

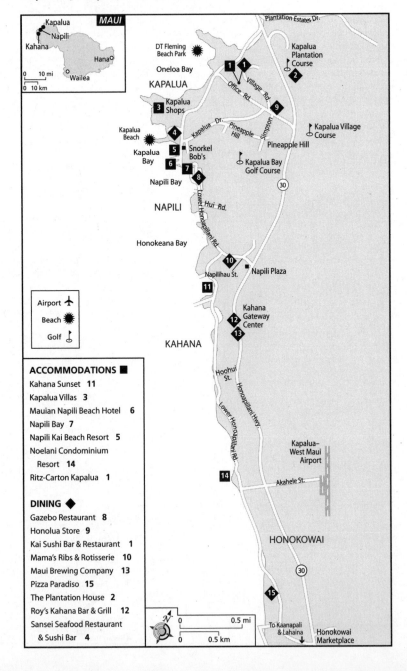

Airport ✈
Beach ✳
Golf ⛳

ACCOMMODATIONS ■

Kahana Sunset **11**
Kapalua Villas **3**
Mauian Napili Beach Hotel **6**
Napili Bay **7**
Napili Kai Beach Resort **5**
Noelani Condominium
　Resort **14**
Ritz-Carton Kapalua **1**

DINING ◆

Gazebo Restaurant **8**
Honolua Store **9**
Kai Sushi Bar & Restaurant **1**
Mama's Ribs & Rotisserie **10**
Maui Brewing Company **13**
Pizza Paradiso **15**
The Plantation House **2**
Roy's Kahana Bar & Grill **12**
Sansei Seafood Restaurant
　& Sushi Bar **4**

Accommodations and Dining in West Maui: Lahaina and Kaanapali

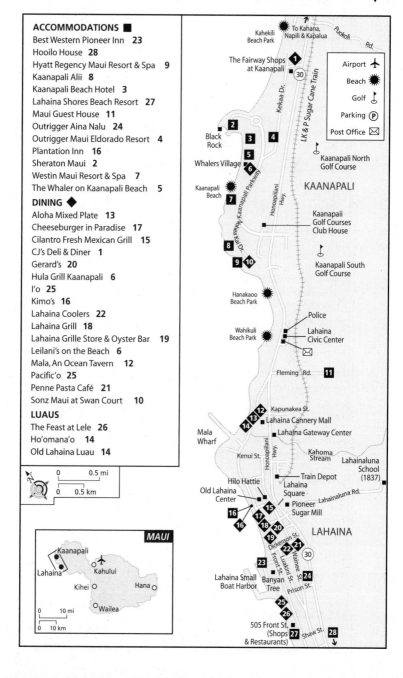

ACCOMMODATIONS ■
Best Western Pioneer Inn **23**
Hooilo House **28**
Hyatt Regency Maui Resort & Spa **9**
Kaanapali Alii **8**
Kaanapali Beach Hotel **3**
Lahaina Shores Beach Resort **27**
Maui Guest House **11**
Outrigger Aina Nalu **24**
Outrigger Maui Eldorado Resort **4**
Plantation Inn **16**
Sheraton Maui **2**
Westin Maui Resort & Spa **7**
The Whaler on Kaanapali Beach **5**

DINING ◆
Aloha Mixed Plate **13**
Cheeseburger in Paradise **17**
Cilantro Fresh Mexican Grill **15**
CJ's Deli & Diner **1**
Gerard's **20**
Hula Grill Kaanapali **6**
I'o **25**
Kimo's **16**
Lahaina Coolers **22**
Lahaina Grill **18**
Lahaina Grille Store & Oyster Bar **19**
Leilani's on the Beach **6**
Mala, An Ocean Tavern **12**
Pacific'o **25**
Penne Pasta Café **21**
Sonz Maui at Swan Court **10**

LUAUS
The Feast at Lele **26**
Ho'omana'o **14**
Old Lahaina Luau **14**

Accommodations in South Maui

Best Western Maui
Oceanfront Inn **7**
Fairmont Kea Lani Maui **13**
Four Seasons Resort Maui
at Wailea **12**
Grand Wailea Resort & Spa **10**
Koa Lagoon **2**
Koa Resort **1**
Mana Kai Maui **6**
Maui Coast Hotel **4**
Outrigger Palms at Wailea **7**
Punahoa Beach Apartments **3**
ResortQuest at the
Maui Banyan **5**
Wailea Beach Villas **11**
Wailea Beach Marriott
Resort & Spa **9**

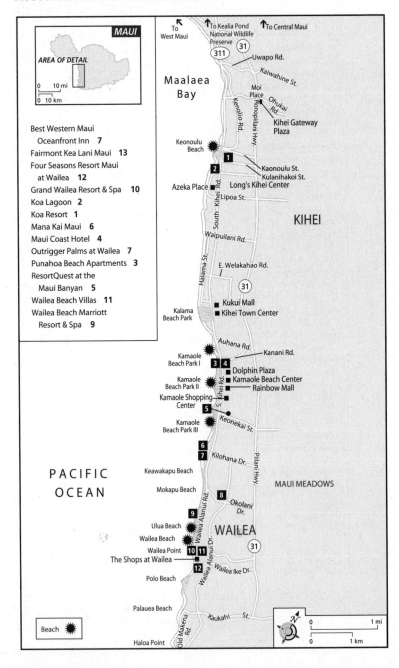

Accommodations and Dining in Upcountry and East Maui

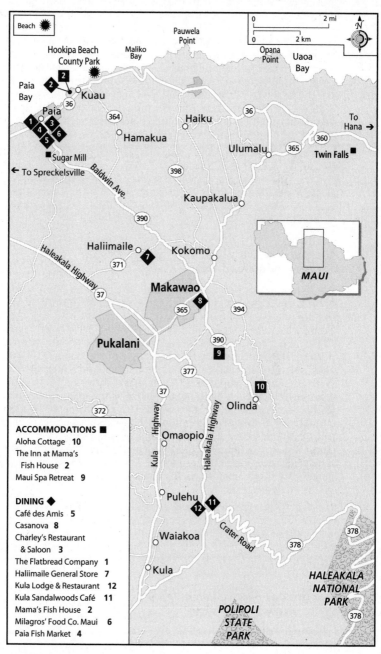

Beach ☀

0   2 mi
0   2 km
N

Pauwela Point

Maliko Bay

Opana Point   Uaoa Bay

Hookipa Beach County Park

Paia Bay

2

The Inn at Mama's

36   Kuau

1 **3**
4 **6**
5

Paia

364

Haiku

36

To Hana →

Hamakua

Ulumalu   365

360

Sugar Mill

← To Spreckelsville

Baldwin Ave.

398

Twin Falls

Kaupakalua

390

Haliimaile   **7**   Kokomo

Haleakala Highway

371

Makawao

37

8

365   394

Pukalani

390

9

377

37

10

372

Olinda

Kula Highway

Haleakala Highway

Omaopio

MAUI

Pulehu

12 **11**

Waiakoa

Crater Road

378

Kula

378

HALEAKALA NATIONAL PARK

378

POLIPOLI STATE PARK

ACCOMMODATIONS ■
Aloha Cottage **10**
The Inn at Mama's
  Fish House **2**
Maui Spa Retreat **9**

DINING ◆
Café des Amis **5**
Casanova **8**
Charley's Restaurant
  & Saloon **3**
The Flatbread Company **1**
Haliimaile General Store **7**
Kula Lodge & Restaurant **12**
Kula Sandalwoods Café **11**
Mama's Fish House **2**
Milagros' Food Co. Maui **6**
Paia Fish Market **4**

a winning combination. Rooms are small and on the dark side, but they're cool, pretty, and comfortable, with modern tiled bathrooms and coffeemakers. Deluxe rooms also have wet bars with minifridges, and suites add an additional Murphy bed. The quietest rooms face the garden courtyard pool or the massive banyan tree next door. A few have harbor views that heighten the maritime experience. Front Street–facing rooms are noisy, but shaded and furnished lanais give you a ringside seat for the sidewalk party. The hotel has an appealing indoor-outdoor restaurant and bar on site; the beach is a drive away, but the town couldn't be more convenient. All in all, the Best Western Pioneer Inn isn't Maui's roomiest or quietest place to stay, but it's a real charmer. This is best for those who prefer walkable access to in-town conveniences such as dining, shopping, and nightlife.

See map p. 120. At Lahaina Pier, 658 Wharf St. (at Front Street), Lahaina. ☎ *800-457-5457 or 808-661-3636. Fax: 808-667-5708.* www.pioneerinnmaui.com *or* www.bestwestern.com. *Parking: Free (but 2 blocks away). Rack rates: $149–$195 double; from $200 suite. Deals: Discounts for AAA and AARP members, seniors (55-plus) and military; inquire about BestRates discounts and other special packages. AE, DC, DISC, MC, V.*

Fairmont Kea Lani Maui
$$$$$ South Maui (Wailea)

This fanciful Moorish palace is just as pricey as Maui's other luxury resorts, but it gives you so much more room for your money. Spread out and enjoy a giant one-bedroom suite, complete with a gorgeous living room with a full entertainment center (CD and DVD players, plus a second TV in the bedroom); a wet bar with coffeemaker and microwave; a mammoth marble bathroom with a soaking tub big enough for two, double sinks, separate shower, and terrific toiletries; and a furnished lanai that's ideal for an alfresco breakfast. The two- and three-bedroom villas are even more luxurious, each boasting a gourmet kitchen; a washer and dryer; a gas barbecue and plunge pool on the private patio; and a prime, on-the-sand location. Amenities include three swimming pools (one for adults only), two Jacuzzis, an excellent spa (second only to the neighboring Grand Wailea's), a fitness center, a full beach activities center, and a wealth of daily activities and kids' programs. The hotel's excellent dining options include the ultraromantic **Nick's Fishmarket** (see p. 171). It's a first-rate choice on every level.

See map p. 120. 4100 Wailea Alanui Dr., Wailea. ☎ *800-441-1414 or 808-875-4100. Fax: 808-875-1200.* www.kealani.com. *Valet parking: $18. Self-parking: Free. Rack rates: $450–$1,200 suite; $1,100–$2,500 2- or 3-bedroom villa. Deals: Many available specials, including golf and spa packages, and breakfast-inclusive deals; be sure to check the Web site or ask. AE, DC, DISC, MC, V.*

Four Seasons Resort Maui at Wailea
$$$$$ South Maui (Wailea)

I personally prefer the neighboring Fairmont or Grand Wailea, but there's no doubting the Four Seasons brand for a premier luxury experience.

Averaging an extra-large 640 square feet (although the Kea Lani's suites are even more spacious), the guest rooms here are done in soft, warm tones and feature cushy furnishings, grand and gorgeous bathrooms (among the best in Hawaii), and big lanais. About 80 percent have ocean views, but beware those that overlook the driveway — it's a real mood killer. You're better off with a gardenview room overlooking the lovely sculpture gardens and waterfalls (and most of these have a bit of an ocean view anyway). The mountainview rooms are a good value for pricey Maui, considering the cream-of-the-crop quality of the accommodations and service. The gorgeous grounds overflow with first-rate facilities — including the only Hawaii branch of Wolfgang Puck's legendary **Spago** restaurant (p. 176) and a sublime spa offering yoga, Pilates, and a wide variety of pampering treatments. The beach is one of Maui's finest, and the service is exceptional. If you prefer to lounge poolside, you can recline in comfort under a shaded cabana or on a grassy lawn; a pool attendant will even bring you chilled towels and spritz you with Evian if you break a sweat. Don't be surprised if you see Misha, Jessica, Cameron, or another big star lounging poolside — this resort is a big-time Hollywood favorite. The kids will be duly pampered in an excellent activities program.

See map p. 120. 3900 Wailea Alanui Dr., Wailea. ☎ *800-334-6284 or 808-874-8000. Fax: 808-874-6449.* www.fourseasons.com/maui. *Rack rates: $475–$1,005 double; $1,045–$5,510 suite. Valet parking: $18. Deals: Multiple package deals almost always on offer, including room-and-car, bed-and-breakfast, golf, spa, and others. Also ask about 5th-night-free deals and special family rates. AE, DC, DISC, MC, V.*

Grand Wailea Resort & Spa
$$$$$ South Maui (Wailea)

Now part of the prestigious Waldorf=Astoria collection of luxury hotels, this palatial resort is just too glorious to deny. This monument to monied excess won me over with its lush, art-filled grounds (boasting works by such masters as Botero, Legér, Picasso, and Warhol) and its exclusive tropical-theme-park vibe. The fantastic 50,000-square-foot Spa Grande is the island's ultimate temple to the pampered life, whereas the pool complex is Hawaii's best water playground, a fantasy of falls, rapids, slides, grottos, hidden hot tubs, and swim-up bars, plus the world's only water-powered elevator. Rooms are huge and elegantly appointed, with luxurious marble bathrooms. If you can afford it, stay in the Napua Tower; this exclusive 100-room hotel-within-a-hotel offers personalized concierge service plus free continental breakfast. Restaurants, shops, and lounges abound. What's more, both food and service are first-rate, making this resort the place to stay if you can afford to live large. And bring the kids — they'll think that they've died and gone to heaven, especially after they see the whopping 20,000-square-foot kids' camp. But despite the resort's grandness, you'll still feel comfortable roaming around in your beach togs. This elegant fantasyland is an ideal place to tie the knot, too, because it's home to a picture-perfect seaside wedding chapel. Minimalists, on the other hand, should book elsewhere.

See map p. 120. 3850 Wailea Alanui Dr., Wailea. ☎ *800-888-6100 or 808-875-1234. Fax: 808-874-2442.* www.grandwailea.com. *Valet parking: $20. Rack rates: $625–$1,180* double; $1,900–$17,710 suite. Mandatory $25-per-night "resort fee" for "free" self-parking, "free" local and toll-free calls, in-room coffee, daily fitness classes, and other resort extras. Deals: Numerous packages are usually available, including bed-and-breakfast, 7th night free, spa, golf, kids, and more; from $499 at press time. AE, DC, DISC, MC, V.

Hana Oceanfront Cottages
$$$ Hana

Housed in two plantation-style buildings built by friendly California refugees Dan and Sandi Simoni, these two marvelous one-bedroom units are fully outfitted for Hana living. Each comes complete with a living room, a fully appointed gourmet kitchen (no worrying about that pesky where-to-dine problem), super-comfortable furniture (including artfully made beds), a full bath, a TV with VCR and DVD player, a CD player, and a big lanai with ocean views. The Beach Suite gives you a bit more space, while the Beach Cottage gives you a bit more privacy and puts you closer to the surf. The property boasts lush, mature tropical grounds. Best of all, paradise-like Hamoa Beach, East Maui's finest swimming spot — which James Michener called "the most beautiful beach in the world" — is just steps away. Enjoy a simply delightful place to stay, whether or not you can afford the luxurious Hotel Hana-Maui down the road. Be sure to say "hello" if you see Dan and Sandi's next-door neighbor (Oprah Winfrey owns the adjacent 4 acres).

See map p. 120. Hana Highway, Hana. ☎ 808-248-7558. www.hanaoceanfront cottages.com. Parking: Free. Rack rates: $250–$275. 10 percent discount available for weeklong stays; 3-night minimum for stays booked within 2 months of arrival, 4-night minimum for more advanced bookings. $75 cleaning fee. MC, V.

Heavenly Hana Inn
$$–$$$ Hana

This gorgeous Japanese-style inn was originally built in the 1950s and completely renovated in the '90s — with no dollar or detail spared. It's utterly beautiful, luxuriously comfortable, and totally serene. Every room exhibits stunning woodwork and the impeccable taste of the innkeepers. The suites boast sitting rooms, little lanais, big baths with deep soaking tubs, and platform beds adorned in lavish textiles and deep, cushy futons. The two outside acres are landscaped Japanese-style, with a bamboo fence, tiny bridges over a meandering stream, and lava-rock paths. The $16 two-course continental breakfast is an expanded gourmet feast served *kaiseki* style, and picnic lunches and afternoon tea service can be prepared to order with advance notice. Though the inn is impeccable, I have received a few complaints that the innkeepers are a bit remote and the rules can feel strict, so don't expect a warm-and-fuzzy experience. Note that no children under age 15 are accepted. Following Japanese and Hawaiian traditions, the owners ask that you remove your shoes when entering. A friendly cocker spaniel and two cats live on the premises.

See map p. 120. Hana Highway (between mile markers 32 and 33), Hana. ☎/Fax: 808-248-8442. www.heavenlyhanainn.com. Parking: Free. Rack rates: $190–$260 *suite. Full gourmet breakfast available for $16 per person. Ask about special rates. 2-night minimum stay. AE, DISC, MC, V.*

Hooilo House
$$$$ West Maui (Lahaina)

Perched on a breezy hill above the West Maui coast is this elegant bed-and-breakfast, coined Hooilo House by its innkeepers, who sought refuge from the colder climes of the Pacific Northwest and Alaska and chose Maui as their ultimate escape (*hooilo* means "winter"). The house was built as a bed-and-breakfast, so all of the six suites have been designed with guests in mind. Each features a comfortable, custom, king-size bed, an extra-large marble bathroom with a tub, a private outdoor shower lined in lava rock, and a lanai furnished for lounging with tranquil garden or ocean views.

The house is designed and decorated Balinese-style. Practically every wall is a window that opens to the breeze; the hallways are open-air bridges that cross koi-filled streams, and each guest room is entered through an imported Balinese door inlaid with mother-of-pearl that sets the mood for something special, including such creative details as showerheads crafted from stone-carved masks and bamboo. The owners live in an adjacent cottage, so guests feel free to lounge or play a board game in the house's common area, which overlooks a lovely 4-foot-deep pool with panoramic ocean views. This is the site for the morning buffet spread, which you can enjoy at your leisure. I also like the full daily maid service, which isn't a given at all home-style accommodations. However, I do have a few quibbles: The bedrooms are a hair's breadth smaller than I wish they were. The outdoor shower is delightful, except when the wind kicks up and then I wish I had a shower option indoors. In a place with this much attention to detail, I don't understand why the small TVs have VCRs rather than DVD players. In a luxury B&B designed for romance, there should really be a hot tub, as well as a pool designed for more than dipping. And I think the innkeepers are a bit too aloof — but you may actually prefer the hands-off approach. Still, Hooilo House is a tranquil, romantic retreat, and a convenient drive to beaches and the restaurants and nightlife of Lahaina. Not suitable for children.

See map p. 120. 138 Awaiku St. (off Kai Hele Ku Road, 1 mile uphill from Honoapiilani Highway, Highway 30), Lahaina. ☎ 808-667-6669. www.hooilohouse.com. Parking: Free. Rack rates: $345 double. Deals: 15 percent discount for stays of 5 nights or longer. AE, MC, V.

Hotel Hana-Maui
$$$$$ Hana

The Hotel Hana-Maui, a breathtaking oceanfront property that had languished in disrepair for too many years, was gloriously reborn a few years ago, I'm happy to report. The same folks behind Big Sur's amazing Post Ranch Inn have transformed this property into one of Maui's most magical resorts, making it reason enough to cruise to the end of the road to Maui's remote eastern shore. The small hotel has just 66 rooms and suites nestled in one-story Hawaiian-style cottages; its expansive and meticulously land-scaped grounds slope gently down to glorious Hana Bay, allowing for plenty of privacy and quiet relaxation. Both the setting and the warm-hearted staff exude an old-Hawaii feeling. Accommodations, on the other hand, boast only the most luxe comforts: warm and welcoming interiors featuring indigenous island materials, textiles, and patterns. These gener-ously apportioned units are at once designer-stylish and sigh-inducingly comfortable. The duplex Sea Ranch cottages are the most luxurious, with cathedral ceilings, gorgeous oversize bathrooms, and private lanais; about half have patio Jacuzzis. But you can't go wrong with the low-rise Bay View suites, a little farther up the slope, if your wallet is tighter. A lack of TVs, radios, and air-conditioning (you don't need it out here) suits the mood perfectly; no one travels to the end of the road in Hana to watch CNN. (The common Club Room has a giant-screen TV and Internet access if you really need a fix.) A wealth of marvelous outdoor activities — from cultural walks and horseback riding to sunbathing at — will keep you content, as does the utterly pampering and peaceful Honua Spa. The one downside is that you may get tired of the cuisine after a time — there are no other restau-rants in Hana besides the hotel's own.

See map p. 120. At Hana Ranch, Hana Highway, Hana. ☎ *800-321-HANA (800-321-4262) or 808-248-8211. Fax: 808-248-7202.* www.hotelhanamaui.com. *Valet park-ing: Free. Rack rates: $495–$525 Bay cottage for 2; $650–$1,625 Sea Ranch cottage for 2; $1,675 2-bedroom suite; $4,000 2-bedroom Plantation guesthouse. Deals: Numerous value-added packages available, with oceanview Sea Ranch cottages from $495 at press time; call or check the Web site for current offers. AE, DC, DISC, MC, V.*

Hyatt Regency Maui Resort & Spa
$$$$–$$$$$ West Maui (Kaanapali)

If you like the idea of a fantasy megaresort but can't swing the price tag at the Grand Wailea, also consider this often-less-expensive alternative, located on 40 oceanfront acres at the quieter south end of Kaanapali Beach. This opulent fantasyland is dotted with a riot of tropical foliage, rushing waterfalls, sparkling lagoons, and exotic wildlife. Though not quite as fab as the Grand Wailea's, the half-acre pool complex is no slouch here, either; there's a lava tube slide and a rope bridge for the kids, and even a man-made beach, in case the spectacular sands out front are too crowded.

The spacious guest rooms are warmly decorated in rich colors, floral prints, and Asian accents (a welcome change from the chain-standard beiges that often plague Hawaii resorts), and feature separate sitting areas and furnished lanais. The Hyatt is an excellent choice for restless vaca-tioners, because activities include a rooftop astronomy program, tennis, world-class golf within walking distance, beach and ocean activities, and a nightly luau complete with fire dancers. When it's time to relax, give your-self over to the soothing oceanfront Spa Moana (reserve your treatments well in advance). Cascades features marvelous views and superb sushi, while the romantic Son'z Maui at Swan Court offers innovative cuisine, an extensive wine list, and impeccable service. Although it's not exactly an intimate experience — how could it be with 806 guest rooms? — it's a very satisfying choice nonetheless.

See map p. 120. 200 Nohea Kai Dr., Kaanapali. ☎ *800-233-1234 or 808-661-1234. Fax: 808-667-4498.* www.maui.hyatt.com. *Valet parking: $20. Rack rates: $400–$735 double; call for suite rates. $15-per-night "resort fee" includes self-parking, "free" local and toll-free calls, in-room coffee, health club access, tennis, and other extras. Deals: Special deals (including 5th night free and breakfast included) and packages galore. Discounts available for AAA members. AE, DC, DISC, MC, V.*

The Inn at Mama's Fish House
$$ East Maui (On the Road to Hana)

These tropical cottages on one of Maui's most gorgeous oceanfront lots are ideal for those who want a quiet but still-central location. Nestled in a coconut grove on secluded Kuau Cove — just a ten-minute drive from the airport — six beautifully furnished vacation rentals feature rattan furnishings, lovely local artwork, terra-cotta floors, and complete kitchens (even dishwashers). Extras like big TVs with DVD players, CD players, Weber gas barbecues, laundry facilities, and tons of beach toys make this a great place to stay with friends or family. The one-bedrooms can sleep up to four — two on the queen-size bed in the bedroom, two on the sleeper sofa. The two-bedrooms can sleep up to six: One bedroom has a queen-size bed, and the second has a full bed or two twin beds, plus a sleeper sofa in the bedroom. Two-bedrooms also benefit from a prime beachfront location, and the one-bedrooms are just steps from the beach, nestled in colorful tropical foliage. Service is thoughtful, friendly, and efficient. The divine **Mama's Fish House** — my favorite Maui restaurant (see p. 168) — is next door, and inn guests benefit from discounts at lunch and dinner. Just down the road is hip-as-can-be Paia, the fun and funky surf town that serves as the gateway to the road to Hana. The only downside? Despite the on-the-beach location, only the luxury beachfront cottage benefits from an ocean view.

See map p. 120. 799 Poho Place (off the Hana Highway in Kuau), Paia. ☎ *800-860-4852 or 808-579-9764. Fax: 808-579-8594.* www.mamasfishhouse.com. *Parking: Free. Rack rates: $175 garden studio; $225 garden 1-bedroom unit; $325 garden 2-bedroom unit; $525 luxury beachfront unit. 3-night minimum stay. AE, DISC, MC, V.*

Kaanapali Alii
$$$$–$$$$$ West Maui (Kaanapali)

If you want luxury living and condo conveniences, this high-rise beachfront complex is the place for you. These condos are Maui's finest, and they're well worth the high price tag. Each is privately owned, so décor varies, but owners are held to a high standard. The one- and two-bedroom apartments are universally large (1,500–1,900 sq. ft.); each comes with a fully equipped gourmet kitchen, huge living room and dining room, two TVs and VCR and/or DVD player, two full bathrooms (even in the one-bedrooms), washer/dryer, and private lanai. The luxuriant grounds feature a fitness room, tennis courts, a smallish heated pool with hot tub and poolside snack service, plus a separate kids' pool, a beach activities center, and poolside gas grills for fun family meals. Among the resortlike amenities are daily maid service; concierge, bell, valet, and room service; complimentary kids' club activities in summer; yoga classes; on-the-beach cabana rentals; and even grocery delivery and a resident tennis pro. Service is friendly and accommodating. Best of all, the location — oceanfront at the southern end of fabulous Kaanapali Beach — simply can't be beat. An excellent choice on all fronts, and one of my all-time Hawaii favorites.

See map p. 120. 50 Nohea Kai Dr., Kaanapali. ☎ *800-642-6284 or 808-661-3339. Fax: 808-667-1145.* www.classicresorts.com. *Parking: Free. Rack rates: $425–$695 1-bedroom; $590–$975 2-bedroom. 3- to 5-night minimum stay, depending on the date. Deals: Numerous deals are usually on offer, including 5th-night-free, room-and-car, and romance packages; 1-bedrooms from $316 at press time. AE, DC, MC, V.*

Kaanapali Beach Hotel
$$–$$$$ West Maui (Kaanapali)

The Kaanapali Beach Hotel is the last hotel left in Hawaii that gives you a real resort experience in this price range. It's older, and it's not luxurious, but it boasts a genuine spirit of aloha that's absent in so many other hotels. Set beachfront around a wide, grassy lawn with a whale-shaped pool, three low-rise wings house spacious, well-maintained rooms. They may be rather motel-like, but they're perfectly comfortable and feature all the conveniences, plus lanais overlooking the pretty yard or beach. Tiki torches, hula, and music create an irresistible Hawaiian ambience every evening, and the service is some of the friendliest around. An extensive Hawaiian program goes beyond the standard hula lessons to include lauhala weaving, lei making, and cultural tours. A kids' program, three just-fine restaurants, and coin-op laundry are also on-site. It's one of my all-time favorites. *Travel + Leisure* agrees with me: The magazine has dubbed this Hawaii's top hotel for value, and second-best hotel in the world for less than $200 a night. Unfortunately, rates have begun to climb, but they remain relatively affordable considering the excellent location and warm spirit of aloha.

See map p. 120. 2525 Kaanapali Pkwy., Kaanapali. ☎ *800-262-8450 or 808-661-0011. Fax: 808-667-5978.* www.kbhmaui.com. *Self-parking: $9. Valet parking: $11. Rack rates: $199–$355 double; $277–$485 suite. Most rates can be selected with or without breakfast included. Deals: Free-car, free-night, golf, and romance packages are almost always available, as well as senior (50-plus) and corporate discounts and Internet specials. AE, DC, DISC, MC, V.*

Kahana Sunset
$$–$$$$ West Maui (Kahana/Napili)

These oceanfront condos are an excellent value, one of Maui's best. The attractive wooden complex stair-steps down pretty terraced grounds to a petite but perfect swimming cove fringed with white sands. The apartments are roomy enough to accommodate families (especially if you book one of the two-bedroom units, which boast two full bathrooms). Each unit has nice island-style furniture; a complete kitchen with a dishwasher, a microwave, and a refrigerator with an ice maker; washer/dryer; air-conditioning and ceiling fans; a DVD player and sleeper sofa in the living room; and a big lanai with a terrific view. Nestled between the coastline and the road above, the complex is much more private than many on this condo coast. On-site is a lovely heated pool and Jacuzzi, a separate kids' pool, barbecues, and beach showers. Furthermore, daily maid service (not a given in condos) makes it actually feel like you're on vacation.

See map p. 120. 4909 Lower Honoapiilani Hwy., at the northern end of Kahana (8 miles north of Lahaina). ☎ *800-669-1488 or 808-669-8700. Fax: 808-669-4466.* www.kahana sunset.com *or* www.premier-hawaii.com. *Parking: Free. Rack rates: $165–$290 1-bedroom; $225–$465 2-bedroom. 2-night minimum. Deals: Car-and-condo packages, special rates, and Internet offers often available, so always mine for discounts. AE, MC, V.*

Koa Resort
$ South Maui (Kihei)

These unfancy but nice condos sit right across the street from the ocean and make a good choice for active families on tight budgets. There are two on-site tennis courts, a very nice swimming pool, a hot tub, and an 18-hole putting green. The spacious, privately owned one-, two-, and three-bedroom units are fully equipped and have plenty of room for even a large clan. Each comes with a full kitchen — complete with dishwasher, microwave, and coffeemaker — and a large lanai with ceiling fans, and washer/dryer. The majority of two- and three-bedroom units have multiple bathrooms. The smaller units have showers only, so ask for one with a tub if it matters to you. Also, for maximum peace and quiet, ask for a unit removed from Kihei Road.

See map p. 120. 811 S. Kihei Rd. (between Kulanihakoi Street and Namauu Place), Kihei. Reservations c/o Bello Realty. ☎ *800-541-3060 or 808-879-3328. Fax: 808-875-1483.* www.bellomauivacations.com. *Parking: Free. Rack rates: $99–$115 1-bedroom; $100–$140 2-bedroom; $160–$240 3-bedroom. AE, MC, V.*

Koa Lagoon
$$ South Maui (Kihei)

This delightful condo complex just may be the top bargain of the Kihei coast. This midrise building has 42 units — each with a breathtaking oceanfront setting with views that most visitors have to pay much more to enjoy. Each large one-bedroom (700 sq. ft. plus lanai) or two-bedroom (975 sq. ft. plus lanai) apartment is nicely decorated and smartly outfitted and includes a large, furnished lanai; a full all-electric kitchen with dishwasher and microwave; washer/dryer; TV with VCR or DVD; a sofa bed in the living room; and air-conditioning (not the best, but you're unlikely to need it). Unlimited free local calls and free high-speed Internet access are nice pluses. On the impeccably maintained grounds, you'll find a heated pool and gas barbecues to share with your fellow residents — plus those wonderful ocean views, which come alive during the day, with winter whale sightings, and nightly year-round at the sunset hour (the building is west-facing). Unit no. 503 is particularly popular thanks to its spectacular sight-lines. The whole place is consistently clean and well taken care of, with friendly and professional service. I also like the location at the north end of Kihei, which is relatively quiet and convenient to the rest of the island's sights and attractions. All in all, one of Maui's finest values.

See map p. 120. 800 S. Kihei Rd., Kihei. Reservations c/o Bello Realty. ☎ 800-367-8030 or 808-879-3002. Fax: 808-874-0429. www.koalagoon.com. *Parking: Free. Rack rates: $140–$180 1-bedroom; $170–$210 2-bedroom; $160–$240 3-bedroom. AE, MC, V.*

Lahaina Shores Beach Resort
$$–$$$ West Maui (Lahaina)

This dated but pleasant plantation-style complex of studios and one-bedroom suites sits right on the sand at the quiet end of Lahaina, within easy walking distance of restaurants, shopping, and entertainment, but nicely out of the noisy fray. The hotel is more basic than stylish, but the units are comfortable and decently outfitted, and the price is right, especially considering the on-the-beach location. Even the smallest unit is a spacious 550 square feet. Each one comes with a fully equipped kitchen (with microwave), a sitting and dining area, and a furnished lanai. Obviously, those units overlooking the waves and the island of Lanai across the channel are best, but the mountain views aren't shabby either; still, given the all-around good value, splurge on an ocean view if you can. Do know, however, units are individually owned and can vary in quality; some have been recently updated, while others need renovation attention. When you book, inquire about the specific quality and features of your unit. Outside is a lovely grassy lawn with a small pool, hot tub, and lounge chairs; just beyond it is a narrow stretch of swimming beach. (First-time surfers often learn on the low-riding waves here.) Other amenities include on-site laundry facilities, and tennis courts just across the street. This in-town, close-to-conveniences location is best for those wanting a good price. Note that units can be rented through two different brokers (see the following paragraph), so I highly recommend that you price compare.

See map p. 120. 475 Front St. (near Shaw Street), Lahaina. ☎ 800-367-5242 (Condominium Rentals Hawaii), 800-642-6284 (Classic Resorts), or 808-661-4835. Fax: 808-667-1145. www.crhmaui.com *or* www.lahainashores.com. *Parking: $3. Rack rates: $167–$215 studio; $240–$340 1-bedroom; $290–$370 penthouse. $35 reservation fee added to every booking. Deals: 7th-night-free and room-and-car specials offered at press time. Discounts available for stays longer than 1 week. AE, MC, V.*

Mana Kai Maui
$–$$ South Maui (Kihei)

Situated on a beautiful white-sand beach with excellent snorkeling, this eight-story hotel-condo hybrid is one of my favorite affordable choices. About half of the units are hotel rooms, which are smallish but offer great value. The larger one- and two-bedroom apartments feature up-to-date full kitchens, nice island-style furnishings, well-maintained bathrooms, and open living rooms that lead to small lanais with ocean views. These are older units, but they're clean and comfortable, thanks to daily maid service. A coin-op laundry is located on each floor, a restaurant and lounge is downstairs, and a nice pool and a grassy lawn with beach chairs complement that fabulous beach. Management is friendly and conscientious. But the Mana Kai's real ace in the hole is its location: It lies on Wailea's doorstep, on the prettiest, quietest end of Kihei, away from the strip-mall fray. Maui Yoga Path operates an open-air studio on the Mana Kai grounds, offering daily classes by the ocean.

See map p. 120. 2960 S. Kihei Rd., Kihei (just before Wailea). ☎ *800-367-5242 (800-663-2101 from Canada) or 808-879-2778. Fax: 808-879-7825.* www.crhmaui.com. *Parking: Free. Rack rates: $120–$201 double hotel room; $205–$377 1-bedroom; $255–$438 2-bedroom. $35 reservation fee added to every booking. Deals: 7th-night-free and room-and-car specials offered at press time. Discounts available for stays longer than 1 week. AE, MC, V.*

Mauian Napili Beach Hotel
$$ West Maui (Kahana/Napili)

These simple studio units have a pleasing old-fashioned Hawaiian style. The family-run Mauian is perched above a beautiful half-mile-long, white-sand beach with great swimming and snorkeling. It has a pool with lounge chairs, umbrellas, and tables on the sun deck, and the verdant grounds are bursting with tropical color. The rooms feature hardwood floors, Indonesian-style furniture, full kitchens with fridges and coffeemakers (in most units), and big lanais with great sunset views. The rooms don't have phones or TVs (this place really is about getting away from it all), but the large *ohana* (family) room does have a TV with a VCR and an extensive library of videos, plus free Wi-Fi access. Complimentary coffee, coin-op washer/dryers, and phones and fax service are available. Great restaurants are just a five-minute walk away, and Kapalua Resort is up the street. All in all, this is an excellent beachfront choice for the price.

See map p. 120. 5441 Lower Honoapiilani Rd., Napili. ☎ *800-367-5034 or 808-669-6205. Fax: 808-669-0129.* www.mauian.com. *44 units. Parking: Free. Rack rates: $155–$180 gardenview double; $195–$230 oceanview double; $250–$200 oceanfront double. Rates include continental breakfast. Extra person $10. Children 4 and under stay free in parent's room. Deals: Check for Internet specials, which were as low as $110 double at press time. AE, DISC, MC, V.*

Maui Coast Hotel
$$ South Maui (Kihei)

This affordable hotel is recommended for its good package deals, and its central (if rather less-than-pretty) location, about a block from the beach and a short walk away from restaurants, shopping, and nightlife. This isn't the Four Seasons, so don't expect luxury — but the clean, modest rooms feature good-value extras, including sitting areas, coffeemakers, minifridges, Nintendo game systems, and furnished lanais. The one-room alcove suites are a bit larger; each has a separate sitting area with a cafe table and chairs for enjoying your morning coffee. Add a fairly good restaurant, room service, free use of laundry facilities, a nice pool (plus one for the kids) with poolside service, two Jacuzzis, a restaurant, and tennis courts (with lights for night play), and you end up with a full-service hotel at a bargain price. The suites offer families excellent value, especially if you can find a package to suit you.

See map p. 120. 2259 S. Kihei Rd. (at Ke Alii Alanui Drive), Kihei. ☎ *800-895-6284, 800-663-1144, or 808-874-6284.* www.mauicoasthotel.com *or* www.coasthotels.com. *Parking: Free. Rack rates: $215–$245 double or 1-room alcove suite with a separate sitting area; $275–$320 suite. Deals: Inquire about breakfast, golf, romance, room-and-car, and 5th-night-free packages (from $195 with a compact car at press time); also ask about AAA, senior (55-plus) and best-available rates (from $184, suites from $204 at press time). Special holiday rates may apply. AE, DC, DISC, MC, V.*

Maui Guest House
$$ West Maui (Lahaina)

This appealing and professionally run bed-and-breakfast is an excellent value and offers more amenities than many of the "full-service" hotels just down the road in Kaanapali. The spacious home offers four guest accommodations, all mostly suited to couples looking for romance at a budget rate. All rooms have queen beds (three have an extra twin bed if you're traveling with a child or a friend), plus a private bathroom, a large plasma TV with DVD player, air-conditioning, a fridge, and — the crowning glory — a private lanai with its own private Jacuzzi. You're welcome to make yourself at home throughout the house, which boasts parquet floors, floor-to-ceiling windows, a large and lovely swimming pool with comfortable lounging chairs and a hammock, a well-outfitted kitchen and barbecue grill for your use, a 300-plus DVD library, and laundry facilities (no quarters needed). The house even has a wireless network throughout for laptop toters, plus a computer you can use if you just want to check your e-mail once or twice during your trip. A generous continental breakfast is laid out each day, and the owners can help you arrange just about every island activity. The nearest beach is about a block away. Here you'll enjoy a clean, quiet, and utterly charming place to stay.

See map p. 120. 1620 Ainakea Rd. (off Fleming Road), Lahaina. ☎ *800-621-8942 or 808-661-8085.* www.mauiguesthouse.com. *Parking: Free. Rack rates: $169 double. AE, DC, DISC, MC, V.*

Maui Spa Retreat
$$ Upcountry Maui

Boasting a majestic perch on the slopes of Haleakala, this hidden gem can reward you with one of the finest spa days you'll ever enjoy, as well as a comfortable place to stay. The sloping property is a beautifully manicured aromatherapy farm, and the proprietor blends all her own body scrubs, wraps, and healing oils from the garden for use during the spa treatments.

There are two simple, charming cottages to rent for a complete Upcountry experience. Best is the spacious one-bedroom, two-story cottage, which features a comfortable and nicely furnished living room, a fully equipped kitchen with gorgeous koa cabinetry, a king-size Tempur-Pedic bed in the upstairs bedroom, a nicely outfitted bathroom, and sensational views from both levels. Up to four guests can be accommodated on futons in the living room. A petite, octagonal-shaped, studio-style cottage is also available for rent. This unit features a king bed, a nice studio-style kitchen with granite countertops, a dining area for two, a TV with DVD player, a rustic but pleasant bathroom with an open shower, and a nicely furnished deck where you can enjoy a morning cup of Hawaii's famous Kona coffee. Since this is a vacation rental, no breakfast is provided, and services are minimal, but the cottages are well outfitted and nicely maintained. On-site is a saltwater lap pool and a hot tub, both with panoramic views. Restaurants are just a short drive down the hill in Makawao, and beaches are another 15 minutes beyond that. You'll truly be away from civilization at this pleasant getaway. Check the Web site for details on spa packages available.

See map p. 120. 1860 Olinda Rd., Olinda. ☎ *877-877-MAUI (877-877-6284).* www.aroma therapyfoundationofmaui.org *or* www.mauisparetreat.com. *Parking: Free. Rack rates: $175 studio double; $225 1-bedroom cottage double. $90–$125 cleaning fee. Ask about nights free for longer stays. Cash or check only.*

Napili Bay
$–$$ West Maui (Kahana/Napili)

This excellent bargain sits on Napili's beautiful, half-mile white-sand beach. This small, two-story complex is perfect for an affordable romantic getaway; the sound of the waves creates a comfortable and relaxing atmosphere. The studio apartments are definitely small, but still, you have a full kitchen (with fridge and coffeemaker), a queen-size bed, a queen-size sleeper sofa that lets you sleep two more (if you don't mind lots of togetherness), a TV with DVD, a CD player, and a spacious lanai where you can sit and watch the sun set. Each unit is individually owned, so furnishings can vary, but the quality is consistently good. Louvered windows and ceiling fans keep the units cool during the day. You have plenty of restaurants and a convenience store within walking distance, and you're about 10 to 15 minutes away from Lahaina and some great golf courses. Coin-op washer/dryers and a barbecue are nice features. The beach right out front is one of the best on the coast, with great swimming and snorkeling right at your door. Book early, because this place fills up fast. Note that you have two sources for booking: Maui Beachfront Rentals and Aloha Condos both allow you to book directly through the owners. Both Web sites feature pictures of available units so you can choose the one you like. If your idea of paradise does not include being unplugged from e-mail or the Internet, be aware that only a few units have high-speed Internet access, so ask for one if you want it.

See map p. 120. 33 Hui Dr. (off Lower Honoapiilani Highway), Napili. Bookings handled by Maui Beachfront Rentals or Aloha Condos, 256 Papalaua St., Lahaina. ☎ *888-661-7200 or 808-661-3500. Fax: 808-661-2649.* www.mauibeachfront.com *or* www.alohacondos.com. *Parking: Free. Rack rates: $120–$280 studio. Check minimum-stay requirements; usually 7 nights minimum, but may vary depending on rental source. MC, V.*

Napili Kai Beach Resort
$$$–$$$$ West Maui (Kahana/Napili)

Make yourself right at home at this complex of bright one- and two-story units embracing its own wonderful white-sand snorkeling beach. There are a handful of basic hotel rooms with minifridges and coffeemakers, but most units have lovely tropical-modern décor, large lanais, DVD players, and kitchenettes (all with microwave, some with dishwasher). The one-bedrooms have sleeping accommodations in both rooms — usually a king-size bed in one room, two twin beds in the other — making this a great configuration for families; some even have a second bathroom. The two-bedroom units can sleep as many as six or seven, and all have a second bathroom. The Khaka suites unite two or three adjoining hotel rooms or studios in one value-priced package for families or shares. Most, but not all, units offer air-conditioning, so ask if you want it (you'll need it only in summer); otherwise, ceiling fans do the trick. The complex has a restaurant and bar with a great view; however, I've heard too many complaints that it's overpriced for what you get, and most guests don't dine here more than once. The beach pagoda serves daytime snacks and drinks and doles out snorkel gear for your free use. You also get daily maid service, four pools and a hot tub, barbecues, a fitness room, an 18-hole putting green, and a basic spa. During family seasons (Easter/spring break, summer, and Christmas), kids 6 to 10 can enjoy the supervised Keiki Club, with two hours of activities daily (except Sun), plus Wednesday-night movies. All in all, a nice place to stay, if not a bargain.

See map p. 120. 5900 Honoapiilani Rd., Napili (at the extreme north end of Napili, next to Kapalua). ☎ *800-367-5030 or 808-669-6271. Fax: 808-669-0086.* www.napili kai.com. *Parking: Free. Rack rates: $230–$280 hotel room double; $285–$385 studio; $430–$700 1-bedroom or 2-room Keaka suite; $625–$1,050 2-bedroom or 3-room Keaka suite. Deals: Ask about room-and-car, 5th-night-free, bed-and-breakfast, and spa packages. AE, MC, V.*

Noelani Condominium Resort
$–$$ West Maui (Kahana/Napili)

I stand by all my recommendations, but that doesn't mean I don't get a teensy bit nervous when my boss says that she's going to take me up on one. So I was thrilled when she came home from Maui confirming my own observations — that this top-notch oceanfront condo is a stellar value and a great place to stay. All the well-maintained apartments sport kitchens, VCRs, ceiling fans (no air-conditioning), and spectacular ocean views; all but the studios have dishwashers and washer/dryers, too (self-service laundry facilities are available for studio dwellers). Best is the Antherium building, where apartments have ocean-facing lanais just 20 feet from the surf. Concierge and midweek maid service, two freshwater pools (one heated for night swimming), and an oceanfront Jacuzzi round out the good value. You're invited to a continental breakfast orientation on the first day of your stay. Don't miss mai tai parties in the evenings; oceanfront barbecues are ideal for family outings. Next door is a sandy cove that's popular with snorkelers, but you may find yourself driving to a prettier beach — at these prices, you won't mind. All in all, one of the best values the island has to offer.

See map p. 120. 4095 Lower Honoapiilani Rd., Kahana. ☎ *800-367-6030 or 808-669-8374. Fax: 808-669-7904.* www.noelani-condo-resort.com. *Rack rates: $125–$175 studio; $175–$197 1-bedroom; $240–$290 2-bedroom; $330–$357 3-bedroom. 3-night minimum. Parking: Free. Deals: Check for 5 percent Internet booking discount, weekly discounts for seniors and AAA members, and honeymoon specials. AE, MC, V.*

The Old Wailuku Inn at Ulupono
$$ Central Maui (Wailuku)

If you're charmed by the notion of old-time Hawaii, book into this 1920s home, located in the historic town of Wailuku. Innkeepers Tom and Janice Fairbanks have restored the house (a cross between Craftsman and plantation style) very nicely, although a few negatives — such as yellow safety tape on the hardwood stairs — undermine the ambience. Janice has used her impeccable eye to fill the home with island-style bamboo and Asian antiques. Each of the seven guest rooms in the main house is decorated with a Hawaiian heirloom quilt and top-quality everything, including an oversize luxury bathroom; unfortunately, housekeepers took the gorgeous quilt off the bed the first time they made up my room, folded it inside out and stored it for the duration of my week's stay, so I never got to enjoy it. Though the bathrooms are large, they tend to lack storage space. Still, the furnishings are oversize, cushy, and invite you to kick back and make yourself at home.

Three units occupy a modern annex called the Vagabond's House (named to honor Don Blanding, the "vagabond poet laureate" of Hawaii). Sig Zane, Hawaii's premier fabric designer, created custom linens inspired by Hawaiian flowers for each of these wonderful rooms. These units are a better option for light sleepers, because noise can travel a bit in the main house. The beach is a drive away, but the central location puts Maui within easy reach — plus, for people in an acquisitive mood, Wailuku is lined with antiques shops.

See map p. 120. 2199 Kahookele St. (at High Street), Wailuku. ☎ *800-305-4899 or 808-244-5897. Fax: 808-242-9600.* www.mauiinn.com. *Parking: Free. Rack rates: $165–$195 double. Rates include full gourmet breakfast. Additional person $20. 2-night minimum stay. Deals: Ask about discounts on rental cars from Dollar and Avis. MC, V.*

Outrigger Aina Nalu
$$–$$$ West Maui (Lahaina)

Run by Outrigger, the value-minded, Hawaii-based hotel chain, this well-managed plantation-style complex makes a nice place to stay, especially when you can score a good deal (which you usually can). The newly redeveloped property offers petite studios and more spacious one- and two-bedrooms with fresh, contemporary island-style décor that is more attractive than you might expect; Outrigger did a very nice job here. Studios have a microwave and minifridge; all other units have fully outfitted kitchens. All

units have lush garden views, air-conditioning, and video games. The one-
and two-bedroom apartments have dishwashers, sofa beds and their own
washer/dryers. Note that bathrooms have showers only, no tubs. The well-
manicured grounds feature barbecues, a hot tub, and a nice pool. The larger
units are perfect for families; your kids will love the heart-of-Lahaina location, and you'll appreciate the tranquil ambience that results from a peaceful side-street location (a rarity in Lahaina). The complex is generally very
quiet but you should ask for a unit away from the highway for minimum
intrusion. Note that this two-story building has no elevators.

*See map p. 120. 660 Wainee St. (between Dickenson Street and Prison Street),
Lahaina. ☎ 800-688-7444 or 808-667-9766. Fax: 808-661-3733.* www.outrigger.
com. *Parking: $15. Rack rates: $229–$265 studio; $299–$335 1-bedroom; $369–$415 2-
bedroom. 2-night minimum. Deals: Outrigger is one of Hawaii's best dealmakers;
better-than-average discounts for AAA and AARP members and seniors (50-plus), plus
corporate, government, and military discounts; from $129 at press time. Ask about
bed-and-breakfast, room-and-car, and other package deals. AE, DC, DISC, MC, V.*

Outrigger Maui Eldorado Resort
$$$ West Maui (Kaanapali)

These spacious condos — all with full kitchens, washer/dryers, and daily
maid service — were built back in the good old days when land in
Kaanapali was cheap, contractors took pride in their work, and visitors
expected spacious accommodations with views from every window. It may
be of late-'60s vintage, but the Outrigger chain keeps quality and mainte-
nance high. This resort is a wonderful choice for families, with big, comfy
units, grassy areas that are perfect for running off all that excess kid
energy, and a shoreline that's usually safe for swimming. Three pools, bar-
becue areas, shops, and a coin-op laundry round out the appeal.

*See map p. 120. 2661 Kekaa Dr., Kaanapali. ☎ 888-339-8585, 800-688-7444, or 808-
661-0021. Fax: 808-667-7039.* www.outrigger.com. *Parking: Free. Rack rates:
$219–$345 studio double; $239–$405 1-bedroom (sleeps up to 4); $565–$625 2-bedroom
(up to 6). 2-night minimum stay. Deals: Many discounted rates and package deals
available, including 5th-night-free, frequent-flier, and room-and-car packages.
Discounts also available for seniors and military personnel. AE, DC, DISC, MC, V.*

Outrigger Palms at Wailea
$$$ South Maui (Wailea)

This villa-style apartment complex is a very nice choice if a sunny Wailea
location appeals to you, but you just don't want to shell out for one of
those ridiculously expensive resorts. The smart and pleasing complex
boasts contemporary Southwestern-style buildings spread over tidy
greens. The modern apartments are well-furnished and feature all the
expected amenities, including a fully outfitted kitchen, furnished lanai,
VCR, and washer/dryer. On-site is a very nice pool and hot tub, and championship Wailea golf and tennis facilities are right at hand. Daily maid service and concierge-style desk service are part of the package. The only
downsides are that it's about a 10- to 15-minute walk to a good swimming

beach, and air-conditioning is in the master bedroom only; you'll have to pay extra for a portable unit in the other spaces. You won't normally need it, but it can get warm in summer. The elegant, open-air Shops at Wailea is also a short walk away.

See map p. 120. 3200 Wailea Alanui Dr., Wailea. ☎ *888-294-7731, 800-688-7444, or 808-879-5800. Fax: 808-874-3723.* www.outrigger.com. *Parking: Free. Rack rates: $249–$329 1-bedroom; $259–$425 2-bedroom. 2-night minimum stay. Deals: Better-than-average discounts for AAA and AARP members and seniors (50-plus), plus corporate, government, and military discounts. Romance and room-and-car packages regularly on offer. AE, DC, DISC, MC, V.*

Plantation Inn
$$–$$$ West Maui (Lahaina)

This charming Victorian-style hotel in the heart of Lahaina offers both in-town convenience and old-fashioned romance. It's actually of 1990s vintage, but modern extras like soundproofing (a plus in downtown Lahaina), VCRs, fridges (a few have kitchenettes), and private bathrooms (some with shower only) don't detract from the period appeal. Deluxe rooms in the Lanai category are the way to go for romance-seeking couples, because this is where the décor really starts to have distinctive detail and personality; tell the reservationist your tastes and she'll likely be able to match you with one that best suits your style. The lower-category rooms are a bit more budget-basic. The inn wraps around a nice, large tiled pool and deck with a hot tub. On-site are coin-op laundry facilities and Gerard's, a top-notch French restaurant. The staff is excellent. You'll have to drive to a good beach, but Lahaina Harbor is a walk away (great for early-morning snorkel cruises). Guests here have full privileges at the Kaanapali Beach Hotel, a sister property reviewed earlier in this section. Not perfect, but a good choice for travelers who want both wallet-friendly rates and accommodations with personality.

See map p. 120. 174 Lahainaluna Rd. (between Wainee and Luakini streets), Lahaina. ☎ *800-433-6815 or 808-667-9225. Fax: 808-667-9293.* www.theplantationinn. com. *Parking: Free. (A rarity in Lahaina.) Rack rates: $169–$245 double; $265–$290 suite. Rates include continental breakfast. 2-night minimum stay at Halloween; 7-night minimum at Christmas. Deals: Ask about gourmet, honeymoon, rental-car, and other packages, and check for great Internet specials. AE, DC, DISC, MC, V.*

Punahoa Beach Apartments
$$ South Maui (Kihei)

With the best location in Kihei, this friendly little complex is a bona fide beachfront bargain. The setting — off noisy, traffic-congested Kihei Road, on a quiet side street that faces the ocean — is fabulous: A grassy lawn extends down to the sand, where great offshore snorkeling awaits, and a popular surfing spot sits just next door. A coin-op laundry is on-site, and markets and restaurants are but a stroll away. The apartments aren't fancy, but they're nicer than you'd expect for the money; each has a fully equipped kitchen and a lanai with great ocean views. Studios have

Murphy-style queen-size beds, one-bedrooms have king beds, and corner-unit two-bedrooms have a queen-size bed in the master and twin beds in the second bedroom. Only a few units have air-conditioning, but ceiling fans draw in the trade winds. Guests keep coming back, so reserve your bargain unit as far in advance as possible.

See map p. 120. 2142 Iliili Rd. (off South Kihei Road, near Kamaole Beach Park I), Kihei.
☎ *800-564-4380 or 808-879-2720. Fax: 808-875-9147.* www.punahoabeach.com. *Parking: Free. Rack rates: $116–$150 studio; $160–$231 1-bedroom; $198–$263 2-bedroom. 5-night minimum. Deals: 10 percent discount on stays of 10 nights or more Apr to mid-Dec; 15 percent discount on stays of 21 nights or more year-round. AE, DC, DISC, MC, V.*

Making yourself at home: Condos

Condominium apartments are some of Maui's most appealing and cost-effective accommodations options. They're outfitted like a full-service home and can accommodate anywhere from two to eight vacationers in one, two, or three bedrooms. Even couples enjoy the extra space and home-style amenities.

Well-developed Maui abounds with condo developments. I review my favorites in this chapter, but there are more. Real-estate agencies tend to manage individual units throughout an area's assorted complexes. Expand your choices by contacting one of the following agencies, which can match you with the unit that meets your needs and budget.

In addition to those already listed — including the **Kaanapali Alii, ResortQuest at the Maui Banyan,** and **The Whaler on Kaanapali Beach,** just to name a few — a number of booking agencies offer one-stop shopping for condo rentals all over the island.

The **Hawaii Condo Exchange** (☎ 800-442-0404 or 323-436-0300; www.hawaiicondoexchange.com) is a Southern California–based agency that acts as a consolidator for condo properties throughout the islands, including a number of excellent choices on Maui. The Exchange works to match you up with the place that's right for you and tries to get you a good deal.

For a complete selection of upscale condos throughout sunny, luxury-minded Wailea, contact **Destination Resorts Hawaii** (☎ 866-384-1365 or 808-891-6249; www.destinationresortshi.com). Destination Resorts generally handles first-class one-, two-, and three-bedroom condos boasting deluxe amenities, including daily maid service, concierge service, grocery delivery service, and preferential rates at the area's first-class tennis facilities and championship golf courses. Prices start as low as $225 for a one-bedroom. Value-added packages, such as fifth-night-free and car-condo deals, are available regularly.

Destination Resorts's **Wailea Beach Villas** (☎ 866-901-5207 or 808-891-4500; www.waileabeachvillas.com) have set a new standard for condominium luxe on Maui. Since around June 2006, these 98 glorious villas and penthouses blend luxurious, home-style comforts with first-class resort services (even fully stocked kitchens and personal chef services) and a wonderful Wailea Beach location. Rates run $880 to $3,000 nightly for the 1,900- to 3,100-square-foot residences, with a five-night mini-mum stay.

If you like the sound of the tranquil Kapalua resort but the Ritz-Carlton is out of your price range (or your style), consider renting an elegant condo or vacation home at **Kapalua Villas** (☎ **800-545-0018**, 800-227-6054 or 808-665-5400; www.kapalua villas.com). Nightly rates range from $279 for a one-bedroom apartment with a fairway view to $759 for an oceanfront two-bedroom apartment — not bad, consid-ering you enjoy the same delicious perks and spectacular views of your much-higher-paying neighbors (including Kelsey Grammer, who owns his own Kapalua spread). The three- to five-bedroom freestanding luxury vacation homes run from $1,700 to $7,500 nightly. Whether you go large or small, you're sure to be pleased with your first-class accommodations.

Bello Realty (☎ **800-541-3060** or 808-879-3328; www.bellomauivacations.com) represents affordable condos throughout the Kihei/Wailea area, with prices starting as low as $99 in the low season and $115 in the high season. I've received plenty of good feedback from vacationers who've used Bello and come away with an excel-lent beachfront bargain and good service results, so I'm quite confident about the quality and values that Bello offers. Be sure to check out **Koa Resort** and **Koa Lagoon**, two of Maui's best bargains (reviewed earlier in this chapter).

Condominium Rentals Hawaii (☎ **800-367-5242** or 808-879-2778; www.crhmaui.com) has moderately priced condos throughout Maui, with a concentration in Kihei, and handles the **Mana Kai** (reviewed earlier in this chapter). The car-and-condo pack-ages and other regular specials can really add to the value of these units.

You can choose from a range of good-value apartments along West Maui's condo coast through **Maui Beachfront Rentals** (☎ **888-661-7200** or 808-661-3500; www.maui beachfront.com). The best deal for budget-minded couples is at the **Napili Bay**, which start out between $145 and $167. Two of my favorite Kaanapali Beach condo complexes are **The Whaler** and **Kaanapali Alii** (reviewed earlier in this chapter). Ask about packages that include a free night or a rental car.

You can cut out the middleman and rent directly from the owner at a number of qual-ity condo resorts on Maui, including the terrific **Napili Bay, The Whaler,** and a few other good-quality condo resorts, by visiting **Aloha Condos Hawaii** (www.aloha condos.com), a cooperative of owner-managed units.

Most companies that offer all-inclusive travel packages to Maui can book you into any number of condos, as can your travel agent. See Chapter 5 for details on booking a pay-one-price travel package.

ResortQuest at the Maui Banyan
$$–$$$ **South Maui (Kihei)**

Skip the standard hotel rooms, if you can, and go straight for a condo unit — which offers much more value for your dollar — at this very nice apartment-like complex situated across Kihei Road from Kamaole (kam-a-*oh*-lay) Beach Park II. The roomy, open-plan one- and two-bedroom units are all decently outfitted and well maintained; a few three-bedroom units are also available. They've all feature contemporary island-style furniture, full kitchens with microwave, washer/dryers, and furnished lanais. Light daily maid service is included, and two pools, tennis courts, and a Jacuzzi are on-site. The building sits perpendicular to the coast, so partial ocean views are the best you can do; most upper units overlook the parking structure or the building next door. Still, this complex is a good value, especially if you can score one of the many price breaks.

ResortQuest offers a number of additional good choices in West Maui and Kihei, in South Maui, for travelers looking for reasonably priced accommodations. For information on additional choices, call ☎ **877-997-6667** or 866-774-2924, or visit www.resortquesthawaii.com.

See map p. 120. 2575 S. Kihei Rd., Kihei. ☎ 877-997-6667, 866-774-2924, or 808-875-0004. Fax: 808-874-4035. www.resortquest.com. Parking: Free. Rack rates: $175–$225 double; $215–$295 1-bedroom; $275–$395 2-bedroom; $415–$520 3-bedroom. Deals: Excellent opportunities for discounts; Internet-only e-Special rates as low as $139 double or 1-bedroom, $231 2-bedroom at press time; ask for AAA, senior (50-plus), and corporate discounts, as well as packages that include airfare and other special rate programs. AE, DC, DISC, MC, V.

Ritz-Carlton Kapalua
$$$$$ West Maui (Kapalua)

Situated at the end of the road in glorious Kapalua, Maui's most gorgeous planned community, the Ritz is a destination resort by virtue of its location alone. But you won't need to hop in the car every day in search of fun, because everything is right at hand: a small but fabulous beach and activities galore, including Kapalua's 54 holes of world-class, tournament-quality golf, as well as its justifiably renowned art school for vacationers who want to feed a creative appetite. The natural setting — on 50 terraced oceanfront acres, surrounded by century-old Norfolk pines and ironwood trees — is breathtaking.

Thanks to a multimillion-dollar renovation completed in early 2008, the hotel is more glorious than ever. Designed to look like a grand plantation house, it's airy and graceful, with a gracious pool area, two hot tubs, and a professional croquet lawn. The spacious and tropically gorgeous rooms surpass the chain's usual high standard with heavenly featherbeds, extra-large marble bathrooms and gorgeous island-inspired décor. The dining is excellent, especially the superb sushi bar, Kai, and the gorgeous, Asian-inspired Banyan Tree restaurant). The amenities are extensive (including a full-service spa that was dramatically expanded and upgraded as part of the renovation, a new state-of-the-art fitness center, the outstanding Ritz Kids program as well as an environmental education center for kids and teens, and a full-time cultural advisor who imbues the service and programming with genuine respect for the culture), and the service is unsurpassed. Still, some may find it a tad too formal for Hawaii. Furthermore, you might expect an on-the-beach location for these prices, but the hotel is situated slightly uphill. You may find it worthwhile to spend a few extra dollars for a club-level room; club guests enjoy individualized concierge service and five — yes, five — complimentary food presentations throughout the day, including a generous morning continental spread. Ask about the brand-new one- and two-bedroom residential suites, if you can afford to do so.

See map p. 120. 1 Ritz-Carlton Dr., Kapalua. ☎ 800-542-8680 or 808-669-6200. Fax: 808-669-1566. www.ritzcarlton.com. *Self-parking: Free. Valet parking: $18. Rack rates: $499–$699 double; $799–$1,500 suite. Mandatory $20-per-night "resort fee" covers such amenities as "free" self-parking, resort shuttle service, use of fitness center, wireless Internet access, kids' program, and other extras. Deals: Romance, golf, room-and-car, and other packages often available; available rates from $395 at press time. AE, DC, DISC, MC, V.*

Sheraton Maui
$$$$$ **West Maui (Kaanapali)**

This expansive resort hotel boasts the ideal location on Kaanapali Beach: on a spectacular stretch of sand at the foot of Black Rock, one of Maui's best offshore snorkel spots. Much like its Kauai sister, this Sheraton is great for those who don't care for the forced formality or over-the-top excesses that often go hand-in-hand with resort vacations. The Sheraton Maui has an easygoing, open style, and great facilities for families and active types, including a nice fitness center and an open-air spa. The lagoonlike pool features lava-rock waterways, wooden bridges, and an open-air whirlpool. You're greeted with a lei upon arrival, and then the valet takes you and your luggage straight to your room so you don't need to stand in line — a smooth, personalized touch. The big, island-style rooms are attractive and comfortable, with such nice features as the aptly named Sheraton SweetSleeper bed, flat-panel TVs, minifridges, coffee-makers, and private lanais. Building 6 is the place to be during whale-watch season; the rooms directly overlook one of the whales' favorite playpens. A class of oversized two-room Ohana suites is designed with families in mind; the junior suites can also suit families well, or make a great splurge for couples looking for room to spread out in luxury. Restaurants and bars (including the fun and flavorful Teppan-yaki Dan's for Japanese hibachi-style dining), a nightly torch-lighting and cliff-diving show, a terrific year-round kids' program, a spa, tennis courts, and lots of other extras further the appeal, and the location just can't be beat. A terrific hotel from start to finish — it's no surprise that this was Sheraton's North American "Hotel of the Year" in 2007.

See map p. 120. 2605 Kaanapali Pkwy., Kaanapali. ☎ 800-782-9488 or 808-661-0031. Fax: 808-661-0458. www.sheratonmaui.com. *Valet parking: $12. Self-parking: Free. Rack rates: $500–$770 double; $900–$1,000 family or junior suite; $1,100–$5,000 luxury suite. Mandatory "resort fee" of $20 per day for "free" self-parking, local and toll-free phone calls, high-speed Internet access, yoga and Pilates classes, and free dining for kids under 5, plus dining discounts for kids 6–12. Deals: Special rates and/or package deals are almost always available, including family, romance, 7th-night-free, and rental-car deals. Also ask for AAA-member and senior discounts, and look for Internet specials, which were as low as $299 at press time. AE, DC, DISC, MC, V.*

Wailea Beach Marriott Resort & Spa
$$$$$ South Maui (Wailea)

This appealing property has an airy, comfortable feel, and it's looking better than ever after a $60-million total renovation was completed in 2006. Eight buildings, all low-rise except for an eight-story tower, are thoughtfully spread over 22 gracious acres, with lots of open parklike space and a half-mile of prime oceanfront. The spacious guest rooms have all been completely redecorated with a sleeker and more elegant look. There's a comprehensive kids' program for *keiki* ages 5 to 13, plus five pools — including a kid-friendly water-activities playground complete with a pair of water slides — and a terrific beach out front. A good indoor/outdoor restaurant and nightly Hawaiian entertainment, a coin-op laundry, a fitness center, and the full-service Mandara Spa and salon make life easier for the grown-ups in your group, too. My biggest complaint is that the resort fee is too high, and it irks me to have to pay extra to access the Internet — but if you leave your computer at home, you won't notice.

See map p. 120. 3700 Wailea Alanui Dr., Wailea. ☎ *888-228-9290, 888-236-2427, or 808-879-1922. Fax: 808-874-7888.* www.marriotthawaii.com. *Valet parking: $18. Self-parking: Free. Rack rates: $350–$525 double; $450–$3,250 suite. Mandatory "resort fee" of $30 a day includes discounts on hotel services, spa services, and dining, as well as unlimited local and long-distance calls to the U.S. and Canada, and self-parking; Internet access is an extra charge. Deals: Seniors (62-plus) receive 15 percent discount. AAA, government, and military discounts plus Hertz rental-car upgrades available. Marriott Rewards members also qualify for special discounts and other perks (25 percent off, plus a $25-per-day resort credit at press time). Also check for packages, which usually abound. AE, DC, DISC, MC, V.*

Westin Maui Resort & Spa
$$$$$ West Maui (Kaanapali)

This hotel isn't quite as fabulous as the Grand Wailea (reviewed earlier in this chapter), but it's often cheaper, and your kids will be in water-hog heaven here, too, thanks to an 87,000-square-foot "Aquatic Playground," complete with swim-through grottos, waterfalls, and a 128-foot water slide. (There's also an adults-only pool and a secluded Jacuzzi.) Rooms are on the smallish side, but they're stylishly contemporary in the W Hotels mode. Each and every one boasts a truly celestial Heavenly Bed, which keeps me coming back to Westin every time. The Heavenly Shower adds to the luxury in the bathroom, while your youngest ones can enjoy Westin's own plush-as-can-be Heavenly Cribs. A prime stretch of Kaanapali Beach and a wealth of facilities are on hand, including a well-outfitted fitness center with an array of classes, a gorgeous 13,000-square-foot spa, and a full children's program. The stylish Tropica restaurant isn't the best on Maui, but the innovative fare is just fine, and the oceanfront setting is designer-sleek and romantic at the same time. Beware the timeshare salesperson in the lobby — and if you get suckered in, don't say I didn't warn you.

See map p. 120. 2365 Kaanapali Pkwy., Kaanapali. ☎ *866-716-8112 or 808-667-2525. Fax: 808-661-5764.* www.westinmaui.com. *Valet parking: $10. Self-parking: Free.*

Rack rates: $515–$795 double; $1,000–$3,500 suite. Mandatory "resort fee" of $20 per day for "free" self-parking, high-speed Internet access, shuttle service, bottled water (2 per day, replenished daily), an outdoor portrait sitting and free 4-x-6-inch photo, and fitness center access. Deals: Inquire about family, golf, wedding-and-honeymoon, and other packages, as well as special promotions that may include a rental car. Promotional rates from $350 at press time. AE, DC, DISC, MC, V.

The Whaler on Kaanapali Beach
$$$–$$$$$ West Maui (Kaanapali)

Not only would I stay at this beachfront midrise condo complex again, but I'd move in here if I could. The Whaler was built in the '70s and still sports a few "Me Decade" hallmarks, but in a good way — it feels like the kind of place where Jack Lord would keep his neighbor island bachelor pad. The relaxing atmosphere starts in the clean-lined open-air lobby and continues in the impeccably kept apartments. They're privately owned and individually decorated, but all have fully equipped kitchens, VCRs, marble bathrooms, and big, blue-tiled lanais. Many one-bedrooms have two full bathrooms, making them great for small families or shares. Most units have some kind of ocean view, but the garden views are also pleasant. Luxuries include daily maid service, plus bell and concierge services. The grounds are private and well-manicured, and on-site extras include an oceanfront pool and spa, five tennis courts, an exercise room, and great dining and shopping at neighboring Whalers Village. Both property managing agents are reliable, so go with the best rate; I often find that ResortQuest has the best deals.

See map p. 120. 2481 Kaanapali Pkwy., Kaanapali. ☎ *808-661-4861. Fax: 808-661-8315. Reserve through either of the following companies: Premier Resorts:* ☎ *800-367-7052.* www.the-whaler.com. *ResortQuest:* ☎ *877-997-6667.* www.whaler kaanapali.com *or* www.resortquesthawaii.com. *Parking: $12. Rack rates: $315–$345 studio; $305–$455 1-bedroom; $400–$880 2-bedroom. Deals: Car-and-condo packages and other bargains often available through both booking agents, so always mine for specials and off-season discounts; Internet-only e-Special rates from $35 at press time through the ResortQuest Web site; ask for AAA, senior (50-plus), and corporate discounts, and other special rate programs. AE, DC, MC, V.*

Index of Accommodations by Location

South Maui (Wailea)
Fairmont Kea Lani Maui ($$$$$)
Four Seasons Resort Maui at Wailea
($$$$$)
Grand Wailea Resort & Spa ($$$$$)
Outrigger Palms at Wailea ($$$)
Wailea Beach Marriott Resort & Spa
($$$$$)

Upcountry
Aloha Cottage ($$–$$$)
Maui Spa Retreat ($$)

West Maui (Kaanapali)
Hyatt Regency Maui Resort and Spa
($$$$–$$$$$)
Kaanapali Alii ($$$$–$$$$$)
Kaanapali Beach Hotel ($$–$$$)
Outrigger Maui Eldorado Resort ($$$)
Sheraton Maui ($$$$$)
Westin Maui Resort & Spa ($$$$$)
The Whaler on Kaanapali Beach
($$$–$$$$$)

West Maui (Kahana/Napili)
Kahana Sunset ($$–$$$)
Mauian Napili Beach ($$)
Napili Bay ($–$$)
Napili Kai Beach Resort ($$$–$$$$)
Noelani Condominium Resort ($–$$)

West Maui (Kapalua)
Ritz-Carlton Kapalua ($$$$$)

West Maui (Lahaina)
Best Western Pioneer Inn ($$)
Hooilo House ($$$$)
Lahaina Shores Beach Resort ($$–$$$)
Maui Guest House ($$)
Outrigger Aina Nalu ($$–$$$)
Plantation Inn ($$–$$$)

East Maui/Paia
The Inn at Mama's Fish House ($$)

Index of Accommodations by Price

$$$$$
Fairmont Kea Lani Maui (South Maui/
Wailea)
Four Seasons Resort Maui at Wailea
(South Maui/Wailea)
Grand Wailea Resort & Spa (South
Maui/Wailea)
Hotel Hana-Maui (Hana)
Hyatt Regency Maui Resort and Spa
(West Maui/Kaanapali)
Kaanapali Alii (West Maui/Kaanapali)
Ritz-Carlton Kapalua (West Maui/
Kapalua)
Sheraton Maui (West Maui/Kaanapali)
Wailea Beach Marriott Resort & Spa
(South Maui/Wailea)
Westin Maui Resort & Spa (West
Maui/Kaanapali)
The Whaler on Kaanapali Beach
(West Maui/Kaanapali)

$$$$
Hooilo House (West Maui/Lahaina)
Hyatt Regency Maui Resort and Spa
(West Maui/Kaanapali)
Kaanapali Alii (West Maui/Kaanapali)
Napili Kai Beach Resort (West Maui/
Napili)
The Whaler on Kaanapali Beach
(West Maui/Kaanapali)

$$$
Aloha Cottage (Upcountry)
Hana Oceanfront Cottages (Hana)
Heavenly Hana Inn (Hana)
Kaanapali Beach Hotel (West Maui/
Kaanapali)
Kahana Sunset (West Maui/Kahana)
Lahaina Shores Beach Resort (West
Maui/Lahaina)
Napili Kai Beach Resort (West Maui/
Napili)

Outrigger Aina Nalu (West Maui/Lahaina)

Outrigger Maui Eldorado Resort (West Maui/Kaanapali)

Outrigger Palms at Wailea (South Maui/Wailea)

Plantation Inn (West Maui/Lahaina)

ResortQuest at the Maui Banyan (South Maui/Kihei)

The Whaler on Kaanapali Beach (West Maui/Kaanapali)

$$

Aloha Cottage (Upcountry)

Best Western Maui Oceanfront Inn (South Maui/Kihei)

Best Western Pioneer Inn (West Maui/Lahaina)

Heavenly Hana Inn (Hana)

The Inn at Mama's Fish House (East Maui: On the Road to Hana)

Kaanapali Beach Hotel (West Maui/Kaanapali)

Kahana Sunset (West Maui/Kahana)

Koa Lagoon (South Maui/Kihei)

Lahaina Shores Beach Resort (West Maui/Lahaina)

Maui Coast Hotel (South Maui/Kihei)

Mana Kai Maui (South Maui/Kihei)

Mauian Napili Beach Hotel (West Maui/Napili)

Maui Guest House (West Maui/Lahaina)

Maui Spa Retreat (Upcountry)

Napili Bay (West Maui/Napili)

Noelani Condominium Resort (West Maui/Kahana)

The Old Wailuku Inn at Ulupono (Central Maui/Wailuku)

Outrigger Aina Nalu (West Maui/Lahaina)

Plantation Inn (West Maui/Lahaina)

Punahoa Beach Apartments (South Maui/Kihei)

ResortQuest at the Maui Banyan (South Maui/Kihei)

$

Koa Resort (South Maui/Kihei)

Mana Kai Maui (South Maui/Kihei)

Napili Bay (West Maui/Napili)

Noelani Condominium Resort (West Maui/Kahana)

Chapter 11

Dining Out around Maui

● ●

In This Chapter

▶ Choosing among Maui's best restaurants

▶ Finding the finest luaus if you're in the hula mood

● ●

*M*aui's dining scene is excellent, with amazing scope and innovation. The lovely and charismatic Valley Isle has attracted so many top chefs from around the globe that it's tough to choose among their outposts. But be prepared to pay for the privilege of dining on Maui. The island is overflowing with restaurants, so choice isn't a problem — but you have to navigate a minefield of overpriced, mediocre-quality restaurants in order to get value for your dollar. The listings in this chapter offer a recommendable course of action, whether you're looking for a splurge-worthy special-occasion restaurant or a satisfying casual meal that relieves the pressure on your wallet.

Lahaina, on Maui's west shore, sits at the heart of the island's dining scene. Luckily, it's quite convenient — no more than a half-hour drive or so from any of the beach resorts (45 minutes from Wailea). Many of its restaurants — even the affordable ones — boast front-row, on-the-water seats for spectacular sunset-watching. But nowhere is the minefield of mediocrity more explosive, so choose carefully.

Chapter 18 gives you a fun and easy overview of Maui's dining scene, with tips on local specialties and the astounding variety of seafood on island menus.

Maui's Best Restaurants

In the restaurant listings that follow, each restaurant name is followed by a number of dollar signs, ranging from one ($) to five ($$$$$). The dollar signs are meant to give you an idea of what a complete dinner for one person — with appetizer, main course, a drink, tax, and tip — is likely to cost. The price categories are outlined in Table 11-1.

Table 11-1	Key to Restaurant Dollar Signs
Dollar Sign(s)	*Price Range*
$	Cheap eats — less than $20
$$	Still inexpensive — $20–$34
$$$	Moderate — $35–$49
$$$$	Pricey — $50–$74
$$$$$	Ultraexpensive — $75 or more

Of course, how much you spend depends on how you order, so stay away from the surf and turf or the north end of the wine list if you're watching your wallet. To give you a better idea of how much you can expect to spend, I also include the price range of main courses in the listings. (Prices can change at any time, of course, but restaurants usually don't raise their prices by more than a dollar or two at any given time.)

The state adds roughly 4 percent in taxes to every restaurant bill. The percentage may vary slightly depending on the county you're in, and may be embedded in the total purchase price or shown as an independent line item on your bill. A 15 percent to 20 percent tip for the server is standard, just like back home.

At the end of the chapter, I index the restaurants in three different ways: by location, cuisine, and price. Also, use the maps in this chapter to get a more specific fix on where each restaurant is located in relation to your accommodations.

Aloha Mixed Plate
$ West Maui (Lahaina)   LOCAL HAWAIIAN

This charming, cheap patio restaurant specializes in traditional pan-cultural foods of Hawaii: great saimin (ramen noodle soup), teriyaki chicken, finger-lickin' Korean-style *kalbi* barbecue ribs, coconut shrimp, mahimahi sandwiches, stir-fry, and other local staples, plus burgers (both taro and beef) and a kalua pig sandwich. Succulent roast duck, stir-fry, and chow fun noodle dishes reveal the Chinese influence. Most dishes are served as complete meals (a style called *plate lunch*), accompanied by "two scoop" rice and a scoop of macaroni salad; they can be ordered mini, regular, or sumo-size to customize to your appetite. Brought to you by the people behind the Old Lahaina Luau (the top luau in the islands, described later in this chapter), this colorful place serves up the best local food around. Don't expect gourmet — this is Hawaii's version of paper-plate eats, and the setting is super-casual but island colorful and friendly. Aloha Mixed Plate offers real value — and in an oceanfront setting to boot! The restaurant even has

Dining in Maui

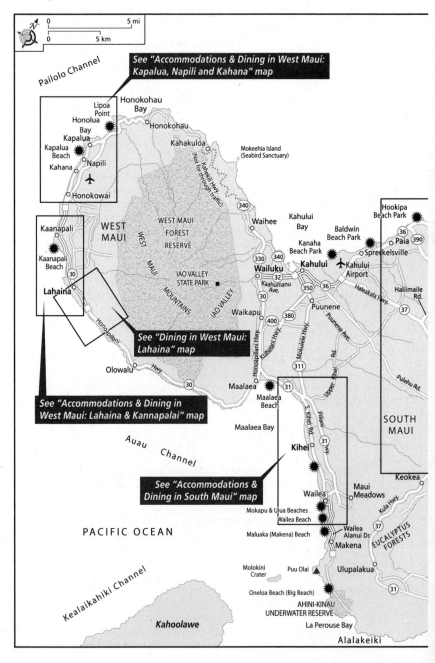

See "Accommodations & Dining in West Maui: Kapalua, Napili and Kahana" map

Pailolo Channel

Lipoa Point

Honokohau Bay

Honolua Bay

Kapalua

Kapalua Beach

Kahana

Napili

Kahakuloa

Mokeehia Island (Seabird Sanctuary)

Honokowai

Honokohau

Kahekili Hwy. (Not for through traffic)

340

WEST MAUI FOREST RESERVE

Waihee

Kahului Bay

Kanaha Beach Park

Baldwin Beach Park

Hookipa Beach Park

36

390

Paia

Spreckelsville

Kaanapali

Kaanapali Beach

WEST MAUI

WEST MAUI MOUNTAINS

IAO VALLEY STATE PARK

330

340

Kahului

Wailuku

32

Kaahumanu Ave.

Kahului Airport

350

36

Haleakala Hwy.

Haliimaile Rd.

37

Lahaina

30

Honoapiilani Hwy.

See "Dining in West Maui: Lahaina" map

Waikapu

30

400

380

Puunene

Puunene Ave.

Mokulele Hwy.

Kahekili Hwy.

Olowalu

Honoapiilani Hwy.

30

See "Accommodations & Dining in West Maui: Lahaina & Kannapalai" map

Maalaea

Maalaea Beach

311

31

S. Kihei Rd.

Piilani Hwy.

Upper Kihei Rd.

Pulehu Rd.

SOUTH MAUI

Auau Channel

Maalaea Bay

See "Accommodations & Dining in South Maui" map

Kihei

31

Wailea

Maui Meadows

Keokea

Kula Hwy.

PACIFIC OCEAN

Mokapu & Ulua Beaches

Wailea Beach

Maluaka (Makena) Beach

Wailea Alanui Dr.

Makena

37

EUCALYPTUS FORESTS

Molokini Crater

Puu Olai

Ulupalakua

31

Oneloa Beach (Big Beach)

AHINI-KINAU UNDERWATER RESERVE

La Perouse Bay

Kealaikahiki Channel

Kahoolawe

Alalakeiki

0   5 mi

0   5 km

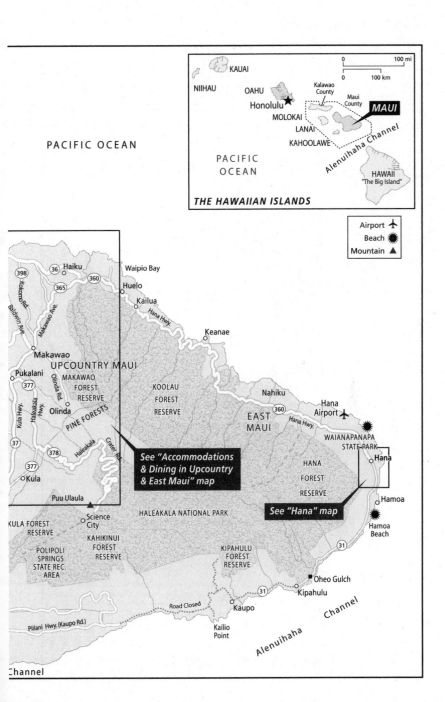

THE HAWAIIAN ISLANDS

KAUAI

NIIHAU

OAHU
Honolulu

MOLOKAI
LANAI
KAHOOLAWE

Kalawao
County

Maui
County

MAUI

HAWAII
"The Big Island"

PACIFIC OCEAN

PACIFIC
OCEAN

Alenuihaha Channel

0   100 mi
0   100 km

Airport ✈
Beach ☀
Mountain ▲

(398)
(36) Haiku
(360)
(365)

Waipio Bay

Huelo

Kailua

Hana Hwy.

Keanae

Kolomo Rd.

Makawao Ave.

Baldwin Ave.

Makawao

Pukalani

(377)

Olinda Rd.

Olinda

UPCOUNTRY MAUI

MAKAWAO
FOREST
RESERVE

KOOLAU
FOREST
RESERVE

Nahiku

EAST
MAUI

(360)
Hana Hwy.

Hana
Airport ✈

Kula Hwy.

Haleakala Hwy.

(37)

(378)

(377)

Haleakala

Crater Rd.

PINE FORESTS

See "Accommodations
& Dining in Upcountry
& East Maui" map

WAIANAPANAPA
STATE PARK

☀
Hana

Kula

Puu Ulaula ▲

HALEAKALA NATIONAL PARK

HANA
FOREST
RESERVE

See "Hana" map

Hamoa

☀
Hamoa
Beach

KULA FOREST
RESERVE

Science
City

KAHIKINUI
FOREST
RESERVE

POLIPOLI
SPRINGS
STATE REC.
AREA

KIPAHULU
FOREST
RESERVE

(31)

Oheo Gulch

(31)
Kipahulu

Road Closed

Kaupo

Channel

Piilani Hwy. (Kaupo Rd.)

Kailio
Point

Alenuihaha

Channel

Dining in West Maui: Lahaina

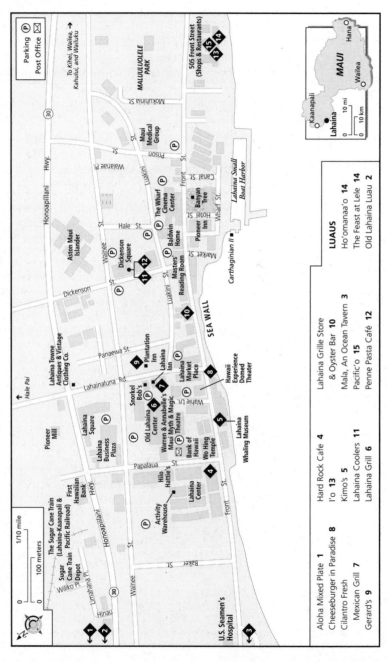

Parking P
Post Office ⊠

LUAUS
Ho'omanaa'o **14**
The Feast at Lele **14**
Old Lahaina Luau **2**

Lahaina Grille Store
& Oyster Bar **10**
Mala, An Ocean Tavern **3**
Pacific'o **15**
Penne Pasta Café **12**

Hard Rock Cafe **4**
I'o **13**
Kimo's **5**
Lahaina Coolers **11**
Lahaina Grill **6**

Aloha Mixed Plate **1**
Cheeseburger in Paradise **8**
Cilantro Fresh
Mexican Grill **7**
Gerard's **9**

a bar, so you can celebrate the sunset with a tropical cocktail or wash down your hearty meal with an ice-cold beer, as long as you take a seat on the upper deck; both levels have lovely ocean views. Fruit juices and smoothies are available, too. Corn dogs and grilled cheese are available for *keikis* (kids), but the minisize plate lunches suit smaller appetites, too.

See map p. 154. 1285 Front St. (across from Lahaina Cannery Mall), Lahaina. ☎ *808-661-3322.* www.alohamixedplate.com. *Reservations not accepted. Main courses: $4–$13. MC, V. Open: Daily 10:30 a.m.–10 p.m.*

Café des Amis
$–$$ Central Maui (Paia)   MEDITERRANEAN AND INDIAN

This charming indoor/outdoor cafe in the heart of Paia town is a local favorite; at least three islanders recommended it to me in the course of my recent visit to Maui. I can see why: Café des Amis delivers a satisfying trifecta of quality, creativity, and value. It's casual indoors, with a baker's counter and colorful chalkboard menus on the walls, plus a lovely outdoor seating area alongside. The menu is an interesting cross-section of Mediterranean and Indian cuisines; Indian curries reside alongside Greek salads, Italian antipasti, and crepes, making for a small but highly satisfying menu. The morning starts with both egg and sweet crepes. Lunchtime brings savory crepes, such as ham and gruyere, or brie and avocado with apple and black pepper; flavorful Indian curries with beef and mushrooms, chicken, or mahimahi for an island flair; and a bountiful Mediterranean plate, with such goodies as house-made hummus, olives, feta, and fresh pita bread with a variety of salads and dips. The beverage menu runs the gamut from smoothies in Indian *lassi* yogurt drinks to wine and beer. Service is attentive and friendly.

See map p. 125. 42 Baldwin Ave., Paia. ☎ *808-579-6323. Reservations not accepted. Main courses: Breakfast $4–$10; lunch and dinner $8.50–$17. AE, MC, V. Open: Daily 8:30 a.m.–8:30 p.m.*

Capische
$$$$$ South Maui (Wailea)   MEDITERRANEAN-ITALIAN

Nestled in a little-known hilltop resort that caters largely to Japanese guests, this dreamy hideaway is one of Maui's true hidden gems. Capische boasts majestic coastal vistas, an ultraromantic ambience, and service that's both friendly and professional. The menu showcases the culinary delights of the Mediterranean. Book a table on the lanai or the lovely alfresco terrace, and come for sunset to maximize the views and your enjoyment. I find the starters to be the stars of the menu; begin with the delectable quail saltimbocca wrapped in apple-smoked bacon, the to-die-for *kabocha* pumpkin gnocchi in sage brown butter, or a garden-fresh *caprese* salad of buffalo mozzarella, sweet baby basil, and local Kula tomatoes. Follow with a seafood-rich cioppino, a gorgonzola-crusted filet mignon with Maui onion jus, or one of the delightful daily specials. A pianist often adds to the ambience, sometimes accompanied by a sultry jazz singer. There's also a sexy martini lounge if you're in the mood for something shaken or stirred. Winner of the *Wine Spectator* Award of Excellence for four years running, Capische also received Chef of the Year for owner-chef Brian Etheredge and Most Romantic restaurant kudos from readers of the *Maui No Ka Oi* magazine in 2008. This really is the most romantic spot on Maui.

If you're in the mood for the ultimate splurge, consider a private dining, personal chef and wine pairing experience at Il Teatro at Capische; call for details.

In the Diamond Hawaii Resort & Spa, 555 Kaukahi St., Wailea. ☎ **808-879-2224.** www.capische.com. *Reservations recommended. Main courses: $32–$45. AE, DC, MC, V. Open: Daily 5:30 p.m. until closing.*

Casanova
$$–$$$ Upcountry Maui ITALIAN

Located in the cowboy-boutique town of Makawao, Casanova is a spacious, casual spot with great Italian food and music beloved by both locals and visitors looking for something different. Look for a tiny veranda with a few stools next to a deli at Makawao's busiest intersection. The restaurant contains a stage, dance floor, and long bar; it's the setting for some of Maui's liveliest nightlife (see Chapter 15 for details).

The pasta is homemade, and the selections are first-rate — try the zesty spaghetti *fra diavolo,* the spinach gnocchi in a fresh tomato–Gorgonzola sauce, or the *tagliolini al salmone* (thin pasta sautéed in a saffron cream sauce with naturally smoked salmon, leeks, and green peas). Other choices include a huge and satisfying pizza selection, both traditional and creative; grilled lamb chops in a porcini mushroom marinade; Cornish game hen marinated in citrus, grilled under a brick, and served with fresh Kula-grown veggies; nightly fish specials with an Italian flair; and Maui's best tiramisu. It's easy to modulate your bill depending on how you order. The pleasant deli serves soups, salads, hot panini, pizza by the slice, pastries, espresso, and that terrific tiramisu all day, for eat in or take out.

See map p. 125. 1188 Makawao Ave. (at Baldwin Avenue), Makawao. ☎ **808-572-0220.** www.casanovamaui.com. *Reservations recommended for dinner. Main courses: $10–$28; 12-inch pizzas $12–$20. DC, MC, V. Open: Restaurant Mon–Sat 11:30 a.m.–2 p.m. and 5:30–9:30 p.m., Sun 5:30–9:30 p.m.; deli daily 7:30 a.m.–5:30 p.m.*

Charley's Restaurant & Saloon
$–$$ Central Maui (Paia) AMERICAN/INTERNATIONAL

Before I set out on any drive to Hana, I always make time for a hearty breakfast at Charley's (which was named after the owner's Great Dane). This casual restaurant is my favorite breakfast place on Maui, thanks to over-stuffed breakfast burritos, fluffy omelets, macadamia-nut pancakes, and eggs Benedict with perfectly puckery hollandaise. Lunch and dinner bring burgers, kiawe-smoked ribs and marlin, calzones baked fresh to order, and a variety of vegetarian delights, from veggie lasagna to bounteous salads and stir-fry. Expect nothing in the way of ambience, but service is friendly and prices are low, making Charley's worth the half-hour drive from Kihei, for an affordable and unpretentious meal, even if you're not heading to Hana. The adjacent roadhouse-style bar serves up a good selection of microbrews.

See map p. 125. 142 Hana Hwy. (at Baldwin Avenue), Paia. ☎ *808-579-9453. Reservations not taken. Main courses: Breakfast and lunch $6–$14, dinner $12–$26. AE, DC, DISC, MC, V. Open: Daily 7 a.m.–1 a.m.*

Cheeseburger in Paradise/Cheeseburger Island Style
$–$$ West Maui (Lahaina)/South Maui (Wailea)   AMERICAN

This oceanfront burger joint (not affiliated with singer Jimmy Buffett's mainland chain, but with sister locations in Waikiki) is a perennial favorite thanks to an always-lively atmosphere, consistently good food, and million-dollar views, all at bargain-basement prices. At the original Lahaina location — the first in the burgeoning minichain — the second-level open-air room offers a prime ocean view from every seat. The Wailea outpost is set back farther from the surf, but an upstairs location gives it its own terrific ocean vistas, and the retro-hip décor sets just the right mood. No matter which location you choose, the tropical-style burgers are big, juicy mounds of natural Angus beef, served on fresh-baked buns and guaranteed to satisfy. Chili dogs, fish and chips, crispy onion rings, and spiced fries broaden the menu. Dieters and vegetarians can opt for the excellent garden and tofu burgers, a lean chicken breast sandwich, or a meal-size salad. Two full bars boast a festive, first-rate menu of tropical drinks (including one of the best piña coladas in the islands). There's lively music every night to round out the party-hearty appeal at both locations. You can even launch your day oceanside with hearty omelets, French toast, eggs Benedict, and other morning faves. Beware: The Lahaina location has been plagued by a report or two of uneven food and service of late.

In Lahaina: 811 Front St. (oceanside near the end of Lahainaluna Road), Lahaina. ☎ *808-661-4855.* www.cheeseburgermaui.com. *See map p. 154. In Wailea: At the Shops at Wailea, 3750 Wailea Alanui Dr., 2nd Floor.* ☎ *808-874-8990.* www.cheeseburgerland.com. *Reservations not accepted. Main courses: $9–$14. AE, DISC, MC, V. Open: Daily 8 a.m. to close.*

Cilantro Fresh Mexican Grill
$ West Maui (Lahaina)   MEXICAN

Cilantro Grill promises "a fresh take on Old Mexico," and delivers at incredible prices. Here's living proof that fast food doesn't have to be unhealthy and overprocessed. Chef Paris Nabavi has re-created authentic recipes from Mexico's heartland, and reinvented them with local island ingredients (for example, combining a dash of grilled pineapple salsa with the succulent adobo roasted pork found in the tacos *al pastor*). Each dish is bursting with flavor. Tired of plain old guacamole? Then try Cilantro Grill's guacamole tom-tom, which combines chopped tomatoes and tomatillos with avocados and onions, and then livens things up with the zing of lime, cilantro, and Serrano chile. The clean-lined, zesty-hued interior is a step up from other quick-service restaurants, too.

See map p. 154. In the Old Lahaina Shopping Center, 170 Papalaua Ave., Lahaina. ☎ *808-667-5444.* www.cilantrogrill.com. *Reservations not accepted. Most items $3.50–$10. MC, V. Open: Mon–Fri 11 a.m.–9 p.m.; Sat 11 a.m.–10 p.m.; Sun 11 a.m.–8 p.m.*

CJ's Deli & Diner
$ **West Maui (Kaanapali)   AMERICAN**

"Comfort food at comfort prices" — that's the motto at CJ's, and this cheap-chic diner keeps its word. An extensive chalkboard menu hangs from the brightly colored wall above the open-air kitchen. Menu items include generous, farmer-style breakfasts; hearty, veggie-packed salads; half-pound burgers; classic Reubens; roasted chicken; pot roast; and fresh-grilled fish. There's a pleasing local flair to the offerings, including a host of homemade baked goodies. Don't miss the hot *malasadas,* a light and flaky sweet pastry, sort of like a powdered-sugar-covered doughnut hole, which is one of the islands' favorite sweet treats; CJ's can be downright addictive. Food can be prepared for takeout or plated to enjoy in the casual, colorful dining room; you can even order one of their "chefs to go" meals that's completely prepped to be thrown on the grill when you get back to the condo. There's even an Internet-connected computer so you can check your e-mail while you wait. Stop by for a box lunch to go if you're heading to Hana, Haleakala, or the beach. There's also a kids' menu on hand. Considering the high dining prices that run rampant on Maui, CJ's is a very good choice if you're watching your wallet.

See map p. 123. At The Fairway Shops at Kaanapali, 2580 Keka'a Dr. (facing Honoapiilani Highway, on the access road), Kaanapali. ☎ *808-667-0968.* www.cjs maui.com. *Reservations not accepted. Main courses: $8–$15. MC, V. Open: Daily 7 a.m.–8 p.m.*

Da' Kitchen
$ **South Maui (Kihei)/Central Maui (Kahului)   LOCAL HAWAIIAN**

Da' Kitchen is the place to come for local grinds. The simple but comfortable Kihei closet is the original; come for the food, not the mood. Place your order at the counter and then grab one of the handful of tables to chow down on the extra-hearty eats. All the classic Hawaiian plate lunches come with two scoops of rice, plus potato *and* macaroni salad (you can request a green salad instead) — trust me, you won't leave here hungry. Good choices include pulled kalua pork, slow-cooked until tender and seasoned with Hawaiian salt; chicken *katsu,* breaded in panko crumbs and served with Japanese barbecue sauce; and *loco moco,* a hamburger patty grilled, topped with two fried eggs, and smothered in gravy (a dieter's delight!). Also recommended are a yummy lemon chicken and a couple of teriyaki dishes for more mainstream tastes, plus big Asian-style noodle bowls, hamburgers, and a better-than-you'd-expect Chinese chicken salad. Some locals complain that this is local food "for tourists," but I continue to see plenty of locals here, especially at the Kahului location. The colorful Kahului location is more cafe-style, with full table service.

In Kihei: In Rainbow Mall, 2439 S. Kihei Rd. (at the south end of town). ☎ *808-875-7782. In Kahului: In Triangle Square, 425 Koloa St. (off Dairy Road).* ☎ *808-871-7782.* www.da-kitchen.com. *Reservations not taken. Main courses $7–$12. No credit cards. Open: Kihei daily 9 a.m.–9 p.m.; Kahului Mon–Fri 11 a.m.–8:30 p.m., Sat 11 a.m.–4 p.m.*

The Flatbread Company
$–$$ Central Maui (Paia)   PIZZA

This utterly delightful new entry to the Maui dining scene is well worth the drive to Paia (about ten minutes east of Kahalui, along the Hana Highway) for its terrific value, excellent fare, and all-around satisfying dining experience. As you might expect, the Flatbread Company specializes in pizza. Its all-natural, wood-fired pizzas are baked right in the center of the colorful, high-rafted open dining room, in a massive clay oven. You can watch the night's baker (a small chalkboard announces his name — ours was Bob) nurture the flatbreads and other dishes to kiawe-charred perfection. All ingredients that can be organic and/or island grown are, including free-range and chemical-free meats; the dough is even made fresh daily from 100 percent organically grown wheat.

The menu features two main sections: salads and flatbreads. However, the wide variety of combinations will keep everyone in your party engaged. You can choose from one of the creatively designed pizzas — such as Mopsy's Kalua Pork, topped with smoked free-range pork shoulder, homemade organic mango barbecue sauce, organic red onions, Maui pineapple, local Surfing Goat Dairy chèvre, Maui Sprout Farm scallions, premium mozzarella, imported parmesan, and herbs — or design your own. Pizzas come 12- and 16-inch, while salads can be built appetizer or entree size, depending on what you dress yours with. I've found that a salad with a few add-on items and a 16-inch pie are plenty for two hungry diners.

Both the room and service is colorful and very friendly, with a contemporary, surfer-hippie vibe that's just right for Paia. There's a full, very competent bar that makes a convivial place to sit if you have to wait a few minutes for your table, plus an affordable list of wines by the bottle or glass. Great for families, too. From start to finish, my new favorite spot on Maui.

See map p. 125. 89 Hana Hwy., Paia. ☎ *808-579-8989.* www.flatbread company.com. *Reservations not taken. Main courses: $10–$20. AE, MC, V. Open: Daily 11:30 a.m.–10 p.m.*

Gazebo Restaurant
$ West Maui (Napili)   LOCAL

Tucked in the back of the Napili Shores Resort, this simple, oceanfront gem is well worth waiting in line for. Breakfast and lunch are served simultaneously throughout the morning and lunch hour in a simple, open-air setting, offering stunning views and service brimming with aloha. Happy diners are glad to stand in line, chat, and enjoy the views while they wait for a table and the opportunity to dig into macadamia-nut pancakes dressed with the restaurant's own dream-worthy whipped cream and coconut syrup; hearty omelets served with Portuguese sausage, an island breakfast staple; island-style lunch plates starring such local favorites as kalua pork slow-cooked in traditional luau-style; and burgers and salads. This is good, unfancy food made with care. The kitchen moves quickly, so the line does, too. One of the island's best — and one of its best dining bargains, too.

See map p. 122. In the Napili Shores Resort, 5315 Lower Honoapiilani Hwy., Napili. ☎ *808-669-5621. Reservations not accepted. Main courses: $7–$11. MC, V. Open: Daily 7:30 a.m.–2 p.m.*

Gerard's
$$$$$ West Maui (Lahaina) FRENCH

This traditionalist's haven boasts an ultraromantic setting that includes a charming, slightly frilly dining room, tables on the lanai, and a lovely garden patio. A regular winner of the *Wine Spectator* Award of Excellence and named "Maui's little French jewel" by *Bon Appétit* magazine, Gerard's offers refined cuisine that seldom disappoints, as long as you're not paying too much attention to price. Gerard Reversade excels at seeking out the freshest local ingredients and preparing them in traditional Gallic style. My favorite among the starters is the shiitake and oyster mushrooms in puff pastry, but the foie gras terrine is a must for those who indulge. A wealth of meat and poultry dishes is at hand (including a terrific rack of lamb in mint crust), plus divine daily fresh fish preparations that depend on what the boats bring in. Inventive desserts provide a memorable finale, unless you opt for a cheese plate, served with toasted country bread and poached pears. Service is appropriately attentive. Very expensive, but a nice choice for special-occasion diners who prefer the classics over contemporary dining experiences.

See map p. 154. In the Plantation Inn, 174 Lahainaluna Rd. (between Wainee and Luakini streets), Lahaina. ☎ *808-661-8939.* www.gerardsmaui.com. *Reservations highly recommended. Main courses: $35–$50. AE, DC, DISC, MC, V. Open: Daily 6–9 p.m.*

Haliimaile General Store
$$$$ Upcountry Maui HAWAII REGIONAL

This attractive plantation-style restaurant continues to be one of the best not only in Maui, but in all of Hawaii — and my top recommendation for those who prefer to sample top-quality, island-style cooking in a refreshingly casual and pretension-free setting. Star chef Bev Gannon, the queen of Hawaii Regional Cuisine, presents a heartier-than-average Hawaii Regional menu full of American home-style favorites prepared with an island spin and a few generous dashes of fun. I love to start with the rock shrimp tempura, served in a Chinese "to go" with popcorn (popcorn shrimp — get it?), and accompanied by a trio of dipping sauces that include a heavenly truffle honey. On the main-course menu, look for such signature satisfiers as succulent barbecued pork ribs; long-simmering coconut fish and shrimp curry; and New Zealand rack of lamb prepared

Going for a post-Haleakala-sunrise breakfast

Rising at o'dark thirty to drive two hours Upcountry to catch the glorious sunrise from atop Haleakala Crater is one of Maui's greatest pastimes (see Chapter 13). But the real treat comes after, in the form of a hearty, country-style breakfast. Two wonderful breakfast stops sit at the base of the mountain, in a tiny town called Kula that you'll pass through on your way back to the beach.

Kula Sandalwoods Cafe, 15427 Haleakala Highway ($; Highway 377; ☎ 808-878-3523; www.kulasandalwoods.com; see map p. 125), is a family-run restaurant that starts serving home-baked pastries, omelets prepared with fresh-from-the-chicken-coop eggs and garden-fresh veggies, and eggs Benedict topped with hollandaise sauce (made from scratch) every day at 7:30 a.m. All the home-style breakfasts and lunches are hearty and delicious; I especially like the French toast made from home-baked Portuguese sweetbread. You can choose to eat in the large dinerlike room or out on the lanai if it's not too chilly. It's open Monday through Friday 7:30 a.m. to 3 p.m. and Sunday 7:30 to 11:30 a.m.

For slightly more upscale dining, head down the road to **Kula Lodge & Restaurant** ($$; ☎ 800-233-1535 or 808-878-1535; www.kulalodge.com; see map p. 125), whose cozy, lodgelike dining room features a big stone fireplace; breakfast is served from 6:30 a.m. Picture windows with lush panoramic views on three sides let the outside in as you enjoy eggs scrambled with bacon and sausage or the justifiably famous banana-macadamia-nut pancakes.

Hunan-style. No matter what you order, you won't be disappointed. The desserts — created by Bev's daughter Teresa Gannon, now a well-known chef in her own right — are better than Mom used to make; I never miss the light and tangy *lilikoi* (passion fruit) tart. The *keiki* menu even comes complete with kid-friendly "cocktails." Well worth the 45-minute drive Upcountry; Bev never disappoints. (If you're in South Maui, you can head to sibling restaurant Joe's Simply Delicious Food for a different type of experience; see review later in this chapter.)

See map p. 125. 900 Haliimaile Rd., Haliimaile (ha-lee-ee-my-lee). From the Hana Highway (Highway 36), take Highway 37 for 4½ miles to Haliimaile Road (Highway 371); turn left and drive 1½ miles to the restaurant. ☎ 808-572-2666. www.bev gannonrestaurants.com. *Reservations recommended. Main courses: Lunch $10–$24; dinner $24–$42. AE, DC, MC, V. Open: Mon–Fri 11 a.m.–2:30 p.m. and 5:30–9:30 p.m.; Sat–Sun 5:30–9:30 p.m.*

Hula Grill Kaanapali
$–$$$ West Maui (Kaanapali)   STEAK/SEAFOOD

This attractive and bustling Kaanapali restaurant features a killer beach-front setting and a midrange island-style steak-and-seafood menu brought to you from the people behind Waikiki's renowned Duke's Canoe Club. Kissed by the trade winds, the patio is the ideal setting for sunset watchers, and tiki torches make for after-dark magic. The wide-ranging menu has something for everyone, including superb wood-grilled or macadamia-crusted fresh island fish, yummy barbecued pork ribs in mango barbecue sauce, or succulent lemon-ginger roasted chicken. Those on a budget can stick to the bar menu, which features Merriman's famous *poke* rolls (filled with seared fresh *ahi*), kiawe-fired pizzas, and creative salads and sandwiches. Hawaiian music, hula dancing at sunset, and well-blended tropical drinks dressed up with umbrellas round out the carefree island vibe. If you want a patio table, you should request one when you book. The more casual Barefoot Bar invites you to sit with your toes in the sand while you enjoy burgers, fish, pizza, and salads.

See map p. 123. In Whaler's Village, 2435 Kaanapali Pkwy., Kaanapali Beach. ☎ *808-667-6636.* www.hulapie.com. *Reservations recommended for dinner. Main courses: $20–$35 (most less than $25); Barefoot Bar menu $9–$18. AE, DC, DISC, MC, V. Open: Restaurant daily 5–9:30 p.m.; Barefoot Bar daily 11 a.m.–11 p.m.*

I'o
$$$$ West Maui (Lahaina) NEW PACIFIC

You can't get closer to the ocean than I'o's alfresco tables, some of which sit just feet from the surf (request one when you book). Overseen by award-winning chef James McDonald — and awarded a gold award in 2006 as one of Maui's best restaurants by *Honolulu* magazine — I'o is a multi-faceted joy, with winningly innovative fusion cuisine, first-rate service, and a top-notch wine list that has won the *Wine Spectator* Award of Excellence. The seafood-heavy menu features copious Pacific Rim accents, plus a few creative twists, courtesy of the Western hemisphere: Maine lobster tails are stir-fried and served with sweet potatoes flambéed in a dark rum and mango Thai curry sauce; the grilled lamb chop is spiced with madras curry and topped with a pineapple demi-glace; and the fresh catch gets a crust of foie gras for the ultimate decadence. Each dish is paired with a recommended wine for easy ordering. Skip the silken purse appetizer, though — it's an overrated signature. A full, friendly bar (including a tempting array of specialty martinis) makes this restaurant an all-around terrific choice.

See map p. 154. 505 Front St. (on the ocean at Shaw Street), Lahaina. ☎ *808-661-8422.* www.iomaui.com. *Reservations recommended. Main courses: $29–$34 ($66 for lobster tails). AC, MC, V. Open: Daily 5:30–10 p.m.*

Joe's Simply Delicious Food
$$$$ South Maui (Wailea) NEW AMERICAN/HAWAII REGIONAL

Joe's is a little slicker than its Upcountry sibling, Haiilimaile General Store, and serves a similarly pleasing menu of American home cooking with an island-regional twist, this time without the strong Asian influence. Top choices include the signature grilled applewood salmon, smoky and sublime; pumpkinseed-crusted fresh catch accompanied by chipotle honey butter and whipped potatoes; and innovative preparations of such classics as meatloaf, rack of lamb, and center-cut pork chops. Specialty martinis are concocted behind the handcrafted 43-foot copper bar. The wood-paneled room is casual and welcoming, rock-'n'-roll memorabilia lines the walls (Joe Gannon, husband of acclaimed chef Bev Gannon, managed Alice Cooper for years), and open-air views take in the tennis action below. At night, low lighting and well-spaced tables make for a surprisingly romantic ambience, but the room takes on a laid-back liveliness after it fills up. The service is top-notch.

At the Wailea Tennis Center, 131 Wailea Ike Place (between Wailea Alanui Drive and Piilani Highway), Wailea. ☎ *808-875-7767.* www.bevgannonrestaurants.com. *Reservations recommended. Main courses: $23–$42. AE, DC, DISC, MC, V. Open: Daily 5:30–9 p.m.*

Kai Sushi Restaurant
$$$$ West Maui (Kapalua)   JAPANESE

This lovely sushi bar just off the lobby at the tony Ritz-Carlton is a hit for its fresh-off-the-boat fish lovingly prepared by Chef Tadashi Yoshino and his team of well-trained sushi chefs. If Sansei is a bastion of sushi creativity, Kai is a temple to traditionalism. Usually at least 20 varieties of raw fish are on the menu, depending on what's freshest and best that day. On my last visit, we enjoyed dense, rich, buttery *hamachi* (yellowtail) and melt-in-your-mouth *toro* (fatty tuna), which is always worth the splurge if it's on the menu. The chef breaks tradition on the creative appetizer menu; the braised short-rib potstickers were a delectable delight. There's a full menu of classic and creative martinis and margaritas, as well as a fine selection of wine, beer and sake. The room is spacious, bright and modern, warmed by natural fibers and glowing woods, and service is everything you should expect from Ritz-Carlton. Well worth the trip to Kapalua for those who love quality sushi.

See map p. 122. 1 Ritz-Carlton Dr., Kapalua. ☎ *808-669-6200.* www.ritzcarlton.com. *Reservations recommended. Main courses: Sushi/sashimi $6–$24; rolls $7–$20; sushi/sashimi combos $20–$47. AE, DC, DISC, MC, V. Open: Daily 5–9 p.m.*

Ka'uiki
$$$$ East Maui (Hana)   CONTINENTAL/ISLAND FUSION

Under the guiding hand of Executive Chef John Cox, the Hotel Hana Maui's main dining room reigns supreme as the best restaurant in this part of the island. Christened Ka'uiki (for the nearby peninsula where Hawaii's Queen Kaahumanu was born in 1768), the restaurant marries fresh island ingredients with sophisticated, contemporary preparations. Chef Cox works closely with local farmers and fishermen in a never-ending quest to procure the finest ingredients on Maui, and the menu changes daily to reflect what's fresh and in season. The very good cuisine is a perfect match for the simple elegance of the dining room, with gleaming hardwood floors, well-spaced tables, and glorious ocean views. The room is graced with original island-inspired art that includes the breathtaking *Red Sails* painting, with its imagery of the first Hawaiians voyaging to the islands.

Another dining option in Hana

Hana's other option is the more casual and affordable **Hana Ranch Restaurant** ($–$$$;
☎ **808-248-8255** or 808-270-5280; Open: Daily 7–10 a.m. and 11a.m.–3 p.m.; Wed and
Fri–Sat 6–8:30 p.m. Takeout counter open Sun–Tues and Thurs 6 a.m.–7p.m.; Wed and
Fri–Sat 6 a.m.–4 p.m.), in town on the mountain side of Hana Highway. At lunchtime,
choose between the informal takeout window, serving up local fare, such as teriyaki
chicken and hot dogs that you can enjoy at outdoor picnic tables, and a casual sit-
down lunch menu inside comprised of burgers and sandwiches ($9–$15). The restau-
rant is also open for sit-down dinner on Wednesday and Friday evenings for such fare
as New York strip steaks, burgers and grilled fish ($14–$20). The dining room is casual
and attractive. Reservations are highly recommended for dinner.

Breakfast is much better than in needs to be, with such yummy dishes as
a Heirloom spinach omelet dressed with Big Island goat cheese, Maui
onions, and Pohole fern salad, or Brioche French toast served with chicken
mango sausage that's its own savory treat. Lunch brings a fine grilled Kobe
burger, fresh-caught fish, and salads crafted from locally grown greens.
Come for dinner on Friday to enjoy a Hawaiian buffet dinner accompanied
by live, island-style music and dance.

 If you're coming for light fare or cocktails in the adjacent Paniolo Lounge,
please adhere to the restaurant's dress code: collared shirts and slacks or
dress shorts for men, skirts or slacks for women. The Paniolo Lounge also
offers an alternative, more affordable dinner option, with *pupus* and main
courses ($10–$22) served from 2:30 to 9 p.m.

See map p. 229. In the Hotel Hana-Maui, Hana Highway, Hana. ☎ *800-321-4262 or
808-248-8211.* www.hotelhanamaui.com. *Reservations recommended for dinner.
Main courses: Breakfast and lunch $12–$20; dinner $28–$42. Friday dinner buffet: $50
adults, $35 kids 12 and under. AE, DC, MC, V. Open: Daily 7:30 a.m.–9 p.m.*

 Kimo's
$$$ **West Maui (Lahaina)**   STEAK/SEAFOOD

This casual waterfront restaurant boasts a winning combination of affordable prices, good food, and great ocean views. The menu isn't quite as
innovative as that of sister restaurant Hula Grill, but it still offers a reliable
and satisfying selection of fresh fish preparations (you can choose from a
good half-dozen), hefty sirloins served with garlic mashed potatoes, and
such island favorites as Koloa pork ribs with plum barbecue sauce. With
Caesar salads and sides included, dinners make for a very good deal, and
there's nightly entertainment to boot. Dessert lovers should save room for
Kimo's own Hula Pie — macadamia-nut ice cream in a chocolate-wafer
crust with fudge and whipped cream — a decadent island delight. The
open-air patio is a great place for better-than-you'd-expect sunset cocktails and *pupus.*

See map p. 154. 805 Front St., Lahaina. ☎ **808-661-4811.** www.kimosmaui.com.
*Reservations recommended for dinner. Main courses: Lunch $8–$13; dinner $18–$32
(most under $25). AE, MC, V. Open: Daily 11 a.m.–10 p.m.*

Lahaina Coolers
$$ **West Maui (Lahaina)** **AMERICAN/ECLECTIC**

Billing itself as "The Cheers of the Pacific," this lively, friendly spot serves
up affordable eats at breakfast, lunch, and dinner that are a step above the
standard. Despite its side-street location, this happy-hour favorite main-
tains an appealingly laid-back tropical vibe. Start the morning with an over-
stuffed breakfast burrito with black beans and rice or fluffy Portuguese
sweetbread French toast. Lunch on one of the tropical pizzas (I love the
Evil Jungle Pizza, with grilled chicken and spicy Thai peanut sauce), or per-
haps a grilled portobello mushroom sandwich on focaccia bread. The
fresh fish tacos or the homemade pastas are satisfying dinner choices, or
maybe you'll just opt for cheap draft beers and affordable *pupus* like the
crispy calamari. The full dinner menu is served until midnight (tropical
cocktails until 2 a.m.), making Lahaina Coolers a Hawaii late-night rarity.
Live music — often blues, sometimes folk or rock — adds to the lively
atmosphere on Saturdays and on the occasional weeknight.

See map p. 154. 180 Dickenson St. (between Front and Wainee streets), Lahaina.
☎ **808-661-7082.** www.lahainacoolers.net. *Reservations accepted. Main
courses: Breakfast and lunch $8.50–$14; dinner $9–$25 (most less than $20). AE, DC,
DISC, MC, V. Open: Daily 8 a.m.–2 a.m.*

Lahaina Grill
$$$$–$$$$$ **West Maui (Lahaina)** **NEW AMERICAN/HAWAII
REGIONAL**

This nearly perfect restaurant is a bastion of warm island sophistication
in ticky-tacky, party-hearty Lahaina, racking up numerous awards and stel-
lar ratings from dining bible *Zagat's.* Locals and visitors alike have regu-
larly named it as their Maui favorite since it opened its doors in 1990 —
and I'm thrilled to report that even though David Paul's name is no longer
on the door, it's still as divine as ever. In actuality, David Paul hasn't been
involved in the restaurant for nearly a decade now; chef/owner Jurg Munch
continues Paul's culinary tradition, and continues to steward the restau-
rant to success.

The dining room is one of Hawaii's prettiest. It's stylish yet delightfully
homey, with high pressed-tin ceilings, elegantly dressed tables, golden
wood floors, vibrant original art by spirited Maui colorist Jan Kasprzycki,
and a generous bar at the center of the room that adds just the right
amount of lively bustle to the scene. The kitchen excels at distinctive fla-
vors that are bold without being overpowering. Signature dishes remain
the stars of the menu, including kalua duck — a duck confit leg bathed in
reduced plum wine sauce — which is rich, fork-tender, and greaseless. I'm
also wowed by the Kona coffee–roasted rack of lamb, dressed in a light

cabernet demi-glace. Lahaina Grill also shines with seafood; start with the Cake Walk, a delectable trio of Kona lobster crab cake, zesty Louisiana rock shrimp cake, and seared *ahi* cake. The celestial seared *ahi* and foie gras pairing with fig compote will prove that foie gras is far from passé. The wine list is excellent, and the all-pro waitstaff offers welcome relief from Lahaina's usual surfer style.

See map p. 154. At the Lahaina Inn, 127 Lahainaluna Rd. (1 block inland from Front Street), Lahaina. ☎ *808-667-5117.* www.lahainagrill.com. *Reservations highly recommended. Main courses: $33–$48; chef's tasting menu $78 per person. AE, DC, DISC, MC, V. Open: Daily from 6 p.m. to closing.*

Lahaina Store Grille & Oyster Bar
$$$–$$$$ West Maui (Lahaina)   NEW AMERICAN

This upstairs restaurant is most notable for its glorious setting, on the rooftop of the historic (built in 1916) Lahaina Store. Reserve a table on the twinkle-lit outdoor deck, which boasts glorious ocean views and an infinity fountain that drowns out the street noise from below and sets a romantic tone. The menu up here is on the pricey and more sophisticated side, boasting such entrees as pan-seared *walu* (Hawaiian butterfish) served with grilled bacon-wrapped scallops; macadamia nut–crusted mahimahi dressed in a mango *beurre blanc;* and a range of steaks and lamb chops. The food is good if not great; my favorite part of the meal was the well-prepared fresh *ahi poke* and fresh raw oysters from the oyster bar, which flies in mollusks from around the world. You can also sit in the inside dining room and bar, where a less expensive menu is available, featuring good burgers, fish and chips, and other casual dishes, as well as oysters, sushi, ceviche, and other specialties from the oyster bar. We experienced perfectly satisfactory service, but word is that it can be spotty.

See map p. 154. 744 Front St. (on the second floor, between Lahainaluna and Dickenson streets), Lahaina. ☎ *808-661-9090.* www.lahainastoregrille.net. *Reservations recommended. Main courses: Lunch $10–$18; dinner $10–$44 (most under $31). AE, MC, V. Open: Daily 11 a.m.–10 p.m.*

Leilani's on the Beach
$$$ West Maui (Kaanapali)   STEAK/SEAFOOD

The Hula Grill's next-door sister restaurant is a very nice alternative for diners who want good-quality steak-and-seafood fare in an equally lovely oceanfront setting that's a bit more relaxed and suitable for quiet conversation. Downstairs, the Beachside Grill serves an affordable all-day menu similar to that at the Hula Grill's Barefoot Bar. Upstairs is Leilani's, a spacious and comfortable open-air dining room that's dressed in dark woods and simple ornamentation; the fantastic beach and ocean views offer all the necessary window dressing. On my last visit, I was extremely pleased with the quality of my filet mignon, which was crusted in cracked Hawaiian sea salt and pepper, flash-grilled to keep the juices in, and served with a delectable papaya béarnaise. My husband, a prime-rib connoisseur, was equally pleased with his slow-roasted version, with accompanying au jus and horseradish crème for dipping. Of course, fresh catches are always available in a variety of preparations; my favorite is the straightforward broil, dressed in grilled pineapple salsa and cilantro lime vinaigrette. Service is casual, friendly, and prompt. The cocktails are everything they should be, as are the sunset views.

See map p. 123. Whaler's Village, Kaanapali. ☎ *808-661-4495.* www.leilanis.com. *Reservations recommended for dinner. Main courses: Beachside Grill $10–$20; dinner at Leilani's $19–$32. AE, DC, DISC, MC, V. Open: Daily 11 a.m.–midnight. Beachside Grill daily lunch and dinner; Leilani's daily dinner only.*

Maalaea Waterfront Restaurant
$$$$ South Maui (Maalaea)   CONTINENTAL/SEAFOOD

Family-run for many years, this decidedly unhip seafood restaurant is a traditionalist's delight, and continues to please diners year after year. The European-style waitstaff, who serve every dish with a professional flourish, regularly win the annual "Best Service" and "Best Seafood" awards from the *Maui News.* A half-dozen fresh catches — delivered straight off the boat from local fishermen — are usually on hand, and you can choose the preparation you'd prefer. Your choices include a la meunière; baked and stuffed with Alaskan king crabmeat; Provençal style (sautéed with olives, peppers, and tomatoes in garlic and olive oil); and Cajun spiced. But my absolute favorite is the *en Bastille,* in which the fish is "imprisoned" (get it?) in grated potato and sautéed, and then crowned with scallions, mushrooms, tomatoes, and meunière sauce — yum! Meat and poultry are on hand for non–seafood eaters, including a well-prepared steak Diane and slowly simmered pork *osso buco.* The bread comes with a delectable beer cheese spread (how retro is that?), and your server prepares your Caesar salad tableside if you ask. Book a table on the lanai before sunset for pretty harbor views.

In the Milowai Condominium, 50 Hauoli St., Maalaea (north of Kihei). ☎ *808-244-9028.* www.waterfrontrestaurant.net. *Reservations recommended. To get there: From Highway 30, take the second right into Maalaea Harbor, and then turn left. Main courses: $19–$38 (some seafood at market price). AE, DC, DISC, MC, V. Open: Daily 5–10 p.m.*

Mala, An Ocean Tavern
$$$–$$$$ West Maui (Lahaina)   HEALTHY ECLECTIC

The Valley Isle has applauded the return of hometown chef Mark Ellman to the gourmet dining fold. After shutting the doors on Avalon a few years back, Ellman focused his energy on expanding his successful Maui Tacos quick-service chain, and otherwise stayed out of sight. In 2006, he reentered the full-service restaurant business with a bang. *Mala* means "garden" in the Hawaiian language; it's an apt moniker thanks to the restaurant's bounteous menu, which bursts with exciting choices. The menu is built around small plates and sharing, so you can enjoy a variety of taste sensations in the course of your meal. The focus is on healthy eating, so expect whole grains and organic whenever possible. This won't dull your pleasure; highlights from the regular menu include a divine Kobe beef cheeseburger with applewood smoked bacon and Maytag blue cheese, a wok-fried *moi* (a fish once reserved for Hawaiian royalty) sautéed in a delectable black-bean sauce, and an exotic Indonesian stir-fry with fresh island fish. However, the real treat is the daily specials menu, where Mark puts his creativity to full use, making the most of what's market fresh that day. Vegetarians will feel well cared for.

Mala boasts a delightfully casual-contemporary setting where you can feel perfectly comfortable showing up in your shorts; with its over-the-water location and waves crashing just below, the tiki torch–lit lanai is one of Maui's most thrilling open-air dining rooms. Start your meal with a house special mojito or sangria, and the evening is yours. Weekend brunch is its own delight.

Mala now boasts a sister location in South Maui, **Mala Wailea,** at the Wailea Beach Marriott Resort & Spa, 3700 Wailea Alanui Dr., Wailea (☎ **808-875-9394**), which boasts its own wonderful oceanfront setting. It's open for breakfast and dinner daily.

See map p. 154. 1307 Front St., Lahaina (at the north end of town; take the Front Street exit off Highway 30). ☎ 808-667-9394. www.malaoceantavern.com. *Reservations recommended. Main courses: Brunch $8–$16; lunch $8–$15; dinner $15–$28. AE, DC, DISC, MC, V. Open: Mon–Fri 11 a.m.–9:30 p.m.; Sat–Sun 9 a.m.–9:30 p.m.*

Mama's Fish House
$$$$$ Central Maui (Paia)   SEAFOOD

Okay, it's true: Mama's Fish House is just slightly touristy, and you'll have to pay through the nose. Despite those caveats, Mama's is my hands-down top choice on Maui and one of my all-time favorite Hawaii restaurants — and one of its most popular, too. The tiki-room setting is an archetype of timeless Hawaii cool. The beach-house dining room has ambience in excess, with lavish tropical floral arrangements, sea breezes ruffling the tapa tablecloths, soft lighting, and gorgeous views galore. Fresh island fish simply doesn't get any better than this; it's all caught locally, with the provenance indicated on the menu ("Opakapaka caught by Earle Kiawi bottom-fishing outside his homeport of Hana Bay"). The day's catches are the stars of the show, and you choose from four preparations. My favorite is the Pua Me Hua Hana, two of the day's fresh catches steamed gently and served traditional luau style, with purple Molokai sweet potato, baked banana, fresh island fruit, and a fresh young coconut — plates just don't get prettier than this. The service is sincere if a bit serious ("And what will the lady have?"), but somehow it suits the mood. A lengthy list of tropical drinks (dressed with umbrellas, of course) completes the tropical-romantic picture. A kids' menu is on hand for families. A real island-style delight!

See map p. 125. 799 Poho Place, Paia (just off the Hana Highway, 1½ miles past Paia town). ☎ 808-579-8488. www.mamasfishhouse.com. *Reservations recommended for lunch, required for dinner. Main courses: Lunch $25–$35; dinner $32–$49. AE, DC, DISC, MC, V. Open: Daily 11 a.m.–2 p.m.; 2:30–4:30 p.m. (light menu only); 4:30–9:30 p.m.*

Mama's Ribs & Rotisserie
$ West Maui (Napili) BARBECUE

This simple, family-owned storefront specializes in freshly prepared, quick, and affordably priced home-style barbecue. The takeout cafe is bright and clean, with a few cafe tables and chairs outside. The rotisserie chicken (prepared traditional, teriyaki, or my favorite, the teriyaki citrus style) is moist and delicious, as are the slow-cooked pork ribs — not greasy or fatty, painted with tangy, but not spicy, house-special sauce. All dinners come with your choice of two sides: steamed rice, macaroni salad, or divine barbecue baked beans. The only misstep is the coleslaw made with raisins and apples — yuck! The polite, friendly staff is happy to pack your plated meal in a Styrofoam box, which makes it perfect for a beach lunch or take-home dinner back at the condo.

See map p. 122. Napili Plaza, 5095 Napilihau St. (at Honoapiilani Highway), Napili. ☎ *808-665-6262. Main courses: Plated meals $6–$20 (most under $15). No credit cards. Open: Mon–Sat 11 a.m.–8 p.m.*

Mañana Garage
$$ Central Maui (Kahului) LATIN AMERICAN

Locals and visitors alike flock here from all corners of the island, drawn by the winning indoor/outdoor setting and creative, nicely prepared Latin American cuisine that scores on all fronts. The boldly colored restaurant can be described as retro-industrial — it's cute and fun — but the groovy patio is the place to be. Paying for chips and salsa is a drag, but all is forgiven after the basket arrives with its trio of zesty "samba" salsas. Everything just gets better. At lunchtime, I like the adobo barbecued duck and sweet potato quesadilla, mildly spiced with delicate green chilies, and the classic pressed Cuban sandwich. At dinner, you may start with green tomatoes, fried just right with smoked mozzarella and slivered red onions, or zesty ceviche, made with fresh island fish. For your main course, consider the citrus-jalapeño-glazed salmon, a black-pepper-rubbed New York strip steak grilled with chipotle-wine demi-glace, or the skewered jumbo prawns glazed with pineapple rum and served with mashed sweet potatoes. You can't go wrong with anything on the menu; every pan-Latin dish sings with flavor. No wonder Rachel Ray named Mañana Garage a Maui favorite on her Food Network "$40 a Day in Maui" show. A real winner!

33 Lono Ave. (at Kaahumanu Avenue), Kahului. ☎ *808-873-0220. Reservations recommended, especially for Fri–Sat dinner. Main courses: Lunch $7–$15; dinner $16–$28. AE, DC, DISC, MC, V. Open: Mon, Wed, Sat 11a.m.–1:30 a.m.; Tues and Thurs 11 a.m.–9 p.m.; Fri 11 a.m.–10:30 p.m.; Sun 5–9 p.m.*

Marco's Grill & Deli
$–$$ Central Maui (Kahului) AMERICAN/ITALIAN

This Central Maui stalwart has been the island's go-to diner for anytime dining for nearly two decades. The expansive menu features a something-for-everyone mix of American diner favorites (burgers, salads, pastrami on rye) and Italian-style dishes (meatball subs, shrimp scampi, homemade ravioli in pink cream sauce, veal parmesan). Service can be short, but the food is satisfying. A wide range of breakfast choices — including steak and eggs, a classic Benedict, apple-cinnamon pancakes, and indulgence-worthy chocolate-cinnamon French toast — is served daily until noon, and until 1 p.m. on weekends. A good stop if you're starving and on your way to or from the airport.

444 Hana Hwy. (at Dairy Road). ☎ *808-877-4446. Reservations not accepted. Main courses: $9–$26 (most under $20). AE, MC, V. Open: Daily 7 a.m.–10 p.m.*

Maui Brewing Company
$$$ West Maui (Kahana)   STEAK/SEAFOOD

This restaurant has all the style of a bad toupee (luckily, a mid-2008 remodel will be complete by the time you arrive), but I like it anyway — part brewpub, part sports bar (with live nightly music), and part clubby restaurant. The fare is straight-ahead seafood and grill fare. Start with a half-dozen oysters on the half-shell or maybe the kiawe-grilled brewer's sausage, and then move on to a first-rate fresh catch or something meatier, if you've eaten your fill of seafood in Hawaii. The kitchen prepares fish to your taste, one of four ways: blackened Cajun style, habanero-cornmeal crusted, seven-spiced with soy mirin glaze, and "just plain" grilled. Beware of the seven spices — five of them are peppers. I like the "just plain" best because it lets the quality of the fish shine. The 10-ounce kiawe-smoked prime rib is a high-quality cut and beautifully prepared. The rotisserie also produces a lovely herb-rubbed chicken with a golden crust. You can also opt for more casual fare, such as pizzas and burgers. All the house-made beers are terrific — particularly the amber-hued Plantation Pale Ale and the dark, robust Wild Hog Stout — and the service is easygoing but attentive. A kids' menu is on hand for family meals, plus there's a late-night menu of casual bar fare in case the munchies strike between 10 p.m. and 1 a.m. Look for great happy-hour deals on drinks and appetizers from 3 to 4:30 p.m.

See map p. 122. In the Kahana Gateway Shopping Center, 4405 Honoapiilani Hwy. (Highway 30), Kahana. ☎ *808-669-3474.* www.mauibrewingco.com. *Reservations recommended. Main courses: Lunch $7–$14; dinner $13–$36. AE, DC, DISC, MC, V. Open: Daily 11 a.m.–10 p.m.; late-night menu 10:30 p.m.–1 a.m. During football season (Sept–Jan) brunch Sun 7:30 a.m.–3 p.m.*

Milagros Food Co. Maui
$$ Central Maui (Paia)   SOUTHWESTERN

This charmingly artsy indoor/outdoor place is a great stop for innovative island-style riffs on south-of-the-border fare, top-shelf margaritas, and more. The fish tacos — flavored with secret sauce — are fabulous, as are the chile rellenos with grilled *ahi* and Kula greens. But the chef reaches beyond the standard, offering a nightly fresh *ahi* creation and other Southwestern specialties with a local flair. The outdoor patio is a nice place to start your day with huevos rancheros, or you can wind up the drive to Hana with a late-afternoon plate of piled-high nachos and a beer. This place draws a Gen-X crowd, so expect to be surrounded by laid-back surfer dudes and other Paia hipsters.

See map p. 125. 3 Baldwin Ave. (at Hana Highway), Paia. ☎ *808-579-8755. Main courses: $6–$22. MC, V. Open: Daily 8 a.m.–11 p.m.*

Nick's Fishmarket
$$$$ South Maui (Wailea)   MEDITERRANEAN/SEAFOOD

This expensive Mediterranean-accented seafood restaurant is just gorgeous. It's not on the beach, but the ambience is ultraromantic anyway; I prefer the vine-covered terrace with its sparkling lights, but the gorgeous, dimly lit dining room (which features a spectacular aquarium and a 2,000-bottle wine display) doesn't disappoint, either. The straightforward preparations let the clean, fresh flavor of the top-quality seafood shine: Kona-raised lobster is perfectly steamed and shelled at your table; mahimahi is kiawe-grilled and dressed with a cabernet sauce and white truffle oil; and an elegant *opaka-paka* (pink snapper) is sautéed with meaty rock shrimps and lightly dressed with lemon butter and capers. The young, elegantly dressed servers have been schooled as pros, and it shows; you'll want for nothing here. The wine list is pricey but excellent. One caveat: I've had only excellent experiences here, but lately I've heard quibbles about unevenness. A nice kids' menu is at hand if an upscale family dinner is in your plans.

In the Fairmont Kea Lani Maui, 4100 Wailea Alanui Dr., Wailea. ☎ *808-879-7224.* www.tristarrestaurants.com. *Reservations highly recommended. Main courses: $30–$55. AE, DC, DISC, MC, V. Open: Daily 5–9:45 p.m.*

Pacific'o
$$$$ West Maui (Lahaina)   NEW PACIFIC

I'o (see the review earlier in this chapter) has an equally divine, equally pricey, and equally well-situated sister restaurant. Star chef James McDonald also oversees Pacific'o. I don't know which of the two restaurants you'll like better; frankly, they're not all that different. I'o is the more postmodern in terms of décor, while Pacific'o is more middle-of-the-road contemporary. Pacific'o's menu has a more distinct Asian influence and features more red-meat and fowl dishes for non–fish eaters. The Hapa/Hapa Tempura is a don't-miss for *ahi* tuna lovers. There's an excellent wine list (with many selections available by the glass), but tropical drinks and specialty martinis are also available.

See map p. 154. 505 Front St., Lahaina. ☎ *808-667-4341.* www.pacificomaui.com. *Reservations recommended. Main courses: Lunch $12–$16; dinner $30–$40. AE, DC, MC, V. Open: Daily 11:30 a.m.–4 p.m. and 5:30–10 p.m.*

Paia Fish Market
$–$$ Central Maui (Paia)   SEAFOOD

This hugely popular restaurant serves some of the freshest and best-prepared seafood on the island. It's nothing fancy — colorful and crowded, with happy diners elbow to elbow at picnic tables, chowing down on whatever's fresh off the day's boat, served on disposable dishware. But whatever you order, it's bound to be fresh, well prepared, and delicious. Place your order at the counter, and then find a seat. The mahimahi fish and chips is always lightly breaded and perfectly crisp, and the generous portion is a bargain at $13. The charbroiled fish is always what it should be; if *ono* is in season, don't miss the opportunity to enjoy this firm and moist local fish. Even though the house specialty is seafood, the chicken selection or burger (also locally supplied, by the Maui Cattle Company) are also well prepared if there's a fish-phobe in your group — a testament to this place's commitment to serving quality food. There's a good beer and wine selection, too. Well worth the drive, especially if you're tired of resort prices.

See map p. 125. 100 Hana Hwy. (at Baldwin Avenue), Paia. ☎ *808-579-8030.* www.paiafishmarket.com. *Reservations not taken. Main courses: $9–$21. MC, V. Open: Daily 11 a.m.–9:30 p.m. (until 4:30 p.m. July 4, Oct 31, Dec 24, Dec 31). Closed Jan 1, Thanksgiving, Dec 25.*

Peggy Sue's
$ South Maui (Kihei)   AMERICAN

Step back in time to the fabulous '50s at this gleaming retro-style diner. Cherry cokes, egg creams, beefy burgers, and old-fashioned shakes are the order of the day. This place is old-fashioned all the way, and I love it. But it's not just about nostalgia: The burgers are juicy; the fries, crispy; and the malts, as creamy as they come. It's a good choice for a satisfying, affordable, all-American meal. Don't miss the opportunity to spin some vintage tunes on the genuine Wurlitzer jukebox!

In Azeka Place II shopping center, 1279 S. Kihei Rd. (at the north end of South Kihei Road, at Piikea Avenue), Kihei. ☎ *808-875-8944.* www.peggysues-maui.com. *Main courses: $6–$15. DC, MC, V. Open: Sun–Thurs 11 a.m.–9 p.m.; Fri–Sat 11 a.m.–10 p.m.*

Penne Pasta Cafe
$ West Maui (Lahaina)   ITALIAN

This casual, wallet-friendly walk-up cafe is a welcome antidote to Lahaina's largely high-priced dining scene. Housed in a charming, simple storefront a couple of blocks from bustling Front Street, it's the brainchild of long-time Maui chef Mark Ellman (see Mala, an Ocean Tavern, reviewed earlier in this chapter), who decided that gourmet food doesn't have to be expensive or overly fussy. As you might expect, the specialties of the house are beautifully prepared homemade pastas, which have always been perfectly cooked on my visits. I like the slow-simmered penne *puttanesca* in Mark's own *pomodoro* sauce; baked penne New York style, with provolone, parmesan, mozzarella, and braised beef; excellent linguine in buttery clam sauce; and the unusual but terrific entree-size niçoise salad, prepared with garlic *ahi* and tossed in a red-onion Dijon vinaigrette. Pizzas, sandwiches, and traditional Italian desserts, such as *panna cotta* and tiramisu, round out a very good, value-priced menu. A kids' menu is also available. Thank you, Mark!

See map p. 154. 180 Dickenson St., Lahaina. ☎ *808-661-6633.* www.pennepasta cafe.com. *Reservations not accepted. Main courses: $6–$15 (most under $13). AE, DC, DISC, MC, V. Open: Mon–Fri 11 a.m.–9:30p.m.; Sat–Sun 5–9:30 p.m.*

Pizza Paradiso
$ West Maui (Honokowai)   ITALIAN

This sit-down pizzeria serves up top-quality pies that manage to wow even skeptical New Yorkers (really!). In addition to a long list of create-your-own traditional toppings, Pizza Paradiso also offers a variety of theme pies — from the Maui Wowie (with ham and pineapple) to the Jimmy Hoffa (mozzarella buried under tons of pepperoni) — plus pastas; fresh, bounteous salads; and surprisingly good desserts (including a lovely homemade tiramisu). It's a terrific choice for bargain-hunting families, or anybody who needs a break from high-priced *ahi* for a while. The Kaanapali location is an express takeout joint, but you can enjoy your pie at a table in the adjacent Whaler's Village food court. Both locations offer free delivery in the immediate area.

See map p. 122. In the Honokowai Marketplace (next to the Star Market), 3350 Honoapiilani Rd., Honokowai (south of Kahana). ☎ *808-667-2929.* www.pizza paradiso.com. *Main courses: Full-size pizzas $12–$26; pastas and sandwiches $6–$12. MC, V. Open: Daily 11 a.m.–10 p.m.*

The Plantation House
$$$$–$$$$$ West Maui (Kapalua)   HAWAII
REGIONAL/MEDITERRANEAN

Overlooking luxuriant golf greens and the stunning Kapalua coastline, the Plantation House may have the most glorious setting on Maui. The open, airy country club–style dining room features crisp white linens; teak wood chairs, hand-carved with a pineapple motif; and soft tropical colors. At night, a glowing fireplace adds to the romance. Chef Alex Stanislaw and his team have crafted a one-of-a-kind Asian-Mediterranean fusion menu that changes frequently to take advantage of fresh seasonal produce. Expect to find such dishes as a Tuscan-style rib-eye steak with garlic mashed potatoes and goat's milk Gorgonzola cheese; macadamia nut and goat cheese salad with Kula greens, Kalamata olives, and passion-fruit vinaigrette; or roasted Molokai pork tenderloin with caramelized Maui onions. Fresh-caught island fish is the star of the menu, with several preparations available, including the divine Rich Forest option. (The fish is pressed with bread crumbs and porcini mushroom powder, sautéed, and nestled in garlic-braised spinach and mashed potatoes.) Chef Alex even lends his descriptive thoughts to the impressive wine list, one of the finest on the island. I've heard some complaints recently that the service can be pretentious, but I haven't had a problem. Book a terrace table and come at sunset for maximum enjoyment.

See p. 122. In the Plantation Course Clubhouse, 200 Plantation Club Dr., Kapalua. ☎ *808-669-6299.* www.theplantationhouse.com. *Reservations highly recommended for dinner. Main courses: $8–$18 at breakfast and lunch; $26–$42 at dinner. AE, DC, MC, V. Open: Daily 8 a.m.–3 p.m.; 3–5:30 p.m. (cafe menu in lounge only); 5:30–9 p.m. (6–9 p.m. May–Sept).*

Roy's Kahana Bar & Grill/Roy's Kihei
$$$–$$$$ **West Maui (Kahana)/South Maui (Kihei)**   **HAWAII REGIONAL**

Roy Yamaguchi is the most famous name in Hawaii Regional Cuisine. He has expanded his empire on the mainland, where he hasn't quite been able to re-create the magic he conjures up in Hawaii. But his island restaurants continue to shine. You won't notice any striking difference between these two bustling siblings, one in South Maui and one in West Maui. They share the same executive chef, the same basic menu, and the same lively, sophisticated vibe. Thanks to an oversized menu of dim sum, appetizers, and *imu*-baked pizzas, you can easily eat affordably in either dining room. The daily menu revolves around a few standards, such as sublime Szechuan baby-back ribs and blackened *ahi* with a delectable soy-mustard butter. The service is always attentive, even when the dinner hour is packed and buzzing, and Roy's well-priced, private-label wines are an excellent value (though you may be tempted to sample the outstanding private-label sakes instead).

See map p. 122. **Roy's Kahana:** *In the Kahana Gateway Shopping Center, 4405 Honoapiilani Hwy. (Highway 30), Kahana.* ☎ *808-669-6999.* **Roy's Kihei:** *In the Piilani Shopping Center, 303 Piikea Ave., Kihei.* ☎ *808-891-1120.* www.roys restaurant.com. *Reservations highly recommended. Appetizers and pizzas: $8.50–$16. Main courses: $18–$41 (most under $35). AE, DC, DISC, MC, V. Open: Daily 5:30–10 p.m.*

A Saigon Cafe
$$ **Central Maui (Wailuku)**   **VIETNAMESE**

This family-run restaurant, in decidedly untouristy Wailuku, serves up outstanding Vietnamese cuisine that's worth seeking out, especially if you're looking for a high-quality culinary return on your dollar. The wide-ranging menu features a dozen different soups (including a terrific lemongrass version), a complete slate of hot and cold noodle dishes, and numerous wok-cooked Vietnamese specialties, starring island-grown produce and fresh-caught fish. Expect a taste sensation no matter what you order; every authentic dish bursts with piquant flavor. Ambience is minimal, but the quality of the food, low prices, and caring service more than compensate.

1792 Main St. (between Kaniela and Nani streets), Wailuku. To get there: Take Kaahumanu Avenue (Highway 32) to Main Street; it's the white building under the bridge. ☎ *808-243-9560. Reservations recommended for 4 or more. Main courses: $7.50–$17. DC, MC, V. Open: Mon–Sat 10 a.m.–9:30 p.m.; Sun 10 a.m.–8:30 p.m.*

Sansei Seafood Restaurant & Sushi Bar
$$$ West Maui (Kapalua)/South Maui (Kihei)   JAPANESE/PACIFIC RIM/SEAFOOD

Chef D.K. Kodama's superstar sushi bars offer some of Maui's finest dining — especially for serious sushi lovers. Best of all, the restaurants are casually comfortable, service is always a delight, and it's easy to keep the bill within reason. Composed primarily of pan-Asian seafood dishes with multicultural touches, Sansei's innovative menu has won raves from fans around the globe. Entrees are available, but I recommend assembling an adventurous family-style meal from the sushi rolls and small plates: The rock shrimp cake in ginger-lime chili butter, topped with crispy Chinese noodles, and Thai *ahi* carpaccio in a red pepper–lime sauce are both standouts. You really can't go wrong with anything. I love the beautifully presented flower sushi; don't miss it if you're a fish head. For premier sushi service, cozy up to the bar at the bustling Kihei location; you won't be disappointed. For more creative taste-testing, head to the Kapalua location, where wunderkind chef Ivan Pahk brings his own innovative spin to the nightly specials. Even the desserts are divine at this easy-going, Japanese-style place. Book in advance so that you don't miss out. Take advantage of late-night dining and live karaoke from 10 p.m. to 1 a.m. on Thursdays and Fridays (Sat as well at the Kihei location), and early-bird and late-night specials can take the sting out of the bill. It's really impossible to go wrong with Sansei. It's a real winner!

See map p. 122. In Kapalua: 600 Office Rd. (near the Honolua Store). ☎ *808-669-6286. In Kihei: Kihei Town Center (near Foodland), 1881 S. Kihei Rd.* ☎ *808-879-0004.* www. sanseihawaii.com. *Reservations highly recommended. Sushi and sashimi: $3–$24. Main courses: $11–$43. AE, DISC, MC, V. Open: Kapalua Sat–Wed 5:30–10 p.m., Thurs–Fri 5:30 p.m.–1 a.m.; Kihei Sun–Wed 5:30–10 p.m., Thurs–Sat 10 p.m.–1 a.m.*

Sarento's on the Beach
$$$$–$$$$$ South Maui (Kihei)   ITALIAN/MEDITERRANEAN

The Maui outpost of a Honolulu special-occasion favorite has won over legions of well-dressed couples with its first-class service and its gorgeous setting, which seamlessly fuses white-linen elegance and white-sand romance. The sophisticated Italian-Mediterranean cuisine and first-class service round out a wonderful package. The stellar chopped salad is an excellent way to begin any meal. Veal lovers rave without fail about the *osso buco,* served on a bed of saffron risotto. I love the swordfish "saltim-bocca," dressed with prosciutto and porcinis, and the cioppino, with Kona lobster, diver scallops, and Alaskan king crab. If you don't want to splurge on dinner, go to the sexy bar to revel in a perfectly poured cocktail and stupendous sunset views.

At the Maui Oceanfront Inn, 2980 S. Kihei Rd. (at the south end of Kihei, just north of Kilohana Street), Kihei. ☎ **808-875-7555.** www.tristarrestaurants.com. *Reservations highly recommended. Main courses: $30–$49. AE, DC, DISC, MC, V. Open: Daily 5 p.m.–midnight.*

Sonz Maui at Swan Court
$$$$$ West Maui (Kaanapali)   HAWAII REGIONAL/PACIFIC RIM

Kudos to the Hyatt Regency for adding this genuinely inspired restaurant to the Kaanapali dining scene. Sonz occupies the resort's attractive Swan Court, where soaring ceilings, dim lighting, generously spaced tables terraced to maximize appreciation for the swan-filled pond, and impeccable service that falls refreshingly shy of formal set a romantic tone. (I saw not one but two wedding parties here on my last visit.) But the real draw is the first-rate cuisine, which focuses on using local delicacies and Maui-grown produce in artful, often European-inspired dishes. Consider starting with the Surfing Goat cheese ravioli, stuffed with "Purple Rain" cheese from the local Surfing Goat dairy (see Chapter 13) and delicately dressed in Kula corn, Hamakua mushrooms, edamame, prosciutto and a sherry vinegar pan sauce, or opt to begin with the escargot profiterole, whose alii oyster mushrooms add a genuinely Hawaii flair. Move on to the Hawaiian *opakapaka picatta*, a flaky local pink snapper adorned in fresh veggies and a slow-roasted tomato puree; a beef tenderloin from the Maui Cattle Company, marinated in Maui coffee, beautifully grilled and accompanied by crispy parmesan-garlic fries and "Mauishire" steak sauce; or the steak-like *ahi* "prime rib," seared medium rare, drizzled in lemongrass "au jus," and paired with green beans, wasabi potatoes, and a popover. With 3,000 bottles and an insightful staff, the wine cellar won't disappoint either. Expensive, but ideal for a special occasion.

See map p. 123. At the Hyatt Regency Maui Resort & Spa, 200 Nohea Kai Dr. (at the south end of Kaanapali Resort), Kaanapali. ☎ **808-667-4506.** www.sonzmaui.com. *Reservations highly recommended. Main courses: $29–$50 (most under $43). AE, DC, DISC, MC, V. Open: Daily 5:30–10 p.m.; bar daily 5 p.m. to midnight.*

Spago
$$$$$ South Maui (Wailea)   CALIFORNIA/HAWAII REGIONAL

America's first celebrity chef, Wolfgang Puck, goes Hawaiian at this Maui outpost of his world-famous Beverly Hills restaurant. Puck's signature cutting-edge, California style showcases fresh, local Hawaii ingredients. The fabulous dining room is a sleek, modern open-air setting overlooking the blue Pacific. The menu features a heavenly coconut soup with local lobster, kefir, chili, and galangal; a whole steamed fish served with chili, ginger, and baby choy sum; and an incredible Kona lobster with sweet-and-sour banana curry, coconut rice, and dry-fried green beans. Spago has an extensive and thoughtful wine list. Save room for dessert (perhaps a warm chocolate truffle purse with Big Island vanilla bean ice cream). Be prepared for super-high prices and a sleek, L.A.-inspired attitude.

In the Four Seasons Resort Maui, 3900 Wailea Alanui Dr., Wailea. ☎ *808-879-2999.* www.wolfgangpuck.com. *Reservations required well in advance. Main courses: $32–$52. AE, DC, DISC, MC, V. Open: Daily 5:30–9:30 p.m.*

If you're in the mood for an elegant dinner in South Maui but suspect that Spago is a bit too style-conscious for you, opt instead for the Four Seasons' sister restaurant, **Ferraro's Bar e Ristorante** ($$$$; ☎ **808-874-8000;** www.fourseasons.com/maui). South Maui's only outdoor beachside restaurant turns into a twinkling seaside paradise in the evening. Ferraro's has built a deserved buzz with authentic Italian *cucina rustica* (the scrumptious focaccia is baked over a wood fire). It's a gorgeous sunset setting, with live evening entertainment. Casual poolside fare dominates during the daytime.

Stella Blues Cafe
$$–$$$ South Maui (Kihei)   NEW AMERICAN

Stella Blues began life as a Deadhead-themed deli, but it has reinvented itself in recent years as a stylish and sophisticated grown-up restaurant. The rock-'n'-roll memorabilia still dresses the walls, but now it adds a pleasingly funky touch to an airy dining room dressed in rich colors and warm woods, with an open, stainless-steel kitchen and a big, backlit bar. Tiki torches add romance to the outdoor patio after dark. But the great thing about Stella Blues is that it's still friendly, unpretentious, and affordable. You'd be hard-pressed to find another restaurant in the islands that offers this much panache and good cooking at such affordable prices.

Start your day with a hearty create-your-own omelet and then move on to a French dip or another hefty sandwich at lunch. The place really comes alive at dinner: Start with the surprisingly good Caesar salad, the delectable homemade hummus served with hot pita, or the funky nachos (blue and yellow corn chips layered with mahimahi, *ahi,* jalapeños, Jack cheese, and guacamole). Choose from a range of creative pizzas, pastas, and big plates for your main course; the New York steak (homegrown by the Maui Cattle Company) is as good as most cuts of beef that are twice the price. Late-night dining (until midnight weekdays, to 1:30 a.m. Fri and Sat nights) is another plus. Good job, Stella — you go, girl!

In Azeka Mauka Shopping Center, 1279 S. Kihei Rd. (at the north end of Kihei). ☎ *808-874-3779.* www.stellablues.com. *Reservations not necessary. Main courses: Breakfast and lunch $6–$15; dinner $12–$28. DISC, MC, V. Open: Daily 7:30 a.m.–11 p.m.*

Tommy Bahama's Tropical Cafe
$$$$ South Maui (Wailea)   CARIBBEAN

Housed in the Tommy Bahama's fashion emporium at the Shops at Wailea, this delightful restaurant perfectly embodies the tropical haberdasher's breezily sophisticated style. The open-air room is a mélange of bamboo, rattan, and tropical prints that come together in a postmodern plantation style. Although the food is very well prepared, it's too expensive — but that's the story of this pricey resort coast. I love Tommy Bahama's best for cocktails, which are some of the island's most creative and satisfying, or a relaxed lunch, when the menu focuses on Caribbean-inspired sandwiches and bounteous entree-size salads. Pleasing choices include the Habana Cabana pulled-pork sandwich, finished with the restaurant's own blackberry brandy barbecue sauce; and the Aruba Arugula salad, tossed in a tamarind vinaigrette and garnished with Caribbean-zested shrimp and scallops. Dinner brings more substantial fare, such as maple-brined and chargrilled pork tenderloin topped with a dried-berry merlot chutney, and pan-seared sashimi-grade *ahi* dressed in sweet chili oil, cilantro, and lemongrass. All in all, a really satisfying dining choice, if you can overlook the tab. As good as the food is, Tommy Bahama's Tropical Cafe is really about soaking up the carefree mood, along with a few fruity cocktails. Come early for dinner, because the second-level setting enjoys gorgeous sunset views.

At the Shops at Wailea, 3750 Wailea Alanui Dr., 2nd floor. ☎ *808-875-9983.* www.tommybahama.com. *Reservations recommended. Main courses: Lunch $16–$21; dinner $32–$40. AE, MC, V. Open: Daily 11 a.m.–11 p.m.*

WokStar
$ **South Maui (Kihei)   INTERNATIONAL**

This cheerful new spot has brought welcome color, flavor, personality, and dining value to the Kihei scene. It's situated in a cute plantation-style cottage, with most of the restaurant residing on the covered patio. The setting is ultracasual and pleasant, dressed in a cute, island-modern style and a vibrant palette. Place your order at the inside counter, take a seat, and your food will be brought to you by an attentive waitstaff. The menu is comprised of an international array of noodle bowls, from an Indonesian peanut stir-fry — freshly sautéed veggies in a spiced peanut sauce with thick egg noodles, topped with cilantro and sprouts — to a great version of the local favorite saimin — chow mein noodles in a miso broth, topped with barbecued pork, fried Spam (an island favorite, and tastier than you'd think), fish cake, and boiled egg. I also like the Maui fried rice, a local version of the classic with sweet onion and island pineapple, and the yummy Thai red curry. Beef, pork, chicken, shrimp, or tofu can be added to any dish. You can start your meal with chicken satay or pan-fried potstickers, and follow with banana *jaffel,* an Indonesian toasted sandwich with toasted peanut butter, banana, and honey on Hawaiian sweet bread. Breakfast *jaffels* means you can start your day here, too.

1913-D South Kihei Rd. (just south of Kihei Town Center and Foodland), Kihei. ☎ *808-495-0066. Reservations not taken. Main courses: $5–$9. AE, DISC, MC, V. Open: Daily 7 a.m.–midnight.*

Luau!

Maui is Hawaii's hands-down winner in the luau department. These lavish feasts are a splurge, but they're an only-in-Maui experience.

You need reservations for the luaus that I list in this section. Make reservations as far in advance as possible — preferably before you leave home — because all these first-rate beach parties are often fully booked a week or more in advance, sometimes two.

Don't give up if you're trying to make last-minute plans, though; it never hurts to call and ask whether a few spots have opened up due to cancellations. Also, if you're booking at the last minute or you want more island luaus to choose from, check with **Tom Barefoot's Tours** (☎ **888-222-3601;** www.tombarefoot.com), a very reliable Maui-based activities center that can hook you up with a number of other luaus on Maui, and sometimes even save you a few bucks in the process.

The Feast at Lele

This partnership between the folks behind the stellar Old Lahaina Luau and star chef James McDonald of I'o and Pacific'o (see earlier in this chapter) is a winning concept. It's ideal for those diners who don't mind paying extra for a more intimate oceanfront setting and a private table. An excellent five-course meal is prepared by a skilled chef and served at your own table (no standing in line at an all-you-can-eat buffet). You'll experience a lovely flower-lei greeting but no traditional *imu* ceremony or craft demonstrations (as at the Old Lahaina Luau). The performance troupe is smaller, but they're held to the same exacting standards.

This feast celebrates not only Hawaii but also three more Polynesian islands — Tonga, Tahiti, and Samoa — so the structure diverges from your standard luau. Each course is dedicated to an island culture — comprised of gourmet versions of foods from the native cuisine, followed by a native song-and-dance performance. Not only does this creative approach offer you the opportunity to sample plenty of well-prepared dishes — steamed *moi* (island trout) from Hawaii; lobster, octopus, and *ogo* salad from Tonga; steamed chicken and taro leaf in coconut milk from Tahiti; and so on — but it also highlights the nuances among the unique but related Polynesian groups. Furthermore, because Samoa is represented, the dazzling show can both stay culturally correct and feature crowd-pleasing fire-knife dancers.

Although the Feast at Lele welcomes all visitors, it tends to cater to a more sophisticated, kid-free grown-up crowd than most luaus, making it an ideal choice for romance-seeking couples or anyone wanting a more refined experience. You can choose from a full wine list and tropical cocktail menu in addition to the included well cocktails; and you can expect your two dedicated servers to be friendly, knowledgeable, and attentive.

See map p. 154. 505 Front St. (on the ocean at Shaw Street), Lahaina. ☎ *866-244-5353 or 808-667-5353.* www.feastatlele.com. *Open: Nightly at 6 p.m. (at 5:30 p.m. Oct–Mar). Admission: $110 adults, $80 kids 2–12. Prices include cocktails, but not tax and tip.*

Old Lahaina Luau

Old Lahaina Luau is Hawaii's most authentic and acclaimed luau and my absolute favorite. The oceanfront luau grounds provide a stunning setting, both the luau feast and riveting entertainment serve as a wonderful intro-duction to genuine island culture, and the staff exudes aloha. When you book, choose between Hawaiian-style seating on mats and cushions set at low tables at the foot of the stage or traditional seating at generously pro-portioned common tables with comfortable wooden chairs; all tables have great views, but earlier bookings garner the best seats.

You're welcomed with a fresh flower lei (the yellow plumeria is the fragrant one) and greeted with a tropical cocktail. Arrive early so that you have plenty of time to stroll around the grounds — watching craftspeople at work and taking in the gorgeous views — before the *imu* ceremony, in which the luau pig is unearthed from the underground oven. The tradi-tional buffet spread is excellently prepared and well labeled, so you know what you're eating (although the sit-down Feast at Lele, which I describe earlier in this section, should be the choice for gourmands).

Following dinner, the luau's excellent show begins, featuring authentic hula and traditional chants accompanied by an intelligent narrative charting the history of Hawaii from the first islanders to modern day. Don't mistake this narrative for a deadly-dull history lesson — it's compelling entertain-ment, and the male and female dancers are all first-rate performers. (Don't expect fire dancers, though, because ancient Hawaiians didn't play with fire.) It's well worth the money, a joy from start to finish, and an excellent choice for families, groups, and couples alike.

See map p. 154. 1251 Front St. (on the ocean side of the street, across from Lahaina Cannery Mall), Lahaina. ☎ *800-248-5828 or 808-667-1998.* www.oldlahainaluau. com. *Open: Nightly at 5:45 p.m. (at 5:15 p.m. Oct–Mar). Admission: $92 adults, $62 kids 2–12. Prices include cocktails, but not tax and tip.*

Old Lahaina Luau is now offering a special three-hour daytime event called Ho'omana'o, which brings the authentic luau experience to the morning meal. You'll enjoy a Hawaiian-style breakfast, an aloha welcome chant followed by a hula show, and interactive cultural encounters — poi pounding, *hukilau* (throw-net fishing), *kapa*-cloth making, and much more — in three villages styled after ancient Hawaii. Ho'omana'o is offered on the Old Lahaina Luau grounds on Tuesday and Friday morn-ings at 9 a.m. The cost is $69 adults, $49 kids 2 to 12. As with all Old Lahaina Luau offerings, advance reservations are recommended.

Index of Establishments by Location

Central Maui
(Kahului/Wailuku/Paia)

Cafe des Amis (Mediterranean/Indian, $–$$)
Charley's Restaurant & Saloon (American/International, $–$$)
Da' Kitchen (Local Hawaiian, $)
The Flatbread Company (Pizza, $–$$)

Mama's Fish House (Seafood, $$$$$)
Mañana Garage (Latin American, $$)
Marco's Grill & Deli (American/Italian, $–$$)
Milagros Food Co. Maui (Southwestern, $$)
Paia Fish Market (Seafood, $–$$)
A Saigon Cafe (Vietnamese, $$)

East Maui (Hana)

Hana Ranch Restaurant (American, $–$$$)
Ka'uiki (Continental/Island Fusion, $$$$)

South Maui (Maalaea/Kihei)

Da' Kitchen (Local Hawaiian, $)
Maalaea Waterfront Restaurant (Continental/Seafood, $$$$)
Peggy Sue's (American, $)
Roy's Kihei (Hawaii Regional, $$$–$$$$)
Sansei Seafood Restaurant & Sushi Bar (Japanese/Pacific Rim/Seafood, $$$)
Sarento's on the Beach (Italian/Mediterranean, $$$$–$$$$$)
Stella Blues Cafe (New American, $$–$$$)
WokStar (International, $)

South Maui (Wailea)

Capische (Mediterranean-Italian, $$$$$)
Cheeseburger Island Style (American, $–$$)
Ferraro's Bar e Ristorante (Italian, $$$$)
Joe's Simply Delicious Food (New American/Hawaii Regional, $$$$)
Mala Wailea (Healthy Eclectic, $$$–$$$$)
Nick's Fishmarket (Mediterranean Seafood, $$$$$)
Spago (California/Hawaii Regional $$$$$)
Tommy Bahama's Tropical Cafe (Caribbean, $$$$)

Upcountry Maui

Casanova (Italian, $$–$$$)
Haliimaile General Store (Hawaii Regional, $$$$)
Kula Lodge & Restaurant (Breakfast, $$)
Kula Sandalwoods Cafe (Breakfast, $)

West Maui (Kaanapali)

CJ's Deli & Diner (American, $)
Hula Grill Kaanapali (Steak/Seafood, $–$$$)
Leilani's on the Beach (Steak/Seafood, $$$)
Sonz Maui at Swan Court (Hawaii Regional/Pacific Rim, $$$$$)

West Maui (Kahana/Napili/Honokowai)

Gazebo Restaurant (Local, $)
Mama's Ribs & Rotisserie (Barbecue, $)
Maui Brewing Company (Steak/Seafood, $$$)
Pizza Paradiso (Italian, $)
Roy's Kahana Bar & Grill (Hawaii Regional, $$$–$$$$)

West Maui (Kapalua)

Kai Sushi Restaurant (Japanese, $$$$)
The Plantation House (Hawaii Regional/Mediterranean, $$$$–$$$$$)
Sansei Seafood Restaurant & Sushi Bar (Japanese/Pacific Rim/Seafood, $$$)

West Maui (Lahaina)

Aloha Mixed Plate (Local Hawaiian, $)
Cheeseburger in Paradise (American, $–$$)
Cilantro Fresh Mexican Grill (California-Mexican, $)
The Feast at Lele (Luau, $$$$$)
Ho'omana'o (Luau, $$$$)
Gerard's (French, $$$$$)
I'o (New Pacific, $$$$)
Kimo's (Steak/Seafood, $$$)
Lahaina Coolers (American/Eclectic, $$)
Lahaina Grill (New American/Hawaii Regional, $$$$–$$$$$)
Lahaina Store Grille & Oyster Bar (Contemporary, $$$–$$$$)
Mala, An Ocean Tavern (Healthy Eclectic, $$$–$$$$)
Old Lahaina Luau (Luau, $$$$$)
Pacific'o (New Pacific, $$$$)
Penne Pasta Cafe (Italian, $)

Index of Establishments by Cuisine

American

Charley's Restaurant & Saloon (Central Maui/Paia, $–$$)
Cheeseburger Island Style (South Maui/Wailea; $–$$)
Cheeseburger in Paradise (West Maui/Lahaina; $–$$)
CJ's Deli & Diner (West Maui/Kaanapali; $)
Lahaina Coolers (West Maui/Lahaina, $$)
Marco's Grill & Deli (Central Maui/Kahului, $–$$)
Peggy Sue's (South Maui/Kihei, $)

Barbecue

Mama's Ribs & Rotisserie (West Maui/Napili, $)

Breakfast

Café des Amis (Central Maui/Paia, $–$$)
Charley's Restaurant & Saloon (Central Maui/Paia, $–$$)
Cheeseburger Island Style (South Maui/Wailea; $–$$)
Cheeseburger in Paradise (West Maui/Lahaina; $–$$)
CJ's Deli & Diner (West Maui/Kaanapali; $)
Gazebo Restaurant (West Maui/Napili, $)
Ho'omana'o (West Maui/Lahaina, $$$$)
Kula Lodge & Restaurant (Upcountry, $$)
Kula Sandalwoods Restaurant (Upcountry, $)
Lahaina Coolers (West Maui/Lahaina, $$)
Marco's Grill & Deli (Central Maui/Kahului, $–$$)
The Plantation House (West Maui/Kapalua, $$$$–$$$$$)
Stella Blues Cafe (South Maui/Kihei, $$–$$$)
WokStar (South Maui/Kihei, $)

California

Spago (South Maui, Wailea, $$$$$)

Caribbean

Tommy Bahama's Tropical Cafe (South Maui/Wailea, $$$)

Continental

Ka'uiki (Hana, $$$$)
Maalaea Waterfront Restaurant (South Maui/Kihei, $$$$)

Eclectic

Lahaina Coolers (West Maui/Lahaina, $$)
Mala, An Ocean Tavern (West Maui/Lahaina; also South Maui/Wailea, $$$–$$$$)

French

Gerard's (West Maui/Lahaina, $$$$$)

Hawaii Regional

Haliimaile General Store (Upcountry, $$$$)
Joe's Simply Delicious Food (South Maui/Wailea, $$$$)
Lahaina Grill (West Maui/Lahaina, $$$$–$$$$$)
The Plantation House (West Maui/Kapalua, $$$$–$$$$$)
Roy's Kahana Bar & Grill (West Maui/Kahana, $$$–$$$$)
Roy's Kihei (South Maui/Kihei, $$$–$$$$)
Sonz Maui at Swan Court (West Maui/Kaanapali, $$$$$)
Spago (South Maui/Wailea, $$$$$)

Indian

Café des Amis (Central Maui/Paia, $–$$)

International
Charley's Restaurant & Saloon
(Central Maui/Paia, $–$$)
WokStar (South Maui/Kihei, $)

Island Fusion
Ka'uiki (Hana, $$$$)

Italian
Capische (South Maui/Wailea, $$$$$)
Casanova (Upcountry, $$–$$$)
Ferraro's Bar e Ristorante (South
Maui/Wailea, $$$$)
Marco's Grill & Deli (Central
Maui/Kahului, $–$$)
Penne Pasta Cafe (West Maui/
Lahaina, $)
Sarento's on the Beach (South
Maui/Kihei, $$$$–$$$$$)

Japanese
Kai Sushi Restaurant (West
Maui/Kapalua, $$$$)
Sansei Seafood Restaurant & Sushi Bar
(West Maui/Kapalua and in South
Maui/Kihei, $$$)

Latin American
Mañana Garage (Central Maui, $$)

Local/Hawaiian
Aloha Mixed Plate (West
Maui/Lahaina, $)
Da' Kitchen (South Maui/Kihei and
Central Maui/Kahului, $)
Gazebo Restaurant (West Maui/
Napili, $)
Hana Ranch Restaurant (East Maui/
Hana, $)

Luau
Ho'omana'o (West Maui/Lahaina,
$$$$)
The Feast at Lele (West Maui/Lahaina,
$$$$$)
Old Lahaina Luau (West Maui/Lahaina,
$$$$$)

Mediterranean
Café des Amis (Central Maui/Paia,
$–$$)
Capische (South Maui/Wailea, $$$$$)
Nick's Fishmarket (South Maui/Wailea,
$$$$$)
The Plantation House (West Maui/
Kapalua, $$$$–$$$$$)
Sarento's on the Beach (South Maui/
Kihei, $$$$–$$$$$)

Mexican/Southwestern
Cilantro Fresh Mexican Grill (West
Maui/Lahaina, $)
Milagros Food Co. Maui (Central Maui/
Paia, $$)

New American
Joe's Simply Delicious Food (South
Maui/Wailea, $$$$)
Lahaina Grill (West Maui/Lahaina,
$$$$–$$$$$)
Lahaina Store Grille & Oyster Bar
(West Maui/Lahaina, $$$–$$$$)
Stella Blues Cafe (South Maui/Kihei,
$$–$$$)

Pacific Rim
I'o (West Maui/Lahaina, $$$$)
Pacific'o (West Maui/Lahaina, $$$$)
Sansei Seafood Restaurant & Sushi Bar
(West Maui/Kapalua and in South
Maui/Kihei, $$$)
Sonz Maui at Swan Court (West Maui/
Kaanapali, $$$$$)

Pizza
The Flatbread Company (Central
Maui/Paia, $–$$)
Pizza Paradiso (West
Maui/Honokowai, $)

Seafood
Maalaea Waterfront Restaurant (South
Maui/Kihei, $$$$)
Mama's Fish House (Central Maui/
Paia, $$$$$)

Nick's Fishmarket (South Maui/Wailea, $$$$$)

Paia Fish Market (Central Maui/Paia, $–$$)

Sansei Seafood Restaurant & Sushi Bar (West Maui/Kapalua and in South Maui/Kihei, $$$)

Steak/Seafood

Hana Ranch Restaurant (East Maui/Hana, $$$)

Hula Grill Kaanapali (West Maui/Kaanapali, $–$$$)

Kimo's (West Maui/Lahaina, $$$)

Leilani's on the Beach (West Maui/Kaanapali, $$$)

Maui Brewing Company (West Maui/Kahana, $$$)

Vietnamese

A Saigon Cafe (Central Maui, $$)

Index of Establishments by Price

$$$$$

Capische (South Maui/Wailea, Mediterranean-Italian)

The Feast at Lele (West Maui/Lahaina, Luau)

Gerard's (West Maui/Lahaina, French)

Lahaina Grill (West Maui/Lahaina, New American/Hawaii Regional)

Mama's Fish House (Central Maui/ Paia, Seafood)

Nick's Fishmarket (South Maui/Wailea, Mediterranean/Seafood)

Old Lahaina Luau (West Maui/Lahaina, Luau)

The Plantation House (West Maui/ Kapalua, Hawaii Regional/Mediterranean)

Sarento's on the Beach (South Maui/Kihei, Italian/Mediterranean)

Sonz Maui at Swan Court (Hawaii Regional

Spago (South Maui/Wailea, Hawaii Regional/Pacific Rim)

$$$$

Ferraro's Bar e Ristorante (South Maui/Wailea, Italian)

Haliimaile General Store (Upcountry, Hawaii Regional)

Ho'omana'o (West Maui/Lahaina, Luau)

I'o (West Maui/Lahaina, New Pacific)

Joe's Simply Delicious Food (South Maui/Wailea, New American/Hawaii Regional)

Kai Sushi Restaurant (West Maui/Kapalua, Japanese)

Ka'uiki (East Maui/Hana, Continental/Island Fusion)

Lahaina Grill (West Maui/Lahaina, New American/Hawaii Regional)

Lahaina Store Grille & Oyster Bar (West Maui/Lahaina, New American)

Maalaea Waterfront Restaurant (South Maui/Kihei, Continental/Seafood)

Mala, An Ocean Tavern (West Maui/Lahaina; also South Maui, Wailea, Healthy Eclectic)

Pacific'o (West Maui/Lahaina, New Pacific)

The Plantation House (West Maui/ Kapalua, Hawaii Regional/Mediterranean)

Roy's Kahana Bar & Grill (West Maui/Kahana, Hawaii Regional)

Roy's Kihei (South Maui/Kihei, Hawaii Regional)

Sarento's on the Beach (South Maui/Kihei, Italian/Mediterranean)

Tommy Bahama's Tropical Cafe (South Maui/Wailea, Caribbean)

$$$

Casanova (Upcountry, Italian)

Charley's Restaurant & Saloon (Central Maui/Paia, American/International)

Hana Ranch Restaurant (East Maui/ Hana, American)

Hula Grill Kaanapali (West Maui/
Kaanapali, Steak/Seafood)

Kimo's (West Maui/Lahaina, Steak/
Seafood)

Lahaina Store Grille & Oyster Bar
(West Maui/Lahaina, New American)

Leilani's on the Beach (West
Maui/Kaanapali, Steak/Seafood)

Mala, An Ocean Tavern (West Maui/
Lahaina; also South Maui, Wailea,
Healthy Eclectic)

Maui Brewing Company (West
Maui/Kahana, Steak/Seafood)

Roy's Kahana Bar & Grill (West
Maui/Kahana, Hawaii Regional)

Roy's Kihei (South Maui/Kihei, Hawaii
Regional)

Sansei Seafood Restaurant & Sushi Bar
(West Maui/Kapalua and in South
Maui/Kihei, Japanese/Pacific Rim/
Seafood)

Stella Blues Cafe (South Maui/Kihei,
New American)

$$

Café des Amis (Central Maui/Paia;
Mediterranean/Indian)

Casanova (Upcountry, Italian)

Charley's Restaurant & Saloon
(Central Maui/Paia,
American/International)

Cheeseburger in Paradise (West Maui/
Lahaina; American)

Cheeseburger Island Style (South
Maui/Wailea; American)

The Flatbread Company (Central
Maui/Paia; Pizza)

Hana Ranch Restaurant (East Maui/
Hana, American)

Hula Grill Kaanapali (West Maui/
Kaanapali, Steak/Seafood)

Kula Lodge & Restaurant (Upcountry,
Breakfast)

Lahaina Coolers (West Maui/Lahaina,
American/Eclectic)

Mañana Garage (Central Maui, Latin
American)

Marco's Grill & Deli (Central Maui/
Kahului, American/Italian)

Milagros Food Co. Maui (Central Maui,
Southwestern)

Paia Fish Market (Central Maui/Paia,
Seafood)

A Saigon Cafe (Central Maui,
Vietnamese)

Stella Blues Cafe (South Maui/Kihei,
New American)

$

Aloha Mixed Plate (West Maui/
Lahaina, Local Hawaiian)

Café des Amis (Central Maui/Paia;
Mediterranean/Indian)

Cheeseburger in Paradise (West Maui/
Lahaina; American)

Cheeseburger Island Style (South
Maui/Wailea; American)

Cilantro Fresh Mexican Grill (West
Maui/Lahaina; Mexican)

CJ's Deli & Diner (West Maui/
Kaanapali, American)

Da' Kitchen (South Maui/Kihei, also in
Central Maui/Kahului; Local Hawaiian)

The Flatbread Company (Central
Maui/Paia; Pizza)

Gazebo Restaurant (West Maui/Napili;
Local)

Hana Ranch Restaurant (East
Maui/Hana, American)

Hula Grill Kaanapali (West Maui/
Kaanapali, Steak/Seafood)

Kula Sandalwoods Cafe (Upcountry,
Breakfast)

Mama's Ribs & Rotisserie (West Maui/
Napili, Barbecue)

Marco's Grill & Deli (Central Maui/
Kahului, American/Italian)

Paia Fish Market (Central Maui/Paia,
Seafood)

Peggy Sue's (South Maui/Kihei,
American)

Penne Pasta Cafe (West Maui/Lahaina,
Italian)

Pizza Paradiso (West Maui/
Honokowaii; Pizza)

WokStar (South Maui/Kihei;
International)

Part IV
Exploring Maui

The 5th Wave
By Rich Tennant

"That's Maui. You can tell because it resembles a man looking to the right in a panic because he can't find his airline ticket which his wife wisely packed in their carry-on the night before."

In this part . . .

This part is just what you need for your introduction to Maui's famous beaches. I'll show you how to enjoy the waves, and provide you with the lowdown on the best watersports, snorkel spots, cruises, and much more. You'll also discover the island's top adventures: watching the mystical sunrise at Haleakala National Park, cruising the Heavenly Road to Hana, and splashing in tropical waterfalls along the way. (I have all the best golf courses listed here, too, of course.) I'll also show you where to shop, where to toast the perfect sunset, and where to party the night away. As if this weren't enough, a whole world of adventure is waiting for you on Maui's closest neighbors, unspoiled Molokai and upscale Lanai.

Chapter 12

Enjoying Maui's Best Beaches and Watersports

In This Chapter

▶ Locating Maui's best beaches
▶ Playing in the waves: Dive trips, snorkel cruises, and much more
▶ Watching whales
▶ Staying safe while you enjoy the water

*F*or people who love spending time outdoors, Maui is practically paradise. Even if you have no intention of sampling every activity that it has to offer, the bounty of choice will wow you.

See Chapter 13 for detailed information on land sports, including golf, hiking, horseback riding — and even mountain biking down a volcano!

Taking the Plunge: Knowing Where to Start

In order to begin your fabulous Maui adventure, you may want a little local help. Several companies offer reliable personal assistance that can help you choose the activities that are right for you. The best and most reliable activity booker on Maui is **Tom Barefoot's Tours,** 250 Alamaha St. (at Wakea Street, south of the Hana Highway), Kahului (☎ **800-621-3601** or 808-661-1246; www.tombarefoot.com), which may be able to save you a few valuable dollars on many of Maui's activities on land and sea. Unlike most other so-called "activity centers" on Maui, this professional operation has nothing to do with timeshares — activities are their business, and their reps are pros who really know their stuff. I've found the salespeople's recommendations to be consistently good ones. You're welcome to visit the store, but you don't have to; all business can be conducted over the phone or online, even before you arrive in the islands (which I recommend, to ensure that you don't miss out on an activity that matters to you).

Tom Barefoot's offers a 10 percent discount on select activities when you pay with cash, personal check, or traveler's checks, or a 7 percent discount if you pay by credit card. However, if you tell Tom Barefoot's that you want the top-of-the-line snorkel cruise or luau, they'll freely recommend and book you with Trilogy or Old Lahaina, even though they can't offer you a savings and won't make a dime — because they figure that a happy customer is a returning customer. You can book discounted activities from home via their Web site or toll-free number.

Another recommendable activity booker is **Trilogy Ocean Sports,** which maintains a kiosk on Kaanapali Beach in front of the Kaanapali Beach Hotel (☎ **808-661-7789**). A sister business to Trilogy Excursions — which is universally regarded as the finest snorkel-sail operator on Maui (read more about Trilogy Excursions' offerings later in this chapter) — Trilogy Ocean Sports can book you not only onto Trilogy cruises but also with other activity providers they endorse, whether you're looking for a backcountry four-wheeling excursion or a beginning surfing lesson. They've handpicked a top-flight group of activity providers to represent.

Do yourself a favor and avoid those activities bookers that are trying to sell you a timeshare. Believe me, you don't want to spend a half-day of your precious vacation time warding off a salesperson's hard-sell advances to buy a timeshare you don't need in exchange for a "free" snorkel cruise on a cut-rate operator.

Hitting the Beaches

Maui wouldn't be such a glamour girl without its breathtaking array of beaches. All of Maui's fabulous beaches (even those in front of exclusive resorts) are open to the public. Hawaii state law requires all hotels to offer public right-of-way access (across private property) to the beach, along with public parking. So just because a beach fronts a hotel doesn't mean that you can't enjoy the water. However, the hotel may restrict certain areas of private property for guests' use only. Hotels are generally happy to rent you beach gear or sell you refreshments.

Never leave valuables in your rental car while you're at the beach. Knowledgeable thieves like to prey on tourists, and they know how to get into your interior, trunk, and glove box in no time flat. Be especially diligent about leaving your stuff behind at your condo or in your hotel safe when you're heading off to a remote beach.

Also, when it comes to safe swimming conditions, do your homework: Check out the following beach descriptions and, after you're on Maui, make inquiries about local surf conditions. At beaches without lifeguards, keep an eye out for posted signs warning of dangerous currents or conditions. If you see a red flag hoisted at any beach, don't venture into the water because it indicates that conditions are unsafe for swimmers. Even if the waves look placid, trust the warning. And never turn your back on the ocean; big waves can come out of nowhere in a matter of minutes. See the end of this chapter for more on water safety.

Snorkelers should also check out the Snorkeling section under "Discovering Water Fun for Everyone," for some additional recommendations on great snorkel spots.

In West Maui

These fine beaches are easily accessible from the Honoapiilani Highway, which connects the island's commercial heart, Kahului, to Lahaina, Kaanapali, and Kapalua. Each one offers excellent opportunities for whale-watching in humpback season and for sunset viewing at any time of year.

Honolua/Mokuleia Bay Marine Life Conservation District

Snorkelers love this gorgeous cove for its smooth surf, clear waters (which are protected as a marine-life conservation district), excellent coral formations, and abundance of tropical fish, especially on the west side of the bay. The beige-sand crescent is lovely and never too crowded. In winter, stay out of the water — it's too rough and dangerous. Instead, watch daredevil surfers ride the finest breaks in the islands.

Sorry, this beach has no facilities. But nearby **D. T. Fleming Beach Park** has restrooms, showers, picnic tables, and barbecue grills. This quiet, crescent-shaped cove north of the Ritz-Carlton starts at the 16th hole of the Kapalua golf course (Makaluapuna Point) and rolls around to the sea cliffs at the other side. Ironwood trees provide shade. The waters are generally calm enough to offer good swimming and snorkeling.

See map p. 192. At the northernmost end of Honoapiilani Highway (Highway 30), about 2 miles past Office Road (the turnoff for Kapalua); park with the other cars in the available spaces or along the roadside and walk 200 yards down the stairs and to the beach.

Kapalua Beach

This gorgeous, golden crescent bordered by two palm-studded points is justifiably popular for sunbathing, swimming, and snorkeling. The sandy bottom slopes gently to deep water that's crystal-clear. Well-protected from strong winds and currents, Kapalua's calm waters are usually great for swimmers of all ages and abilities year-round, and waves come in just right for easy riding. The rocky points offer good fish-viewing opportunities for snorkelers and offshore divers alike. The beach is also great for offshore whale-watching in winter, too. A shady path and cool lawns edge the beach's inland side. Facilities include showers, restrooms, a rental shack, and outdoor showers. The small parking lot is limited to about 30 spaces, so arrive early.

See map p. 192. On Lower Honoapiilani Road at the south end of Kapalua, just before the Napili Kai Beach Club. To get there: From Honoapiilani Highway, turn left just past mile marker 30, go 1/10 mile to Lower Honoapiilani Road, turn left, and go 8/10 mile to the access point.

Maui's Best Beaches, Snorkel Spots, and Watersports

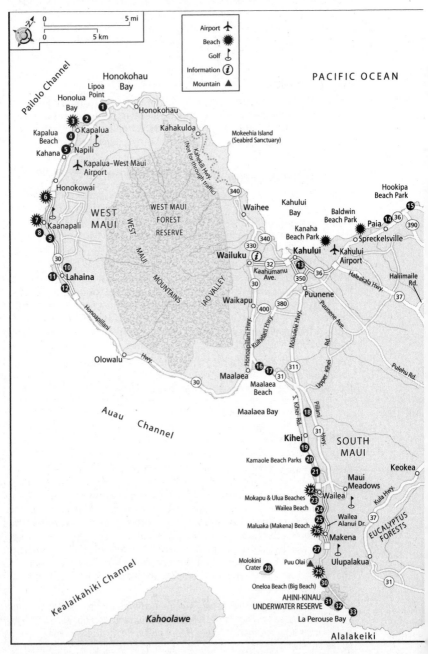

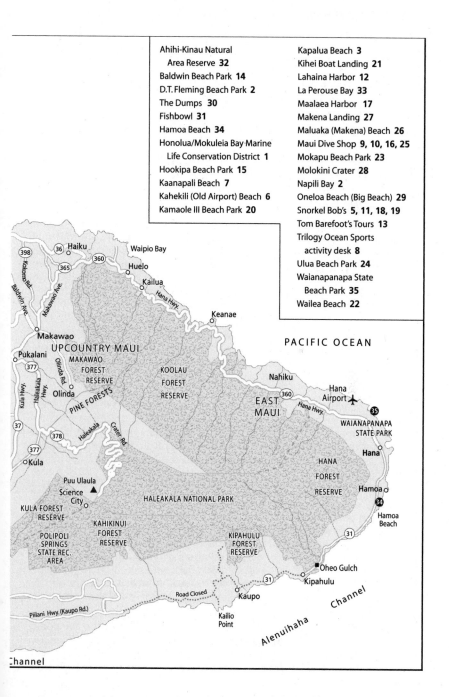

Ahihi-Kinau Natural
   Area Reserve **32**
Baldwin Beach Park **14**
D.T. Fleming Beach Park **2**
The Dumps **30**
Fishbowl **31**
Hamoa Beach **34**
Honolua/Mokuleia Bay Marine
   Life Conservation District **1**
Hookipa Beach Park **15**
Kaanapali Beach **7**
Kahekili (Old Airport) Beach **6**
Kamaole III Beach Park **20**

Kapalua Beach **3**
Kihei Boat Landing **21**
Lahaina Harbor **12**
La Perouse Bay **33**
Maalaea Harbor **17**
Makena Landing **27**
Maluaka (Makena) Beach **26**
Maui Dive Shop **9, 10, 16, 25**
Mokapu Beach Park **23**
Molokini Crater **28**
Napili Bay **2**
Oneloa Beach (Big Beach) **29**
Snorkel Bob's **5, 11, 18, 19**
Tom Barefoot's Tours **13**
Trilogy Ocean Sports
   activity desk **8**
Ulua Beach Park **24**
Waianapanapa State
   Beach Park **35**
Wailea Beach **22**

Kahekili (Old Airport) Beach

This smallish but extremely attractive beach is one of Maui's best snorkel spots for beginners and families with small kids because its waters are shallow, clear, and well protected by an expansive offshore reef that teems with colorful fish. The nice facilities — including very clean restrooms with showers, plus picnic tables — make it a good place to come and spend the day. Don't be surprised if you see groups of divers, because Kahekili is a popular instructional dive spot.

See map p. 192. Off Honoapiilani Highway (Highway 30) at the north end of Kaanapali, just across from the Sugar Cane Train. To get there: From Honoapiilani Highway, turn left at the northernmost access to Kaanapali; look for public beach access and parking on your right.

Kaanapali Beach

Maui's first resort developers were drawn to build on this beach for a good reason: It's absolutely fabulous. Hotels and condos (almost approaching the density of Waikiki) now line Kaanapali's 4 miles of grainy, gold sand, but the not-too-wide beach tends to be populated only in pockets; you can usually find an uncrowded area to spread out your towel even when the hotels are at capacity. Swimming and wave jumping are excellent, but beware of the rough winter *shorebreak* (where the waves break on the shore), which can really kick up.

At the beach's north end, in front of the Sheraton, is Black Rock, the best offshore snorkel spot on Maui. The water is clear, the area is well-protected from rough surf (most of the time), and the clouds of tropical fish are used to finned folks. Well worth seeking out; mornings tend to be calmest and clearest.

A paved beach walk links the hotels and the open-air Whaler's Village shopping and dining complex, a great place to cure the midday munchies or sip a tropical cocktail while scanning for whales or watching the sun set over the Pacific. Lifeguards and beach boys from the resorts man the beach, beach-gear rental shacks are set up right on the sand, and most hotels have outdoor showers (and sometimes restrooms) you can use; restrooms are also available at Whaler's Village.

The only downside is that parking is difficult for those who are not staying in the area. Whalers Village has a paid lot, but beachgoers are discouraged from using it by a NO BEACH PARKING sign; if you do, be sure not to be unloading a giant cooler, beach umbrella or set of chairs from your car, and be sure to buy lunch (or at least some sunscreen) from one of the vendors in the center to count as a shopper. Park with care here, lest you be towed. Another alternative is to pay to park as a visitor at one of the resorts, and do so legitimately by starting your day with a meal there.

There is a small free parking lot for public beach access in the Sheraton Maui's parking structure. Follow the main resort road down to the north end; the entrance is right before the main entrance to the resort itself, on the lower level of the structure at its south end (nearest to the Kaanapali Beach Hotel). Look for the sign that says BEACH ACCESS PARKING, park, and follow the beach access path between the Kaanapali Beach Hotel and the Sheraton. The lot is open daily from 7 a.m. to 7 p.m.; come early to snare your spot in this tiny lot.

See map p. 192. Kaanapali Parkway, off Honoapiilani Highway (Highway 30), Kaanapali.

Along the South Maui Coast

These fabulous beaches are located along Maui's sunny southwest-facing shore, where you find the resort areas of Kihei and Wailea.

Kamaole III Beach Park

Three popular beach parks — Kamaole I, II, and III — face the waves across from South Kihei Road in mid-Kihei. The biggest and best is Kamaole III (or Kam-3, as the locals call it), which boasts a playground and a grassy lawn that meets the finely textured, golden sand. Swimming is generally safe, but parents should make sure that little ones don't venture too far out because the bottom slopes off quickly. Families may prefer the beach's grassy end with shade trees, where the ocean bottom has a fairly gentle slope. Both the north and south ends have rocky fingers that are great for snorkelers, and the winter waves attract bodysurfers. This west-facing beach is also an ideal spot to watch the sun go down or look for whales off-shore in winter. Facilities include restrooms, showers, picnic tables, bar-becues, volleyball nets, and lifeguards. Food and beach-gear rentals are available at the malls across the street — but be careful crossing busy Kihei Road!

See map p. 192. On South Kihei Road, just south of Keonekai Street (across from the Maui Parkshore and Kamaole Sands condos), Kihei.

Mokapu and Ulua Beach Parks

Situated at the north end of Wailea, these lovely, side-by-side sister beaches boast pretty, golden sand, grassy areas for sandless picnicking, and clean facilities, including restrooms and a freshwater shower pole. The ocean bottom is shallow and gently slopes down to deeper waters, making swimming generally safe; snorkelers find Wailea's best snorkeling at the rocky north end. When the surf kicks up, the waves are excellent for body-surfers. Although these beaches are popular with the nearby upscale condo crowd, the sand rarely gets too crowded. The parking lot is tiny, though, so come early.

See map p. 192. On Wailea Alanui Road at Hale Alii Place, between the Wailea Marriott to the south and the Wailea Ekahi Village condos to the north (directly across from the Palms at Wailea condos), Wailea.

Wailea Beach

This ultrafine gold-sand beach is long, wide, and protected on both sides by black lava points with a sandy and sloping bottom, making the clear waters excellent for swimming (and okay for snorkeling, too). The year-round waves are just right for easy board-riding or bodysurfing, but trade winds can kick up in the afternoon, so come early. The view out to sea is gorgeous, with the islands of Kahoolawe and Lanai framing the view. This site is ideal to watch for humpback whales in winter. This stretch of shoreline may feel like it belongs to the ultradeluxe resorts that line it, but it doesn't; just look for the blue SHORELINE ACCESS signs for easiest entry points. Restrooms and showers are available.

See map p. 192. Fronting the Grand Wailea and Four Seasons resorts, Wailea. To get there: The blue SHORELINE ACCESS sign is between the two resorts on Wailea Alanui Drive.

Maluaka (Makena) Beach

This wonderful beach park fronting the Maui Prince Hotel offers a pleasing off-the-beaten-path experience for people in search of first-rate snorkeling, or anybody who wants a break from Maui's ever-present crowds. Short, wide, and palm-fringed, this unspoiled crescent of golden, grainy sand is set between two protective lava points and bounded by big, grassy sand dunes. Snorkelers find surprisingly colorful coral and an impressive array of vibrantly hued reef fish at the beach's rocky south end, past the lava point. Sunbathers and casual swimmers stick to the beautiful strand closer to the hotel, which is virtually empty on weekdays. Facilities include restrooms and showers.

See map p. 192. Makena Road, Makena (south of Wailea). To get there: Follow Wailea Alanui Drive south through Wailea to Makena (where it becomes Makena Alanui Road); go past the Maui Prince Hotel, turn right on Makena Road (where it wraps around) and look for the SHORELINE ACCESS sign near the hotel for public access parking.

Oneloa Beach (Big Beach)

Oneloa means "long sand" in Hawaiian, and locals call it Big Beach. It comes by its name honestly, for this gorgeous crescent of white sand is 3,300 feet long and more than 100 feet wide. Oneloa is a beautiful spot for swimming, sunbathing, surfing, bodysurfing, and body boarding, or just hanging out for the day and strolling along the picture-perfect shoreline. And, true to its nickname, Oneloa is so big that even when it's crowded, it doesn't *feel* crowded — so bring your beach chair and plan to stay a while, playing in the gorgeous surf and light waves. Snorkeling is a bit better down the road, but you'll find decent fish-watching near the north. In winter storm season, beware of fierce waves and a strong rip current that sweeps the sharp drop-off. The area has no facilities except portable toilets, but plenty of parking is available. Well worth seeking out for a picture-perfect Maui day.

See map p. 192. Off Makena Rd., 1⅓ miles south of the Maui Prince Hotel. To get there: Drive past the Maui Prince Hotel 1⅓ miles, where a paved road leads to the parking lot and beach. A second parking lot is available just to the north.

Hanging out at a perfect spot like Oneloa all day can sure make a vaca-tioner hungry. If you find yourself in such a state, head south on Makena Road just a bit to **Makena Grill,** a simple lunch cart on the inland side of the road serving up fantastic fish tacos with pineapple salsa, beautifully wood-grilled chicken and beef kabobs dressed in a pineapple-teriyaki glaze, and one or two other lunch plates, depending on what's fresh and available. The proprietor is a bit Soup Nazi–ish, but her food is great — supposedly, Tony Hawk calls this the best food on Maui. I don't know if I'd go that far, but it's sure good. There's a small but pleasant picnic area where you can enjoy your eats. Makena Grill is usually open daily from 11 a.m. to "4-ish" — but it's a lady with a cart and a few propane tanks, so don't blame me if she's taken the day off.

The Dumps

It's not a sexy name, but the Dumps makes a great spot for serious snor-kelers in search of an off-the-beaten-path experience. This locals' favorite is part of the Ahihi-Kinau Natural Area Reserve, the Dumps isn't a beach, really. Instead, it's an exposed cove with a bit of black sand, lots of lava rock, and a wealth of mature coral offering some great snorkeling when the winds are down and the turquoise water is clear.

Only confident swimmers should explore the Dumps, and then only early in the day, when winds are down and visibility is best. Don't get in the water if the winds are kicking or there's rough surge near the shoreline (folks have been blown out to sea on windy days). Also, be sure to wear reef shoes or other sturdy footwear for your walk out to the shoreline.

See map p. 152. Off Makena Road, just south of Ahihi Cove, just before the lava fields begin; park along the roadside if there's no space in the small lot.

Central and East Maui

These glorious sands are accessible from the Hana Highway, which runs along the island's lush North Shore.

Baldwin Beach Park

Despite the beauty of this gorgeous North Shore beach park — a long ribbon of powdery white sands backed by swaying palms and fringed by white-crested turquoise waves — it's not usually crowded, except on week-ends when local families come. The beach stretches for a good mile, so it has plenty of room for everybody, especially because only locals and intrepid visitors generally end up here. This is a terrific spot for swimmers and body boarders, because the water is silky, warm, and gorgeous. But be careful before venturing into the water and always heed the lifeguard, because the undercurrent can be strong at times; it's best to stay out of the water altogether in the rough winter months. The winter water's not for inexperienced swimmers, but everybody can enjoy the beautiful set-ting at any time of year. Facilities include restrooms and showers.

See map p. 192. On the Hana Highway (Highway 36), just east of Paia.

Hookipa Beach Park

Possibly the most famous windsurfing beach in the world, this small, gold-sand beach at the foot of a grassy cliff attracts top windsurfers and wave jumpers from around the globe with hard, constant winds and endless waves that result in near-perfect wave-riding conditions. Come on weekday afternoons to watch the local experts fly over the waves with their colorful sails; winter weekends host regular competitions. When the winter waves die down, snorkelers and divers explore the reef. Even then, be extremely careful because these waters are rough year-round; summer mornings are best. Facilities include some rustic restrooms and showers, plus pavilions, picnic tables, and barbecues. The lower parking lot is generally reserved for windsurfers and their equipment, so park in the upper lot (see the following directions), where the high, grassy bluff offers a better perch for watching the action anyway.

See map p. 192. Off Hana Highway (Highway 36), 2 miles east of Paia, about 6 miles east of Haleakala Highway (Highway 37). To get there: Drive past the park and turn left at the entrance at the far side of the beach, at the Hookipa Lookout sign.

Hamoa Beach

This remote, half-moon-shaped beach near the end of the Hana Road is one of the most breathtakingly lovely in Hawaii, celebrated in writing by no less than James Michener for its singular beauty. The Hotel Hana-Maui likes to maintain the beach is its own, but it has to share, so feel free to march right down the steps from the lava-rock lookout point and stake out a spot on the open sand. Even if you don't want to swim or sunbathe, come to peek at this stunner from above: You'll find surf that's the perfect color of turquoise, golden-gray sand, and luxuriant green hills serving as the postcard-perfect backdrop. The beach is generally good for swimming and wave-riding in the gentle seasons, but stick close to the shore at any time of year, because you're in open, unprotected ocean. Stay out of the water entirely in winter. The hotel maintains minimal facilities for nonguests, including a restroom.

See map p. 192. Off the Hana Highway (Highway 36), about 2½ miles past Hana town. To get there: Turn at the small white sign that says HAMOA BEACH and go about 1½ miles to the lava-rock lookout point; you can park on the roadside or in the dirt area across the road. The stairs are just beyond the lookout point. (If you reach the steep service road to the beach, you've gone too far.)

Discovering Water Fun for Everyone

If your hotel or condo doesn't provide beach gear or beach toys, you won't have a problem finding a place to rent these items. In addition to offering top-quality snorkel gear, **Snorkel Bob's** (see contact information in the next section) also rents body boards, beach chairs, coolers, and umbrellas at its three Maui stores. Rental shacks on such popular beaches as Kaanapali and Kapalua can also hook you up.

Snorkeling

Maui is justifiably famous for its snorkel cruises to Molokini and Lanai, both of which offer first-class fish-spotting, some of the best in the state (see the "Ocean cruising to Molokini and Lanai and other on-deck adventures," later in this chapter). But anybody who's already perused the "Hitting the Beaches" section earlier in this chapter knows that Maui offers a wealth of terrific snorkel spots that are accessible from shore. Probably the best of these spots is **Black Rock,** at the north end of **Kaanapali Beach;** also excellent are **Honolua Bay,** north of Kapalua; **Mokapu and Ulua beach parks,** in Wailea; one of my lesser-known favorites, **Maluaka** (sometimes called **Makena**) **Beach,** south of Wailea in Makena; and the unsexily named **The Dumps,** a nice choice for experienced snorkelers who want an off-the-beaten-path experience. (See "Hitting the Beaches," earlier.)

In addition, for those staying in West Maui, **Napili Bay** is worth seeking out for its generally well-protected snorkeling and convenient access. Take Highway 30 to mile marker 29, where you'll see the Napili Center; turn left and proceed to Lower Honoapiilani Highway; turn right and proceed a half-mile to the BEACH ACCESS signs on Napili Place and Hui Drive. Park along the streets and take one of the beach access pathways to the golden sand. No facilities.

In South Maui, **Makena Landing,** a popular spot for kayak launching, is also a good spot for snorkelers who want to enjoy easy access. The best offshore snorkeling is around the lava point on the right (north) side; if you're lucky, a short swim will reward you with sea turtles. There's not much beach here, but there are good facilities, including toilets, showers, a small parking lot, and a pretty grassy area. To get there, follow Wailea Alanui Drive until it turns into Makena Alanui Road; bear right at Makena Road and park where you see the vans with the empty kayak carts.

In addition to Makena Landing and The Dumps, there is more good snorkeling worth seeking out to the south. South of Oneloa Beach and The Dumps, you'll cross into black lava fields that mark the beginning of the **Ahihi-Kinau Natural Area Reserve.** The best snorkeling in this area is aptly named **Fishbowl,** a tiny but rich cove off Cape Kinau. It takes some work to get there, however. The trailhead begins about a half-mile past the parking area for the Dumps, where you'll need to park. Walk along the road to the trailhead, and then follow the mile-long lava trail to the shoreline; wear good shoes, not flip-flops, because you'll need toe protection. Go early, before the winds kick up, and stay within the protected cove.

If you drive through the lava fields to the end of the road, you'll eventually reach **La Perouse Bay,** whose black-sand beach and gorgeous turquoise waters are well worth seeking out, even if just for a look. Intrepid snorkelers can swim out to the outer coves for wonderful fish viewing — some of the best on the island, in fact. However, don't bother getting in the water if you're not able or willing to swim out, as the underwater viewing at the end of the road is poor. Go early in the morning, and stay out of the water once the winds kick up. A few portable toilets comprise the extent of the facilities.

Additionally, many of the island's hotels and condo complexes sit on coves excellent for snorkeling — and not just the super-expensive ones. The affordable Mana Kai Maui in Kihei, for example, fronts a snorkeling gem. Your hotel staff is sure to have recommendations.

For the most comprehensive guide to the best snorkel spots around the island, stop into the **Maui Dive Shop** and pick up a copy of the free publication *Maui Dive Guide*. In the centerfold of the magazine-style guide is a map to all the best snorkel spots, with information on level of difficulty, best water access points, facilities information, and all the details you need to get there. Maui Dive Shop has four locations in West Maui, including the new Lahaina Gateway Mall (☎ **808-661-5388**) and Whaler's Village at Kaanapali (☎ **808-661-5117**), and four locations in South Maui, including Maalaea Harbor Village (☎ **808-244-5514**) and the Shops at Wailea (☎ **808-875-9904**). To find the location nearest you, call ☎ **800-542-3483** or ☎ 808-879-1775, or visit www.mauidiveshop.com.

If you want to take advantage of Maui's offshore snorkeling opportunities, you probably need to rent some gear. My favorite rental-gear supplier in Hawaii is **Snorkel Bob's;** it rents the best-quality gear, with friendly service and a refreshing dose of snarky humor thrown in for good measure. Snorkel Bob's maintains four Maui locations, with two in West Maui. One is at Dickenson Square, at the corner of Dickenson and Wainee streets, in Lahaina town (☎ **808-662-0104**). The other West Maui store is almost to Kapalua, in Napili Village, 5425 Lower Honoapiilani Hwy. (☎ **808-669-9603**). In South Maui, find Bob's at Azeka Place 2, 1279 S. Kihei Rd. #310, North Kihei (☎ **808-875-6188**), and at the Kamaole Beach Center at Kihei Marketplace, 2411 S. Kihei Rd., between Rainbow Mall and Dolphin Plaza, across from Kamaole I Beach Park and not too far from Wailea (☎ **808-879-7449**).

The best-quality gear — the "Ultimate Truth" — rents for $8 a day, or $32 a week ($22 per week for kids) for the mask/snorkel/fins set. For $12 more, nearsighted snorkelers can opt for prescription masks (including snorkel and fins set). On the other hand, budget travelers can rent basic gear for just $9 per week. If you can afford it, do yourself a favor and rent the highest-quality gear. Spending the extra bucks is worth getting a mask that doesn't leak and a snorkel that doesn't clog. Wetsuits and life vests are also available. You don't need to reserve gear in advance, but you're welcome to book your gear over the phone at ☎ **800-262-7725** or online at www.snorkelbob.com. The shops are open daily from 8 a.m. to 5 p.m.

When you rent gear from Snorkel Bob's, you can pick up a set of snorkel gear at the start of your trip, carry it with you as you travel throughout the islands, and then return it to another Snorkel Bob's location on Oahu, the Big Island, or Kauai. (All shops offer 24-hour gear return service.)

Any snorkel cruise or kayak outfitter supplies you with gear, but I highly recommend renting your own set and bringing it aboard. Free gear is almost universally bad — and can you think of anything worse than not being able to see sea turtles or other cool creatures because of a crappy mask? Spending the few extra dollars to rent a quality mask and snorkel and fins that fit is worth every penny.

Keep these snorkel tips in mind as you head into the water:

✔ Make mornings your offshore snorkel time on Maui, because the winds often start to kick up around noon, making surf conditions rougher and less conducive to fish-spying.

✔ Always snorkel with a friend and keep an eye on each other.

✔ Look up every few minutes to get your bearings, check your position in relation to the shoreline, and check for any boat traffic.

✔ If you're not a strong swimmer, don't be embarrassed to don a life jacket while you snorkel.

✔ Don't touch anything. Not only can your fingers and feet damage coral, but also the coral can give you nasty cuts. Moreover, camouflaged fish and spiny shells may surprise you.

✔ Before you set out, check surf conditions by calling one of the local dive or snorkel shops, such as Snorkel Bob's, which can give you the latest on local conditions and recommend alternative spots if the prime ones are too rough for snorkeling.

Ocean cruising to Molokini and Lanai and other on-deck adventures

Maui boasts two top day-cruising destinations: the sunken offshore crater **Molokini,** which is hugely popular among snorkelers and divers; and the island of **Lanai,** terrific for snorkelers and sunbathers alike. (Note that only Trilogy and Paragon take their guests onshore at Lanai; other operators just anchor offshore for snorkeling in the surrounding waters.) Both options offer excellent snorkeling opportunities, but I'd choose a Lanai cruise in whale-watching season (from mid-Dec through Apr), because the channel that separates Maui from Lanai is a favorite hangout for wintering humpback whales.

Dramamine or nausea-prevention wristbands are an excellent idea if you're prone to seasickness. A very important tip: If you opt for Dramamine, be sure to take it with plenty of time for it to work, including *before* the boat gears up for the return trip to Maui. After the return sail is underway, it's too late for the drug to do any good.

The outfitters listed in this section hardly scratch the surface of the glut of cruise operators that sail from Maui. I consider these to be the best. If you want additional options, contact the island's most reliable activity center, **Tom Barefoot's Tours,** 250 Alamaha St. (at Wakea Street, south of the Hana Highway), Kahului (☎ **888-222-3601** or 808-661-1246; www. tombarefoot.com), which can also save you a few bucks by booking you with some of the operators that I list.

All the sail-snorkel cruises I recommend are family-friendly, but Trilogy boasts the kid-friendliest crew of them all.

Blue Water Rafting

Blue Water's cruises are distinct for four reasons. First, this outfit takes small groups of guests (no more than 24) out on fast-flying, rigid-hulled inflatable boats for an exciting ride. Second, its Molokini Express cruises arrive at Molokini in between the big boats' trips, so passengers have the perpetually overpopular crater largely to themselves. Third, the speed and extra-maneuverability of its boats allows Blue Water to take you to South Maui's otherwise untouristed Kanaio Coast beyond Makena, where you'll visit sea caves and snorkel in pristine areas favored by sea turtles and spinner dolphins on both Kanaio-only and Molokini-combination tours. And lastly, the low-to-the-water boats put you as close as possible to turtles and dolphins, as well as humpback whales in winter. This cruise is an excellent choice for adventure-seekers in search of something different.

Cruises depart from Kihei Boat Landing, on South Kihei Road just south of Kamaole III Beach Park (between Keonekai Street and Kilohana Drive), Kihei. ☎ *808-879-7238.* www.bluewaterrafting.com. *2- to 5½-hour raft cruises: $55–$119 adults, $45–$99 kids 11 and under. Prices include deli lunch, plus continental breakfast on the 5½-hour tour.*

Maui Classic Charters

This company can offer you Molokini snorkel-sail experiences on two great boats: The *Four Winds II,* a modern 55-foot, 149-person-capacity catamaran featuring a glass-bottom hull for on-ship viewing, a water slide, three swim ladders, and barbecues; and the *Maui Magic,* a super-fast state-of-the-art 54-foot, 71-passenger power catamaran with similarly cool features in a more intimate environment. The *Maui Magic* cruises also include some dolphin spotting on most trips. A naturalist accompanies the whale-watching trips in season.

Cruises depart from Maalaea Harbor (at the Highway 30/130 junction), Maalaea. ☎ *800-736-5740 or 808-879-8188.* www.mauicharters.com. *3½- to 5-hour cruises: $42–$99 adults, $30–$79 kids 12 and under. Prices include continental breakfast and barbecue lunch on longer cruises; beer, wine, and soda on all cruises. 15 percent online discount available at press time for booking at least 7 days in advance.*

Pacific Whale Foundation Eco-Adventures

If you consider yourself to be ecologically minded, you can't do better than to give your snorkel-cruise dollars to the Pacific Whale Foundation. This nonprofit organization has been at the forefront of Maui-based whale research, education, and conservation since the 1970s, and it also happens to host very fine cruises. Its first-rate modern catamaran fleet offers some of the best tours of Molokini and offshore Lanai. Its five-and-a-half-hour Lanai snorkel-sail takes in the island's less visited bays and includes a search for wild dolphins in its regular itinerary. The five-hour Molokai trip is as fine as any and includes a visit to a second snorkel spot, Turtle Arches. Not only is a naturalist (at least one) always onboard, but the entire crew is knowledgeable, ecoconscious, and friendly; the boats (each of which carries 100 people maximum) even burn ecofriendly fuel. What's more, the cruises are great for beginning snorkelers because guides lead fish talks and reef tours, and a wide variety of flotation devices are available. The winter whale-watching cruises are unparalleled, of course. You simply can't go wrong with these folks.

Departures from Maalaea Harbor (at the Highway 30/130 junction), Maalaea, and Lahaina Harbor, on Front Street, Lahaina, depending on cruise. ☎ *800-942-5311 or 808-249-8811.* www.pacificwhale.org. *Cruises: $50–$110 adults, $40–$70 kids 3–12. Kids 2 and under sail free, except on dinner cruise. Some cruises include continental breakfast and/or deli lunch.*

Paragon Sailing Charters

Paragon is noted for its state-of-the-art, high-performance catamarans, intimate gatherings (only 24–38 passengers, depending on the trip), and landing rights at Manele Bay, which give the Lanai trip a special edge. (Trilogy is the only other outfitter that lands on Lanai, and the only one that takes you on an island tour.) This quality outfitter is a nice choice if you want to embark on a Molokini cruise, an easy afternoon snorkel cruise, or a champagne sunset sail from Lahaina, too.

Departures from Maalaea Harbor (at the Highway 30/130 junction), Maalaea, and Lahaina Harbor, on Front Street, Lahaina, depending on cruise. ☎ *800-441-2087 or 808-244-2087.* www.sailmaui.com. *Cruises (which include drinks and hors d'oeuvres or full meals, depending on the outing you choose): $55–$154 adults, $28–$104 kids ages 4–12. Usually free for children 3 and under, but $20 fee applies to some cruises. 15 percent online advance-booking discount available at press time.*

Trilogy Excursions

Book these trips in advance, because Trilogy — the Mercedes of Maui snorkel-sail operators — offers the island's most popular snorkel-sail trips, hands down. They're the most expensive, too, but the quality is high. The trips feature first-rate catamarans, top-quality equipment, great food, and the best crew in the business. What's more, Trilogy is the only Lanai cruise operator other than Paragon (earlier) that's allowed to land on the island's Hulopoe Beach, a terrific marine preserve that's one of the best snorkel and dolphin-watching spots in Hawaii, for a fun-filled day of sailing and snorkeling. It's also the only operator that can offer a ground tour of the island (as part of the deluxe Ultimate Seafari). Certainly a quality experience, but I've heard some complaints recently that Trilogy has become a little too slick and commercial for some tastes; book with a smaller operator, like Paragon, if you want a more intimate experience.

Trilogy also offers terrific half-day snorkel-sail trips to Molokini and unique snorkel-sail trips off Kaanapali Beach. No matter which trip you take, you'll find that the Trilogy crews are knowledgeable (they always have a naturalist on board), and the state-of-the-art boats are comfortable, well-equipped, and meticulously maintained. All trips include a continental breakfast (with home-baked cinnamon buns) and a very tasty barbecue lunch (shipboard on the half-day trip, ashore on the Lanai trip). You should know, however, that they may make you wear a flotation device no matter how good your swimming skills are; if wearing a life jacket is going to bother you, ask when you book.

Scuba upgrades are available for first-timers and certified divers alike on most Trilogy excursions to Molokini ($59–$69).

Departures from Maalaea Harbor (at the Highway 30/130 junction), Maalaea; Lahaina Harbor, on Front Street, Lahaina; or Kaanapali Beach, Kaanapali, depending on cruise. ☎ *888-225-6284 or 808-874-5649.* www.sailtrilogy.com. *Full-day Lanai cruises: $208 adults, $104 kids 3–15, including barbecue lunch and island tour. (Deluxe Ultimate Seafari version with Jeep safari and champagne return sail: $219 adults, $110 kids.) Half-day Molokini or Kaanapali cruise: $121 adults, $61 kids. Scuba add-ons available. Shorter Kaanapali sunset cruise: $65 adults, $33 kids; 2-hour Kaanapali whale-watching cruise: $43 adults, $22 kids. 10 percent online-only 7-day advance-booking discount available at press time.*

Scuba diving

Molokini is one of Hawaii's top dive spots thanks to calm, clear, protected waters and an abundance of marine life at every level, from clouds of yellow butterfly fish to white-tipped reef sharks to manta rays. This crescent-shaped crater has three tiers of diving: a 35-foot plateau inside the crater basin (used by beginning divers and snorkelers), a wall sloping to 70 feet just beyond the inside plateau, and a sheer wall on the outside and backside of the crater that plunges 350 feet below the surface.

Other top dive spots include the pristine waters off the island of **Lanai,** whose south and west coasts are a dream come true for divers looking for a one-of-a-kind setting.

You need to book a dive boat to get to Molokini or Lanai. **Lahaina Divers** (☎ **800-998-3483** or 808-667-7496; www.lahainadivers.com) is a five-star PADI facility that such publications as *Scuba Diving* magazine have lauded as one of Hawaii's top dive operators. The company can take certified divers to Molokini or Lanai aboard one of its big, comfortable dive boats for two- to four-tank dives ranging in price from $109 to $209; West Maui dives start at $109. Instruction is available for divers of all experience levels, and the Discover Scuba package for beginners starts at just $139 (check for Internet specials). Full open-water training packages are also available, as well as specialty training in deep diving, underwater photography, and more. Lahaina Divers is happy to take divers with disabilities, too. They'll also direct experienced, certified divers to Maui's best beach dives.

Or contact **Ed Robinson's Diving Adventures** (☎ **800-635-1273** or 808-879-3584; www.mauiscuba.com/erd1.htm), which caters to certified divers from a South Maui base. A widely published underwater photographer, Ed is one of Maui's best; most of his business is repeat customers. Ed offers personalized two-tank dives, three-tank adventures, Lanai trips, and sunset and night dives; prices start at $130. Custom dives are also available, plus discounts for multiday dives.

For two-tank boat dives to Molokini and nearby Maui waters, I also recommend **Mike Severns Diving** (☎ **808-879-6596**; www.mikeseverns diving.com), which takes 12 divers at a time out from Kihei in two groups of six for a quiet and crowd-free experience. The price is $145, including gear, with discounts available if you have your own equipment or schedule multiday dives. Private charters are also available.

If you've never been scuba diving before but want to discover how, contact either Lahaina Divers or **Bobby Baker's Maui Sun Divers** (☎ **877-879-3337** or 808-879-3337; www.mauisundivers.com). This outfit specializes in training beginners in small groups, and it offers introductory two-tank dives for $110 and multiple-day starter and certification programs.

Ocean kayaking

My favorite kayaking trips are offered by **Maui Eco Tours** (☎ **808-891-2223**; www.mauiecotours.com), which offers a range of wonderful guided kayak tours for beginning and more experienced kayakers and snorkelers alike. I've found their guides to be some of the best out there; ours got in the water with us at snorkel time and knowledgably narrated our underwater tour, for a genuinely rich experience, instead of just leaving us to our own devices to look-see. The three-hour Discovery tour, which departs from South Maui's Makena Landing, is ideal for first-time kayakers and first-time-to-Maui kayakers alike. It's $74 for adults and $37 for kids under 12; there's also an advanced adults-only Makena-area tour called the Xplorer for $84 per person. Summer visitors might consider the terrific Escapade trip, which explores gorgeous Honolua Bay in Kapalua; this adults-only trip is $89 per person. Whale-watching trips are also offered in winter — and there's no getting closer to the magnificent mammoths than on a kayak. Check online for Web specials and on-sale dates, which can save you as much as 25 percent.

Another good kayaking outfitter for beginners and accomplished kayakers alike is **South Pacific Kayaks & Outfitters** (☎ **800-776-2326** or 808-875-4848; www.southpacifickayaks.com). South Pacific offers a range of kayak tours that launch from both South and West Maui and incorporate whale-watching in winter. The excellent guides are all very knowledgeable and ecology minded. What's more, single and double kayaks are both available, which is not always the case when you take a guided tour (doubles are most common); let them know your preference when you book. Tour prices run from $65 to $139 per person, with custom options available.

If you're an experienced kayaker capable of setting out on your own, South Pacific can rent you single or double kayaks for $40 or $60 a day, respectively. They'll meet you at Makena Landing in South Maui at 7 a.m., and be there at noon to pick your kayak back up from you; call at least a day in advance to reserve. Weekly rates and islandwide delivery (for an additional charge) are also available.

If you're hanging out in East Maui, contact **Hana-Maui Sea Sports** (☎ **808-248-7711** or 808-264-9566; www.hana-maui-seasports.com), which offers guided kayak and snorkel tours to one of the healthiest, most vital reefs in Hawaii daily at 11 a.m. for $120 per person. Tours leave from Hana Bay. Advance reservations are highly recommended, because no more than six to eight people are taken out at once. Reservations are also available through the Hotel Hana-Maui activities desk.

Winter whale-watching

From January through April, the world's largest mammals migrate from frigid Alaska to balmy Hawaii. More than any other Hawaiian Island, Maui is your best perch for spotting Pacific humpback whales in winter. Because whales prefer water depths of less than 600 feet, these endangered gentle giants come in relatively close to shore. You can see them regularly from the beach in prime season, spouting and *spyhopping* (peeking above the waterline to "spy" on what's going on). They often prefer the west, or leeward, sides of the islands.

From December through April, virtually all boats that operate from Maui combine whale-watching with their regular adventures, and a good number offer dedicated whale-watching cruises in season. Most notable among the outfitters offering dedicated whale-watching cruises is the **Pacific Whale Foundation Eco-Adventures** (☎ **800-942-5311** or 808-249-8811; www.pacificwhale.org). (See the section "Ocean cruising to Molokini and Lanai and other on-deck adventures," earlier in this chapter.) The channel separating Maui from Lanai and Molokai is a whale-watching hot spot, so Lanai cruises, in particular, are always an excellent bet.

You don't have to shell out the bucks for a pricey cruise to see whales. In season, you can spot them right from shore. Just look out to sea — just about any west-facing beach offers you a prime whale-watching opportunity.

Follow these tips to increase your humpback-spotting chances:

✔ **After you see a whale, keep watching in the same vicinity.** They travel in groups and often stay down for 20 minutes or so and then pop back up to take in some air and play a little. Be patient, and you're likely to see several.

✔ **Bring your binoculars from home.** You see so much more with a little magnification.

✔ **Pick a spot nearly anywhere along the West Maui coast for whale-watching.** Whales love to frolic in the channel separating the Valley Isle from Molokai and Lanai. A great place to park yourself is **McGregor Point Scenic Overlook,** a scenic lookout at mile marker 9 on the Honoapiilani Highway (Highway 30), on the way to Lahaina from Maalaea. Another good West Maui whale-watching perch is the straight part of Honoapiilani Highway, between McGregor Point and Olowalu. However, do yourself and everybody else a favor, and pull over to the side of the road before you look out to sea; whale-spotting along the highway has caused more than a few accidents.

✔ The Pacific Whale Foundation (see earlier in this section) operates a **Whale Information Station** at McGregor Point that's staffed by friendly and knowledgeable whale-expert naturalists, daily from 8:30 a.m. to 3:30 p.m. from December through April. Just stop by — they even have high-powered binoculars you can use, and they're happy to share whale-watching tips and facts galore. Call ☎ **800-WHALE-1-1** (800-942-5311) or 808-249-8811, or visit www.pacific whale.org for more information.

Surfing

If you've always wanted to surf, Maui is a great place to fulfill the dream. Surfers know Maui has the easiest surf in all Hawaii, making it an excellent spot for many first-timers to learn.

The motto at the **Nancy C. Emerson School of Surfing** (☎ **808-244-7873;** www.mauisurfclinics.com) is, "If a dog can surf, so can you!" — a dubious challenge, but a surprisingly comforting one, too. A pro international surfing champ, an instructor since 1973, a stunt performer in movies like *Waterworld,* and a surf teacher to such celebs as Kiefer Sutherland and Beau Bridges, Nancy has pioneered the technique of teaching completely unskilled folks to surf in one two-hour lesson. You can, really — I've seen it happen firsthand. The instructors are professional and personable; you'll probably have your lesson on the beach behind 505 Front St., in Lahaina, where the surf breaks are big enough for beginners but not overwhelming. A beginning lesson starts at $100 per person for a one-hour private lesson, $165 for two hours, or $78 per person for two hours with a group; I recommend going for the group option. Experienced surfers can take full- and multiday private lessons and group clinics with Nancy's skilled instructors.

Action Sports Surf School (☎ **808-871-5857;** www.actionsportsmaui. com), with one location near the Kahului airport and one in Kihei, offers everything from kiddie lessons to extreme tow-in and strap surfing lessons for experienced board riders; beginning lessons start at a very reasonable $69 for a two-hour lesson. If you're hanging out in East Maui, contact **Hana-Maui Sea Sports** (☎ **808-248-7711** or 808-264-9566; www. hana-maui-seasports.com). In addition to their excellent kayak and snorkel tours, this terrific outfitter also offers surfing lessons by an experienced surf instructor and certified lifeguard. Beginners are welcome. Reservations are also available through the Hotel Hana-Maui activities desk.

Book your surfing lesson for early in your stay. That way, if conditions aren't right on your scheduled day, you have plenty of time to reschedule.

Expert surfers visit Maui in winter, when the surf's really up. The best surfing beaches include **Honolua Bay,** north of Kapalua; **Maalaea,** just outside the breakwall of the Maalaea Harbor; and **Hookipa Beach Park** in Paia, where surfers get the waves until noon, when the windsurfers take over. If you have a bit of experience but don't want a serious challenge, head to the **505 Front Street Beach,** next to Lahaina Harbor in Lahaina, where even long-surfing locals regularly catch the easy waves.

Second Wind Sail & Surf, 111 Hana Hwy. (between Dairy Road and Hobron Avenue), Kahului (☎ **800-936-7787** or 808-877-7467; www.second windmaui.com), has the best fleet of rental boards on the island ($20 per day, or $110 for a week), and friendly service to boot.

For daily reports on wind and surf conditions, call the **Wind and Surf Report** at ☎ **808-877-3611.**

Windsurfing and kiteboarding

Expert windsurfers will want to head to Paia's world-famous **Hookipa Beach,** known all over the globe for its brisk winds and excellent waves in the afternoons. When the winds turn northerly, **Kihei** is the spot to be; some days you can see whales in the distance behind the windsurfers. The northern end of Kihei is best. At **Ohukai Park,** the first beach along South Kihei Road, the winds are good, the water is easy to access, and a long strip of grass is available on which to assemble your gear. If you have enough experience to head out on your own but you want manageable waves, head to **Kanaha Beach Park** near the airport in Kahului, which is where all the top schools take their students.

You can find top-quality rental gear for windsurfing and kitesurfing from **Second Wind Sail & Surf,** 111 Hana Hwy. (between Dairy Road and Hobron Avenue), Kahului (☎ **800-936-7787** or 808-877-7467; www.secondwindmaui.com). The company is also an excellent contact if you want to arrange windsurfing lessons, for beginners and experienced windsurfers alike, as well as kiteboarding lessons for experienced wave riders. **Action Sports Maui** (☎ **808-871-5857;** www.actionsportsmaui.com) also offers lessons in windsurfing and kiteboarding, as well as paragliding for high-soaring adventurers.

Book your windsurfing or kiteboarding lesson for early in your stay. That way, if conditions aren't right on your scheduled day, you have plenty of time to reschedule.

Sportfishing

Are you ready to head out on the open waves in search of big-game fish, such as marlin, tuna, and wahoo? **Hawaii Fishing Adventures and Charters** (☎ 877-388-1376; www.sportfishhawaii.com) can book a first-class charter for you out of Maalaea or Lahaina harbors on Maui. Half-day private charters start at $600.

Playing Safely in the Ocean

Even people with ocean experience should know a few things before they plunge into Maui's waters.

- ✔ **Never, ever turn your back to the ocean.** Big waves can come seemingly out of nowhere and travel far upshore in a matter of minutes. Always keep one eye on the waves, even if you're just beach-combing or taking a casual stroll along the water's edge. Never let a younger child go into the ocean alone and always keep an eye on your older children.

- ✔ **Get out of the water when the swells come.** Ocean conditions can change in a few hours. Surf that was placid and safe for swimming one day can be dangerous the next.

- ✔ **Use the buddy system.** Always swim with a partner.

- ✔ **Swim at beaches with lifeguards.** When swimming at an unfamiliar beach, ask the lifeguard about the current conditions, and where the safest place to swim is. If the beach doesn't have a lifeguard, ask other beachgoers, some of whom are likely to be locals. If no one is around to ask, stay out of the water: Hidden rip currents, undertows, and submerged rocks may turn a pleasant dip into a disaster.

Shark!

Sharks aren't a big problem in Hawaii. In fact, they're so seldom seen that locals actually *look forward* to spotting one. Since 1882, Hawaii has only had 113 shark attacks, around 15 of which have been fatal (the last one, at this writing, in 2004). When you realize that about 7.5 million visitors play in Hawaii's waters every year (not to mention the locals), that number is infinitesimal.

Still, just to be on the safe side, use these good shark-avoidance tips:

- ✔ **Don't swim at sunrise, sunset, or where the water is murky.** Sharks may mistake you for lunch.

- ✔ **Don't swim alone.** It's never a good idea.

- ✔ **Refrain from excessive splashing.**

> ✔ **Don't swim with open wounds, or where bloody fish are in the water.** Surprise, surprise: Sharks become aggressive around blood.
>
> ✔ **Get out of the water if turtles and fish are fleeing the area.** As you might expect, they're pretty savvy about these things.

Avoiding things that sting

Most people manage to hang out in tropical waters without incident. But if you do happen to run into a jellyfish, the pointy spine of a sea urchin, or some sharp coral, take the following advice.

According to Hawaiian folklore, in order to treat certain ocean injuries, the injured party should — I'm not making this up — urinate on the wound. However, urinating on any sort of ocean wound (or probably any wound, for that matter) won't help, so don't let anybody talk you into it.

Portuguese man-of-war

Portuguese man-of-war stings are painful and a nuisance but rarely harmful; fewer than one in a thousand requires medical treatment. The best prevention is to watch for these jellyfish as you snorkel or swim: They're a bluish-purple floating bubble with a long tail (look for the hanging tentacles below the surface). Get out of the water if anyone near you spots one because they tend to hang out in clusters. Also pay attention when walking near the water because even beached man-of-wars can deliver a nasty sting.

Reactions to stings range from mild burning and reddening to severe welts and blisters. Pick off any visible tentacles with a gloved hand, a stick, or anything handy, rinse the sting with saltwater or fresh water, and apply ice to prevent swelling and fight pain. Most man-of-war stings disappear in 15 to 20 minutes. If pain persists or a rash or other symptoms develop, see a doctor.

Box jellyfish

These transparent, square-shaped bell jellyfish are nearly impossible to see in the water. Fortunately, they seem to follow a monthly cycle: Eight to ten days after the full moon, they appear in the waters on the *leeward* side (the side away from the wind) of each island and hang around for about three days. Also, they seem to sting more in the morning hours, when they're on or near the surface. The best prevention is to get out of the water if you spot one.

Stings range from no visible marks to red hivelike welts, blisters, and pain (a burning sensation) lasting from ten minutes to eight hours. To treat a sting, start by pouring regular household vinegar on the affected area; this action stops additional burning. Don't rub the area with anything. Then pick off any vinegar-soaked tentacles with a stick and apply an ice pack for pain. Most box-jellyfish stings disappear by themselves without any treatment, but see a doctor if you experience shortness of breath, weakness, palpitations, muscle cramps, or any other severe symptoms.

Punctures

Most sea-related punctures come from stepping on or brushing against the needlelike spines of sea urchins. Be careful when you're in the water; don't put your foot down (even if you have booties or fins on; the sea urchin's spines can puncture a wetsuit) if you can't clearly see the bottom.

A sea-urchin sting can result in burning, aching, swelling, and discoloration (black or purple) around the area where the spines broke off. Pull out any protruding spines; the body absorbs any spines within 24 hours to three weeks, or the remainder of the spines will work themselves out. Again, if people recommend vinegar or urine, ignore them.

Cuts

The most common cuts are from corals. Take seriously any cut you get in the ocean. Contrary to popular belief, coral can't grow inside your body; however, bacteria can — and very often does. The best way to prevent cuts is to wear a wetsuit, gloves, and reef shoes. Never, under any circumstances, should you touch coral. And *never* walk on coral, even when you are wearing reef shoes. Not only can you cut yourself, but also you can damage a living organism that took decades to grow.

The symptoms of a coral cut can range from a slight scratch to severe welts and blisters. Gently pull the edges of the skin open and remove any embedded coral or grains of sand with tweezers. Rinse the cut well with fresh water (*not* ocean water). If the cut is bleeding, press a clean cloth against it until it stops. If bleeding continues or the edges of the injury are jagged, find a doctor.

Landlubbers' curse: Seasickness

You're not alone: Some 90 percent of the population tends toward seasickness. The waters in Maui can range from calm as a lake to downright frightening (in stormy conditions), but they usually fall somewhere in between. Generally, expect rougher conditions in winter than in summer. Afternoon seas can be very choppy year-round; the channel between Maui and Lanai has caused at least a few snorkelers to upchuck their barbecue lunch.

If you've never been out on a boat before, or if you've found yourself seasick in the past, take the following precautions:

The day before . . .

> ✔ Avoid alcohol, caffeine, and citrus and other acidic juices, as well as greasy, spicy, or other hard-to-digest foods.
>
> ✔ Get a good night's sleep.

That day . . .

> ✔ Use whatever seasickness prevention works best for you — pills, a patch, an acupressure wrist band, ginger-root tea or capsules, or any combination — *before* you board. After you set sail, using these preventive measures generally isn't going to help.
>
> ✔ After you're onboard, stay as low and as near the center of the boat as possible. Avoid the fumes (especially if it's a diesel boat); stay in the fresh air and watch the horizon. Don't read.
>
> ✔ If you start to feel queasy, drink clear fluids like water and eat something bland, such as a soda cracker.

Chapter 13

Exploring the Island

●●●

In This Chapter

▶ Watching the magical sunrise or sunset at Haleakala National Park

▶ Cruising the Heavenly Road to Hana

▶ Sightseeing via tour, on foot, or by helicopter

▶ Discovering Maui's history

▶ Golfing, horseback riding, and playing tennis

●●●

*M*aui is home to two of Hawaii's most renowned attractions: Haleakala National Park, a remarkable, otherworldly crater at the heart of the island that offers an incredible, mystical view of sunrise and sunset (not to mention one-of-a-kind hiking and biking fun); and the Heavenly Road to Hana, one of the most scenic drives in the United States.

Visiting Haleakala National Park

Haleakala (*ha*-lay-*ah*-kah-la) — the House of the Sun — is the massive 10,023-foot-high mountain that forms the core of Maui. It's also one of Hawaii's two U.S. national parks (the other is the Big Island's Hawaii Volcanoes National Park), designated as such in 1961, and Maui's biggest natural attraction. Each year, some 2 million people drive to the summit of Haleakala to peer down into the crater of the world's largest dormant volcano. (Its official status is "active but not currently erupting," even though Haleakala has remained dormant since 1790.) The crater is impressive. At 3,000 feet deep, 7½ miles long by 2½ miles wide, and encompassing 19 square miles, it could hold half of Manhattan. More than anything, it resembles a barren moonscape.

This stark, rugged place is breathtakingly beautiful in its own way: a desolate, otherworldly canyon painted in hues of blue and green and red. Just driving up the mountain is an experience in itself: The road climbs from sea level to 10,000 feet in just 37 miles, and the views are magnificent along the entire route. At first glance, the landscape looks like nothing more than a dry and barren wasteland. But soon, a fascinating, multihued geologic world emerges — a surprisingly fragile one that supports a number of the world's rarest examples of flora and fauna.

Among the rare endangered species that call Haleakala home are the nene (*nay*-nay), a gray-brown Hawaiian goose that doesn't migrate, prefers rock-hard lava beds to lakes, and is now protected as the state bird, and the silvery-green, porcupiney silversword plant, which grows only in Hawaii, lives for about 50 years, blooms once in a beautiful purple bouquet, and dies.

Nene like to hang out around park headquarters, so you can spot one or two there — if you don't hear their distinctive call ("Nay! Nay!") first. Kalahaku Overlook (see the "Driving back down the mountain" section, later in this chapter) is a good place to see silverswords. Please don't feed the nene and leave the silverswords where you see them.

Haleakala is best known for its mystical sunrise vistas. Crowds of visitors drive here in the dark, predawn hours to watch the spectacle of dawn breaking over the crater. If you decide to join the early-morning crowds, stick around after sunrise for some excellent hiking opportunities. Or do what a lot of people do: Hop on a bike and coast down the switchback road to the base of the mountain, enjoying magnificent views as you go.

Sunrise at Haleakala has become so popular that the park was experiencing theme-park crowds and L.A.-style gridlock in the predawn hours, seriously damaging both the mood and the protected natural environment. In response, the National Park Service instituted policies in late 2005 that limited the number of vehicles allowed into the summit parking lots. You should know that if lots are too crowded, there's a chance — albeit a small one — that you may be turned away at the entrance gate.

That's the bad news. The good news is that the premium value of getting up in the middle of the night to greet sunrise atop Haleakala is largely a myth. Many — including yours truly — believe that sunset is actually Haleakala's finest hour. The crater is in shadow at sunrise; by sunset, it has positioned itself to bring the colors of Haleakala into their full, vibrant hues. Many consider Haleakala to offer the finest sunsets in Hawaii — and sunset doesn't offer the risk that sunrise holds, since the cloud cover that might block a sunrise view can be difficult to evaluate under cover of darkness. And best of all, you won't be too exhausted to enjoy the fabulous views. (Another option is go up at night, when stargazing from the summit can be spectacular. You might bring your binoculars or rent a pair, and make the ascent if the sky is clear.)

The park actually contains two separate and distinct destinations: Haleakala Summit and the Kipahulu Coast. Lush, green, and tropical, Kipahulu is a world apart from the summit — and accessible only from the east side of the island, near Hana. No road links the summit and the coast, so Hana is a completely separate outing. I concentrate solely on the summit-related info in the following sections. For a discussion of Kipahulu and its biggest attraction, Oheo (oh-*hay*-oh) Gulch, see "Driving the Heavenly Road to Hana," later in this chapter.

Haleakala National Park

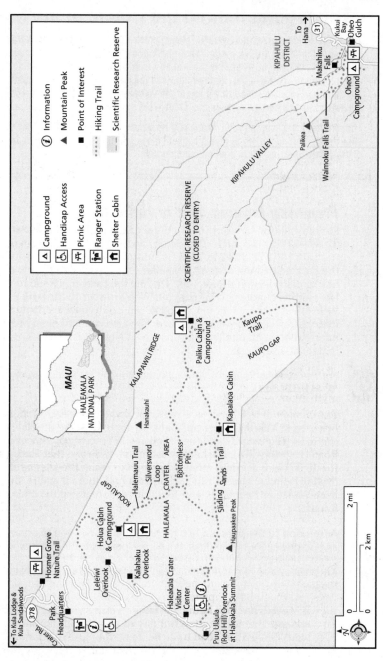

The legend behind the House of the Sun

The name *Haleakala* actually means "House of the Sun." The story of how this wild-looking volcano got such a magnificent name goes like this: One day, a mom complained that the sun sped across the sky so quickly that her tapa cloth didn't have enough time to dry. So in the predawn hours of the next morning, her thoughtful son, the demi-god Maui, climbed to the top of the volcano. When the sun rose above the horizon, Maui lassoed it, bringing it to a halt in the sky.

The sun begged Maui to let go. Maui said he would, on one condition: That the sun slow its trip across the sky to give the island more sunlight. The sun agreed. In honor of the agreement, islanders dubbed the mountain "House of the Sun."

Preparing for your visit to Haleakala

For information before you go, contact **Haleakala National Park** at ☎ **808-572-4400** for information on the Haleakala-summit (main) area of the park (dial ☎ **808-248-7375** for information and the ranger station at the park's Kipahulu district, near Hana, which is a completely separate outing discussed in the section "Driving the Heavenly Road to Hana," later in this chapter). Or point your Web browser to the park's official Web site at www.nps.gov/hale. You can call to have camping and hiking information sent to you in advance. You also can find plenty of useful information at an unofficial but excellent site, www.haleakala. national-park.com.

For the sunrise time and viewing conditions at Haleakala summit, call ☎ **808-877-5111.**

The summit of Haleakala is 37 miles, or about a one-and-a-half-hour drive, from Kahului in Central Maui. To get there, take the Haleakala Highway (Highway 37 and then Highway 377) to wiggly Haleakala Crater Road (Highway 378), the heavily switchbacked road that leads you to the 10,000-foot summit. Allow two hours to reach the summit if you're driving from Lahaina or Kihei, two and a half hours if you're arriving from Wailea or Kaanapali, and 15 minutes more if you're coming from Kapalua.

Admission to the park is $10 per car, which allows you to come and go as you please for seven days. It's $5 per person for individual walk-ins.

Keep these tips in mind as you plan your visit to Haleakala National Park:

> ✔ **If Maui is the first Hawaiian island you're visiting, schedule your sunrise visit for the first full day of your trip.** Your body clock won't be on Hawaii time yet, so it shouldn't be too hard to get up at 3 a.m. — because your body will still think that it's anywhere from

5 to 9 a.m. if you're from the mainland. If Maui is the last island on your itinerary, schedule your sunrise visit for the final day of your trip, because you need to start reacclimating yourself to your at-home hour anyway. Or, as I recommend earlier, simply opt for a visit later in the day, so as not to disturb your normal sleep patterns.

✔ **Dress warmly, in layers, no matter what time of year you visit.** Temperatures at the summit usually range between 40°F and 65°F but can drop below freezing any time of year after you factor in the wind chill, especially in the predawn hours. Wear a hat and sturdy shoes and bring a blanket if you don't have a warm jacket. The weather is unpredictable at the summit, so be prepared for wind and rain in winter, no matter what the time of day. Don't be fooled by the coastline conditions. Call ☎ 808-877-5111 for the summit forecast.

✔ **Bring drinking water.** You need plenty of water on hand, especially if you plan on hiking.

✔ **Remember that this locale is a high-altitude wilderness area.** The thinness of the air makes some people dizzy; you may also experience lightheadedness, shortness of breath, nausea, headaches, and dehydration. The park recommends that pregnant women and people with heart or respiratory problems consult a doctor before ascending to high elevations.

✔ **Fill up your gas tank before you head to Haleakala.** The last gas station is 27 miles below the summit at Pukalani. Fill up the night before if you're going for sunrise, because finding an open gas station at 4 a.m. is nearly impossible.

If you want to explore the park thoroughly, you may want to consider booking a Haleakala day hike with **Hike Maui, Maui Eco-Adventures** or **Maui Hiking Safaris;** see the section "Enjoying Guided Nature Hikes," later in this chapter. If you're interested in a stay near the park for a few nights so that you can explore it more fully, you'll find some accommodations that fill the bill in Chapter 10.

Arriving at the park and making the drive to the summit

About a mile from the entrance is the **Park Headquarters Visitor Center,** open daily from 8 a.m. to 3:45 p.m. It's a great place to pick up park information, including the latest schedule of guided walks and ranger talks. If, however, you arrive before dawn, all you can do here is use the round-the-clock restrooms; the ones here are much nicer than the ones at the summit, so I highly recommend making a pit stop on the way up. Drinking water is also available.

Traveling along Haleakala Crater Road, you pass two scenic overlooks on the way to the summit. Stop at the one just beyond mile marker 17, **Leleiwi Overlook,** if only to get out, stretch, and get accustomed to the heights. From the parking area, a short trail leads to a panoramic view of the lunarlike crater. (The other overlook, Kalahaku, is most easily accessible on the descent. Check out the "Driving back down the mountain" section, later in this chapter.)

Continue on, and you'll soon reach **Haleakala Visitor Center,** 11 miles from the park entrance (open daily 6:30 a.m.–3:30 p.m.), which offers spectacular views and some bare-bones restrooms. Park rangers also offer excellent, informative, and free naturalist talks daily throughout the day from the center. (Call ahead to confirm the next day's schedule.)

The actual summit — and the ideal sunrise-viewing perch — is beyond the turnoff for the visitor center, at **Puu Ulaula Overlook** (Red Hill). At Puu Ulaula, a triangular glass building serves as a windbreak and the best sunrise-viewing spot. After the spectacle of sunrise, you can often see all the way to the snowcapped summit of Mauna Kea on the Big Island if it's clear. Haleakala Observatories (nicknamed Science City), which isn't open to the public, is also located there. This is also one of the park's best sunset-viewing perches.

Hitting the park's trails

If you want to hike the park, I strongly suggest going with a guide. The park is an outlandishly huge, empty place. You can view it better with someone who can lead you in the right direction and help you understand what you're seeing. Park rangers offer a range of free guided hikes; call for the latest schedule (☎ **808-572-4400**) and to find out what to wear and bring. (Sturdy shoes and water are musts.)

Also consider taking one of the guided Haleakala Crater hikes offered by **Hike Maui, Maui Eco-Adventures,** and **Maui Hiking Safaris.** I really like the extended views of the crater that professional guides offer on these private tours. See the section "Enjoying Guided Nature Hikes," later in this chapter.

If you're a regular hiker and you're prepared for a challenge, consider the **Sliding Sands Trail.** Its Hawaiian name is Keoneheehee Trail, but this arduous trail is better known for its powdery cinder sands. The trail starts at the bulletin board by the entrance to the summit parking lot. It's a 4-mile hike, descending a steep 2,800 feet to the valley floor. Your best bet for a challenging but rewarding day hike is to take the trail 2½ miles in to Ka Luu o ka Oo, the first cinder cone along the trail, where the shifting sands illuminate with vibrant color. This is a difficult trail and weather shifts dramatically at the summit, so be sure to come prepared with good hiking shoes, layered clothing (including rain protection), and plenty of sun protection and water.

If you don't want to bother with a serious hike but just want a glimpse of the park's peculiar brand of natural beauty, take a half-hour walk down the half-mile **Hosmer Grove Nature Trail,** which anybody can do. The trail is well-marked, with placards that point out what you're seeing along the way. Ask the ranger at the visitor center to direct you to the trailhead.

If you want to strike out on your own along the park's more serious trails, you can preview your options online at www.haleakala. national-park.com (click on Hiking Guide) or call ahead. Rangers are always happy to provide you with complete trail information.

Driving back down the mountain

Put your rental car in low gear on the way down so that you don't ride your brakes.

Around mile marker 24 is **Kalahaku Overlook,** the best place to spot the spiky, alien-like silversword plant, and to take in some fabulous panoramic views.

At the mountain's base, where you turn onto Haleakala Crater Road from the Haleakala Highway, is **Kula,** the closest resemblance to a gateway town that Haleakala has. Kula is most notable for its two restaurants, Kula Sandalwoods Cafe and the Kula Lodge & Restaurant, both of which serve great post-sunrise breakfast and lunch. (See Chapter 11 for more information.)

Exploring the volcano by horseback

My absolute favorite way to explore Haleakala Crater is with **Pony Express Tours** (☎ **808-667-2200;** www.ponyexpresstours.com), which offers guided trail rides down the crater's Sliding Sands Trail, which descends from the crater rim 2,500 feet to the crater floor, for a majestic 7½-mile round-trip ride. The guides are friendly experts, and the horses are good natured and extremely well taken care of; mine was an agreeable red-haired boy named Leo, and my day exploring Haleakala with him was the highlight of my last trip to Maui. These all-day Haleakala trail rides are $182 per person, and require you to have at least minimal riding experience; this is strictly a nose-to-tail ride, so as long as you know the basics, you'll be in good shape. Rides start daily at 8:30 a.m., with a second ride offered on days that demand it. A two-hour *paniolo* ranch ride is also offered for $110. Book well in advance — ideally, before you leave home — in order to secure your spot on this terrific trip.

At press time, Pony Express was offering 10 percent off for those who booked their trips online.

Biking down the volcano

Another great way to experience Haleakala is to cruise down it, from summit to base, on a bicycle. The guided ride is quite an experience, with stunning views the entire way. And you don't need to be an expert cyclist to do it; you just have to be able to ride a bike. In fact, you barely have to pedal — you'll coast down at a nice, leisurely pace. (The constant switchbacks keep you from picking up too much speed.)

These tours used to be offered from Haleakala's summit at sunrise and throughout the day, but the National Park Service has suspended all tours from within Haleakala National Park following a glut of increased traffic. As of this writing, most bike tours start at 6,500 feet elevation, just outside the park entrance. The trips are still quite fun, but you have to start the day atop Haleakala on your own. I'm sure that the big outfitters will reinstate full service as soon as the National Park Service allows; check the outfitters' Web sites or call for further information.

Maui's oldest downhill company is **Maui Downhill** (☎ **800-535-2453** or 808-871-2155; www.mauidownhill.com). Maui Downhill offers a variety of guided Haleakala bike "safaris" at sunrise, midday, and sunset, running from $125 to $195 per person. Other reliable companies include **Maui Mountain Cruisers** (☎ **800-232-6284** or 808-871-6014; www.maui mountaincruisers.com) and **Mountain Riders** (☎ **800-706-7700** or 808-242-9739; www.mountainriders.com). Prices usually include hotel pickup, transport to the top, all equipment, meals, and drop-off. Generally, riders have to be at least 12 and at least 4'10" tall. Younger kids and pregnant women can usually ride along in the van.

At press time, you could save a bundle on most of these tours by booking in advance via most of these companies' own Web sites (for example, Maui Downhill was offering $30-per-person discounts on its $125 tours!).

Coasting down Haleakala can be an incredible ride, and thousands of people come home from Maui every year claiming that it was the highlight of their trip. Still, you should know a few things before you book one of these trips. I'm not trying to discourage you, by any means; I just want you to know exactly what to expect:

- ✔ Virtually all the outfitters advertise these trips as safe, no-strain bicycle rides that anyone can do, even Grandma. However, these downhill bike tours do require some stamina, particularly in winter. Conditions can be harsh, and you have to stay in line and keep pace with the other riders as cars go by. (Drivers are usually quite respectful, so you don't have to worry about dodging traffic.) Even from 6,500 feet, the trip makes for a quite a long day.

- ✔ Summer and fall — when drive conditions and relatively mild temperatures usually prevail — are the best seasons for Haleakala downhill rides. Even though the better outfitters provide you with slick jumpsuits and headgear to protect you from the rain that you'll almost inevitably encounter at some point, count on getting cold and wet in winter and spring.

Driving the Heavenly Road to Hana

No road in Hawaii is more celebrated than the Hana Highway (Highway 36), the supercurvaceous, two-lane highway that winds along Maui's northeastern shore, offering some of the most scenic natural sightseeing in the entire state.

The Hana Highway winds for approximately 52 miles east from Kahului, in Central Maui, crossing more than 50 one-lane bridges, passing greener-than-green taro patches, magnificent seascapes, gorgeous waterfalls, botanical gardens, and rain forests before passing through the little town of Hana and ultimately ending up in one of Hawaii's most beautiful tropical places: the Kipahulu section of Haleakala National Park. Kipahulu is home to Oheo Gulch, a stunning series of waterfall pools that tumble down to the sea. (See the section "Venturing beyond Hana: Hamoa Beach and Oheo Gulch," later in this chapter.)

Despite the draws at the end of the road, this drive is about the journey, *not* the destination. The drive from end to end takes at least three hours, but allow all day for it. If you race along just to arrive in Hana as quickly as you can, you'll be as perplexed as so many others who just don't understand all the hype. Start out early, take it slow and easy, stop at the scenic points along the way, and let the Hana Road work its magic on you. It will — I promise.

Take these points into consideration as you plan your Hana Road trip:

- ✔ **Leave early.** Get up just after dawn, have an early breakfast (Charley's in Paia opens at 7 a.m.; see Chapter 11), and hit the road by 8 a.m. If you wait until midmorning to leave, you'll get stuck in bumper-to-bumper Hana Road traffic, you won't have enough time to enjoy the sights along the way, and you'll arrive at Oheo Gulch too late in the day to take a hike or a dip. To make the most of the daylight hours, leave early, particularly in the winter when days are shortest.

- ✔ **Consider booking a place to stay in Hana if you really want to take your time.** If you book a room, you can head out to Hana against the traffic in the afternoon, stay for a couple of nights so that you have a full day to enjoy East Maui's attractions (including an abundance of peace and quiet), and meander back at your own pace (once again avoiding the traffic) on the morning of the third day. (See Chapter 10 for recommendations.)

- ✔ **Fill up on gas before you set out.** If all else fails, make sure that you stop in Paia, just east of Kahului, because the next gas station is in Hana — 44 miles, 50-some bridges, and 200-plus hairpin turns down the road.

- ✔ **Don't bother if it's been raining heavily.** The Hana Highway is well paved and well maintained but can nevertheless be extremely dangerous when wet — and you can easily get stuck in muddy shoulders and pull-offs.

- ✔ **Bring your bathing suit in warm weather.** You'll find a number of waterfall pools along the way that are ideal for a refreshing dip, and folks love to swim in Oheo Gulch's placid summer pools.

The Heavenly Road to Hana

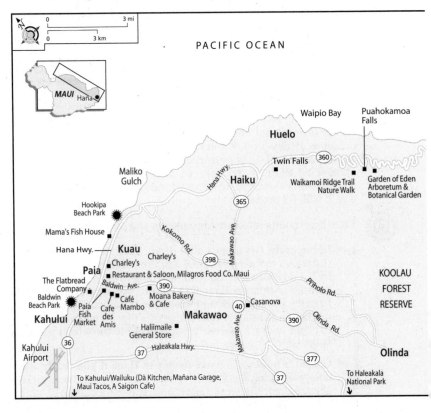

- ✔ **Only enter waterfall pools in the calmest ranger-approved conditions.** A mainland visitor was washed away to sea during a seemingly innocuous Oheo Gulch photo op in 2002. Always check with the rangers before you go in the pools. And if water seems to be running between the pools at all, stay out.

- ✔ **Bring mosquito repellent.** Lush East Maui is a buggy place.

- ✔ **Leave your road rage on the mainland.** Practice aloha as you drive the Hana Road: Give way at the one-lane bridges. Wave at passing motorists. Let the locals who drive this road with jaw-dropping speed and who pass on blind curves have the right-of-way. If the guy behind you blinks his lights, let him pass. And don't honk your horn — it's considered rude in Hawaii.

There's one exception to the no-horn-honking rule: If you reach a blind curve, *do* honk your horn to indicate that you're coming around the bend — and proceed slowly.

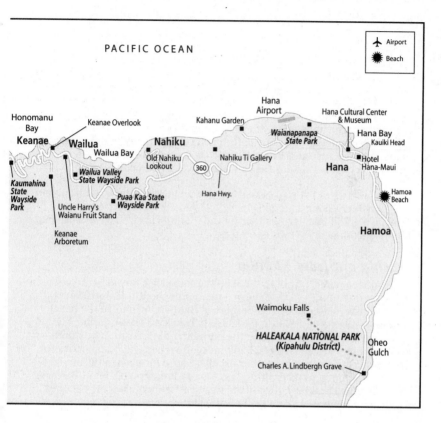

PACIFIC OCEAN

Airport
Beach

Honomanu Bay
Keanae Overlook
Keanae
Wailua
Wailua Bay
Kahanu Garden
Hana Airport
Nahiku
Old Nahiku Lookout
(360)
Nahiku Ti Gallery
Waianapanapa State Park
Hana Cultural Center & Museum
Hana Bay
Kauiki Head
Kaumahina State Wayside Park
Wailua Valley State Wayside Park
Uncle Harry's
Waianu Fruit Stand
Puaa Kaa State Wayside Park
Hana Hwy.
Hana
Hotel Hana-Maui
Hamoa Beach
Keanae Arboretum
Hamoa

Waimoku Falls

HALEAKALA NATIONAL PARK (Kipahulu District)
Oheo Gulch

Charles A. Lindbergh Grave

If you want some narration to accompany what you're seeing along the road to Hana, pick up a **Hana CD Guide** on your way out of town. The 90-minute CD is $20 at the **Hana Cassette Guide Shop** in Kahului on Dairy Road (Highway 380), next to the Shell service station just before the Hana Highway (☎ **808-572-0550**). It also comes with an accompanying detailed map of the coast and a flora guide that's worth the value of the purchase alone. I highly recommend using it in tandem with the text in this chapter because it covers many more sights and gives much more background than I have the space to include. Along with the recorded tour, you get the Hana Road map and flower guide. The Hana CD Guide Shop also has a recorded guide to Haleakala available; it opens daily at 3 a.m. to accommodate the earliest risers.

Try this route-reversal strategy: Drive directly to Oheo Gulch, at the end of the road, without stopping. Explore Hana and Oheo Gulch in the morning. Head out of Hana right after lunch and do your meandering on the way home, against traffic. The disadvantage of this strategy is that, for some, the gorgeous scenery can lose some of its magic by afternoon: You're tired, and you've been in the car a long time — you know how it goes.

The south route to and from Hana — which is officially Highway 31, but most folks call it the **Kaupo** (*cow*-po) **Road** — was closed at press time due to 2006 earthquake damage. If you're interested in checking it out as a route back to the resorts from Hana, check with your hotel or rental-car company regarding potential reopening and current road conditions. It's usually fine if the weather has been clear, but stay away if it's been raining because unpaved sections of the road can wash out. And check with your rental-car company before you set out; many rental contracts actually *forbid* customers from driving their cars on Kaupo Road, so if you get stuck, the cost for the tow will be your responsibility.

If you want to see the Hana Road but you just don't want to drive it yourself, consider taking a guided van or bus tour. See the section called "Taking a guided van or bus tour on the road to Hana," later in this chapter, for recommended tour operators.

Setting out from Kahului

A half-dozen miles east of Kahului on the Hana Highway is Paia (pa-*ee*-ah), a former mill town that's now a neohippie, boutique-dotted surf spot. **Charley's Restaurant & Saloon,** at Baldwin Avenue in the heart of town, makes an ideal stop for a hearty breakfast (see Chapter 11). Afterward, you can bop around the corner to 30 Baldwin Ave., where **Café Mambo** (☎ **808-579-8021**) offers sandwiches and box lunches for you to take on the road. Another excellent stop for a morning muffin, coffee, or a lunch to take with you is **Moana Bakery & Cafe,** 71 Baldwin Ave. (☎ **808-579-9999**). I enjoy the heavenly mango-blueberry scones here, but the whole Moana menu is delightful.

After you leave Paia, the road bends into an S-turn, where you see the entrance to **Mama's Fish House,** marked by a restored boat with Mama's logo on the side. Mama's is one of my favorite Maui restaurants, even though it's pricey; see the review in Chapter 11. Mama's also has an inn (see Chapter 10).

Just beyond Paia is **Hookipa Beach Park,** one of the greatest windsurfing spots on the planet; see Chapter 12. World-championship contests are held there, but on nearly every windy afternoon, you can watch dozens of colorful windsurfers dancing in the breeze. To watch them, don't stop on the highway, but go past the park and turn left at the entrance on the beach's far side. You can park on the high, grassy bluff or drive down to the sandy beach and park alongside the pavilion. The park also has restrooms, a shower, picnic tables, and a barbecue area.

The road narrows to one lane in each direction and starts winding around mile marker 3. But at mile marker 16, the curves really begin, one right after another. Slow down and enjoy the bucolic surroundings.

Following the road to Hana

After mile marker 16, the highway number changes from 36 to 360 and the mile markers start again at 0 (I have no idea why). I follow suit and include the 0 in this section.

At mile marker 2: The first great place to stop is **Twin Falls,** on the road's inland side; the Twin Falls Fruit Stand marks the spot. Hop over the short ladder on the right side of the red gate and walk about 3 to 5 minutes to the waterfall off to your left, or continue on another 10 to 15 minutes to the second, larger waterfall. You may notice a NO TRESPASS-ING sign at the gate, but the sign doesn't seem to bother the crowds. If it bothers you, skip Twin Falls altogether; you have plenty more to see that's not so marked farther down the road.

Just before mile marker 4: On a blind curve, look for a double row of mailboxes on the left-hand side by the pay phone. Down the road lies the remote, rural community of **Huelo,** embraced by Waipo and Hoalua bays. This fertile area was once home to a population of 75,000. Today, only a few hundred live in this serene small town, where you find a few B&Bs and vacation rentals (see Chapter 10).

After mile marker 4: The vegetation grows lusher as you head east. This area is the edge of the **Koolau Forest Reserve,** where the branches of 20- to 30-foot-tall guava trees are laden with green (not ripe) and yellow (ripe) fruit, and introduced eucalyptus trees grow as tall as 200 feet.

The upland forest gets 200 to 300 inches of rainfall annually, so you begin to see waterfalls around just about every turn as you head east from here. The one-lane bridges start, too; so drive slowly, and yield to oncoming cars.

After mile marker 6: Just before mile marker 7 is a forest of waving bamboo. Bamboo was originally brought to Hawaii by the early Polynesians for construction purposes; during the plantation era, Chinese laborers used bamboo for food and construction alike. The sight of this grove is so spectacular that drivers are often tempted to take their eyes off the road, so be very cautious. Just after mile marker 7, you can pull over at the **Kaaiea Bridge,** which offers a terrific view of the bamboo grove.

At mile marker 8: Mountain Apple trees grow along the ocean side of the road near here. Don't be surprised if you see locals fishing ripe fruit from the trees with long poles. In the summer months, the trees shed their flowers, covering the surrounding ground in a deep red hue. There's another grove on the ocean side of the road near mile marker 11.

At mile marker 9: The sign says Koolau State Forest Reserve, but the real attraction is the **Waikamoi Ridge Trail,** an easy and well-marked ¾-mile loop. This place is great to stretch your legs; look for the turnout on the right. There's another picturesque grove of bamboo just before this mile marker.

At mile marker 10: Park at the bridge and take the short walk up the stone wall–lined trail to 30-foot **Puohokamoa Falls,** tucked away in a fern-filled amphitheater surrounded by banana trees, colorful heliconias, and fragrant ginger. It isn't always running, but the gorgeous pool is a great place to take a plunge.

As you continue on the Hana Highway, the road winds through banana patches, cane grass blowing in the wind, vibrant ferns, and forests of guava trees, avocados, kukui trees, palms, and Christmas berry.

Between mile markers 10 and 11: At the halfway point, on the road's inland side, is the **Garden of Eden Arboretum and Botanical Garden** (☎ 808-572-9899; www.mauigardenofeden.com), with more than 500 exotic plants, flowers, and trees from around the Pacific (including several wild ginger plants and an impressive palm collection) on 26 acres. You can drive through the garden in about five minutes, walk its main loop in about 20 minutes, or stay a bit longer and follow any number of nature trails. The garden is open daily from 8 a.m. to 3 p.m., and admission is $10 per person. A fruit and smoothie stand offers refreshments at the gate.

Just beyond mile marker 12: Kaumahina State Wayside Park has portable toilets and picnic tables at the large parking area, plus a gorgeous view of the rugged coastline across the road.

Near mile marker 14: One of my favorite stops on the entire drive is **Honomanu Bay,** a stark rocky beach popular with net fishermen that faces a beautiful bay. Tear your eyes away, and you find incredible golden-green cliffs forming an intense backdrop as you look inland and up. The turnoff is on the left, at the stop sign just after the mile marker; don't attempt the rutted and rocky road if it has been raining recently. Swimming is best in the stream inland from the ocean because of strong rip currents offshore.

Between mile markers 16 and 17: Farther along the winding road, between mile markers 16 and 17, is a cluster of bunkhouses composing the **YMCA Camp Keanae** (☎ 808-242-9007; www.mauiymca.org). The bunkhouses, which sleep 4 to 60, are available to budget travelers; there is also an affordable oceanview cottage available for rent. A quarter-mile down is the **Keanae Arboretum,** an excellent spot to experience the tropical flora of the islands. The region's botany is divided into three parts: native forest; introduced forest; and traditional Hawaiian plants, food, and medicine. You can swim in the pools of Piinaau Stream or walk a mile-long trail into Keanae Valley, where a lovely tropical rain forest waits at the end.

If you have time to spare, the old Hawaiian village of **Keanae** stands frozen in time, one of the last coastal enclaves of native Hawaiians. They still grow taro in patches and pound it into poi (the staple of the old Hawaiian diet), pluck *opihi* (limpet) from tide pools along the jagged coast, and cast throw nets at schools of fish. The turnoff to the Keanae

Peninsula is on the left, just after the arboretum. The road passes by farms and banana bunches as it hugs the peninsula. Where the road bends, you notice a small beach where fishermen gather to catch dinner. A quarter-mile farther is the **Keanae Congregational Church,** built in 1860 of lava rocks and coral mortar, standing out in stark contrast to the green fields. Beside the church is a small beachfront park, with false kamani trees against a backdrop of black lava and a rolling turquoise ocean.

Just beyond mile marker 17: Keanae Overlook is a wide spot on the road's ocean side where you can see the entire Keanae Peninsula jutting out into the sea, with its checkerboard pattern of green taro fields and its ocean boundary etched in black lava. If time is precious, though, wait to stop after mile marker 19, where the view from the **Wailea Valley** viewpoint is even better.

Between mile markers 17 and 18: The road widens, and fruit and flower stands begin to line the road. Many of these operate on the honor system: You select your purchase and leave your money in the basket. I recommend stopping at **Waianu Fruit Stand,** on the mountain side of the road just past Keanae Arboretum, or **Uncle Harry's Fruit Stand,** just beyond the old Keanae School on the ocean side of the road. Harry Kunihi Mitchell was a legend in his time, an expert in native plants who devoted his life to the Hawaiian-rights and nuclear-free movements.

A quarter-mile after mile marker 19: For the best view of the **Wailua Peninsula** and its verdant taro fields, stop at the **Wailua Overlook** and parking area on the road's ocean side, where sun-dappled picnic tables serve up great views.

A bit farther down the road, just before the bridge on the inland side, is a pretty waterfall view.

Between mile markers 22 and 23: At **Puaa Kaa** (poo-*ah*-ah *ka*-ah) **State Wayside Park,** the splash of waterfalls provides the soundtrack for a small park area with restrooms and a picnic area. On the opposite side of the road from the toilets is a well-marked and paved path that leads through a patch of sweet-smelling ginger to the falls and a swimming hole.

At mile marker 24: A pretty **waterfall** on the mountain side of the highway offers a nice roadside photo op.

After mile marker 25: After the mile marker, turn toward the ocean at the steep turnoff just before the one-lane bridge and follow the well-paved but winding road 2½ miles down to the **Old Nahiku Lookout,** one of the very few points along the entire route that lets you get close to the ocean, and the finest picnic spot on the entire route. A small, grassy lawn faces rocky lava points and crashing turquoise surf for a breathtaking, up-close view. Don't swim there, but you can walk down to the rocky beach at the backside of the parking lot.

Near mile marker 29: A series of locally operated **open-air shopping stalls** sit alongside the **Nahiku Ti Gallery,** on the ocean side of the highway. The gallery is rife with low-cost, nothing-special souvenirs and a small take-away cafe, but the shopping stalls contain some real gems. You'll find fruit stands with fresh-from-the-trees tropical bounty, plus homemade coconut candy coated in pure Hawaii cane sugar; this local sweet treat is simply delicious. There's also an island **taco stand** featuring yummy fresh-caught fish, chicken, and slow-cooked kalua pig tacos (open daily except Thurs).

At mile marker 31: Turn toward the ocean on Ulaino Road and go a half-mile to **Kahanu Garden,** one of four National Tropical Botanical Gardens in Hawaii (☎ 808-248-8912; www.ntbg.org). Surrounded by a native pandanus forest (the leaf that *lauhala* products are woven from), the garden features a remarkable collection of ethno-botanical plants from the Pacific islands (with a particular concentration on plants of value to the people of Polynesia and Micronesia), plus the foundation of Poolanihale Heiau, the largest Hawaiian temple in Hawaii. The self-guided walking tour is $10 (free for kids 12 and under) and takes 30 to 40 minutes to complete; it's open Monday through Friday from 10 a.m. to 2 p.m. The road that leads to the garden entrance is rough and unpaved, but not bad; still, don't bother if it's been raining.

At mile marker 32: The turnoff for 122-acre **Waianapanapa** (why-*ah*-na-pa-*na*-pa) **State Park,** on the ocean side of highway, leads to shiny black-sand **Waianapanapa Beach,** overlooking Pailoa Bay, whose bright-green jungle backdrop and sparkling cobalt water make for quite a stunning view. On hand are picnic pavilions, restrooms, trails, and fruit stands lining the road, so come down to take a peek. The beach isn't for swimming, though. A blowhole appears when the winter surf kicks up. This natural hole in the rocks is configured so that when harsh surf kicks up, water shoots through the hole like a spout — quite an interesting sight. There's also a nice little loop trail leading to **Waianapanapa Caves.**

Arriving in Hana

Postage stamp–size Hana is a lush and charming little hamlet, but frankly, the town doesn't have much to see. As I state elsewhere in this chapter, the drive to Hana is more about the *drive* and less about *Hana.*

The few attractions include the **Hana Coast Gallery,** on the Hana Highway adjacent to the Hotel Hana-Maui (☎ 808-248-8636; www.hana coast.com), an excellent showcase for fine arts and island-made products hewn by master craftspeople, including gorgeous woodworks. The quirky **Hasegawa General Store** (☎ 808-248-8231) is worth stopping in for kicks (look for the Spam sushi vending machine near the entrance) or to use the ATM, but the prices on practical items and munchies are better across the road and up the hill at the **Hana Ranch Store** (☎ 808-248-8261). If you want a meal, there's the casual **Hana Ranch Restaurant** or the gourmet **Ka'uiki,** the main dining room at the Hotel Hana-Maui (for details, see Chapter 11).

Hana

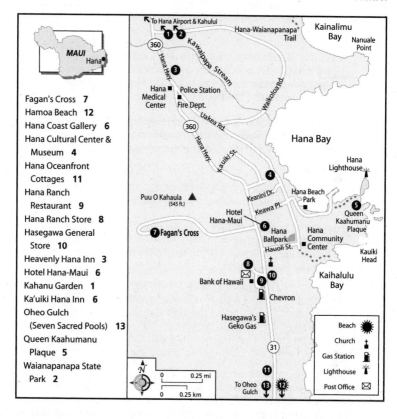

Fagan's Cross **7**
Hamoa Beach **12**
Hana Coast Gallery **6**
Hana Cultural Center &
   Museum **4**
Hana Oceanfront
   Cottages **11**
Hana Ranch
   Restaurant **9**
Hana Ranch Store **8**
Hasegawa General
   Store **10**
Heavenly Hana Inn **3**
Hotel Hana-Maui **6**
Kahanu Garden **1**
Ka'uiki Hana Inn **6**
Oheo Gulch
   (Seven Sacred Pools) **13**
Queen Kaahumanu
   Plaque **5**
Waianapanapa State
   Park **2**

Across the street from the Hotel Hana-Maui is a cattle pasture dominated by a hill. Crowning the hill is a majestic stone cross known as **Fagan's Cross.** The cross was built in honor of Paul Fagan, who saved the Hana economy following the death of the sugar industry by introducing cattle ranching to the region. A paved path leads across the pasture and around the hill to the summit, offering a cardio-stimulating walk and a captivating view over Hana as a reward. This hotel is on Hana Ranch land, so hikers are welcome to cross the gate to reach the path. The walk takes brisk hikers about an hour round-trip; be sure to bring water and wear a hat, because the sun can get harsh, even on mild days, and there's little cover along the path.

History buffs may want to head toward Hana Bay; overlooking the bay is the **Hana Cultural Center and Museum,** 4974 Uakea Rd., near the turnoff to Hana Bay (☎ **808-248-8622;** www.hookele.com/hccm), open daily from 10 a.m. to 4 p.m. (most of the time). This charming museum is dedicated to preserving the history of Hana, with exhibits showcasing traditional Hawaiian quilts and such implements of life as poi boards and fish hooks carved out of the tusks of wild pigs. Also on-site are the Old Hana Courthouse and Jailhouse and four *hale* (living structures), where you can see what it was like to live in the style of Hana's earliest settlers. Admission is $2 (free for kids 12 and under).

Hana Bay is a favorite playground of locals, although visitors tend to prefer prettier Hamoa Beach, a bit farther down the road. Protecting the far east side of the Hana Bay is **Kauiki Head,** an ironwood-covered hill that also marks the birthplace of Hawaii's Queen Kaahumanu in 1768.

If you want to see more of what's available in town, pick up a copy of the **Hana Visitors Guide,** a foldout map and pamphlet that's available free around town. If you don't run across one, stop into Hasegawa's to pick one up.

If you're spending some time in these parts, you'll be glad to know that a number of active adventures are available:

- ✔ **Hang Gliding Maui** (☎ 808-572-6557; www.hanggliding maui.com) offers tandem instructional flights aboard its engine-powered ultralight aircraft. Prices are $130 for a 30-minute lesson, $220 for an hour-long lesson.

- ✔ **Hana Lava Tube** (☎ 808-248-7308; www.mauicave.com) offers the chance to take a 30- to 45-minute self-guided tour ($12 adults, free for kids 5 and under) through Hana's ancient underground lava-tube system. Open Monday through Thursday 10:30 a.m. to 3:30 p.m. No reservations are needed, but call a day ahead just to confirm that the caves will be open; occasionally, they're open on Sunday, too.

- ✔ If you're in Hana on a Monday or Thursday afternoon and you fancy organically grown fruits, consider a tour of **Ono Organic Farms** (☎ 808-248-7779; www.onofarms.com). This certified organic farm offers guided tasting tours of its fruit orchards and coffee farm twice a week (usually Mon and Thurs) at 2:30 p.m. The cost is $35 per person; kids 9 and under visit for free. Reservations are required.

Taking a guided van or bus tour on the road to Hana

If you've rented a car and can get around easily on your own, driving around the island is definitely the preferable way to go.

But you may want to hook up with a guided tour if your mobility is limited, if you're traveling solo and don't want to make the drive to Hana on your own, or if you just want to kick back and let somebody else take the wheel.

The downside of taking a guided tour is that you have little or no control over where you go and how long you stay, and your time communing with nature at some of Hawaii's finest natural spots may be limited. Still, for some people, a guided tour is the best way to see Haleakala National Park or take in the glories of the Heavenly Road to Hana.

For small-scale, local-led van tours of the Heavenly Road to Hana and Haleakala National Park, book your guided trip with family-owned **Ekahi Tours** (☎ **888-292-2422** or 808-877-9775; www.ekahi.com). One of the great advantages of its Hana tour is that it's a circle island tour when weather permits; if the going's good, you'll not only drive the road to Hana, but also experience the desert landscape of the little-traveled back road on the return trip, which takes you along the south coast and around the back side of the Haleakala volcano. Ekahi can take you not only to Hana but also to hidden Keanae, a halfway-to-Hana tour that offers an insightful look at Maui's rural past and present. Sunrise tours of Haleakala Crater are also on offer. Ekahi tour prices range from $101 to $130 adults, $75 to $99 kids 10 and under, depending on the tour you choose; prices include a deli lunch. Discounts are available for seniors 61 and over.

Now offering guided bus tours statewide, **Polynesian Adventure Tours** (☎ **800-622-3011** or 808-877-4242; www.polyad.com) was the first to offer guided tours along the Heavenly Road to Hana and is still going strong. In addition to the Hana option, it offers both Haleakala sunrise and Iao Valley tours in minivans, big-windowed minicoaches, and full-size luxury buses. Prices run $76 to $99 for adults, $52 to $60 for kids ages 3 to 11. Book your Polynesian Adventure Tour online to get a 10 percent price break.

Venturing beyond Hana: Hamoa Beach and Oheo Gulch

About 2½ miles past Hana is the turnoff for **Hamoa Beach,** one of the most gorgeous beaches in all Hawaii — and great for swimming, to boot (in summer, anyway). For details, see Chapter 12.

About 10 luxuriant miles past Hana along the highway is **Oheo Gulch,** a dazzling series of waterfall pools cascading into the sea. Some folks call this the Seven Sacred Pools, even though it has more like two dozen. This area is the Kipahulu district of Haleakala National Park (www.nps.gove/hale), and a **ranger station** located at the back of the unpaved parking lot (☎ **808-248-7375**) is staffed daily from 9 a.m. to 5 p.m. Restrooms are available, but no drinking water, so pick some up in Hana if you're out. You don't have to pay a fee to visit the park.

The easy, half-mile **Kuloa Point Loop Trail** leads to the lower pools, where you can take a dip when the weather is warm and the water is placid. This well-marked 20-minute walk is a must for everyone.

Stay out of the Oheo Gulch pools in winter or after a heavy rain, when the otherwise placid falls can wash you out to sea in an instant, to the waiting sharks below. (No kidding — they actually do hang out in the brackish water at the foot of the falls.) No matter what the season, if you do take a dip, always be extra vigilant; keep an eye on the water in the streams. Even when the sky is sunny near the coast, upland rain can cause floodwaters to rise in minutes, so if the water seems to be running

Maui's Top Attractions

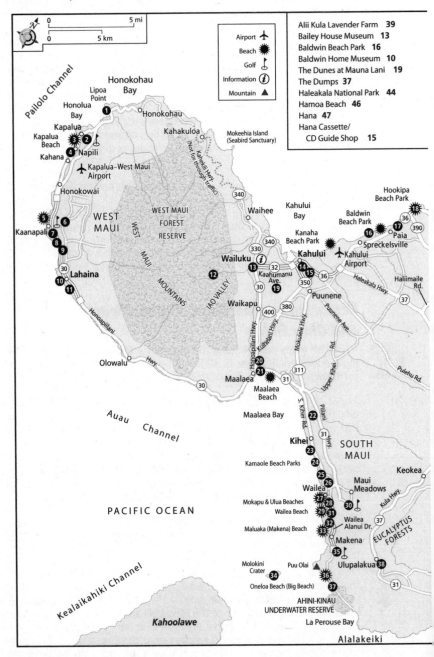

Alii Kula Lavender Farm **39**
Bailey House Museum **13**
Baldwin Beach Park **16**
Baldwin Home Museum **10**
The Dunes at Mauna Lani **19**
The Dumps **37**
Haleakala National Park **44**
Hamoa Beach **46**
Hana **47**
Hana Cassette/
  CD Guide Shop **15**

Airport ✈
Beach ✻
Golf ⛳
Information (i)
Mountain ▲

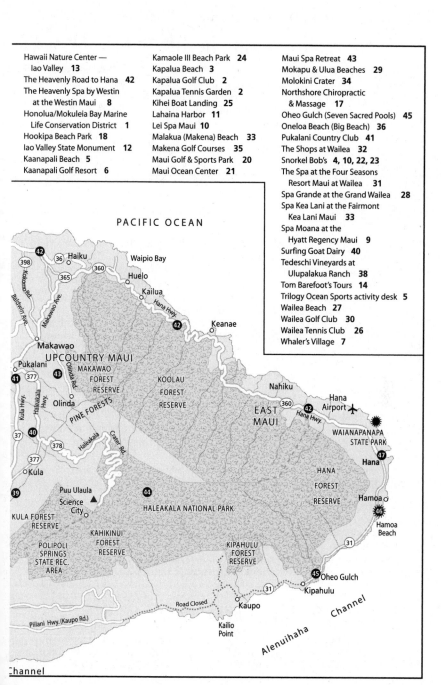

Horseback riding in Kipahulu

If you want to explore the lush Kipahulu District on horseback, contact **Maui Stables** (**☎ 808-248-7799**; www.mauistables.com), which offers a genuine island experience, rich with history and culture, as you explore the gorgeous scenery from your mount. Choose a morning or afternoon three-hour tour; prices are $150 per person, including a deli lunch; discounts are available for kids and seniors. Reservations are a must, as are closed-toed shoes and long pants. The stables are accessible from the Haleakala Highway (Highway 37) from the west side of the island, along the dry southern route to Hana about 25 miles past Tedeschi Winery, as well as directly from Hana. Expect the drive to take about two and a half hours if you're coming from the west side of the island.

between the pools at all, stay out. As I mentioned earlier, a mainland visitor was washed away to sea from Oheo Gulch in May 2002. Don't let this terrible tragedy be repeated; always check with the rangers before you go in the pools. The 2-mile (each way), moderate **Pipiwai Trail** leads upstream to additional pools and 400-foot Waimoku Falls. The often muddy but rewarding uphill trail leads through taro patches and bamboo, guava, and mango stands to the magnificent falls. The trail is unmarked but relatively easy to follow. Wear sturdy shoes, bring water, and don't attempt the trek in the rain.

A mile past Oheo Gulch on the road's ocean side is **Lindbergh's Grave.** First to fly across the Atlantic Ocean, Charles Lindbergh found peace in Hana, where he died of cancer in 1974. The famous aviator is buried under river stones in a seaside graveyard behind the 1857 **Palapala Hoomau Congregational Church,** where his tombstone is engraved with his favorite words from the 139th Psalm: "If I take the wings of the morning and dwell in the uttermost parts of the sea. . . ."

Heading back to the resorts

Before departing Hana, don't forget to check your gas gauge no matter which road west you're traveling. There's nowhere to fill up along either route back to civilization. If you need gas, stop at one of the town's two service stations, Chevron and Hasegawa's Hana Geko Gas, which sit nearly side by side on the right side of the Hana Highway as you leave town. (Prepare for sticker shock at the pump, though!)

Seeing the Sights in Central Maui

These attractions are located in and around the commercial heart of the island, Kahului, and nearby Wailuku, the charming county seat. Wailuku offers a few funky places to shop for antiques and Hawaiiana (see Chapter 14).

Bailey House Museum

This 19th-century missionary and sugar planter's home — built in 1833 on a royal Hawaiian site — is a treasure trove of Hawaiiana that includes a notable collection of precontact Hawaiian artifacts as well as items from post-missionary times. Excellently curated, island-themed temporary exhibits are also part of the mix. This little museum is well worth a half-hour stop for history buffs. It boasts lovely gardens and a wonderful gift shop, neither of which require admission.

2375-A Main St., just west of the Kaahumanu Avenue/Honoapiilani Highway (Highway 32/30) intersection, Wailuku. ☎ *808-244-3326.* www.mauimuseum.org. *Admission: $5 adults, $4 seniors, $1 kids 7–12. Open: Mon–Sat 10 a.m.–4 p.m.*

Hawaii Nature Center — Iao Valley

Before heading into Iao (*ee*-ow) Valley, families may want to stop into this small, kid-centered interactive science center, which features great hands-on exhibits and displays relating to the park's natural history. The center also has a nice gift shop if you're in the market for nature-themed toys.

Call ahead to reserve a spot on Hawaii Nature Center's daily Rainforest Walk through Iao Valley, offered Monday through Friday at 11:30 a.m. and 1:30 p.m. and Saturday and Sunday at 11 a.m. and 2 p.m. Your guide can offer historical, cultural, and natural insight that you just can't gain on a self-guided tour. The price is $30 for adults, $20 for kids (prices include museum admission; children must be at least age 5 to join the Rainforest Walk). Be sure to wear closed-toe shoes suitable for an uneven trail.

At the gateway to Iao Valley State Monument, 875 Iao Valley Rd. ☎ *808-244-6500.* www.hawaiinaturecenter.org. *Admission: $6 adults, $4 kids 11 and under. Open: Daily 10 a.m.–4 p.m.*

Iao Valley State Monument

As you head west to Iao Valley, the transition between town and wild is so abrupt that most people who drive up into the valley don't realize they're suddenly in a rain forest. The walls of the canyon rise, and a 2,250-foot needle pricks gray clouds scudding across the blue sky. The Iao Needle is an erosional remnant of rock. This is Iao Valley, a place of great natural beauty and a haven for Mauians and visitors alike.

You can see everything in an hour or two, though it's a lovely place to bring a picnic and linger. Two paved walkways loop the 6-acre park; a leisurely ⅔-mile loop walk takes you past lush vegetation and lovely views of the fabulously impressive Iao Needle (called Kukaemoku in Hawaiian), a fabulously impressive spire jutting 2,250 feet above sea level. This is the spot of the battle of Kepaniwai, where Kamehameha I conquered the Maui army in 1790 as part of his unification of the Hawaiian islands. An architectural park of Hawaiian heritage houses — including a Japanese teahouse with a lovely koi pond, a Chinese pagoda, a New England–style mission house, a Hawaiian *hale,* and a Portuguese garden — stands in harmony by Iao Stream at Kepaniwai Heritage Garden, near the park's entrance; it makes an excellent place for a picnic, because tables are at hand. You'll see ferns, banana trees, and other native and exotic plants in the streamside botanic garden.

On Iao Valley Road (at the end of Main Street/Highway 32), Wailuku. www.hawaii stateparks.org. *To get there: From Kahului, follow Kaahumanu Avenue east directly to Main Street and the park entrance. Admission: Free. Open: Daily 7 a.m.–7 p.m.*

Exploring Lahaina Town

You may not believe it, seeing today's Lahaina overrun with contemporary tourist schlock, but anyone who has read James Michener's *Hawaii* knows that back in the whaling and missionary days, Lahaina was the capital of Hawaii and the Pacific's wildest port. Now Lahaina is a party town of a different kind and has lost much of its historic vibe, but history buffs with an interest can unearth a half-day's worth of historic sites.

Your best bet is to start at the **Baldwin Home Museum,** a beautifully restored 1838 missionary home at the corner of Front and Dickenson streets, where the **Lahaina Restoration Foundation (☎ 808-661-3262;** www.lahainarestoration.org) is headquartered in the adjacent Master's Reading Room. Stop in any day between 10 a.m. and 4:30 p.m. to pick up the free self-guided walking tour brochure and map of Lahaina's most historic sites. All are within easy walking distance of one another. Stops include the **Brig Carthaginian II,** a replica of the 19th-century whaling ship that brought the first missionaries to Hawaii, docked at Lahaina Harbor; the **banyan tree,** planted as a sapling in 1873 and now a massive 60 feet high and spanning two-thirds of an acre; an 1850s prison, the inside of which the rowdiest whalers no doubt saw on a regular basis; and a number of other interesting sites, including some lovely Buddhist missions and temples.

History aside, Lahaina is the real center of tourism on the island, with hotels, B&Bs, restaurants, T-shirt shops, and a gallery on nearly every block. Expect the town to be rather congested and expect to battle for a parking spot. Paid lots abound, but you can usually find an available free lot at the far south end of town, near the 505 Front St. shops on the mountain side of the street.

Touring South Maui

These terrific attractions are located in Maalaea Harbor Village, at the northernmost end of South Maui.

Maui Ocean Center

This state-of-the-art aquarium is way too pricey for its own good — it's no Monterey Bay Aquarium, after all. If you can overlook the cost, it's a pretty cool place. All exhibits feature the creatures that populate Hawaii's waters.

Lahaina

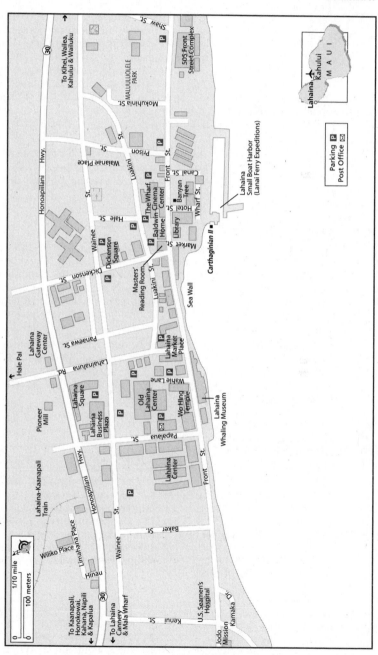

Start at the surge pool, where you'll see such shallow-water marine life as spiny urchins and cauliflower coral, and then move on to the reef tanks and a turtle lagoon (where you'll meet some wonderful green sea turtles). A "touch" pool features tide-pool critters, and a stingray pool is populated by graceful bottom dwellers; the whale discovery exhibit (no live creatures) is disappointing, though. Then you get to the star of the show: the 600,000-gallon main tank, which features tiger, gray, and white-tip sharks, as well as tuna, surgeon fish, triggerfish, and other large-scale tropicals. The neatest thing about the tank is that it's punctured by a clear acrylic tunnel that lets you walk right through it, giving you a real idea of what it might be like to stand at the bottom of the deep blue sea. Allow about two hours for your visit.

In Maalaea Harbor Village, 192 Maalaea Rd. (at the triangle between Honoapiilani Highway [Highway 31] and Maalaea Road), Maalaea. ☎ *808-270-7000.* www.maui oceancenter.com. *Admission: $24 adults, $21 seniors (65-plus), $17 kids 3–12. Open: Daily 9 a.m.–5 p.m. (until 6 p.m. July–Aug).*

Maui Golf & Sports Park

This first-class miniature golf playland boasts two courses that have been designed with both fun and duffing precision in mind. It also has bumper boats with water cannons (great on a hot day), a rock climbing wall, and an "xtreme" trampoline; all activities carry separate charges, or you can bundle them into a package deal. Tiki torches set the mood after dark, and the staff is very friendly. The park is ideal for both family fun and an after-dinner date.

In Maalaea Harbor Village (at the triangle between Honoapiilani Highway [Highway 31] and Maalaea Road; the entrance is on Maalaea Road), Maalaea. ☎ *808-242-7818.* www.mauigolfandsportspark.com. *Activity prices: $15 adults, $12 kids for unlimited miniature golf; other activities $9 adults, $7 kids. Package rates available. Open: Daily 10 a.m.–9 p.m.*

Going Upcountry

The biggest attraction in Upcountry (the area on the slopes of Maui's 10,000-foot Haleakala volcano) is, of course, **Haleakala National Park,** which is so huge that it's discussed in a separate section at the beginning of this chapter. The rural Upcountry also has a handful of other appealing features, most notably Maui's only commercial winery (see the listing later in this section) and some interesting shops in the cowboy-turned-boutique-town of **Makawao** (see "Upcountry Maui: Makawao and Kula" in Chapter 14 for more information).

Alii Kula Lavender Farm

This tranquil, lovely farmstead is the brainchild of "Lavender Engineer" Alii Chang, who figured out that Maui boasted the perfect growing conditions for myriad varieties of the world's lavender (despite the fact that no varieties are native to the island). The expansive, rolling, gorgeously kept gardens now boast some 45 types of lavender, some of which bloom nowhere else on the planet on a year-round basis. The business has grown into a booming enterprise, with a slate of tours and a wealth of lavender-flavored, -scented, and -infused products; in addition to being an inspired horticulturist, Ching has also proven to be a masterful entrepreneur, partnering with some of the islands' finest product manufacturers to create custom lavender products.

The most common tour is the 30-minute guided garden walking tour, which are offered five times daily; afterward, you're welcome to enjoy lavender-scented tea and scones complemented with lavender-infused honey, served on the charming terrace of Chang's home. The guide-led tour really immerses visitors in the beauty and fascinating horticulture of growing gorgeous global collection of lavender. You can also combine your guide-led tour with a lunch basket reserved in advance, filled with lavender-seasoned treats that you're welcome to enjoy on the grounds; the kind folks in the shop will even lend you a picnic mat. For a more in-depth exploration of the garden, reserve a spot on an exclusive cart tour with Alii Chang; the lavender grower escorts up to five guests across a wide swath of the garden on his golf cart, educating and talking story. Or just come on your own for tea and scones at your leisure, pick up a self-guided walking tour map and explore the gardens of your own. A charming shop sells a lovely range of beautifully packaged lavender goods, from spice rubs to creamy hand lotions. Special tea services and seasonal tours — including fun, arts-and-craftsy wreath-making tours — are bookable for small groups.

1100 Waipoli Rd., Kula. ☎ *808-878-3004.* www.aliikulalavender.com. *To get there: From the Hana Highway (Highway 36), turn right onto Haleakala Highway (Highway 37 south); in about 30 minutes, you will pass Kula Elementary School on the right, and then Rice Memorial Park; take the second left after the park and drive about ¼ mile; after you round the bend, take a quick right up Waipoli Road; turn right immediately before the cattle guard. 30-minute lavender garden guided tours ($12 per person) daily at 9:30, 10:30, and 11:30 a.m., and 1 and 2:30 p.m. Reservations for tour recommended at least 24 hours in advance, required if you want to reserve a luncheon basked ($37 per person, guided tour included). Exclusive cart tour with Alii Chang ($25 per person) usually offered daily at 10 a.m. and 2 p.m.; reservations are required. Open: Teahouse and store daily 9 a.m.–4 p.m.*

Surfing Goat Dairy

This delightful place is a must on any foodie's tour of the Valley Isle. German expatriates Thomas and Eva Kafsak came to Maui, purchased 42 verdant acres on the sunny slopes of Haleakala volcano, and opened the finest goat dairy in the Pacific, with 11 national cheese awards under its belt (and counting). The Surfing Goat Dairy is now a thriving business with a herd of 80 goats that Eva, Thomas, and their small staff care for as if they were their children; the result is some of the finest goat cheese you'll ever taste. The farm is also home to three friendly dogs, three cats, and one large, and very spoiled, potbellied pig. Eva and Thomas open their blissful farm to visitors, who come to learn about the practice of goat farming and the craft of artisan goat-cheese making — and, above all else, to pet the utterly charming goat kids, each of whom has its own personality and cute name.

The casual 20- to 30-minute tour is offered every day, generally about every half-hour; just show up during the open hours, and Eva or a tour guide will show you around, give you a brief overview of the process, and introduce you to the goats; the fun culminates in a cheese tasting. For a more detailed experience — including an opportunity to feed and milk the goats and an extended play period with the kids — sign on for the three-hour Grand Tour, which is available on most weekend mornings by appointment. There's also a delightful Evening Chores tour offered three times a week — usually Tuesday, Thursday, and Saturday afternoons.

You can also enjoy a simple farm-style lunch while you're at the farm, and/or order some of the gourmet goat cheeses — which come in a variety of hard, soft, and herb-infused flavors — to carry out or send home. Surfing Goat's cheeses are European style — lighter, more delicate than most domestic goat cheeses — making them appealing to a wider range of palates. The unbaked, German-style *lilikoi* cheesecake is a delightful sweet treat. Don't miss this wonderful spot if you can manage it; if you can't, you can also order cheeses and other goodies online.

3651 Omaopio Rd., Kula. ☎ *808-878-2870.* www.surfinggoatdairy.com. *To get there: From the Hana Highway (Highway 36), turn south on Pulehu Road (Highway 370), and then turn left on Omaopio Road (Highway 372); the entrance will be about 1½ miles on your right. Half-hour Casual Tours ($7, minimum 2 people): Mon, Wed, and Fri 10 a.m.–4 p.m.; Tues, Thurs, and Sat 10 a.m.–3:15 p.m.; Sun 10 a.m.–1 p.m. Evening chores and milking tour ($12): Tues, Thurs, and Sat at 3:15 p.m. 2-hour Grand Tour ($25): every other Sat at 9 a.m. (call for reservations). Custom group tours also available. Dairy store open Mon–Sat 10 a.m.–5 p.m.; Sun 10 a.m.–2 p.m.*

Maui pineapples: *No ka oi!* (The best!)

Everybody thinks of the pineapple as a genuine Hawaiian treat, but the sad fact is that not many pineapples are grown in Hawaii these days. However, the **Maui Pineapple Company** — one of the last real vestiges of Hawaii's plantation era — still harvests some of the world's sweetest, most succulent pineapples in the rich uplands of Kapalua. On the Pineapple Express Tour, you can tour this 23,000-acre working plantation in the company of the company's own field workers, learning about the history of the pineapple in Hawaii and the unique cultivation of these sun-sweet fruits. You even have an opportunity to pick your own luscious fruit to take home. This tour isn't a touristy, faux plantation experience — it's the real deal for folks who are genuinely interested in Hawaii's pineapple history. The two-hour tours are offered weekdays at 9 and 11:45 a.m.; tickets are $40, $32 for children under 12. A three-and-a-quarter-hour Pineapple Experience Signature Tour includes a short hike and lunch at either the Plantation House or Pineapple Grill restaurants in Kapalua; tickets are $65 adults, $58 kids 11 and under. Kids must be at least 5 years old to attend, and everyone should wear closed-toe shoes. Call ☎ 808-665-5491 for reservations or go to www.mauipineapple.com.

Tedeschi Vineyards at Ulupalakua Ranch

Maui's only winery is worth visiting less for its wines — which aren't going to cause the Napa Valley to lose sleep anytime soon — and more for the stunning mountain drive it takes to get there, and the pretty pastoral view you find after you arrive. Sitting on the little-visited south slopes of Haleakala at 2,000 feet elevation, these rolling, golden-hued ranchlands are like no other place you'll find on the island. The ranch dates back to the mid-19th century (the tasting room is housed in a lovely 1874 stone cottage built for a visit by King David Kalakaua), so it has a wonderful historic feeling and well-established grounds that are fine for picnicking; buy a bottle — red, white, or sparkling — to accompany lunch, but skip the silly pineapple wine. Allow an hour each way for the drive from most resorts. Free tastings and guided tours (daily at 10:30 a.m., 1:30 p.m., and 3 p.m.) make this destination surprisingly popular.

On the Kula Highway (Highway 37), Ulupalakua. ☎ *877-878-6058.* www.mauiwine. com. *To get there: Follow the Haleakala Highway south to the Kula Highway; after you reach Keokea, go 5 miles past the Henry Fong Store. Admission, tastings, and tours: Free. Open: Daily 9 a.m.–5 p.m.*

Hitting the Links: Maui's Best Golf

If you love golf, don't miss the opportunity to play on Maui. The Valley Isle boasts a wealth of championship courses designed to make 18-hole memories.

Always book your tee times well in advance (a week or even more) on popular Maui, especially in high season. Weekdays are best for avoiding the crowds and securing the tee times you want. Note that golf carts are required on all Maui golf courses.

The **Maui Golf Shop,** 357 Huku Lii Place, Kihei (☎ **800-981-5512** or 808-875-4653; www.golf-maui.com), can book discounted tee times for you at many of Maui's finest courses (including, at press time, the Dunes, Kaanapali, and Makena, all in the following section). If you want to schedule your tee times before you leave home, you can submit your requests online (where you also find information and insider tips on playing a wealth of Maui links) up to 30 days in advance. After you arrive, the shop is the best place on the island to rent clubs and stock up on gear; you can find it just off the Piilani Highway (Highway 31) at Ohukai Road (behind Tesoro Gas Express).

You can also check out discounter **Tee Times Hawaii.com** (☎ **888-675-GOLF** [888-675-4653] or 866-927-1453; www.teetimeshawaii.com).

Play in the afternoon, when discounted twilight rates are in effect. I can't guarantee that you'll get 18 holes in, especially in winter when it's dark by 6 p.m., but you'll have an opportunity to experience these world-famous courses at half the usual fee. I note discount times in the listings that follow.

A terrific guide to all of Maui's golf courses is available from the Maui Visitors Bureau. Just call ☎ **800-525-MAUI** (800-525-6284) and request a copy of *Maui's Golf Coast*. You can also download a PDF version at www. visitmaui.com.

Maui-based golfers who would also like to experience the celebrated championship challenges on the island of Lanai can take the Expeditions Lanai ferry over to the private island for a day of world-class golf. **Expeditions Maui-Lahaina** (☎ 800-695-2624; www.go-lanai.com) offers service between Lahaina and Lanai's Manele Harbor five times daily; there's also twice-daily service from Maui's Maalaea Harbor, north of Kihei on Maui's neck. The one-way fare is $25 for adults; golf packages are available for $260 per golfer, including greens fees and round-trip ferry service; 6:45 a.m. and 9:15 a.m. departures are available from Lahaina, and there's a 7 a.m. departure from Maalaea. For more on Lanai's two terrific courses, see Chapter 17.

The Dunes at Maui Lani

This dramatic British links-style course was completed in 1997, but it plays like an old pro. Inspired by the old-growth links of Ireland, Honolulu-based course architect Robin Nelson built this public course on the former home of a sand-mining operation, which has allowed the fairways to mature in record time. Several blind and semiblind shots give this all-around, enjoyable course an edge. Considering the course's quality, the rates are a veritable bargain. Private lessons and half-day schools at the PGA pro–taught golf school even make improving your swing a comparatively affordable endeavor.

1333 Mauilani Pkwy., Kahului. ☎ *808-873-0422.* www.dunesatmauilani.com. *Greens fees: $99, $75 after 2 p.m.*

Kaanapali Golf Resort

Both of these popular, rolling resort courses pose a challenge to all golfers, from high handicappers to near pros. In December 2006, the Tournament North Course emerged from a major renovation that has slightly retooled the layout and left the course looking better than ever. It's a true Robert Trent Jones, Jr., design (one of only two in Hawaii), with an abundance of wide bunkers; several long, stretched-out tees; the largest, most contoured greens on Maui; and one of Hawaii's toughest finishing holes. The par-70, 6,400-yard Resort South Course is an Arthur Jack Snyder design that was renovated in 2005 by renowned course architect Robin Nelson, who designed new deep bunkers and landscaping. Although the course still demands challenging shots, the refreshed layout brings the short game and shot selection into play — including a series of forward tees for women, juniors, and beginners — making it a satisfying outing for a wide spectrum of players. Trade winds tend to add an extra level of challenge later in the day. The course is fun to play and boasts great panoramic views, including lovely views of Molokai, Lanai, and even Oahu on clear days. Facilities include a driving range, putting green, clubhouse, and comprehensive golf academy.

2290 Kaanapali Pkwy. (off Highway 30), Kaanapali. ☎ *866-454-GOLF (866-454-4653) or 808-661-3691.* www.kaanapali-golf.com. *Greens fees: $195–$235 ($150–$290 for Kaanapali resort guests), $75–$95 after 1:30 p.m.*

Kapalua Golf Club

These three spectacularly sited championship courses are worth the sky-high greens fees for the magnificent ocean views alone. Resort golf hardly gets finer — *Hawaii* magazine regularly names the Bay and the Plantation courses two of the top nine courses in Hawaii. An Arnold Palmer/Francis Duane design, the par-72, 6,600-yard Bay Course is a bit forgiving thanks to generous and gently undulating fairways, but even the pros have trouble with the 5th, which requires a tee shot over an ocean cove. The breathtaking — and breathtakingly difficult — Ben Crenshaw/Bill Coore–designed Plantation Course is prime for developing your low shots and precise chipping; this 7,263-yard, par-73 showstopper is home to the PGA's annual Mercedes Championship. The par-71, 6,632-yard Village Course, a Palmer/Ed Seay design and the most scenic of the three courses, suits beginners and pros alike, but winds can make for a challenging day among the Cook and Norfolk pines. Facilities include locker rooms, a driving range, and a restaurant.

The first-rate **Kapalua Golf Academy** (☎ 877-527-2582 or 808-665-5455), designed with the input of golf legend Hale Irwin, just may be Hawaii's best place to improve the swing of beginner and almost-pro alike.

Check for money-saving seasonal specials and golf packages at Kapalua's Web site.

Off Honoapiilani Highway (Highway 30), Kapalua. ☎ *877-527-2582 or 808-669-8044.* www.kapaluamaui.com. *Greens fees: $215–$295 ($175–$200 for Kapalua resort guests), $185–$255 midday (11 a.m.–1:50 p.m.) Apr–Sept, $130–$150 after 2 p.m.*

Makena Golf Courses

Robert Trent Jones, Jr., was in top form when he designed these 36 holes. The par-72, 7,017-yard oceanside South Course is considered the more forgiving of the two but has a couple of holes you'll never forget: Running parallel to the ocean, the par-4 16th has a two-tiered green that slopes away from the player, while the par-5, 502-yard 10th is one of Hawaii's best driving holes. With tight fairways and narrow doglegs, the par-72, 6,914-yard North Course is more difficult and more spectacular because it sits higher up the slope of Haleakala. Facilities include a clubhouse, driving range, two putting greens, a pro shop, lockers, and lessons. Additional bonuses include a gorgeous rural setting and spectacular views.

5415 Makena Alanui Dr., Makena (south of Wailea). ☎ *808-879-4000 or 808-875-5817.* www.makenagolf.com. *Greens fees: $155–$200 ($125–$130 for Makena resort guests), $135–$155 after 1 p.m.*

Pukalani Country Club

This par-72, 6,962-yard course (at a cool elevation of 1,100 feet) offers a break from the resorts' sky-high greens fees, and it's really fun to play. The 3rd hole offers golfers two different options: a tough iron shot from the tee (especially into the wind), across a gully to the green; or a shot down the side of the gully across a second green into sand traps below. (Most people choose to shoot down the side of the gully; it's actually easier than shooting across a ravine.) High handicappers love this course, and more-experienced players can make it more challenging by playing from the back tees. Facilities include club and shoe rentals, practice areas, lockers, a pro shop, and a restaurant.

360 Pukalani St., Pukalani (south of Haliimaile on Highway 37, Upcountry). ☎ *808-572-1314.* www.pukalanigolf.com. *Greens fees, including cart: $78 for 18 holes before 11 a.m.; $73 11 a.m.–1 p.m.; $63 after 1 p.m. ($44 for 9 holes after 1:30 p.m.). Take the Hana Highway (Highway 36) to Haleakala Highway (Highway 37) to the Pukalani exit; turn right onto Pukalani Street and go 2 blocks.*

Wailea Golf Club

Most difficult among Wailea's courses is the par-72, 7,070-yard Gold Course, home of the Wendy's Championship Skins Game. This classic Robert Trent Jones, Jr., design boasts a rugged layout, narrow fairways, several tricky dogleg holes, daunting natural hazards, and only-in-Hawaii features, such as lava outcroppings and native grasses. Both the Old Blue and the Emerald are easy for most golfers to enjoy, but the par-72, 6,407-yard Emerald Course — another Trent Jones, Jr., design — is both the prettiest and easiest for high handicappers to enjoy. The par-72, 6,700-yard Old Blue Course, an open course designed by Arthur Jack Snyder, has wide fairways that also appeal to beginners, but bunkers, water hazards, and undulating terrain make it a course that all can enjoy. Facilities include two clubhouses, two pro shops, restaurants, lockers, club rentals, and a complete training facility.

Call to inquire about discounted afternoon rates, money-saving triple- and unlimited-play passes, and other specials, including junior golf rates.

Off Wailea Alanui Drive, Wailea. ☎ *888-328-MAUI (800-328-6284), 800-322-1614, or 808-875-7450.* www.waileagolf.com. *Greens fees: $225 ($130 for the Old Blue Course), $180–$190 for Wailea Resort guests, twilight rates $99–$135.*

Enjoying Guided Nature Hikes

Maui Eco-Adventures (☎ 877-661-7720 or 808-661-7720; www.ecomaui.com) was recognized as Hawaii's Eco-Tourism Operator of the Year in 2005, and deservedly so. This well-run operation specializes in guided cultural and hiking adventures that explore unspoiled areas of the Valley Isle — including the little-known Maunalei Arboretum; Kahakuloa Village, a rare vestige of old Hawaii; and Nakele Point, the northernmost point on Maui — on a variety of compelling journeys for intrepid travelers of all hiking abilities. A selection of wonderful waterfall hikes can make your island dreams come true; the six-hour Rainforest/Waterfall hike is my favorite for the access it provides into the breathtakingly lush, otherwise hidden heart of Maui. A Haleakala crater hike really brings the majestic yet barren landscape to life. Hike/kayak combos are also available for those who want a multifaceted experience, as are custom-designed tours that can add helicopter tours, sailboat adventures, and four-wheeling into the mix. Prices run $80 to $160 per person, including continental breakfast, lunch, a day's supply of water, and pickup from West Maui hotels (expect to pay more for a custom-designed tour). It's an excellent way to see Maui at its natural best.

Maui's oldest guided hiking company is Ken Schmitt's **Hike Maui** (☎ 866-324-MAUI [866-324-6284] or 808-879-5270; www.hikemaui.com). Hike Maui has been universally lauded for the quality of its hikes. The expert guides are all trained naturalists who really know their stuff. Hike Maui offers an array of outings from easy to strenuous, but most fall in the moderate category. Two rain-forest and waterfall hikes are available, as well as two Haleakala Volcano hikes that offer an excellent way to see this splendid national park, which can be difficult to appreciate if you don't know what you're seeing. If you're an accomplished hiker and fit for it, don't miss the longer hike. It takes you all the way to the crater floor — which looks so much like the moon that the lunar astronauts trained here — for an otherworldly experience. Outings range from $75 to $154 per person, including equipment and transportation from the company's Central Maui headquarters and a simple, healthy lunch of sandwiches and fruit. You can book as late as a couple of days in advance, but your best bet is to call before you arrive on the island.

Maui Hiking Safaris (☎ 888-445-3963 or 808-573-0168; www.maui.net/~mhs), another reputable company, offers guided hikes for all levels, including waterfall hikes and guided hikes of Haleakala. Prices run from $59 to $139 per person.

Maui Hiking Safaris extends 10 percent discounts to hikers who book online and to groups of six or more.

Getting a Bird's-Eye View: Helicopter Tours

Flightseeing is an excellent way to explore Maui's stunning, untouched natural areas — some magical parts of the island simply can't be seen by any other means. Maui-based helicopter tours also offer you the opportunity to see a neighbor island — Molokai, Lanai, or even the Big Island — from the air, in addition to the Valley Isle.

There are, however, some considerations. Although the company I recommend in this section features skilled pilots and helicopters with excellent safety records, the truth is that flightseeing can be a risky business. A few dozen people have died in commercial helicopter crashes in

Hawaii over the last decade. Of course, just getting into your rental car and driving to dinner — or even getting into the shower in your condo with a renegade bar of soap — is far more dangerous than catching a copter ride. Still, you should make informed decisions.

When reserving a helicopter tour with any company, check to make sure that safety is its first concern. The company should be an FAA-certified Part 135 operator, and the pilot should be Part 135 certified as well. The 135 license guarantees more stringent maintenance requirements and pilot-training programs than those programs that are only Part 91 certified. And any time weather conditions look iffy, reschedule. You can certainly make arrangements before your vacation begins, but it isn't necessary. The concierge at your hotel can help you make an appointment.

Blue Hawaiian Helicopters

This top-notch flightseeing company is my Hawaii favorite. Family-run by David and Patti Chevalier and a loyal, long-employed staff, Blue Hawaiian flies a fleet of superb American Eurocopter AStar 350 helicopters that carry six passengers, providing each with a 180-degree view and a Bose noise-cancelling headset that lets you enjoy a surprisingly quiet ride. A world leader in the flightseeing industry, Blue Hawaiian also flies Hawaii's only EC-130B4 Eco-Stars. These cutting-edge copters lower noise pollution with a superquiet design and maximize comfort and views with state-of-the-art design, technology, and materials. These copters offer one phenomenal ride. (You can choose which kind of copter you'll fly; the Eco-Star tours are more expensive, but they offer a slightly better viewing range through their bubblelike windows.)

A range of available flight options include some or all of the following spectacular sights: the misty, green West Maui Mountains; otherworldly Haleakala Volcano; luxuriant, unspoiled East Maui and Hana; and Molokai, where you fly by the highest sea cliffs in the world. The various tours run from 30 to 90 minutes.

If you can afford it, I suggest booking the fantastic 90-minute Maui Spectacular, which includes a complete island tour as well as a midflight landing at an exclusive perch at the Ulupalakua Ranch, on the grassy slopes of Haleakala. The view is simply stunning, as is the landing and take-off from this remote spot. This trip was one of my best outings in Hawaii *ever* — and I've spent plenty of time in Hawaii. But don't miss out if you can't quite swing the grand tour; opt for a West Maui/Molokai combo, or a Hana/Haleakala tour (especially if you're not going to have time to hit the road to Hana).

Honored annually by the Federal Aviation Administration (FAA) with its Certificate of Excellence, Blue Hawaiian boasts an excellent safety record, as well as a fleet of other top safety and customer-satisfaction certifications and awards. The pilots (mostly decorated veterans) boast thousands upon thousands of flight hours. The pilots are also well-trained and certified tour guides who are extremely knowledgeable narrators. A state-of-the-art, in-flight video is on board in case you want to preserve the sights and sounds of your thrill-a-minute flight for posterity. An expensive adventure, sure, but money well spent.

At press time, Blue Hawaiian was offering a significant price break — about 13 percent — for online bookings.

Blue Hawaiian tours depart from Kahului Airport. ☎ *800-745-2583 or 808-871-8844.* www.bluehawaiian.com. *30- to 90-minute tours: $173–$518 per person (kids under age 2 fly free; others must pay full fare).*

If Blue Hawaiian is booked, try **Sunshine Helicopters** (☎ **800-501-7738** or 808-270-3999; www.sunshinehelicopters.com), which offers a variety of flights, from short hops around the West Maui Mountains to island tours. Prices range from $200 to $465 per person; check for online discounts.

Saddling Up

Maybe you have a tropical fantasy of riding horseback through rugged ranchlands, into tropical forests, and to remote swimming holes. Maui is the place to make that dream come true.

Call ahead to reserve a spot on the trail rides described in this section — group size is limited. Also confirm times, prices, and routes, which are subject to change.

If you want to ride down into Haleakala's crater, contact **Pony Express Tours** (☎ **808-667-2200;** www.ponyexpresstours.com). See "Exploring the Volcano by Horseback" above for more information.

At press time, Pony Express was offering 10 percent off for those who booked their trips online.

Mendes Ranch & Trail Rides, 3530 Kahekili Hwy., 4 miles past Wailuku (☎ **808-871-5222** or 808-244-7320; www.mendesranch.com), is based on the 300-acre Mendes Ranch, a real working ranch complete with waterfalls, palm trees, coral-sand beaches, lagoons, tide pools, a rain forest, and its own volcanic peak. Allan Mendes, a third-generation wrangler, takes you from the rain forest's edge out to the sea. On the way, you cross tree-studded meadows where Texas longhorns sit in the shade and pass a dusty corral where Allan's father, Ernest, a champion roper, may be breaking a wild horse. The two-and-a-half-hour Aloha ride, which leaves at 8:15 a.m. or 12:15 p.m., costs $110; it includes snacks, and you can add on a barbecue lunch for $20.

If you're out in Hana, call **Maui Stables** (☎ **808-248-7799;** www.maui stables.com), which will take you out to explore the lush scenery of the Kipahulu district. Half-day tours are $150 per person, including a deli lunch. Reservations are a must.

If you enjoy your ride, remember to kiss your horse and tip your guide.

Serving Up Some Tennis

Most resorts and nicer condo complexes in Maui offer private tennis courts.

If you need a court in West Maui, contact the **Kapalua Tennis Garden,** Kapalua Resort (☎ **808-665-9112;** www.kapalua.com), which features ten Plexipave courts for day and night play ($16 for nonresort guests, $14 for resort guests), plus group and private instruction.

In South Maui, book a court at the **Wailea Tennis Club** (☎ **808-879-1958;** www.waileatennis.com). Consistently chosen as one of the finest tennis facilities in the country, Wailea has 11 hard courts available for $15 per person, or a maximum of $60 per court for nonresort guests, plus a full calendar of lessons, clinics, round robins, and the like. The club also rents racquets, shoes, and ball machines.

Relaxing at a Spa

What's the icing on the cake of any vacation? A pampering spa day, of course. Hawaii's spas have raised the art of relaxation and healing to a new level, showcasing Hawaiian products and traditional treatments available only in the islands.

They simply don't come any finer than the luxurious **Spa Grande** at the Grand Wailea Resort (☎ **800-888-6100** or 808-875-1234; www.grand wailea.com), which is regularly recognized as one of the top ten spas in the United States. This 50,000-square-foot temple to the good life boasts a massive East-meets-West spa menu, a first-rate army of therapists, and 40 individual treatment rooms (many with ocean views). There's a full Termé hydrotherapy circuit consisting of a variety of healthful baths (including mud, seaweed, aromatherapy, tropical enzyme, and mineral salt, each with its own rejuvenating powers), Roman pools, and Swiss-jet showers that are worth the treatment price of admission alone. (They're included with every treatment, so I recommend coming a full hour or more before your appointment.) For a one-of-a-kind experience, don't miss the celestial Coconut Euphoria bath, a multistep moisturizing treatment that makes you feel like a piña colada–scented queen for a day. Honestly, you can't go wrong anywhere on this menu. Book a full day's package for the ultimate indulgence — you deserve it. Reserve well ahead.

The Spa at the **Four Seasons Resort Maui at Wailea** (☎ **808-874-8000;** www.fourseasons.com/maui) is another good place to spoil yourself with pure pampering. The intimate and sophisticated facility features 13 indoor treatment rooms, a state-of-the-art gym, a healing garden, and three outdoor *hale* with idyllic ocean views. Imagine the sounds of the waves rolling on Wailea Beach as you're soothingly massaged in the privacy of your own thatch-roofed hut, tucked into the beachside foliage.

For an intimate, personalized experience in South Maui, book treatments at **Spa Kea Lani,** at the Fairmont Kea Lani Maui (☎ 808-875-2229; www. fairmont.com/kealani). A terrific signature experience infused with local character is the *Awapuhi Limi* (Ginger Lime) massage, which features whipped aloe butter infused with ginger and lime essential oils and seaweed extracts applied using the Hawaiian *lomilomi* massage technique.

In West Maui, your top choice is **Spa Moana** at the Hyatt Regency Maui (☎ 800-233-1234 or 808-661-1234; www.maui.hyatt.com), a 15,000-square-foot oceanview spa with 15 treatment rooms, a full-service salon with prime views, an open-air relaxation lounge, and an extensive treatment menu that includes some dynamite facials, as well as soothing body work. Two couples suites allow for romantically infused relaxation. The adjacent Moana Athletic Club has the finest views of any fitness center on the island.

Kaanapali's Westin Maui boasts the **Heavenly Spa by Westin** at Westin Maui (☎ 808-661-2588; www.westinmaui.com), with 13,000 square feet of celestial pampering and relaxation. Many treatments are infused with island scents, including Maui-grown lavender.

If you're in Lahaina and in the mood for some storefront pampering, visit **Lei Spa Maui,** in the 505 Front St. complex, at the far south end of Front Street (☎ 808-661-1178; www.leispa.com), which carries a wonderful line of fragrant and rejuvenating Hawaii-made bath-and-body products, and therapists offer massages, body wraps, and facials.

For the ultimate in Upcountry relaxation, contact **Maui Spa Retreat** (☎ 808-573-8002; www.mauisparetreat.com). Boasting a majestic perch on the slopes of Haleakala, this hidden gem can reward you with one of the finest spa days you'll ever enjoy. The petite spa is also an aromatherapy farm, and the proprietor blends all her own body scrubs, wraps, and healing oils. If you book the spa as a couple, you'll have it all to yourself; I recommend a three-hour spa package for two, which includes private use of the outdoor spa, sauna, and outdoor showers. A divine day spent here is like having your own private spa and pampering at the hands of the finest therapists on the island. If you're a spa aficionado, don't miss it. There are also two simple, charming cottages to rent for a complete Upcountry experience (see Chapter 10 for details).

In Paia, if you're looking for an excellent, low-key, and affordable massage, visit **Northshore Chiropractic and Massage,** 16 Baldwin Ave. (☎ 808-579-9134), on the west side of the main street, a few doors from the highway. They charge a mere $65 an hour and have fabulous therapists.

Chapter 14

Shopping the Local Stores

. . . .

In This Chapter

▶ Finding the best places to buy fabulous, colorful aloha wear
▶ Introducing Maui's art galleries
▶ Discovering unique island gifts for the folks back home

. . . .

*T*he shopping scene on Valley Isle is the reigning king among the neighbor islands. Shoppers may really find themselves in paradise.

Central Maui: Wailuku and Kahului

Although Kahului is the island's hub and the place to go for practical items, the historic town of Wailuku, immediately to its west, offers reasonably good hunting grounds for antiques hounds. Like most Maui shopping destinations, Wailuku is a mixed bag — it has never really taken off like some had hoped — but you can find a few quality shops featuring both new and used treasures on North Market Street. To get there, simply go west from Kahului on Kaahumanu Avenue and turn right when you reach Market, in the heart of Wailuku.

Highlights include **Brown-Kobayashi,** 38 N. Market St. (☎ **808-242-0804**), a treasure trove of graceful Asian antiques (mostly large pieces, but affordable prices make the shipping worth it for committed collectors); **Gottling Ltd.,** 38 N. Market St. (☎ **808-244-7779;** www.gottling ltd.com), for an elegant collection of furnishings and antiques; **Bird of Paradise Unique Antiques,** 54 N. Market St. (☎ **808-242-7699**), for a jumble of collectible glassware, pottery, and Hawaiiana; and **If the Shoe Fits,** 12 N. Market St. (☎ **808-249-9710**), for unique footwear.

If you're in the island music mood, **Mele Ukulele,** before the old Wailuku bridge at 1750 Kaahumanu Ave. (☎ **808-244-3938;** www.meleukulele. com), carries Hawaii's largest selection of new and used ukes.

In Kahului, stop by **Hawaiian Island Surf and Sport,** 415 Dairy Rd., Kahului (☎ **800-231-6958** or 808-871-4981; www.hawaiianisland.com), for all your surfing, body-boarding, and water-play needs.

West Maui: Lahaina, Kaanapali, and Kapalua

Shopping in West Maui consists of two main areas: Lahaina and Kaanapali. The following sections give you the lowdown on these areas, as well as one worth-seeking-out site if you're in the Kapalua area.

Lahaina

Lahaina's main drag, Front Street, overflows with surf-wear shops, contemporary art galleries, trendy boutiques, cheesy T-shirt shops, and much more; you'll tire of browsing well before you run out of places to flex your credit card.

Your best bet is to just start at one end of Front Street and browse. Highlights include **Serendipity,** 752 Front St. (☎ 808-879-7100; www. serendipitymaui.com), for casual women's wear in comfortable, loose-fitting island styles. **Honolua Surf Co.,** 845 Front St. (☎ 808-661-8848; www.honoluasurf.com), carries its own fabulous line of surf wear and gear (you'll find additional locations in Whaler's Village, the Lahaina Cannery Mall, Kihei, and the Shops at Wailea). Another excellent stop for surf wear and gear is **Tropix,** 790 Front St. (☎ 808-661-9296), Maui's homegrown surf company. For a wide selection of swimwear, visit **Maui Water Wear,** 850 Front St. (☎ 808-667-2761); there's a second Lahaina location at Lahaina Cannery Mall.

Célébrités, 764 Front St. (☎ 800-428-3338; www.celebrityfineart. com), features art by and about celebrities; expect original art and numbered lithographs by such second-careerists as John Lennon and the Rolling Stones' Ron Wood, plus a wealth of autographed headshots and platinum albums. **Vintage European Posters,** 744 Front St. (☎ 808-662-8688; www.europeanposters.com), boasts a fantastic array of original poster art from 1890 to 1950, mostly European and all in mint condition. (There's a second branch at Whaler's Village at Kaanapali Beach.)

The **Art of Peter Max Gallery,** 716 Front St. (☎ 808-661-7979; www. petermax.com), specializes in the vibrant, multimedia, cartoon-style art of this icon of the 1960s and '70s. The **Bella Vitri Gallery,** 744 Front St. (☎ 808-661-4646; www.mauiartglass.com), features a glorious collection of studio-art glass from such master artists as Dale Chihuly, James Nowak, and Hiroshi Yamano; this one's a dazzler.

Another excellent choice for original art is **Martin Lawrence Galleries,** Lahaina Market Place, at the corner of Front Street and Lahainaluna Road, in the heart of town (☎ 808-661-1788; www.martinlawrence. com). Famous-name artists, from Rembrandt to Warhol, make this collection so fine that window-shopping alone is a joy. You're welcome to browse, even with no intent to buy.

Also worth checking out are the vibrant, three-dimensional natural panoramas of globetrotting photographer Peter Lik, whose **Peter Lik**

Gallery, 712 Front St. (☎ 808-651-6623; www.peterlik.com), is definitely worth a browse.

An island of artistic integrity in the sea of Lahaina kitsch is **Na Mea Hawaii Store,** in the Baldwin House, 120 Dickenson St., at Front Street (☎ 808-661-5707), which sells only fine-quality, island-made crafts and gifts. That doesn't mean expensive, though; you can find a surprising number of affordable prizes among the bounty.

For marine-themed goods and educational gifts for kids, you can't do better than the surprisingly nice nonprofit **Pacific Whale Foundation** store, 612 Front St. (☎ 808-667-7447; www.pacificwhale.org). Members save 15 percent off all whale- and eco-themed goodies, as well as whale-watching cruises and snorkel tours, which can be booked right at the shop, so consider joining up for a good cause.

Old Lahaina Book Emporium, 834 Front St. (☎ 808-661-1399; www.old lahainabookemporium.com), is a wonderful haunt for used and new fiction, nonfiction, music, and videos.

At the far-south end of Front Street, in the 505 Front St. complex, is **Lei Spa Maui** (☎ 808-661-1178; www.leispa.com), which carries a wonderful line of fragrant and rejuvenating Hawaii-made bath and body products, while therapists offer massages, body wraps, and facials.

At the opposite, north end of Front Street are a couple of shopping centers, including **Lahaina Cannery Mall,** 1221 Honoapiilani Hwy. (☎ 808-667-0592; www.lahainacannerymall.com), for practical items. The **Lahaina Center,** 900 Front St. (☎ 808-667-9216; www.lahainacenter. com), is a pleasant open-air mall that boasts **Hilo Hattie,** Hawaii's biggest name in affordable aloha wear, and a multiscreen movie theater — perfect for rainy days.

Newest on the scene is **Lahaina Gateway** (☎ 808-893-0300; www.lahaina gateway.com), a sprawling new complex on the highway, featuring such big names as **Barnes & Noble** and **Outback Steakhouse.** Also on the highway is **Lahaina Music,** 910 Honoapiilani Hwy, on the mountain side (☎ 808-661-7625; www.lahainamusic.com), which features Lahaina's largest selection of ukuleles as well as guitars and accessories.

Kaanapali

On the beach, in Kaanapali, **Whaler's Village,** 2435 Kaanapali Pkwy. (☎ 808-661-4567; www.whalersvillage.com), has blossomed into quite an upscale shopping and dining complex, offering an appealing open-air shopping experience (once you get past the ordeal of parking). Although it has become a chic shopping stop in recent years — with **Coach, Louis Vuitton,** and **Tommy Bahama** all represented — it also has some surprisingly excellent midrange boutiques, including three branches of **Honolua Surf Co.** — including one for kids — whose stylish surf gear and wear I just love; **Sandal Tree,** for an excellent collection of women's footwear, sun hats, and handbags; **The Walking Company,** for a wide selection of the most comfortable shoes out there for men and women; **Blue Ginger** for relaxed and comfortable batik-print resort wear for women and kids; **Na Hoku,** for quality Hawaii-themed and local-style jewelry, including Hawaiian heirloom jewelry; **Totally Hawaiian Gift Gallery** for an artful collection of island-made gifts; **Dolphin Galleries,** for high-quality, island-themed, and locally designed jewelry, including a 14-carat collection designed in a clever petroglyph style; **David & Goliath,** home to the most delightfully snarky collection of cartoon-print tees for the kid and kid wannabe in your life; **Maui Water Wear** for a fine collection of women's swimwear; a branch of **Reyn's,** the Hawaii-based company that makes my second-favorite contemporary aloha wear (after Sig Zane; see Wailuku, earlier in this section); **Lahaina Printsellers** for antique prints, maps, and engravings; and **Martin & MacArthur** for island crafts. Meeting your practical needs are such stops as **The Body Shop,** in case you need to stock up on ecofriendly sunscreen; **Ritz Camera; Maui Dive Shop;** and **Borders Express,** in case you need a fresh beach read.

Kapalua

In Kapalua, stop by the freshly renovated **Honolua Store,** 502 Office Rd. (☎ 808-665-9105), the resort's beloved plantation store, a lone holdover from when this region grew sugar cane and pineapple rather than golfers and sunbathers. In business since 1929, the new Honolua Store has recaptured its vintage feel, marrying it with an ultramodern selection of wine and locally made gourmet food and gift products. There's also an espresso bar and plate lunch counter. Well worth a stop if you're in the area.

South Maui: Wailea

The lovely open-air **Shops at Wailea,** 3750 Wailea Alanui Dr. (☎ 808-891-6770; www.shopsatwailea.com), has been a great addition to the Wailea resort, bringing in much-needed practical retailers and elegant gift outlets alike. Stores run the gamut from **Tiffany & Co., Fendi, St. John, Louis Vuitton, Betsey Johnson, Guess,** and **Gucci** to **The Gap, Banana Republic,** and **White House/Black Market.** Specialty stores worth seeking out include **Footprints,** for an excellent selection of sandals for men, women, and children; the gorgeous **Tori Richard** and **Reyn's,** for high-quality aloha wear in prints that range from subtly sophisticated to fun and funky; **Martin & MacArthur** and **Elephant Walk,** for hand-crafted koa and other Hawaii crafts and gifts; **Na Hoku,** for fine jewelry done in the Hawaiian heritage style, plus beautiful Tahitian pearls; **Blue Ginger,** which has brought batik into the 21st century with its bold prints and flowing modern cuts for women and kids; **Maui Water Wear,** for an excellent collection of swimwear for women, from sexy to sedate; the **Tommy Bahama Emporium,** with tropically sophisticated clothing (also boasting a winning oceanview cafe and bar — see Chapter 11); and much more. Art lovers can find a wealth of upscale art galleries, including outlets of such Lahaina favorites as **Célébrités,** showcasing art by and about, yes, celebrities; and **Ki'i Gallery,** whose large-scale treasures include the monumental art glass of Dale Chihuly; plus **Eclectic Image Gallery** for high-quality photographic art. You find all this and much, much more in a pleasant oceanview setting.

On the Road to Hana: Paia

The hip little surf town of **Paia** (pa-*ee*-ah), just 15 minutes east of Kahului on the Hana Highway (Highway 36), has evolved into one of my favorite Maui shopping stops of late. It makes an eclectic but appealing stop for shoppers looking for funky, fun, and fashion-forward goods. The boutiques sprawl in a T-shape from the intersection of the Hana Highway and Baldwin Avenue, and the choices range from the sublime to the ridiculous.

On the sublime end is **Maui Crafts Guild,** on the ocean side of Hana Highway at no. 43 (☎ 808-579-9697; www.mauicraftsguild.com), an artist-owned cooperative that represents some of the finest artists and craftspeople on Maui; you find artworks and gifts in all price ranges there. **Maui Hands,** 84 Hana Hwy. (☎ 808-579-9245; www.mauihands.com), also specializes in locally made art and crafts.

Also on the Hana Highway, across the street from Maui Hands at no. 83, is **Tamara Catz** (☎ 808-579-9184; www.tamaracatz.com), the first boutique from the Argentine-born, New York–educated Catz, who is married to world windsurfing champ Francisco Goya. The designer specializes in sleek, sexy fashion with a feminine flair, designed for confident women who love body-conscious wear; her store has launched Paia as a burgeoning hub of cutting-edge chic in the islands.

Moonbow Tropics, 20 and 36 Baldwin Ave. (☎ 808-579-8592; www.moonbowtropicsmaui.com), offers the finest contemporary aloha-wear lines available for men and women alike; Moonbow offers what is arguably the best local-style clothing collection on the island. **Nuage Bleu,** 76 Hana Hwy. (☎ 808-579-9792; www.nuagebleu.com), specializes in cutting-edge clothing and accessories for women and children, carrying such brands as Juicy Couture, Miss Sixty, Diane von Furstenberg, and others; *Lucky* magazine recently named Nuage Bleu its favorite Maui boutique, bar none. Another wonderful fashion stop is **Imrie,** 71 Baldwin Ave. (☎ 808-579-8303); a New York City transplant from sisters Tamsin and Caitlin Imrie, fashionistas who have successfully blended urban chic with casual island style for women who like a funky-fun yet fabulous look. Fashion seekers might also check out **Biasa Rose,** 104 Hana Hwy. (☎ 808-579-8602), for chic, casual clothing for men and women from such brands as Betsey Johnson, James Perse, AG, Calypso, Tart, and more.

The island's sexiest bikinis can be found at **Maui Girl Beachwear,** 12 Baldwin Ave. (☎ 800-579-9266 or 808-579-9266; www.maui-girl.com), which is probably the finest swimwear shop in the islands. There's plenty more good stuff; just park and browse.

If you'd like to bring a special Hawaii-themed gift home to Fido or Fluffy, visit **Birken & Bailey's Pet Boutique,** 21 Baldwin Ave. (☎ 808-579-9805), an ultracharming stop for pet lovers in the heart of Paia town.

Upcountry Maui: Makawao and Kula

Just because you're off the beaten path, doesn't mean you won't find great shopping. Shopping fanatics can have a ball in Maui's verdant Upcountry.

Makawao

From Paia, drive on Baldwin Avenue (Highway 390), toward the mountain, and in 7 miles, you reach **Makawao** (ma-_ka_-wow), a cowboy town–turned–New Age village that's another petite shopper's paradise, especially in the local arts category.

The shopping is so good in Makawao that the whole _town_ is a highlight. Serious shoppers should definitely save an afternoon to explore. Seek out **Hurricane,** 3639 Baldwin Ave. (☎ 808-572-5076), a wonderful split-level boutique that carries a well-displayed selection of fine casuals for women, including such fine labels as Sigrid Olsen; and **Tropo,** next door at 3643 Baldwin Ave. (☎ 808-573-0356), Hurricane's boutique for men. **Pink by Nature,** 3663 Baldwin Ave. (☎ 808-572-9576; www.pinkby nature.com), specializes in lovely contemporary fashions for women and children.

The Courtyard, at 3620 Baldwin Ave., houses a number of interesting craft shops of varying quality, including **Maui Hands** (☎ 808-352-4278; www.mauihands.com); **Hot Island Glass Studio & Gallery** (☎ 808-572-4527; www.hotislandglass.com), a fascinating glassblower's studio that's worth a peek; and the **Garcia Studio Gallery,** 3660 Baldwin Ave. (☎ 808-573-5972; www.garciastudiogallery.com), specializing in island-themed art, plus the compellingly multilayered koi portraits of Terry Gilecki.

Altitude, 3660 Baldwin Ave. (☎ 808-573-4733), specializes in high-quality, high-spirited clothing and accessories for women from such brands as Eileen Fisher, Glima, and Hobo; and much, much more. You'll find another beautifully curated, casually elegant collection of women's wear at Isabelle Buell's **Holiday & Co.,** located in the historic K. Matsui Store, at 3681 Baldwin Ave. (☎ 808-572-1470).

Maui Master Jewelers, 3655 Baldwin Ave. (☎ 808-573-5400), specializes in gold, silver, platinum, and semiprecious and precious beaded jewelry by some of the state's finest jewelry designers. Definitely worth a look are the bamboo designs by Carol and Michael Schwartz, as well as the collection of New Zealand jade pieces.

I highly recommend simply parking and browsing Baldwin and Makawao avenues to realize the full creative bounty of this charming town.

The true gem of Makawao is the **Hui Noeau Visual Arts Center,** a mile outside of town, at 2841 Baldwin Ave. (☎ **808-572-5194;** www.huinoeau. com). A tree-lined driveway leads to the 1917 estate that houses the island's most renowned artists' collection and features rotating exhibits plus an excellent shop. The center has a $2 suggested donation for the exhibit gallery.

Kula

Want to send some of those gorgeous Maui flowers back home to someone special — maybe yourself? Head Upcountry to the slopes of Haleakala, to the **Upcountry Harvest Gift Shop,** on Haleakala Highway (Highway 377; ☎ **800-575-6470;** www.upcountryharvest.com), adjacent to the Kula Lodge & Restaurant (see Chapter 11). The stunning protea — those oversized flowers that look like they came to Maui from another planet — are grown on the owners' own Sunrise Protea Farm. The shop also features a nice collection of island-style gifts and local crafts.

For a hand-painted original, visit the **Curtis Wilson Cost Gallery,** at the Kula Lodge & Restaurant, off Highway 377 on the way to Haleakala Crater (☎ **800-810-2678** or 808-878-6544; www.costgallery.com); the Maui-based painter is a landscape traditionalist; his islandscapes are luminescent and alive with detail.

Even if you don't take the tour, you might want to visit **Alii Kula Lavender Farm,** 1100 Waipoli Rd., off Haleakala Highway (Highway 377; ☎ **808-878-3004;** www.aliikulalavender.com), for high-quality lavender-themed gifts fragranced with locally grown versions of the violet herb.

East Maui: Hana

If you make the trip to the far end of the Hana road, don't miss the **Hana Coast Gallery,** on the Hana Highway, adjacent to the Hotel Hana-Maui (☎ **808-248-8636;** www.hanacoast.com), a gorgeous showcase for island-made art and products hewn by master craftspeople, including gorgeous furniture and woodworks.

The quirky **Hasegawa General Store** (☎ **808-248-8231**) is worth stopping in for kicks (look for the Spam sushi vending machine near the entrance) or to use the ATM, but the prices on practical items and munchies are better across the road and up the hill at the **Hana Ranch Store** (☎ **808-248-**8261).

Chapter 15

Living It Up after the Sun Goes Down

*M*aui's nightlife certainly doesn't rival the after-dark scene on the island of Oahu. Many of Maui's restaurants — particularly the oceanfront ones — do double duty as post-dinner hot spots, often hosting lively bar scenes, live music, and dancing. The epicenter of island nightlife is lively Lahaina.

Finding Your Way Out in the Dark

For the most complete calendar of what's happening while you're on Maui, pick up a copy of the weekly *MauiTime Weekly* newspaper, available for free at kiosks all over the island. The week's live music and DJ entertainment is featured in easy-to-scan grid form near the back of the paper. Current movie listings and showtimes are also listed in the paper.

If you're interested in the more refined performing arts, look for a copy of *Centerpiece*, the free bimonthly magazine published by the **Maui Arts and Cultural Center,** the finest cultural venue in the islands; hotel concierges usually have copies. You can also call the center, which is located in Kahului, at ☎ **808-242-7469,** or visit the Web site at www.mauiarts.org for a current schedule. The Maui Arts and Cultural Center dominates the performing-arts scene on the island, featuring a visual-arts gallery, an outdoor amphitheater, a 300-seat theater for experimental performances, and a 1,200-seat main theater. The diverse calendar sometimes features such big names as Melissa Etheridge, David Sanborn, or George Winston; Maui Film Festival screenings; or performances by Hawaii's most renowned musicians. (Don't miss beautiful island songstress Amy Hanaialii Gilliom if she's on the calendar.)

The island's best sunset cruises are offered by **Paragon Sailing Charters** (☎ 800-441-2087 or 808-441-2087; www.sailmaui.com). From Lahaina Harbor (on Front Street), you'll sail into the sunset on a state-of-the-art, high-performance catamaran. These two-hour sails are intimate affairs (only 24 passengers). Prices are $56 adults, $39 kids 4 to 12, with hors d'oeuvres and beverages (including champagne, wine, and beer). Departure times vary seasonally, and cruises aren't offered every day, so call ahead. Discounts are sometimes available if you book online.

And, of course, don't forget that Maui is home to the finest examples of the ultimate island form of after-dark entertainment: the **luau!** I highly recommend planning to participate in one while you're on the Valley Isle, because it's home to the best commercial luaus in all of Hawaii. For details, see Chapter 11.

Partying in West Maui

West Maui is the Valley Isle's party central. **Lahaina,** in particular, takes on a festive atmosphere as sunset nears. The restaurants along ocean-front Front Street boast stellar views and energetic bar scenes, some with live music. Just stroll the street and join whatever party suits your fancy.

Among the best spots to join the party are **Cheeseburger in Paradise/ Cheeseburger Island Style,** 811 Front St. (☎ 808-661-4855), a regular forum for live-and-lively music; the **Hard Rock Cafe,** 900 Front St. (☎ 808-667-7400); **Kimo's,** 845 Front St. (☎ 808-661-4811); and **Moose McGillycuddy's,** 844 Front St. (☎ 808-891-8600). **Mulligan's on the Wharf,** upstairs at the Wharf Cinema Center in the heart of town, at 658 Front St., across from the banyan tree (☎ 808-661-8881; www.mulligans ontheblue.com), offers rollicking live music and Guinness on tap in its casual Irish pub setting. In the same complex is **Cool Cat Cafe** (☎ 808-667-0908; www.coolcatcafe.com), a charming '50s cafe with great burgers and live music nightly.

Every Friday from 7 to 10 p.m., as part of **Friday Night Is Art Night** in Lahaina, the town's dozens of art galleries open their doors for special shows, demonstrations, and refreshments; you can even enjoy strolling musicians wandering the streets.

Lahaina is also home to two nightly shows that are well worth seeking out. Don't pass up an opportunity to see 'Ulalena at the **Maui Myth & Magic Theatre,** in Old Lahaina Center, 878 Front St. (☎ 877-688-4800 or 808-661-9913; www.ulalena.com or www.mauitheatre.com). This incredible, Broadway-quality, 75-minute live show interweaves the natural, historical, and mythological tales of the birth of Hawaii using a near-perfect mix of original contemporary music and dance, ancient chant and hula, creative lighting, gorgeous costumes, visual artistry (including some mind-blowing puppets), and live musicianship. This universally lauded production is bold, mesmerizing, and like nothing Hawaii has ever seen before — sort of like Laurie Anderson hooks up with Cirque du Soleil in Hawaii. The show is staged at 6:30 p.m. Tuesday through Saturday; additional shows may be added in high season. Tickets are $60 to $100 adults, $40 to $70 kids ages 3 to 12 — yes, they'll love *'Ulalena,* too. Don't miss it! Packages that include dinner and/or VIP access to go backstage and meet the performers are now also available.

For something completely different, spend an evening at **Warren & Annabelle's,** 900 Front St., in Lahaina (☎ **808-667-6244;** www.hawaii magic.com). This genuinely fun and surprisingly not cheesy mystery-and-magic cocktail show stars illusionist Warren Gibson and "Annabelle," a ghost from the turn of the 20th century who plays a grand piano — and even takes your requests. Expect the requisite audience participation, of course. Tickets are $56 per person (with food and drinks available for an additional charge); you must be at least 21 to enter. Dinner packages range from $95 per person. The show is very popular, so book at least a few days in advance to avoid disappointment; no shows are performed on Sundays.

An early-evening family-friendly show is sometimes added to the Warren & Annabelle's schedule during major school-holiday periods; call for details.

Kaanapali has its own family-friendly entertainment as well. **Kupanaha** is the terrific magic show at the **Kaanapali Beach Hotel** (☎ **808-667-0128;** www.kbhmaui.com), starring husband-and-wife illusionists Jody and Kathleen Baran and their daughters, child-prodigy magicians Katrina and Crystal. The dazzling show interweaves illusions, Hawaiian hula and chant, and the stories and myths of ancient Hawaii into a show that the whole family will love. No kidding — the show has been a huge hit. Shows are offered Tuesday through Saturday at the family-friendly hour of 4:45 p.m.; dinner is included, and you'll be out by 7:30 p.m. Tickets are $79 to $89 adults, $55 ages 13 to 20, $39 kids 6 to 12, including a three-course dinner; a kids' menu is available. Free for kids 5 and under.

For live music in Kaanapali, head to **Whaler's Village,** on Kaanapali Beach, at 2435 Kaanapali Pkwy., where you can take an open-air seat facing the ocean at the bar at **Hula Grill** (☎ **808-667-6636**), which features Hawaiian music and hula. With tiki torches flickering and the waves rolling in, you can't go wrong here. For a slightly quieter vibe, head next door to **Leilani's on the Beach** (☎ **808-661-4495**), where the Beachside Grill specializes in satisfying tropical cocktails and casual dining; live music sets the tone on Friday, Saturday, and Sunday afternoons.

In Napili, every Wednesday evening comes alive with traditional and contemporary Hawaiian music thanks to the **Masters of Hawaiian Slack Key Guitar Concert Series.** The weekly event hosts the islands' finest musicians, including such local luminaries as Ledward Kaapana, Cyril Pahinui, Dennis Kamakahi, and others, who come to play music and talk story in genuine local style. It's an event not to be missed, especially if you're a live-music fan. Shows take place in the pavilion at the Napili Kai Beach Resort every Wednesday at 7:30 p.m. Check www.slackkey.com for the current performance calendar; call ☎ 888-669-3858 or 808-669-3858 for reservations. Tickets are $45.

In Honokowai, stop by **Java Jazz & Soup Nutz,** 3550 Lower Honoapiilani Hwy. (☎ 808-667-0787; www.javajazz.com), a friendly, artsy cafe and coffee bar offering cocktails and great live jazz in the evening until 9 p.m., plus an affordable fine-dining menu. This is a colorfully laid-back place to hang with locals and visitors alike.

Sipping a Beverage in South Maui

South Maui is quieter overall, but boasts a couple of hopping joints.

Lively **Life's a Beach,** 1913 S. Kihei Rd. (next to Foodland), Kihei (☎ 808-891-8010; www.mauauibars.com), serves up live music nightly, usually starting at 10 p.m.

The casual, easygoing **South Shore Tiki Lounge,** in Kihei Kalama Village, 1913 S. Kihei Rd. (☎ 808-874-6444; www.southshoretikilounge.com), specializes in first-class mai tais and affordable food in a fun 'n' funky tiki setting; DJs set a party atmosphere most nights.

In the mood for a taste o' the Emerald Isle while you're on the Valley Isle? Head on over to **Mulligan's on the Blue** (☎ 808-874-1131; www.mulligansontheblue.com), located on the Wailea Blue Golf Course on Wailea Alanui Drive, across from the Fairmont Kea Lani. Mulligan's is an authentic Irish pub, complete with Guinness on tap, traditional pub fare (in case you're in the mood for bangers and mash or a potato boxty while you're in the islands) and seven TVs complete with satellite sports channels, plus the kind of panoramic ocean view that only Maui can offer. Pubgoers enjoy high-quality live music nightly, with a Celtic spin on Sundays. It's an all-around excellent place to hang out!

With a 10-foot jumbo screen and 30 TV screens around the room, **Moose McGillycuddy's,** 2511 S. Kihei Rd. (☎ 808-891-8644), makes a great place to catch the game.

Hitting the Dance Floor Upcountry

Somewhat unexpectedly, one of the hottest party spots on the island is Upcountry, in the cowboy town of Makawao. The party never ends at **Casanova,** 1188 Makawao Ave., at Baldwin Avenue (☎ 808-572-0220; www.casanovamaui.com), a popular Italian restaurant (see Chapter 11). After the dinner hour on Wednesday, Friday, and Saturday (plus the occasional Thurs and Sun), attention turns from the good Italian food to socializing around the stage and dance floor. Wednesday is traditionally a ladies'-night disco; Fridays and Saturdays bring DJs or live music. Expect good blues, rock, reggae, jazz, Hawaiian, and the top names in local and visiting entertainment, which generally starts at 9:45 p.m. and continues to 1:30 a.m.

East Maui Entertainment

Out in quiet Hana, your best place for entertainment is the Hotel Hana-Maui, where the **Paniolo Bar** (☎ **808-248-8211;** www.hotelhanamaui. com) hosts excellent live Hawaiian music daily, except Friday, from 6:30 p.m., plus hula on Thursday and Saturday nights. On Fridays, the entertainment moves to the hotel's main dining room, **Ka'uiki** (☎ **808-248-8211**), which hosts an entertaining hula show and buffet dinner on Friday nights from 6:30 to 9:30 p.m. Tickets are $50 adults, $35 kids 12 and under; advance reservations are recommended.

Chapter 16

Taking a Side Trip to Molokai

· ·

In This Chapter

▶ Introducing Molokai
▶ Deciding where to stay and dine
▶ Knowing what to see and do

· ·

*B*orn of volcanic eruptions 1.5 million years ago, Molokai remains a sleepy Hawaiian time capsule at the dawn of the 21st century. It has no glitzy resorts, no stoplights, no Starbucks, and no buildings taller than a coconut tree. Molokai is the least developed, most "Hawaiian" of all the islands, making it especially attractive to adventure travelers and those who are willing to venture off the beaten track to find genuine peace and tranquility.

Molokai lives up to its reputation as the most Hawaiian island chiefly through its lineage — more people of Hawaiian blood live here than anywhere else. This slipper-shaped island is the cradle of Hawaiian dance (the hula was born here) and the ancient science of aquaculture. An aura of mysticism clings to the land, and the old ways still govern life. The residents survive by taking fish from the sea, hunting wild pigs and axis deer on the range, and subsistence farming on 40-acre farmstead plots bestowed by the government to residents with pure Hawaiian blood. Some folks even still catch fish in throw nets and troll the reef for squid.

Not everyone loves Molokai. It's a rustic, rural place — you won't find any sophisticated resorts or restaurants, or much in the way of shopping and organized diversions. This is especially true now that the Molokai Ranch — the sole source of luxury-style accommodations and dining on the island, not to mention most of its activities, including the island's main golf course and sole movie theater — is shuttered. Instead, visiting Molokai is all about communing with nature. Molokai rewards you with Hawaii's highest waterfall and its greatest collection of fishponds, its longest barrier reef, and the world's tallest sea cliffs, plus sand dunes, rain forests, hidden coves, and gloriously empty beaches. The slow-paced, simple life and the absence of modern development attract people in search of the "real" Hawaii, which is quickly disappearing on the other islands, if not already gone. If you want rockin' nightlife, you're in the wrong place; Molokai shuts down after sunset. The only public diversions are softball games under the lights of Mitchell Pauole Field and a few restaurants that stay open after dark, often serving local brew and pizza.

Rugged, red-dirt Molokai isn't for everyone, but anyone who likes to explore remote places and seek their own adventures should love it. If that sounds like you, the funky "friendly island" just may enchant you as the real Hawaii of your dreams.

Getting to Know Molokai

Rural, small-town **Kaunakakai** (ka-*oo*-na-ka-*keye*) is the closest thing Molokai has to a business district. Rabang's Filipino Food posts bad checks in the window; antlered deer-head trophies guard the grocery aisles at Misaki's Market; and Kanemitsu's, the town's legendary bakery, churns out fresh loaves of onion-cheese bread daily. Set on a flat, dusty plain, with its Old West–style storefronts laid out in a three-block grid, Kaunakakai is a town from the past. At the end of Wharf Road is Molokai Wharf, the local place to fish, photograph, and just hang out. Kaunakakai is the dividing point between the lush, verdant East End and the dry, arid West End: On the west side of town stand cactuses, while on the east side there's thick, green vegetation.

Molokai's top attraction is **Kalaupapa National Historic Park,** where Father Damien established his famous leper colony. Touring this remote, poignant site is a memorable journey best made on the back of a trusty mule, who will safely carry you down a spectacular, steep trail. It's an all-day adventure, and the trip of a lifetime. Even if you're not staying on Molokai, the mule ride can be done as a day trip from Maui. If you're only visiting Molokai briefly, don't miss it. See "The legacy of Father Damien: Kalaupapa National Historic Park," near the end of this chapter, for complete details. Read about it and decide if you'd like to sign up before you arrive; it's important to make reservations *well* in advance of your visit.

On the **North Coast,** upland from Kaunakakai, the land tilts skyward and turns vibrantly green, lush with scented plumeria and glossy coffee trees, until it blooms into a true forest — and then abruptly ends at a great precipice, falling 3,250 feet to the sea. The green sea cliffs are creased with five deeply veined V-shaped crevices. The North Coast is a remote, forbidding place, with a solitary peninsula — **Kalaupapa** — that was once the final stopping point for exiled lepers. It's now a national historical park that commemorates the peninsula's cruel fate as well as the courageousness of those who were exiled there. This region is easy on the eyes but difficult to visit. It lies at a cool elevation, and rain squalls can blow in from the ocean. In summer, the ocean is calm, providing great opportunities for kayaking, fishing, and swimming; however, during the rest of the year, giant waves come rolling onto the shores.

The **West End** of the island is largely comprised of stark desert terrain, bordered by the most beautiful white-sand beaches in Hawaii. Here is where the 53,000-acre **Molokai Ranch** once operated the island's premier guest facilities, but everything is boarded up now. The rugged rolling land slopes down to Molokai's only resort development, **Kaluakoi,** a cul-de-sac of condos clustered around a seafront hotel (built three decades ago, but also now empty and shuttered) near 3-mile-long **Papohaku,** the island's biggest beach. On the way to Kaluakoi, you find **Maunaloa,** a 1920s-era pineapple-plantation town that was in the process of being transformed into a master-planned community before the Molokai Ranch's Singapore owners pulled out in the face of staunch local opposition to proposed luxury development. It hardly ever rains on the dry West End, but when it does (usually in the winter), expect a downpour and plenty of red mud.

The area **east** of Kaunakakai becomes lush, green, and tropical, with golden pocket beaches and a handful of affordable cottages and condos. With this voluptuous landscape comes rain. However, most storms are brief (15-minute) affairs that blow in, dry up, and disappear. Winter is Hawaii's rainy season, so expect more rain from January through March; but even then, the storms usually are brief and the sun comes back out.

Beyond Kaunakakai, the two-lane road curves along the coast past pig farms, palm groves, and a 20-mile string of fishponds as well as an ancient *heiau* (sacred Hawaiian religious site), Damien-built churches, and a few contemporary condos by the sea. The road ends in the glorious **Halawa Valley,** one of Hawaii's most beautiful valleys.

Settling Into Molokai

The **Molokai Visitors Association** is located in the Moore Center, 2 Kamoi St., Suite 200, in Kaunakakai (☎ **800-800-6367** from the mainland and Canada, 808-553-3876, or 808-553-5221; www.molokai-hawaii.com). The staff can give you all the information you need on what to see and do while you're on the island. Feel free to stop by their office; it's open Monday through Friday. Also check out www.visitmolokai.com for comprehensive visitor information.

Arriving on Molokai

Visitors arrive at **Hoolehua Airport,** also known as the Molokai Airport (MKK). It's on a dusty plain about 6 miles from Kaunakakai town. Multiple flights land daily from the neighbor islands, although there is no direct service to Molokai from the mainland. For interisland service, contact **Island Air** (☎ **800-652-6541** or 808-565-6744; www.islandair.com); you can also book your Island Air flights via codeshare, through **Hawaiian Airlines** (☎ **800-367-5320;** www.hawaiianair.com). You can also book interisland flights with **go! Airlines** (☎ **888-IFLYGO2** [888-435-9462]; www.iflygo.com).

Molokai's Top Attractions

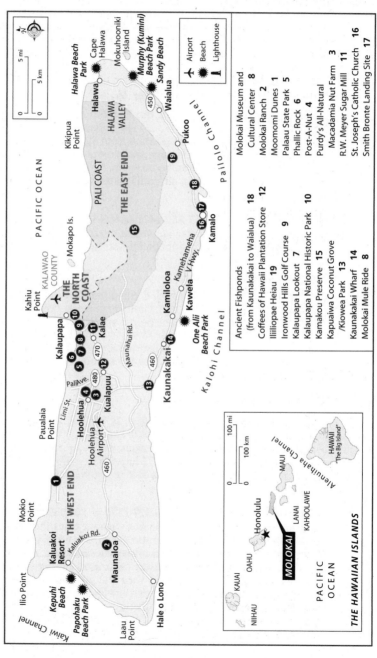

Ancient Fishponds
(from Kaunakakai to Waialua) **18**
Coffees of Hawaii Plantation Store **12**
Iliiliopae Heiau **19**
Ironwood Hills Golf Course **9**
Kalaupapa Lookout **7**
Kalaupapa National Historic Park **10**
Kamakou Preserve **15**
Kapuaiwa Coconut Grove
/Kiowea Park **13**
Kaunakakai Wharf **14**
Molokai Mule Ride **8**

Molokai Museum and
Cultural Center **8**
Molokai Ranch **2**
Moomomi Dunes **1**
Palaau State Park **5**
Phallic Rock **6**
Post-A-Nut **4**
Purdy's All-Natural
Macadamia Nut Farm **3**
R.W. Meyer Sugar Mill **11**
St. Joseph's Catholic Church **16**
Smith Bronte Landing Site **17**

You can also get to Molokai by taking a ferry from Maui. **Molokai Ferry** (☎ **866-307-6524;** www.molokaiferry.com) offers ferry service twice a day, Monday through Saturday, in each direction between Lahaina and Molokai on the *Maui Princess* and the *Molokai Princess.* Travel time is approximately 90 minutes, and the one-way fare is $40 adults, $20 kids 4 to 12. One-day golf and guided sightseeing tours of Molokai are also available.

Molokai day-trip packages from Maui

In addition to daily ferry service, the *Molokai Princess* ferry (☎ 877-500-6284; www.mauiprincess.com) also offers two different package options for Molokai island exploration from Maui: a Cruise-Car package, which includes round-trip passage and a rental car for $191 for the driver, $76 per additional adult passenger, and $38 for children; or the Alii Tour, a guided tour in an air-conditioned van plus lunch for $191 adults, $134 children.

Molokai Outdoors (☎ **877-553-4477** or 808-553-4477; www.molokai-outdoors.com) can also arrange day or overnight packages via air and ferry, including daylong Kalaupapa fly, hike, and mule-ride packages.

Getting around

Getting around Molokai isn't easy if you don't have a rental car, and rental cars are often hard to find. On holiday weekends, car-rental agencies simply run out of cars. Book before you go.

Molokai doesn't have any municipal transit or shuttle service, but a 24-hour taxi service is available (see the section "Taking a taxi or tour" later).

Renting a car

Rental cars are available from **Budget** (☎ **800-527-0700** or 808-567-6877; www.budget.com) and **Dollar** (☎ **800-800-4000,** 800-342-7398, or 808-567-6156; www.dollar.com); both agencies are located at the Molokai Airport. **Molokai Outdoors** (☎ **877-553-4477** or 808-553-4477; www.molokai-outdoors.com) may be able to get you special rates through Dollar; it's worth price-comparing.

Island Kine Auto Rental (☎ **866-527-7368** or 808-553-5242; www.molokai-car-rental.com) often has cheaper rates than the national brands. Barbara Shonely and her son, Steve, will meet you at the Molokai Airport, take you to their office in Kaunakakai, and recommend specific outfitters for your activities. Their used cars are in very good condition and are air-conditioned. Vans and pickup trucks are also available. You don't need a four-wheel-drive vehicle unless you're planning some specialized hiking, but if that's the case, Island Kine has what you're looking for.

Taking a taxi or tour

Molokai Off-Road Tours & Taxi (☎ **808-553-3369;** www.molokai.com/offroad) offers regular taxi service, an airport shuttle, and a full slate of island tours, including a one-day island tour from Maui for $211 per person, including airfare ($154 per person from Oahu). An island highlights tour is $49 per person.

Molokai Outdoors (☎ **877-553-4477** or 808-553-4477; www.molokai-outdoors.com) also offers taxi and shuttle services, plus guided island day tours on Tuesdays, Thursdays, and Saturdays for $167 per person, including a sit-down lunch at the Hotel Molokai. Shorter and custom options are also available; check the Web site for the full suite of offers.

Finding a Place to Stay

Molokai doesn't offer many places to stay, but it's Hawaii's most affordable island when it comes to accommodations. And because few restaurants are on the island, most hotel rooms and condo units come with kitchens, which can save you a bundle on dining costs. If you require anything beyond basic accommodations, you're better off on another island.

In the following listings, each hotel's name is followed by a number of dollar signs, ranging from one ($) to five ($$$$$). Each represents the median rack-rate price range for a double room per night, as follows:

Symbol	Meaning
$	Cheap — less than $150 per night
$$	Still affordable — $150–$224
$$$	Moderate — $225–$324
$$$$	Expensive but not ridiculous — $325–$449
$$$$$	Ultraluxurious — $450 or more per night

Don't forget that the state adds 11.42 percent in taxes to your hotel bill. But parking is free at all of these easygoing properties.

In addition to the choices below, **Molokai Outdoors** (☎ **877-553-4477** or 808-553-4477; www.molokai-outdoors.com) offers access to a range of vacation rentals around the island; check the Web site or call for details on what's available to suit your needs.

A'ahi Place
$ Kaunakakai

Just outside the main town of Kaunakakai and up a small hill lies this simple cedar vacation cottage, complete with a wicker-filled sitting area, a full kitchen (with microwave, coffeemaker, and toaster, but no dishwasher), and two full-size beds. Two lanais make great places to just sit and enjoy the stars at night. Tropical plants, flowers, and fruit trees surround the entire property. For $10 more per night (for two), get all the fixings for a continental breakfast (homegrown Molokai coffee, fresh-baked goods, and fruit from the property) placed in the kitchen so that you can enjoy it at your leisure. A'ahi Place is rather dated and not fancy by any means, but if you want a quiet getaway with no phone or TV to distract you, this is the place. And for people who want to really explore Molokai, the central location is perfect.

If your budget is really tight, ask about the separate no-frills "backpacker's cabin." It's tiny and rather spartan, but you can't argue with a price tag of only $35 per night.

See map p. 269. P.O. Box 528, Kaunakakai. ☎ **808-553-8033.** www.molokai.com/aahi. *Rack rates: $75 double without continental breakfast; $85 double with breakfast. Extra person $20. 3-night minimum stay (or $30 cleaning fee). 7th night free. No credit cards.*

Aloha Beach House
$$$ The East End

Nestled on the lush East End, this pretty Hawaiian-style beach house sits right on the white-sand beach of Waialua. Perfect for families, this impeccably decorated two-bedroom, one-bathroom, 1,600-square-foot beach house can sleep up to five people. The huge living/dining/kitchen area opens out to an old-fashioned porch for meals or just sitting in the comfy chairs and watching the clouds roll by. It's fully equipped, from the complete kitchen (including a dishwasher) and washer/dryer to satellite TV, VCR (plus a library of videos), and CD player to all the beach toys imaginable. Outdoor amenities include a barbecue and outdoor hot shower. Pleasing through and through, and well located near the Neighborhood Store.

See map p. 269. Located just after mile marker 19. ☎ **888-828-1008** *or 808-828-1100. Fax: 808-828-2199.* www.molokaivacation.com. *Rack rates: $290 per night or $2,135 weekly for 2 people, plus $175 cleaning fee. Extra person $20 per night (up to 5 total), with $225 cleaning fee; $2,325–$2,605 per week. 3-night minimum stay. No credit cards.*

Dunbar Beachfront Cottages
$$ The East End

This property is one of the most peaceful, comfortable, and elegant on Molokai's East End, and the setting is simply stunning. Each of these two green-and-white, plantation-style, two-bedroom cottages sits on its own

Molokai Accommodations and Dining

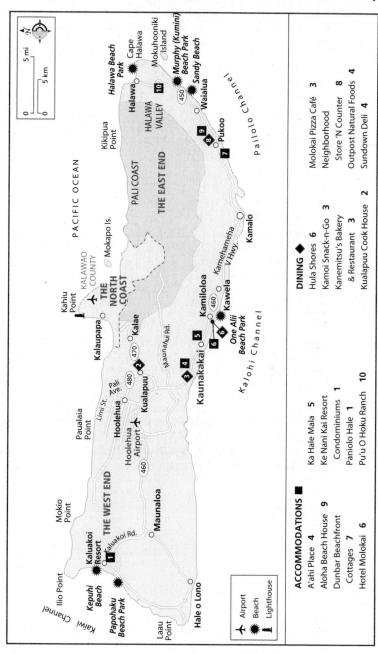

ACCOMMODATIONS ■

A'ahi Place **4**
Aloha Beach House **9**
Dunbar Beachfront
Cottages **7**
Hotel Molokai **6**

Ka Hale Mala **5**
Ke Nani Kai Resort
Condominiums **1**
Paniolo Hale **1**
Pu'u O Hoku Ranch **10**

DINING ◆

Hula Shores **6**
Kamoi Snack-n-Go **3**
Kanemitsu's Bakery
& Restaurant **3**
Kualapuu Cook House **2**

Molokai Pizza Café **3**
Neighborhood
Store 'N Counter **8**
Outpost Natural Foods **4**
Sundown Deli **4**

secluded beach that's good for swimming and snorkeling — you feel like you're on your own private island. The Puunana Cottage has a king-size bed and two twin beds; it sits atop a bluff and has beach access via a single flight of steps. The Pauwalu has a queen-size bed and two twin beds; it sits at beach level, which makes it a better choice for families with small children or anyone with access issues. Each has a full kitchen with microwave, VCR, ceiling fans, a washer and dryer, comfortable tropical furniture, large furnished deck (perfect for whale-watching in winter), outdoor barbecue, and breathtaking views of Maui, Lanai, and Kahoolawe across the channel. There's also a barbecue grill on the shady lawn.

See map p. 269. Kamehameha V Highway, past mile marker 18. ☎ *800-673-0520 or 808-558-8153. Fax: 808-558-8153.* www.molokai-beachfront-cottages.com. *Rack rates: $170 cottage, plus $75 cleaning charge. 3-night minimum stay. No credit cards.*

Hotel Molokai
$$ Kaunakakai

If you love midcentury tiki architecture, the Hotel Molokai is for you. This nostalgic Hawaiian motel complex is gloriously frozen in time. Reminiscent of an old-school Polynesian village, it's composed of a series of modified A-frame units, nestled under coco palms along a narrow but lovely gray-sand beach with a great view of Lanai. The rooms are basic (ask for one with a ceiling fan) but offer lanais. The friendly, caring management has lovingly renovated the hotel. Don't expect luxury, by any means, but you can expect fresh paint, tropical fabrics and furnishings. Every room has cable TV, high-speed Internet, a fridge, a clock radio, and a coffeemaker; few have kitchenettes. A half-dozen still bear the upgraded décor from their days as privately owned units; ask if any are available while you're on the island. The casual Hula Shores dining room has surprisingly good food and cocktails, plus a prime location on the sand. The hotel is the only place on Molokai with nightly entertainment, making this the liveliest spot on the island; Friday nights are especially worth seeking out. There's a petite spa center on site, in case you want a relaxing massage.

See map p. 269. Kamehameha V Highway, Kaunakakai. ☎ *800-535-0085 or 808-553-5347. Fax: 800-477-2329.* www.hotelmolokai.com. *Rack rates: $159–$249 double; from $249 honeymoon suite. AE, DC, DISC, MC, V.*

Ka Hale Mala
$ Kaunakakai

Jack and Cheryl Corbiell offer a spacious and private 900-square-foot, ground-floor apartment in their home that makes a pleasant and affordable place to stay for couples or families. Their home is located in a normal middle-class neighborhood not far from Kaunakakai town. The simple but pleasant suite boasts a fully equipped kitchen with microwave, a comfortable living room, a kitchen and dining area, a double bedroom, and a full bathroom; the living room can accommodate kids on two daybeds. The unit is outfitted with cable TV and CD player. A large lanai furnished for dining overlooks a fragrant tropical garden and orchard; you're welcome to pick from the bounty for your meals, or simply watch the birds that flutter through the garden. Picnic and beach gear is on hand for guests. Breakfasts are hearty, country-style affairs accompanied by fresh fruit, and served on the lanai by your hostess. Cheryl is extremely friendly and full of helpful information for visitors, and the home's central location makes a convenient base for exploring the island. If you're allergic to pet dander, you'll want to keep in mind that there is a cat in residence (though not in the rental unit).

See map p. 269. Off Kamehameha V Highway, just before mile marker 5, Kaunakakai. ☎ *and fax 808-553-9009.* www.molokai-bnb.com. *Rack rates: $90 double with breakfast; $80 double without breakfast. Extra person $20 with breakfast, $15 without breakfast. No credit cards.*

Ke Nani Kai Resort Condominiums
$–$$ The West End

This place is great for families, who appreciate the space. The large apartments are set up for full-time living with real kitchens, washer/dryers, VCRs, attractive furnishings, and breezy lanais. You also have access to a huge pool, a hot tub, a volleyball court, and tennis courts. These condos are farther from the sea than other local accommodations, but still just a brief walk from the beach. Parking and garden areas surround the two-story buildings. The only downside: Maid service is only every third day.

In addition to handling Ke Nani Kai and Paniolo Hale (see later), **Tropical Island Properties** offers some other good-quality rental properties around the island; call ☎ **800-367-2984** or 808-553-8334, or visit www.molokai-vacation-rental.com to peruse their full suite of listings.

See map p. 269. In the Kaluakoi Resort development, Kaluakoi Road, off Highway 460, Maunaloa. ☎ *800-367-2984 or 808-553-8334. Fax: 808-553-3783.* www.molokai-vacation-rental.com. *Rack rates: $104–$155 per night 1-bedroom condo (sleeps up to 4), $652–$1,086 weekly; $119–$225 2-bedroom condo (sleeps 4–6, depending on unit), $750–$1,570 weekly. Cleaning fee varies by unit ($75–$95). 3-night minimum stay. AE, DC, DISC, MC, V.*

Paniolo Hale
$$ The West End

The Paniolo Hale is one of Molokai's most charming lodgings and probably its best value. The two-story, old Hawaiian ranch-house design is airy and homey, with oak floors and walls of folding-glass doors that open to huge screened verandas, doubling your living space. The one- and two-bedroom units come with two bathrooms and easily accommodate three or four people. Some units have hot tubs on the lanai. All are spacious, comfortably furnished, and well equipped, with full kitchens and washer/dryers. The whole place overlooks the now-shuttered Kaluakoi Golf Course, a green barrier that separates these condos from the rest of Kaluakoi Resort. Out front, Kepuhi Beach is a scenic place for walkers and beachcombers, but the seas are too hazardous for most swimmers; swimmable Papohaku Beach is just a few minutes away. A pool, paddle tennis, and barbecue facilities are on the property, which adjoins open grassland. As with most condominiums in a rental pool, the quality and upkeep of the individually owned units can vary widely. When booking, spend some time talking with the friendly people at Tropical Island Properties so that you can get a top-quality condo that has been renovated recently.

See map p. 269. Next door to Kaluakoi Resort, Lio Place, Maunaloa. ☎ *800-367-2984 or 808-553-8334. Fax: 808-553-3783.* www.molokai-vacation-rental.com. *Rack rates: $102–$173 studio, $803–$1,207 weekly; $127–$187 1-bedroom condo, $803–$1,771 weekly; $224–$316 3-bedroom condo, $1,472–$2,213 weekly. Cleaning fee varies by unit ($65–$125). 3-night minimum stay. AE, DC, DISC, MC, V.*

Pu'u O Hoku Ranch
$$ The East End

Escape to a working cattle ranch! *Pu'u o Hoku* ("Hill of Stars") Ranch, which spreads across 14,000 acres of pasture and forests, is the last place to stay before you reach the wild Halawa Valley; it's at least an hour's drive along the shoreline from Kaunakakai. The main lodge building, which sleeps 22, hosts large groups, including retreats, seminars, and family reunions. But you're more likely to be interested in booking the separate cottage or the Grove House.

Two acres of tropically landscaped property circle the ranch's rustic cottage, which boasts breathtaking views of rolling hills and the Pacific Ocean. The 1,050-square-foot wooden cottage features comfortable country furniture, a full kitchen, two bedrooms (one with a double bed, one with two twin beds), two bathrooms, and a separate dining room on the enclosed lanai. The 2,100-square-foot Grove House has four bedrooms (two with queen-size beds and two with two twin beds). It also features a fully equipped kitchen, a fireplace, and an inviting lanai.

You can stargaze at night, hike miles of trails in the afternoon, or relax on a secluded white-sand beach 2 miles down the road. (And, of course, horseback riding is available at the ranch.) TVs and VCRs are available in both units, and guests are usually welcome to use the pool at the main lodge. Both cottages boast stunning views of Maui and marvelous whale-watching in winter.

See map p. 269. Kamehameha V Highway, at mile marker 25, Kaunakakai. ☎ *808-558-8109. Fax: 808-558-8100.* www.puuohoku.com. *Rack rates: Cottage $140 double; Grove House $160 double. Extra person $20. Cleaning fee varies by unit ($75–$100). 3-night minimum stay. MC, V.*

Dining

Molokai is all about adventure, the outdoors, and getting away from it all. When it comes to dining, the offerings are sparse. Mom-and-pop eateries dominate the scene. They're nothing fancy — most of them are fast-food or takeout places, and many feature simple, hearty home cooking. Molokai doesn't cater to food and wine connoisseurs, especially now that the ranch is closed.

Molokai's restaurants are inexpensive or moderately priced, and several of them don't accept credit cards. Regardless of where you eat, you certainly don't have to dress up. In most cases, I list just the town rather than the street address — street addresses are as meaningless on this island as fancy cars and sequins. Reservations aren't accepted unless otherwise noted.

In the restaurant listings that follow, each restaurant name is followed by a number of dollar signs, ranging from one ($) to five ($$$$$). The dollar signs are meant to give you an idea of what a complete dinner for one person — with appetizer, main course, a drink, tax, and tip — is likely to cost. The price categories go like this:

Symbol	Meaning
$	Cheap eats — less than $20 per person
$$	Still inexpensive — $20–$34
$$$	Moderate — $35–$49
$$$$	Pricey — $50 or more

To give you an even better idea of how much you can expect to spend, I also include the price range of main courses or items in the listings. (Prices can change at any time, of course, but restaurants usually don't raise their prices by more than a dollar or two at any given time.)

Note: The restaurants reviewed here are plotted on the "Molokai Accommodations and Dining" map on p. 269.

Hula Shores
$$$ Kaunakakai   AMERICAN/ISLAND

This is my favorite place to dine on Molokai. This open-air dining room with the warm tropical vibe sits right on the ocean — the waves practically lap at your toes — with a view of Lanai, torches flickering under palm trees, and tiny fairy lights lining the room and the neighboring pool area. It's a casual setting for dinner or cocktails, with the most pleasing ambience on the island. Lunch choices stick to hearty island basics, such as salads prepared with Big Island organic greens and sandwiches, from roast beef to grilled mahimahi. I like the Asian salad wrap with char-sui pork. As the sun sets and the torches are lit for dinner, the menu turns to more substantial meats, ribs, fish, and pasta. Try the fresh catch or the Korean *kalbi* ribs. All in all, the food is surprisingly good, as are the tropical cocktails; don't miss the *li hing mui* margarita for a real island treat. This is the only place on the island with live entertainment nightly; Friday night is the most festive night of the week.

See map p. 269. In the Hotel Molokai, on Kamehameha V Highway. ☎ *808-553-5347.* www.hotelmolokai.com. *Reservations recommended for dinner. Main courses:*

Breakfast $6–$12; lunch $8–$11; dinner $15–$25. AE, DC, MC, V. Open: Daily 7–10:30 a.m.; 11 a.m.–2 p.m.; 6–9 p.m. (4–9 p.m. Fri).

Kamoi Snack-N-Go
$ Kaunakakai   ICE CREAM/SNACKS

This is the place to satisfy your sweet tooth. Ice cream made by Dave's on Oahu comes in such flavors as green tea, litchi sherbet, *ube* (a brilliant purple color, made from Okinawan sweet potato), *haupia*, mango, and many other tropical — and traditional — flavors. Schoolchildren and their parents line up for the cones, shakes, sundaes, and popular ICEE floats. This tiny snack shop also has tempting aisles full of candy.

See map p. 269. In Kamoi Professional Center, 28 Kamoi St., Kaunakakai. ☎ *808-553-3742. Ice cream less than $5. MC, V. Open: Mon–Sat 9 a.m.–9 p.m.; Sun noon to 9 p.m.*

Kanemitsu's Bakery & Restaurant
$ Kaunakakai   BAKERY/DELI

Morning, noon, and night, this local legend fills the Kaunakakai air with the intoxicating aroma of fresh-baked bread. Taro *lavosh* and Molokai bread (developed in 1935 in a cast-iron, kiawe-fired oven) are the hot sellers. Flavors range from apricot-pineapple to mango (in season), but the classics remain the regular white, wheat, cheese, sweet, and onion-cheese breads. The bread mixes are a great way to take a taste of Molokai home with you. In the adjoining coffee shop/deli, all sandwiches come with their own freshly baked buns and breads. The hamburgers, egg-salad sandwiches, mahi burgers, and honey-dipped fried chicken are popular and cheap. Ask the locals about the nighttime bread line, which is among the island's finest after-dark activities.

See map p. 269. 79 Ala Malama St., Kaunakakai. ☎ *808-553-5855. Most items under $8. No credit cards. Open: Restaurant Wed–Mon 5:30 a.m. to noon; bakery Wed–Mon 5:30 a.m.–6:30 p.m.*

Kualapuu Cookhouse
$$ En route to north coast   AMERICAN

An old wagon in front of a former plantation house marks this down-home takeout spot, which some consider to be the best food on Molokai now that that Molokai Lodge restaurant is closed. I'm hard pressed to disagree. Local residents flock here, not only for the family atmosphere but also for the oversize servings. Breakfasts feature giant omelets, homemade corned beef hash, and, for diners who dare, The Works — buttermilk pancakes, eggs, and home fries (you'll either be fueled for the day or ready to take a nap). Lunch can either be a burger or sandwich, or one of their humongous plate lunches of pork *katsu* or chicken, served up with rice, of course. Prime-rib Thursdays are worth planning for. No alcohol is served, but you're welcome to bring your own.

See map p. 269. 102 Farrington Ave., 1 block west of Highway 470, Hoolehua. ☎ *808-567-9655. Most items under $18. No credit cards. Open: Mon 7 a.m.–2 p.m.; Tues–Sat 7 a.m.–8 p.m.*

Molokai Pizza Cafe
$$ **Kaunakakai PIZZA**

The excellent pizzas and sandwiches make this a major gathering place for locals. The best-selling pies are the Molokai (pepperoni and cheese), the Big Island (pepperoni, ham, mushroom, Italian sausage, bacon, and vegetables), and the Molokini (plain cheese slices). Pasta, sandwiches, and very good daily fish specials round out the menu; the fresh-baked submarine and pocket sandwiches and the gyro pocket with spinach pie are hits. Sunday is prime-rib day, Wednesday is Mexican, and Hawaiian plates are sold on Thursdays. Coin-operated cars and a toy airplane follow the children's theme, but adults feel equally at home with the very popular barbecued baby-back-rib plate and the fresh fish dinners. Children's art and letters in the tiled dining room add an entertaining and charming touch.

See map p. 269. In Kahua Center, 15 Kaunakaki Place (on the old Wharf Road) Kaunakakai. ☎ *808-553-3288. Large pizzas $14–$25. No credit cards. Open: Mon–Thurs 10 a.m.–10 p.m.; Fri–Sat 10 a.m.–11 p.m.; Sun 11 a.m.–10 p.m.*

Neighborhood Store 'N Counter
$ **The East End AMERICAN**

The Neighborhood Store is nothing fancy, and that's what folks love about it. This store/lunch counter appears like a mirage near mile marker 16, in the Pukoo area, en route to the East End. Picnic tables under a royal poinciana tree are a wonderful sight, and the food doesn't disappoint. The place serves omelets, Portuguese sausage, and other breakfast specials (brunch is very popular) and then segues into sandwiches, salads, mahimahi plates, and varied over-the-counter lunch offerings. Favorites include the mahimahi plate lunch, the chicken *katsu,* and the Mexican plate, each one with a tried-and-true home-cooked flavor. The Neighborhood Store offers daily specials, ethnic dishes, and some vegetarian options, as well as burgers (including a killer veggie burger), saimin, and legendary desserts. Made-on-Maui Roselani ice cream is a featured attraction, and customers rave over the Portuguese doughnut dessert, a deep-fried doughnut filled with ice cream. A Molokai treasure, the Neighborhood Store is also the only grocery store on the East End.

See map p. 269. Kamehameha Highway (at mile marker 16), Pukoo. ☎ *808-558-8498. Main courses: Most items less than $10. No credit cards. Open: Daily 8 a.m–5 p.m.*

Outpost Natural Foods
$ **Kaunakakai VEGETARIAN**

The freshest food on the island is served at this health store's lunch counter, around the corner from the main drag on the ocean side of Kaunakakai town. The tiny store abounds in Molokai papayas, bananas, herbs, potatoes, watermelon, and other local produce, complementing its selection of vitamins, cosmetics, and health aids, as well as bulk and shelf items. But the real star is the closet-size lunch counter. The salads, burritos, tempeh sandwiches, vegetarian potpie, tofu-spinach lasagna, and mock chicken, turkey, and meatloaf (made from oats, sprouts, seeds, and seasonings) are testament to the fact that vegetarian food need not be boring. It's a must for health-conscious diners and shoppers.

See map p. 269. 70 Makaena Place. ☎ 808-553-3377. Main courses: Most items less than $9. AE, DISC, MC, V. Open: Sun–Fri breakfast and lunch.

Sundown Deli
$ Kaunakakai   DELI

From "gourmet saimin" to spinach pie, Sundown's offerings are home-cooked and healthful, with daily specials that include vegetarian quiche, vegetarian lasagna, and club sandwiches. The sandwiches (such as smoked turkey and chicken salad) and several salads (Caesar, oriental, and stuffed tomato) are served daily, with the soup of the day. Vitamins, T-shirts, and snacks are sold in this tiny cafe, but most of the business is takeout.

See map p. 269. 145 Puali St. (across the street from Veteran's Memorial Park). ☎ 808-553-3713. Main courses: Sandwiches, soups, and salads $4–$9. AE, MC, V. Open: Mon–Fri 7:30 a.m.–3:30 p.m.

Having Fun on and off the Beach

With imposing sea cliffs on one side and lazy fishponds on the other, Molokai has little room for beaches along its 106-mile coast — but the beaches that are accessible certainly provide an array of watersports. There's plenty of action on dry land, too, including golf and biking.

If you want to see the most Hawaiian island with a knowledgeable guide, contact **Molokai Outdoors** (☎ 877-553-4477 or 808-553-4477; www. molokai-outdoors.com). Molokai Outdoors offers the most comprehensive suite of guided activities on the island, from biking, hiking, and horseback riding adventures to ocean kayaking and deep-sea fishing adventures; they even offer packaged Kalaupapa sightseeing. Check out the Web site to review its full slate of adventures.

Discovering Molokai's beaches

A big gold-sand beach awaits on the West End, in addition to tiny pocket beaches on the East End. The emptiness of Molokai's beaches is both a blessing and a curse: The seclusion means no lifeguards on any of the beaches.

At the foot of scenic Halawa Valley is **Halawa Beach Park,** a beautiful black-sand beach with a palm-fringed lagoon, a wave-lashed island off-shore, and a distant view of the West Maui Mountains across the Pailolo

Channel. The swimming is safe in the shallows close to shore, but where the waterfall stream meets the sea, the ocean is often murky and unnerving. A winter swell creases the mouth of Halawa Valley on the north side of the bay and attracts a crowd of local surfers. Facilities are minimal; bring your own water. To get there, take King Kamehameha V Highway (Highway 450) east to the end.

Golfers see **Kepuhi Beach,** a picturesque golden strand in front of the closed Kaluakoi Resort and Golf Course, as just another sand trap, but sunbathers like the semiprivate grassy dunes; they're seldom, if ever, crowded. Beachcombers often find what they're looking for there, but swimmers have to dodge lava rocks and risk riptides. Oh, yes — look out for errant golf balls. The beach doesn't have any facilities or lifeguards, so be sure to pack in anything you might need.

Murphy Beach Park was formerly Kumimi Beach Park, and some old-timers still call it Kumimi Beach, but, just to make everything more confusing, some people call it Jaycees Park. No matter what you call it, ironwood trees line this white-sand beach and shade the small, quaint park. Swimming is generally safe. On calm days, snorkeling and diving are great outside the reef. You may spot some fishermen there, looking for _papio_ and other island fish.

One Alii Beach Park, a thin strip of sand, once reserved for the _alii_ (chiefs), is the oldest public beach park on Molokai. You find One (_o-nay_) Alii Beach Park by a coconut grove on the outskirts of Kaunakakai. Safe for swimmers of all ages and abilities, it often draws crowds of families on weekends, but it can be all yours on weekdays. Facilities include outdoor showers, restrooms, and free parking.

Nearly 3 miles long and 100 yards wide, gold-sand **Papohaku Beach** is one of the biggest in Hawaii. It's great for walking, beachcombing, picnics, and sunset-watching year-round. The big surf and riptides make swimming risky except in summer, when the waters are calmer. Go early in the day, when the tropical sun is less fierce and the winds are calm. The beach is so big that you may never see another soul except at sunset, when a few people gather on the shore in hopes of spotting the elusive green flash, a natural wonder that takes place when the horizon is cloud free. Facilities include outdoor showers, restrooms, picnic grounds, and free parking.

Sandy Beach is Molokai's most popular swimming spot — it's ideal for families with small kids. The beach is a roadside pocket of gold sand protected by a reef, with a great view of Maui and Lanai. You'll find it off the King Kamehameha V Highway (Highway 450) at mile marker 20. The beach doesn't have any facilities — just you, the sun, the sand, and the surf.

Enjoying the water

The best places to rent beach toys (snorkels, body boards, beach chairs, fishing poles, kayaks, and more) is **Molokai Outdoors,** in the lobby of the Hotel Molokai, just outside Kaunakakai (☎ **877-553-4477** or 808-553-4477; www.molokai-outdoors.com). Here you'll find everything you need for a day at the beach, plus advice on where it's safe to swim or where the waves are breaking. Another good place to check out is **Molokai Fish & Dive,** Kaunakakai (☎ **808-553-5926**; www.molokaifish anddive.com), a mind-boggling store filled with outdoor gear. You can rent snorkels, fishing gear, and even ice chests. This place is also a hot spot for fishing news and tips on what's running where.

Body boarding and bodysurfing

Molokai has only three beaches that offer rideable waves for body boarding and bodysurfing: Papohaku, Kepuhi, and Halawa. Even these beaches are only for experienced bodysurfers due to the strength of the rip currents and undertows.

You can rent body boards with fins for $5 a day or $20 a week at **Molokai Outdoors,** in the lobby of the Hotel Molokai, just outside Kaunakakai (☎ **877-553-4477** or 808-553-4477; www.molokai-outdoors.com).

Ocean kayaking

During the summer months, when the waters on the North Shore are calm, Molokai offers some of the most spectacular kayaking in Hawaii. However, most of Molokai is for the experienced kayaker. You must be adept in paddling through open ocean swells and rough waves.

Molokai Outdoors, in the lobby of the Hotel Molokai, just outside Kaunakakai (☎ **877-553-4477** or 808-553-4477; www.molokai-outdoors. com), has several different kayak tours, including routes that explore the ancient Hawaii fishponds and the inshore reefs. The standard Downwinder Kayak Adventure is suitable for kayakers from beginning to advanced; you'll paddle about 6 miles inside one of the U.S.'s most pristine reefs for magical snorkeling. The per-person rate is $89, plus $10 if you'd like lunch to be provided.

Molokai Fish & Dive (☎ **808-553-5926**; www.molokaifishanddive. com) also offered guided ocean kayaking tours for all levels of kayakers; their six-hour adventure is $89 per person, including lunch. Kayak rentals are available as well; single boats are $26 per day or $113 per week, while doubles are $39 per day or $167 per week. (Double renters will need to rent an extra paddle for $5 per day or $24 per week.)

Scuba diving

Want to see turtles or manta rays up close? How about sharks? Contact **Molokai Fish & Dive,** Kaunakakai (☎ **808-553-5926**; www.molokaifish anddive.com), can also arrange custom tours for experienced divers along the longest fringe reef in the islands, using top-of-the-line equipment. Two-tank dives are $135, three-tank dives are $275, and Discover Scuba outings for beginners are $195.

Snorkeling

Molokai offers excellent snorkeling. You're like to spot a wide range of butterfly fish, *tangs,* and angelfish. Most of the island's beaches are too dangerous for snorkeling in winter, when big waves and strong currents are generated by storms that sweep down from Alaska. From mid-September through April, stick to Murphy Beach Park (also known as Kumimi Beach Park) on the East End. But in summer (roughly May to mid-Sept), the Pacific Ocean takes a holiday and turns into a flat lake. In these calmer months, the whole west coast of Molokai opens up for snorkeling.

Molokai Outdoors (☎ 877-553-4477 or 808-553-4477; www.molokai-outdoors.com) offers the least-expensive snorkel gear for rent ($6 a day or $24 a week). You can also rent prescription masks in case you have less than 20/20 vision.

For snorkeling tours, contact **Bill Kapuni's Snorkel & Dive,** Kaunakakai (☎ 808-553-9867), which charges $65 for a two-and-a-half-hour trip. Bill also rents snorkeling gear for $10 a day (see "Scuba diving," earlier). Walter Naki of **Molokai Action Adventures** (☎ 808-558-8184) offers leisurely snorkeling, diving, and swimming trips in his 21-foot Boston Whaler for $100 per person for a four- to six-hour custom tour. **Molokai Fish & Dive** (☎ 808-553-5926; www.molokaifishanddive.com) also offer excellent snorkel tours from its 31-foot twin-hull Power Cat for $69 per person.

Sportfishing

Molokai's waters can provide prime sporting opportunities, whether you're looking for big-game sportfishing or bottom fishing. When customers are scarce, Captain Joe Reich, who has been fishing the waters around Molokai for decades, goes commercial fishing, so he always knows where the fish are biting. He runs **Alyce C. Sportfishing** out of Kaunakakai Harbor (☎ 808-558-8377; www.alycecsportfishing.com). A full day of fishing for up to six people is $500, three-quarters of a day is $450, and a half-day is $400. You can usually persuade him to do a whale-watching cruise during the winter months.

For fly-fishing or light-tackle reef-fish trolling, contact Walter Naki at **Molokai Action Adventures** (☎ 808-558-8184). Walter has been fishing his entire life and loves to share his secret spots with visiting fishermen — he knows *the* place for bonefishing on the flats. A full-day trip in his 21-foot Boston Whaler is $350 for up to four people. You're welcome to call Walter even if you don't feel like fishing; he's happy to take you out snorkeling, whale watching in winter, or just sightseeing from the sea. He'll even take you bow or rifle hunting on private land for axis deer, wild boar, or Spanish goats.

For deep-sea fishing, Captain Mike Holmes's **Fun Hogs Hawaii** (☎ 808-336-0047; www.molokaifishing.com) has fishing excursions on a 27-foot, fully equipped sportfishing vessel. For six passengers, both near-shore and deep-sea fishing trips are $428 for four hours, $535 for six hours, and $642 for eight hours. Whale-watching outings are available in season.

If you just want to try your luck casting along the shoreline, **Molokai Outdoors,** located in the lobby of the Hotel Molokai, just outside Kaunakakai (☎ 877-553-4477 or 808-553-4477; www.molokai-outdoors. com), rents fishing poles for $5 a day or $24 per week and can tell you where the fish are biting.

Hitting the links

Now that the Ted Robinson–designed Kaluakoi Golf Course is closed, the island's best option is the **Ironwood Hills Golf Course,** off Kalae Highway (☎ 808-567-6000), Hawaii's very first golf course. You can locate it just before the Molokai Mule Ride Mule Barn, on the road to the Lookout. Del Monte Plantation built Ironwood Hills (named after the two predominant features of the course, ironwood trees and hills) in 1929 for its executives. This unusual course, which sits in the cool air at 1,200 feet, delights with its rich foliage, open fairways, and spectacular views of the island. If you play there, use a trick developed by the local residents: After teeing off on the 6th hole, just take whatever clubs you need to finish playing the hole and a driver for the 7th hole and park your bag under a tree. The climb to the 7th hole is steep — you'll be glad that you're only carrying a few clubs. Greens fees are only $18 for 9 holes and $24 for 18 holes. Twilight specials are available from 3 p.m.; call for twilight rates.

Exploring the island on two wheels

Molokai is a great place to tour by bicycle. The roads aren't very busy, and you can always pull off the road and take a quick, refreshing dip. **Molokai Outdoors,** in the lobby of the Hotel Molokai, just outside Kaunakakai (☎ 877-553-4477 or 808-553-4477; www.molokai-outdoors. com), offers a combination bike-kayak tour of the East End, taking in a healthy dose of local culture and history as you make your way to a spectacular waterfall. If you'd prefer to set out on your own, bike rentals are $26 a day or $113 per week, including a helmet and a bike rack for your car.

Seeing the Sights

Molokai has plenty of history and beauty that you don't want to miss. Let's get started exploring each region of the island. *Note:* The following attractions are plotted on the "Molokai" map on p. 265.

In and around Kaunakakai

Kapuaiwa Coconut Grove/Kiowea Park

This scruffy but still-royal grove — 1,000 coconut trees on 10 acres planted in 1863 by the island's high chief Kapua'iwa (later, King Kamehameha V) — is a major roadside attraction. The shoreline park is a favorite subject of sunset photographers and visitors who delight in a hand-lettered sign that warns: DANGER: FALLING COCONUTS. In its backyard, across the highway, stands Church Row: seven churches, each a different denomination — clear evidence of the missionary impact on Hawaii.

See map p. 265. Along Maunaloa Highway (Highway 460), 2 miles west of Kaunakakai.

Post-A-Nut

Postmaster Margaret Keahi-Leary can help you say "Aloha" with a dried Molokai coconut. Just write a message on the coconut with a felt-tip pen, and she'll send it via U.S. Mail over the sea. Coconuts are free, but postage starts at $4.95 for a mainland-bound 2-pound coconut.

See map p. 265. At the Hoolehua Post Office, Puu Peelua Avenue (Highway 480), near Maunaloa Highway (Highway 460, a half-mile from the Molokai Airport). ☎ *808-567-6144. Open: Mon–Fri 7:30–11:30 a.m. and 12:30–4:30 p.m.*

Purdy's All-Natural Macadamia Nuts (Na Hua O'Ka Aina)

The Purdys have made macadamia-nut buying an entertainment event, offering tours of the homestead and giving lively demonstrations of nutshell cracking in the shade of their towering trees. The tour of the 70-year-old nut farm explains the growing, bearing, harvesting, and shelling processes, so that by the time you bite into the luxurious macadamia nut, you'll have more than a passing knowledge of its entire life cycle. This is a great place to purchase gifts — not only delicious macadamia nuts, but also macadamia blossom honey and macadamia honey-mustard.

See map p. 265. Lihi Pali Avenue (2 miles west of Kualapuu, behind Molokai High School), Hoolehua. ☎ *808-567-6601.* www.molokai-aloha.com/macnuts. *Admission: Free. Open: Mon–Fri 9:30 a.m.–3:30 p.m.; Sat 10 a.m.–2 p.m. Closed on holidays.*

The North Coast

Even if you don't get a chance to see Hawaii's most dramatic coast in its entirety — not many people do — don't miss the opportunity to glimpse it from the **Kalaupapa Lookout** at Palauu State Park. On the way, I've listed a few diversions, arranged in geographical order en route to the North Coast.

Coffees of Hawaii

The defunct Del Monte pineapple town of Kualapuu is rising again — only this time, the crop is coffee, not pineapples. Coffees of Hawaii grows coffee beans on 600 acres of former pineapple land in the cool foothills, irrigating the plants with a high-tech, continuous water and fertilizer drip system. The whole process is designed to be ecologically friendly; you can see it on a somewhat pricey, 90-minute mule-drawn wagon tour or walking tour (call 24 hours in advance to confirm the schedule and reserve a spot). Harvest season, from November through January, makes for a fun visit; the flowering coffee trees are a particularly pretty sight in March and April. Feel free to stop by even if you pass on the tour. The lovely gift shop sells a variety of coffees, plus arts and crafts from Molokai. Stop by the friendly Espresso Bar for breakfast, lunch, or a delicious coffee concoction, such as the Mocha Mama (Molokai coffee, ice cream, and Ghirardelli chocolate). It'll keep you going all day — maybe even all night.

See map p. 265. 1630 Farrington Hwy. (Highway 480, near the junction of Highway 470). ☎ *877-322-FARM (877-322-3276) or 808-567-9490.* www.coffeesofhawaii.net. *Admission: Morning Espresso walking tour $20; mule-drawn wagon tour $35, $10 kids 5–15 (free for kids 4 and under). Also inquire about afternoon hiking adventures offered most weekdays at 3 p.m. Gift shop and espresso bar open daily.*

Molokai Museum and Cultural Center

En route to the California Gold Rush in 1849, Rudolph W. Meyer, a German professor, came to Molokai, married the high chieftess Kalama, and began to operate a small sugar plantation near his home. Now on the National Register of Historic Places, this restored 1878 sugar mill, with its century-old steam engine, mule-driven cane crusher, copper clarifiers, and redwood evaporating pan (all in working order), is the last of its kind in Hawaii. The mill also houses a museum that traces the history of sugar growing on Molokai and features special events, such as wine tastings every two months, taro festivals, an annual music festival, guided hikes, and occasional classes in ukulele making, loom weaving, and sewing. Call for a schedule.

See map p.265. Meyer Sugar Mill, Highway 470 (just after the turnoff for the Ironwood Hills Golf Course, and 2 miles below Kalaupapa Overlook), Kalae. ☎ *808-567-6436. Admission: $2.50 adults, $1 students. Open: Mon–Sat 10 a.m.–2 p.m.*

Palaau State Park

This 234-acre piney-woods park, 8 miles from Kaunakakai, doesn't look like much until you get out of the car and take a hike, which literally puts you between a rock and a hard place. Go right, and you end up on the edge of Molokai's magnificent sea cliffs, with its panoramic view of the well-known Kalaupapa leper colony. Go left, and you come face to face with a stone phallus.

If you have no plans to scale the cliffs by mule or on foot, I highly recommend visiting the **Kalaupapa Lookout,** the only place from which to see the former place of exile. The trail is marked, and historic photos and interpretive signs explain what you're seeing.

The ironwood forest is airy and cool — perfect for a short uphill walk to Molokai's famous **Phallic Rock.** Six feet high, pointed at an angle that means business, Phallic Rock is a legendary fertility tool. According to

Hawaiian legend, a woman who wants to become pregnant need only spend the night near the rock and, *voilà!* It's probably just a coincidence, of course, but Molokai does have a growing number of young, pregnant women.

Phallic Rock is at the end of a well-worn uphill path that passes an ironwood grove and several other rocks that vaguely resemble sexual body parts. There's no mistaking the real thing, though. Supposedly, it belonged to Nanahoa, a demigod who quarreled with his wife, Kawahuna, over a pretty girl. In the tussle, Kawahuna was thrown over the cliff, and both husband and wife were turned to stone. Of all the phallic rocks in Hawaii and the Pacific, this rock is the one to see. The rock is also featured on a postcard you might see around town with a tiny, awestruck Japanese woman standing next to it.

See map p. 265. At the end of Highway 470.

The legacy of Father Damien: Kalaupapa National Historic Park

An old tongue of lava that sticks out to form a peninsula, Kalaupapa became infamous because of the inhumanity unleashed upon victims of a once-incurable contagious disease.

King Kamehameha V sent the first lepers — nine men and three women — into exile on this lonely shore, at the base of ramparts that rise like temples against the Pacific, on January 6, 1866. By 1874, more than 11,000 lepers had been dispatched to die in one of the world's most beautiful — and lonely — places. They called Kalaupapa "The Place of the Living Dead."

Leprosy is actually one of the world's least contagious diseases, transmitted only by direct, repetitive contact over a long period of time. A germ, *Mycobacterium leprae,* which attacks the nerves, skin, and eyes, causes leprosy. The germ is found mainly, but not exclusively, in tropical regions. American scientists found a cure for the disease in the 1940s.

Before science found a cure, Father Damien intervened. Born to wealth in Belgium, Father Damien (born Joseph de Veuster) traded a life of excess for exile among lepers; he devoted himself to caring for the afflicted at Kalaupapa. Father Damien volunteered to go out to the Pacific in place of his ailing brother. Horrified by the conditions he found in the leper colony, Father Damien worked at Kalaupapa for 11 years, building houses, schools, and churches, and giving hope to his patients. He died on April 15, 1889, in Kalaupapa, of leprosy. He was 49.

A hero nominated for Catholic sainthood, Father Damien is buried not in his tomb next to Molokai's St. Philomena Church but in his native Belgium. (Well, most of him anyway: His hand was recently returned to Molokai and was buried at Kalaupapa as a relic of his martyrdom.)

This small peninsula is probably the final resting place of more than 11,000 souls. The sand dunes are littered with grave markers, sorted by the religious affiliation — Catholic, Protestant, Buddhist — of those who died there. But because so many are buried in unmarked graves, no accurate census of the dead exists.

Kalaupapa is now a National Historic Park (☎ 808-567-6802; www.nps. gov/kala) and one of Hawaii's richest archaeological preserves, with sites that date from A.D. 1000. Only a tiny handful of former patients chose to remain in the tidy village of whitewashed houses with statues of angels in their yards. The original name for their former affliction, leprosy, was officially banned in Hawaii by the state legislature in 1981. The name used now is Hansen's disease, for Dr. Gerhard Hansen of Norway, who discovered the germ in 1873. Remaining residents of Kalaupapa still call the disease leprosy, although none are too keen on being called lepers.

Kalaupapa welcomes visitors who arrive on foot, by mule, or by small plane. Father Damien's St. Philomena church, built in 1872, is open to visitors, who can see it from a yellow school bus driven by resident tour guide Richard Marks, an ex-seaman and sheriff who survived the disease. You can't roam freely, and you can only enter the museum, the craft shop, and the church.

Visitors must be 16 years of age or older; you can't bring the kids along for this adventure.

Taking a mule ride to Kalaupapa

Riding a mule to Kalaupapa is quite memorable. The first turn is a gasp, and it's downhill from there. You can close your eyes and hold on for dear life, or slip the reins over the pommel and sit back, letting the mule do the walking down the precipitous path to Kalaupapa National Historic Park.

Even if you have only one day on Molokai, spend it on a mule. This ride is a once-in-a-lifetime adventure. The cliffs are taller than a 300-story skyscraper, but Buzzy Sproat's mules go safely up and down the narrow 3-mile trail daily, rain or shine. Starting at the top of the nearly perpendicular ridge (1,600 ft. high), the surefooted mules step down the muddy trail, pausing often on the 26 switchbacks to calculate their next move — and always, it seems, veering close to the edge. Each switchback is numbered; by the time you get to number four, you'll catch your breath, put the mule on cruise control, and begin to enjoy Hawaii's most awesome trail ride.

The mule tour starts Monday through Saturday at 8 a.m. and lasts until about 3:15 p.m. The tour costs $175 per person for the all-day adventure, which includes the round-trip mule ride, a light picnic lunch, a guided tour of the settlement, a visit to Father Damien's church and grave, lunch at Kalawao, and souvenirs. To go, you must be at least 16 years old, physically fit, and less than 245 pounds. (Wear closed-toe shoes and longer pants.) Contact **Molokai Mule Ride,** 100 Kalae Highway, Suite 104, on Highway 470, 5 miles north of Highway 460 (☎ **800-567-7550** or 808-567-6088 between 8 and 10 p.m.; www.muleride.com). *Note:* Advance reservations (at least two weeks ahead) are required, because space is limited to 18 visitors. They also offer complete packages from Maui that include round-trip airfare, overnight stay, airport transfers, lunch, and the mule tour; inquire about options and prices. Complete packages are also available from Honolulu.

Seeing Kalaupapa by ferry/hiking

From Maui, you can take the *Molokai Princess* ferry to Molokai (☎ **866-307-6524** or 808-662-3355 on Maui; www.mauiprincess.com), where a van meets you and transports you to the top of the 1,700-foot sea cliffs. You then hike down the 3-mile trail to the Kalaupapa National Historic Park. At the park, Damien Tours meets you and gives you a van tour of the peninsula, during which you visit Father Damien's St. Philomena Church and hear the stories of struggle and courage of Kalaupapa's residents. Then you'll have to hike back up the 1,700-foot cliffs, where the van picks you up and returns you to the ferry dock for the trip back to Maui. It takes about an hour hiking down and another 90 minutes to hike back up; it's a serious challenge, so you have to be in good shape to join this tour. The cost for ferry, transportation, tour, and lunch is $277. (As with all the other tours, participants must be 16 years and older. Call ahead to reserve, as the tour is only offered three times a week in season.)

On the northwest shore

Undisturbed for centuries, the **Moomomi Dunes,** on Molokai's northwest shore, are a unique treasure chest of great scientific value. The area may look like just a pile of sand as you fly over on the final approach to Hoolehua Airport, but Moomomi Dunes are much more. Archaeologists have found quarries, ancient Hawaiian burial sites, and shelter caves; botanists have identified five endangered plant species; and marine biologists are finding evidence that endangered green sea turtles are coming out from the waters once again to lay eggs there. The greatest discovery, however, belongs to Smithsonian Institute ornithologists, who have found bones of prehistoric birds — some of them flightless — that existed nowhere else on Earth.

Accessible by Jeep trails that thread downhill to the shore, this wild coast is buffeted by strong afternoon breezes. It's hot, dry, and windy, so take water, sunscreen, and a windbreaker.

At Kawaaloa Bay, a 20-minute walk to the west, you find a broad golden beach that you can have all to yourself. Warning: Due to the rough seas, stay out of the water. Within the dunes, you find a 920-acre preserve accessible via monthly guided nature tours led by the **Nature Conservancy of Hawaii;** call ☎ **808-553-5236** or 808-524-0779 for an exact schedule and details.

To get there, take Highway 460 (Maunaloa Highway) from Kaunakakai, turn right onto Highway 470, and follow it to Kualapuu. At Kualapuu, turn left on Highway 480 and go through Hoolehua Village; it's 3 miles to the bay.

The East End

The East End is a cool and inviting green place that's worth a drive to the end of King Kamehameha V Highway (Highway 450). Unfortunately, the trail that leads into the area's greatest natural attraction in Halawa Valley, the Hipuapua Falls, is off-limits because it's located on private property.

For ranch rides on the vast east side, contact **Molokai Outdoors** (☎ **877-553-4477** or 808-553-4477; www.molokai-outdoors.com), which offers two- and four-hour ranch rides as well as half-day beach adventure rides for $78 to $130 per person, depending on the adventure you choose.

Riding horseback to Iliiliopae Heiau

On horseback (where the elevated view is magnificent), you bump along a dirt trail through an incredible mango grove, bound for an ancient temple of human sacrifice. This temple of doom — right out of *Indiana Jones* — is Iliiliopae, a huge rectangle of stone made of 90 million rocks, overlooking the once-important village of Mapulehu and four ancient fishponds. The horses trek under the perfumed mangoes, and then head uphill through a kiawe forest filled with Java plums to the *heiau* (temple), which stands across a dry streambed under cloud-spiked Kaunolu, the 4,970-foot island summit.

Hawaii's most powerful heiau attracted *kahuna* (priests) from all over the islands. They came to find out the rules of human sacrifice at this university of sacred rites. Contrary to Hollywood's version, historians say that the chosen victims were always men, not young virgins, and that they were strangled, not thrown into a volcano, while priests sat on *Lauhala* mats watching silently. Spooky, eh?

After the visit to the temple, your horse takes you back to the mango grove. Contact **Molokai Horse & Wagon Rides,** King Kamehameha V Highway (Highway 450), at mile marker 15, Kaunakakai (☎ **800-670-6965** or 808-558-8132). The tour and horseback ride are $40 adults, $18 kids 2 to 11. The hour-long ride goes up to the *heiau,* and then beyond it to the mountaintop for those breathtaking views, and finally back down to the beach.

Kamakou Preserve

The nearly mile-high summit receives more than 80 inches of rain a year — enough to qualify as a rain forest. The Molokai Forest, as it was historically known, is the source of 60 percent of Molokai's water. The Nature Conservancy, which has identified 219 Hawaiian plants that grow there exclusively, owns nearly 3,000 acres, from the summit to the lowland forests of eucalyptus and pine. The preserve is also the last stand of the endangered Molokai thrush *(olomao)* and Molokai creeper *(kawawahie).*

To get to the preserve, take the Forest Reserve Road from Kaunakakai. The road is a 45-minute, four-wheel-drive trip on a dirt trail to Waikolu Lookout Campground. From there, you can venture into the wilderness preserve on foot across a boardwalk on a one-and-a-half-hour hike. For more information, contact the **Nature Conservancy (☎ 808-553-5236).**

En route to Halawa Valley

No visit to Molokai is complete without at least a passing glance at the island's **ancient fishponds,** a singular achievement in Pacific aquaculture. With their hunger for fresh fish and lack of ice or refrigeration, Hawaiians perfected aquaculture in 1400, before Christopher Columbus "discovered" America. They built gated, U-shaped stone and coral walls on the shore to catch fish on the incoming tide; they then raised them in captivity. The result: a constant, ready supply of fresh fish.

The ponds, which stretch for 20 miles along Molokai's south shore and are visible from Kamehameha V Highway (Highway 450), offer insight into the island's ancient population. Approximately a thousand people tended a single fishpond, and more than 60 ponds once existed on this coast. All the fishponds are named; a few are privately owned. Some are silted in by red-dirt runoff from south coast gulches, while some folks, who raise fish and seaweed, have revived some.

A 3-foot-high, 2,000-foot-long stone wall surrounds the largest, 54-acre Keawa Nui Pond. You can spot **Alii Fish Pond,** reserved for kings, through the coconut groves at One Alii Beach Park. From the road, you can see **Kalokoeli Pond,** 6 miles east of Kaunakakai on the highway.

The last stop on the way to Halawa Valley is **Mana'e Goods & Grindz,** located at mile marker 16 (☎ **808-558-8498**), a local-style convenience store on the mountain side of the road featuring a lunch counter and deli; it makes a great place to pick up bottled water and a snack or picnic lunch.

Smith Bronte Landing Site

In 1927, Charles Lindbergh soloed the Atlantic Ocean in a plane called *The Spirit of St. Louis* and became an American hero. That same year, Ernie Smith and Emory B. Bronte took off from Oakland, California, on July 14, in a single-engine Travelair aircraft named *The City of Oakland,* and headed across the Pacific Ocean for Honolulu, 2,397 miles away. The next day, after running out of fuel, they crash-landed upside down in a kiawe thicket on Molokai but emerged unhurt to become the first civilians to fly to Hawaii from the U.S. mainland. The 25-hour, 2-minute flight landed Smith and Bronte a place in aviation history — and on a roadside marker on Molokai.

See map p. 265. King Kamehameha V Highway (Highway 450), at mile marker 11, on the makai (ocean) side.

Halawa Valley

Of the five great valleys of Molokai, only Halawa, with its two waterfalls, golden beach, sleepy lagoon, great surf, and offshore island, is easily accessible. Unfortunately, the trail through fertile Halawa Valley — which was inhabited for centuries — and on to the 250-foot Moaula Falls has been closed for some time. The best way to visit the fertile valley is on a guided hike with **Molokai Outdoors** (☎ **877-553-4477** or 808-553-4477; www.molokai-outdoors.com). Molokai Outdoors offers the excellent six- to eight-hour East Molokai Tour and Halawa Cultural Hike, which includes a 2¼-mile hike that is rated moderate to advanced thanks to two river crossings and some rocky areas along the trails. The fee is $188 per person, including pickup at the airport, harbor, or your hotel, plus a picnic lunch.

You can spend a day at the county beach park (see earlier in this chapter), but don't venture into the valley on your own. The valley's private landowners, worried about slip-and-fall lawsuits, have posted NO TRES-PASSING signs on their property.

To get to Halawa Valley, drive north from Kaunakakai on Highway 450 for 30 miles along the coast to the end of the road, which descends into the valley past Jersalema Hou Church. If you want to catch a glimpse of the valley on your way to the beach, take a moment at the scenic overlook along the road: After Puuo Hoku Ranch, at mile marker 25, the narrow two-lane road widens at a hairpin curve, and you find the overlook on your right; the drive is 2 miles more to the valley floor.

Shopping the Local Stores

Because many visitors stay in condos or vacation rentals, it's especially important to find the local grocery stores, so I have included them in this section. But serious shoppers won't find much to do on Molokai.

In downtown Kaunakakai, most of the retail shops sell T-shirts, muumuus, surf wear, and informal apparel. The **Imamura Store** (☎ **808-553-5615**) is a jumble of Hawaiian-print tablecloths, Japanese tea plates, ukulele cases, and even coconut bikini tops. **Molokai Surf,** 130 Kamehameha V Hwy. (☎ **808-553-5093**), offers a broad range of clothing, gear, and accessories for life in the surf and sun.

You can't miss the salmon-colored wooden storefront of the **Friendly Isle Market Center** (☎ **808-553-5595**), on the main drag of Kaunakakai, which has an especially good range of produce and healthy foods — better than standard grocery-store fare. Locals call the Friendly Isle the most affordable stop for groceries on the island, too.

Across from the Friendly Isle Market is **Bamboo Pantry,** 107 Ala Malama St. (☎ **808-553-3300;** www.bamboopantry.com), one of the island's more sophisticated shopping stops, specializing in aloha-style housewares and gifts for home.

Next door to the Molokai Visitor Center is the **Molokai Fine Arts Gallery,** in the Moore Business Center, 2 Kamoi St. (☎ **808-553-8520;** www.molokaifinearts.com). This unassuming but appealing gallery shop offers the best original art and crafts on the island. The bounty runs the gamut from original oil paintings and photography to raku pottery, Hawaiian quilt, Niihau shell leis, and Hawaiian heirloom jewelry. Prices are reasonable.

You can also stock up your kitchen at **Misaki's Grocery and Dry Goods** (☎ **808-553-5505**), established in 1922. You'll find fresh produce, Boca Burgers, a good fish counter, and more. **Molokai Wines & Spirits** (☎ **808-553-5009**) is your best bet on the island for a decent bottle of wine.

And don't forget to treat yourself to a loaf of hot bread from **Kanemitsu Bakery's,** 79 Ala Malama St., Kaunakakai (☎ **808-553-5855**). It's a late-night ritual for local residents, who line up at the bakery's back door beginning at 10 p.m. You can order your fresh bread with butter, jelly, cinnamon, or cream cheese, and the bakers will cut the hot loaves down the middle and slather on the works so that it melts in the bread.

En route to the North Coast, **Coffees of Hawaii,** Highway 480 (near the junction of Highway 470), Kualapuu (☎ **877-322-FARM** [877-322-3276] or 808-567-9490), is a combination coffee bar/store/gallery. You'll find great gifts, including local arts and crafts and island music CDs, as well as a wide variety of excellent coffee and gourmet goodies, such as chocolate-covered coffee beans. A stone's throw away is the **Kualapuu Market** (☎ **808-567-6243**), where you can pick up wine, food, and necessities.

On the West End, the standout store is the **Big Wind Kite Factory** in Maunaloa (☎ **808-552-2364;** www.molokai.com/kites). Not only can you purchase beautifully designed kites (and take free kite-flying classes when conditions are right), but the adjoining gallery features local and Balinese handicrafts and Hawaiian-music CDs. Factory tours are offered daily.

On the East End, the only place for groceries is **The Neighborhood Store 'N Counter,** in Pukoo (☎ **808-558-8498**), where you can enjoy a solid breakfast or lunch at the counter, too.

Enjoying Molokai after Dark

Hula Shores at the Hotel Molokai, in Kaunakakai (☎ **800-367-**5004 or 808-553-5347; www.hotelmolokai.com), offers live entertainment from local musicians, poolside and in the dining room. With its South Seas ambience and poolside setting, the hotel has become the island's premier venue for local and visiting entertainers. Aloha Fridays are especially festive, with a torch-lighting ceremony and traditional artisans on hand. No cover.

Fast Facts: Molokai

Banks

Molokai has several banks, including the Bank of Hawaii, 208 Ala Malama St., Kaunakakai (☎ 808-553-3273; www.boh.com) and American Savings Bank, in the Molokai Center, 40 Ala Malama St., Kaunakakai (☎ 808-553-8391; www.asbhawaii.com). Both are located in Kaunakakai, and both offer ATMs.

Emergencies/Hospitals

Molokai and Lanai are both part of Maui County. For local emergencies, call ☎ 911. For nonemergencies, call the police at ☎ 808-553-5355 or 808-244-6400; the fire department at ☎ 808-553-5601; or Molokai General Hospital in Kaunakakai at ☎ 808-553-5331. You can also find medical care at the Molokai Family Health Center, 39 Ala Malama St., Kaunakakai (☎ 808-553-5353), which is open during regular business hours on weekdays, plus Saturday mornings.

Internet Access

Molokai is not exactly on the cutting edge of cyberspace. The island's only spot for public access to the Internet is Stanley's

Coffee Shop Gallery, 125 Puali St., Kaunakakai (☎ 808-553-9966). They also prepare a decent espresso.

Mail

Downtown Kaunakakai has a post office (☎ 808-553-5845). You can also visit the Hoolehua Post Office, Puu Peelua Avenue (Highway 480), near Maunaloa Highway (Highway 460, a half-mile from the Molokai Airport; ☎ 808-567-6144).

News

Pick up a copy of the *Molokai Island Times*, available free around the island, or check daily goings on at www.molokaitimes.com.

Pharmacies

Head to Molokai Drugs in the Kamoi Professional Center, downtown Kaunakakai (☎ 808-553-5790; www.molokaidrugs.com). Not only can you stock up on essentials, but this drugstore, which has been family-run since 1935, is a friendly stop for guidebooks, books about Molokai, maps, paperbacks, flip-flops, and other handy items.

Chapter 17

Taking a Side Trip to the Island of Lanai

In This Chapter

▶ Introducing Lanai
▶ Deciding where to stay and dine
▶ Knowing what to see and do

*H*ardly more than a former pineapple patch, the petite island of Lanai (lah-*nigh*-ee) now claims to be one of the world's top tropical destinations. It's a bold claim, primarily because there is so little *there* there. Don't expect much, especially when it comes to dining, lodging, or sightseeing options. In fact, Lanai is so quiet that it makes Molokai look like a bustling hub of social activity. Lanai has no stoplight and barely 30 miles of paved road; its biggest draw is its simple serenity.

For generations, Lanai held little more than a small farming community, owned and maintained by the Dole pineapple company for its agricultural workers, surrounded by acres of pineapple fields. Life was virtually untouched by modern civilization throughout much of the 20th century. But all that changed in 1990, when the Lodge at Koele, a 102-room hotel resembling an opulent English Tudor mansion, opened its doors in the island's misty Upcountry, followed a year later by the 250-room Manele Bay Hotel, a Mediterranean-style beach resort overlooking sparkling Hulopoe Bay.

Overnight, the isolated island was transformed: Corporate jets streamed into tiny Lanai Airport, former plantation workers were retrained in the art of dressing pillow-top beds and orchestrating first-class service experiences, and the population swelled to about 3,500 residents. Lanai won a permanent mark on the luxury map when Microsoft billionaire Bill Gates and his bride, Melinda, chose the island for their lavish wedding, buying up every one of its hotel rooms to fend off the media hordes.

In the intervening years, celebrities have opted for more hopping destinations. However, now that the formidable Four Seasons Hotels & Resorts are in charge of the island's two luxury resorts, discriminating travelers are, once again, turning their attention to this otherwise unassuming isle.

The juxtaposition between the big luxury resorts — the island's sole economic engine these days — and the rest of the island's plantation-style, small-town coziness can be a bit jarring. Residents are overwhelmingly friendly, and fishing and working in the garden are considered priorities in life. Lanai is not exactly a cultural destination; rather, it's worth appreciating for its dramatic beauty, quiet, solitude, and communal experience with nature. It's a far cry from the action and development found on Maui. Come to Lanai if you crave the chance to escape in a peaceful tropical setting. The sights can be seen in a day or two; I recommend a short stay unless you're looking to indulge in a real do-nothing vacation.

Getting to Know Lanai

Inhabited Lanai is divided into three parts: Lanai City, Koele, and Manele. The coastal climate zone is hot and dry, while the Upcountry region is cool and misty.

Postage stamp–size **Lanai City** sits at the heart of the island, at 1,645 feet above sea level. It's the only place on the island with any services. Built in 1924, this plantation village is a tidy grid of quaint, tin-roofed cottages in bright pastels, with roosters penned in tropical gardens of banana, *lilikoi,* and papaya. Many of the residents are Filipino immigrants who worked the pineapple fields and imported the art, culture, language, food, and lifestyle of the Philippines. Their colorful clapboard homes seem as if they have been stuck in a time warp.

Norfolk and Cook Island pines line Dole Park Square, where plantation buildings house general stores that sell the basic necessities. Here you'll also find a U.S. Post Office, two banks, and a police station with a jail that consists of three outhouse-size cells with padlocks.

In the nearby, cool, upland district of **Koele** is the Lodge at Koele, standing alone on a knoll overlooking pastures and the sea at the edge of a pine forest, like a grand European manor. The island's other luxurious cocoon, the Manele Bay Hotel, is on the sunny southwestern tip of the island at **Manele.** You get more of what you expect from Hawaii here, including a gorgeously tranquil beach, swaying palms, and poolside mai tais.

If you're not planning to stay on Lanai, you can visit the island on a day trip from Maui. See Chapter 12 for complete details on the highly recommended snorkel cruises to Lanai offered by **Trilogy Excursions.** It's a great way to go, with a stop at Lanai's Hulopoe Beach; for an extra fee, you can add on guided tours of the island as well. Note that these trips are very popular, so you'll need to book your spot well in advance.

Golfers can also ferry over to the private island from Maui for a day of world-class golf. **Expeditions Maui-Lanai** (☎ 800-695-2624 or 808-661-3756; www.go-lanai.com) offers daily ferry service between Maui's

Lahaina and Lanai's Manele Harbor, plus golf packages for $296 per golfer, including greens fees and round-trip ferry service; 6:45 and 9:15 a.m. departures are available. See "Hitting the Links," later in this chapter, for complete descriptions of the island's two championship challenges. Sightseers can also take the ferry over for the day for $25 adults, $20 kids 2 to 11; shuttle service is available to the Dollar Rent-a-Car counter in Lanai City, where you can rent a Jeep for the day (reservations required; see "Getting around," later in this chapter).

Settling Into Lanai

The **Lanai Visitors Bureau** (☎ **800-947-4774** or 808-565-7600; www. visitlanai.net) and the **Hawaii Visitors and Convention Bureau** (☎ **800-GO-HAWAII** [800-464-2924] or 808-923-1811; www.gohawaii. com) provide brochures, maps, and island guides. You can also get information on Lanai from the **Maui Visitors Bureau** (☎ **800-525-6284** or 808-244-3530; www.visitmaui.com).

Arriving on Lanai

There are no flights to Lanai from the mainland — only from Honolulu or Kahului, Maui. From either of these airports, it's a 25-minute trip to Lanai Airport (LNY). **Island Air** (☎ **800-652-6541** or 808-565-6744; www.island air.com) offers several flights a day. You can also book your flights through **Hawaiian Airlines** (☎ **800-367-5320;** www.hawaiianair.com). In addition, you can book interisland flights with **go! Airlines** (☎ **888-IFLYGO2** [888-435-9462]; www.iflygo.com). From the airport, it's about 10 minutes by car to Lanai City and 25 minutes to Manele Bay.

If you prefer traveling by boat, round-trip excursions on **Expeditions Lahaina** (☎ **800-695-2624** or 808-661-3756; www.go-lanai.com) take you between Maui and Lanai for $25 adults, $20 kids 2 to 11 (each way). The ferry service runs five times a day between Lahaina and Lanai's Manele Bay harbor, plus two times a day from Maalaea Harbor, north of Kihei on Maui's neck. The ferry leaves Lahaina at 6:45 a.m., 9:15 a.m., 12:45 p.m., 3:15 p.m., and 5:45 p.m.; the return ferry from Lanai's Manele Bay Harbor leaves at 8 a.m., 10:30 a.m., 2 p.m., 4:30 p.m., and 6:45 p.m. Maalaea ferries depart at 7 a.m. and 3:30 p.m., and leave Manele Bay for Maalaea at 9 a.m. and 5:30 p.m. The 9-mile channel crossing takes 45 minutes to an hour, depending on sea conditions. Reservations are strongly recommended.

Getting around

With so few paved roads on Lanai, you'll need a four-wheel-drive vehicle if you plan on exploring the island's remote shores, its interior, or the summit of Mount Lanaihale. Even if you have only one day on Lanai, rent a four-wheel-drive and see the island.

Four-wheel-drive Jeeps are available at the **Dollar Rent-A-Car** desk at **Lanai City Service/Lanai Plantation Store,** 1036 Lanai Ave. (☎ **800-588-7808** or 800-800-3665 for Dollar reservations, or **808-565-7227** for Lanai City Service; www.dollar.com). Expect to pay up to $139 a day for a four-wheel-drive Jeep; hardtops and convertibles are both available. The kind and knowledgeable staff will provide you with a four-wheeling map and clear guidance as to what sights are accessible while you're on the island.

Don't bother to rent a standard car, because you won't be able to drive anywhere but between town and the resorts. The big resorts offer frequent shuttle service. If you stay at the Lodge at Koele or the Manele Bay Hotel, you need to rent a Jeep only for your sightseeing day. If you stay elsewhere, just rent a Jeep.

Adventure Lanai Ecocentre (☎ **808-565-7373;** www.adventurelanai. com) also has four-wheel-drive Jeeps for rent (complete with towels, masks, fins, snorkel, ice chest, and an island map), usually for $129. You can also arrange two- or four-hour off-road adventure tours with them.

Whether or not you rent a car — which you should — sooner or later you'll find yourself at Lanai City Service/Lanai Plantation Store. This all-in-one grocery store, gas station, rental-car agency, and souvenir shop serves as the island's Grand Central Station. Here's where you can pick up information, directions, maps, and all the local gossip.

Finding a Place to Stay

Above Lanai City is the luxurious Lodge at Koele, while down the hill at Hulopoe Bay is the equally luxurious Manele Bay Hotel. Most accommodations are located "in the village," as residents call Lanai City.

In the following listings, each hotel's name is followed by a number of dollar signs, ranging from one ($) to five ($$$$$). Each represents the median rack-rate price range for a double room per night, as follows:

Symbol	Meaning
$	Cheap — less than $150 per night
$$	Still affordable — $150–$224
$$$	Moderate — $225–$324
$$$$	Expensive but not ridiculous — $325–$449
$$$$$	Ultraluxurious — $450 or more per night

Don't forget that the state adds 11.42 percent in taxes to your hotel bill.

Lanai

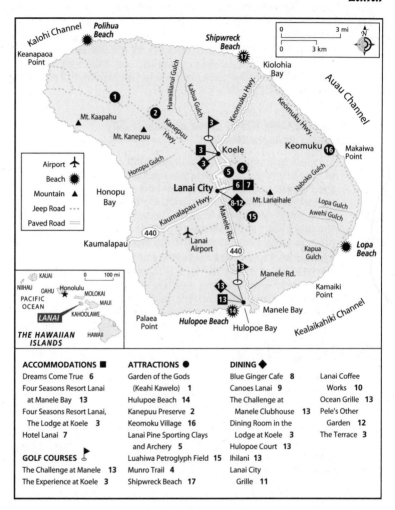

ACCOMMODATIONS ■

Dreams Come True **6**
Four Seasons Resort Lanai
   at Manele Bay **13**
Four Seasons Resort Lanai,
   The Lodge at Koele **3**
Hotel Lanai **7**

GOLF COURSES ⛳

The Challenge at Manele **13**
The Experience at Koele **3**

ATTRACTIONS ●

Garden of the Gods
   (Keahi Kawelo) **1**
Hulopoe Beach **14**
Kanepuu Preserve **2**
Keomoku Village **16**
Lanai Pine Sporting Clays
   and Archery **5**
Luahiwa Petroglyph Field **15**
Munro Trail **4**
Shipwreck Beach **17**

DINING ◆

Blue Ginger Cafe **8**
Canoes Lanai **9**
The Challenge at
   Manele Clubhouse **13**
Dining Room in the
   Lodge at Koele **3**
Hulopoe Court **13**
Ihilani **13**
Lanai City
   Grille **11**

Lanai Coffee
   Works **10**
Ocean Grille **13**
Pele's Other
   Garden **12**
The Terrace **3**

Dreams Come True
$ Lanai City

This quaint plantation house is tucked away among papaya, banana, lemon, and avocado trees in the heart of Lanai City, at 1,620 feet. Hosts Susan and Michael Hunter have filled their house with Southeast Asian antiques collected on their travels. Both are jewelers; they operate a working studio on the premises. Each unit has an Italian marble bathroom with a Jacuzzi tub. Guests are welcome to use the full kitchen and the laundry room. The common area looks out on the garden (which is filled with bountiful tropical fruit trees) and is equipped with a TV and VCR. The Hunters are happy to provide beach toys and help guests arrange for transportation and excursions; the owners themselves offer diving, snorkeling and kayaking tours.

See map p. 295. 1168 Lanai Ave., Lanai City. ☎ *800-566-6961 or 808-565-6961. Fax: 808-565-7056.* www.dreamscometruelanai.com. *Rack rates: $112 double (including breakfast); $450 entire house (does not include breakfast). 2-night minimum stay on weekends. AE, DISC, MC, V.*

Four Seasons Resort Lanai at Manele Bay
$$$$$ **Hulopoe Beach**

Located on a sun-washed southern bluff overlooking Hulopoe Beach, one of Hawaii's best stretches of golden sand, this U-shaped hotel steps down the hillside to the pool and then fans out in oceanfront wings separated by gardens with lush flora, man-made waterfalls, lotus ponds, and streams. A tiki torch–lined path leads to the gorgeous, wide-open sands, while, on the other side, golf greens on a hillside of dry scrub border the hotel. The place is a real oasis against the dry heat of Lanai's arid South Coast.

The hotel is undeniably luxurious but, otherwise, nothing special. The oversize guest rooms are done in the style of an English country house on the beach: sunny chintz fabrics, mahogany furniture, down duvets, Audubon prints, huge marble bathrooms with deep soaking tubs, and semiprivate lanais. Each room features high-speed Internet access, voice mail, CD and DVD players, a coffeemaker, and a refrigerator; the special highlights are the fragrant, French-made L'Occitane toiletries.

This resort is much less formal than the Lodge up the hill. It attracts more families, and shorts and T-shirts are the wardrobe of choice. The small spa offers a variety of massages, facials, and wraps. There's also a fitness center with cardio equipment, free weights, a multistation gym, and yoga classes. Additional amenities include a children's program, 24-hour room service, business services, and twice-daily housekeeping. Several different dining rooms promise variety, though the choices are all upscale and the food is not much more than fine. There's an open-air sports bar with a giant-screen TV and a game room, along with a lounge that features live nightly entertainment.

See map p. 295. 1 Manele Bay Rd., Lanai City. ☎ *800-819-5053, 800-321-4666, or 808-565-2000. Fax: 808-565-2483.* www.fourseasons.com/manelebay. *Rack rates: $495–$1,245 double; $1,400–$7,000 suite. Numerous packages (such as 4th and 5th night free, adventure, golf and spa, four-wheel-drive adventure, and romance) available. AE, DC, DISC, MC, V.*

Four Seasons Resort Lanai, The Lodge at Koele
$$$$–$$$$$ **Lanai City**

Guests come here looking for relaxation in the cool mist of the mountains. Relax on the porch and watch the turkeys mosey across the manicured lawns; stroll through the Japanese hillside garden; or watch the sun sink into the Pacific and the stars light up at night. The Lodge, as folks here call it, stands in a 21-acre grove of Norfolk Island pines at 1,700 feet above sea level, 8 miles from any beach.

The venerable Four Seasons Hotels & Resorts brand undertook a major upgrade of this hotel in 2006, which included a complete renovation of all guest rooms, the creation of a new game room, and the installation of a Chinese pagoda on the grounds. The result of all this investment is an amazing Upcountry luxury experience for Lanai visitors and substantially lower rack rates than you'll pay just down the hill at the beach.

The resort boasts the look and feel of an elegant country estate. The Great Hall sports heavy timbers, beamed ceilings, and the two huge stone fireplaces, along with overstuffed furniture, richly patterned rugs, and museum-quality art. The atmosphere is informal during the day, more formal after sunset.

You have plenty of activities to choose from at the Lodge and at its sister resort down the hill, Manele Bay; guests are treated to the best of both hotels. There's a complimentary shuttle to the acclaimed golf courses, the beach, and the Manele Bay Hotel. Guests also enjoy an on-site swimming pool, plus croquet lawns, horseback riding, Upcountry hiking trails, a sport shooting and archery range, lawn bowling, and a putting green. In keeping with the Four Seasons tradition of outstanding service, the staff will happily help you arrange any kind of adventure outing your heart desires.

See map p. 295. 1 Keomoku Hwy., Lanai City. ☎ ***800-819-5053****, 800-321-4666, or 808-565-4000. Fax: 808-565-4561.* www.fourseasons.com/koele. *Rack rates: $375–$695 double; $850–$1,600 suite. Check the Web site for excellent packages and specials. AE, DC, DISC, MC, V.*

Hotel Lanai
$$ Lanai City

This moderately priced hotel is full of old-fashioned aloha. Built in the 1920s for VIPs, this long, lean, plantation-era, clapboard relic has retained its quaint character and lives on as a simple, charming country inn tucked among the Norfolk pines. The hotel reopened in 2007 after a month of renovations, which included the debut of the new Lanai City Grille, under the direction of Maui celebrity chef Bev Gannon. The ten guest rooms are extremely small, but clean and freshly decorated, with Hawaiian quilts, wood furniture, and ceiling fans (but no air-conditioning or televisions). The most popular are the lanai units, which feature a lanai shared with the room next door. All rooms have ceiling fans and private, shower-only bathrooms. The small one-bedroom cottage, with a TV and bathtub, is perfect for a small family.

See map p. 295. 828 Lanai Ave., Lanai City. ☎ ***808-565-7211****. Fax: 808-565-6450.* www.hotellanai.com. *Rack rates: $159–$179 double; $209 cottage double. Extra person $50. Rates include continental breakfast. 2-night minimum stay (4 nights during holiday periods). AE, MC, V. Airport shuttle $25 round-trip.*

Dining on Lanai

Lanai is a curious mix of innocence and sophistication, with strong cross-cultural elements that liven up its culinary offerings. The tony hotel restaurants require deep pockets (or bottomless expense accounts), and you have only a handful of other options.

In the restaurant listings that follow, each restaurant name is followed by a number of dollar signs, ranging from one ($) to five ($$$$$). The dollar signs give you an idea of what a complete dinner for one person — with appetizer, main course, a drink, tax, and tip — is likely to cost. The price categories go like this:

Symbol	Meaning
$	Cheap eats — less than $20 per person
$$	Still inexpensive — $20–$34
$$$	Moderate — $35–$49
$$$$	Pricey — $50 or more

To give you a further idea of how much you can expect to spend, I've also included the price range of main courses or items in the listings. (Prices can change at any time, of course, but restaurants usually don't raise their prices by more than a dollar or two at any given time.)

Blue Ginger Cafe
$ Lanai City   FRESH LOCAL

Famous for its mahimahi sandwiches and inexpensive omelets, Blue Ginger is a local, casual, and inexpensive alternative to Lanai's fancy hotel restaurants. The four tables on the front porch face the cool Norfolk pines of Dole Park and are always filled with locals who "talk story" from morning to night. The tiny cafe is often jammed from 6 to 7 a.m. with construction workers on their way to work. The offerings are solid, no-nonsense, everyday fare: fried saimin (no MSG, a plus), very popular hamburgers on homemade buns, and mahimahi with capers in a white-wine sauce. Blue Ginger also serves a tasty French toast made with homemade bread, vegetable *lumpia* (the Filipino version of a spring roll), and Mexican specials. The stir-fried vegetables — a heaping platter of freshly cut, perfectly cooked veggies, including summer squash and fresh mushrooms — are a hit. Dinner brings such no-nonsense specialties such as a beautifully prepared pork chop with shrimp and yummy chicken *katsu*, a pounded and *panko*-crusted breast, pan fried to tender perfection. Resort guests are generous with kudos for this simple, charming place. No alcoholic beverages are served.

See map p. 295. 409 Seventh St. (at Lilima Street), Lanai City. ☎ 808-565-6363. Main courses: Breakfast under $8.50; lunch under $12; dinner under $15. No credit cards. Open: Daily 6 a.m.–7 p.m.

Canoes Lanai
$ Lanai City   LOCAL

This mom-and-pop joint has been a landmark since the 1920s. In those days, the tiny storefront (originally called Tanigawa's) sold canned goods and cigarettes; the ten tables, hamburgers, and Filipino food came later. This hole-in-the-wall built its reputation by serving local-style breakfasts. The fare — fried rice, omelets, short stacks, burgers, and simple ham and eggs — is more greasy spoon than gourmet, but it's friendly to the pocketbook.

See map p. 295. 419 Seventh St., Lanai City. ☎ *808-565-6537. Reservations not accepted. Main courses: Breakfast under $8.50; lunch $5–$11. No credit cards. Open: Thurs–Tues 6:30 a.m.–1 p.m.*

The Challenge at Manele Clubhouse
$$ Lanai City   PACIFIC RIM

The view from the alfresco tables here may be the best on the island, encompassing Kahoolawe, Haleakala on Maui, and, on an especially clear day, the peaks of Mauna Kea and Mauna Loa on the Big Island. Your cliff-side perch overlooks the rolling blue Pacific and the emerald-green fairways. Lunchtime features salads and sandwiches, burgers, fish and chips, and seafood chowder. When the midafternoon munchies strike, there's a tempting array of cold and warm *pupu* (appetizers), such as *ahi* sashimi, crab cakes, and even homemade potato chips with a Maui onion dipping sauce. If you've just played a tough 18 holes, the Kona coffee chocolate mousse cake is guaranteed to restore your energy.

See map p. 295. In the Challenge at Manele Clubhouse. ☎ *808-565-2222.* www.four seasons.com/manelebay. *Reservations recommended. Main courses: Most items $12–$24. AE, DC, MC, V. Open: Daily 10:30 a.m.–4:30 p.m.*

Dining Room in the Lodge at Koele
$$$$$ Lanai City   NEW AMERICAN

The setting: a roaring fire, bountiful sprays of orchids, and well-dressed women in pearls sitting across from men in jackets, with wine buckets tableside. The menu highlights contemporary American favorites with intense flavors. Foie gras has a strong presence on the seasonally changing menu, as do venison, local seafood, wild mushrooms, rack of lamb, and the vaunted threadfish. During fall and winter months, expect to see pumpkins, beans, ragouts, and braised items offered in creative seasonal preparations. The Dining Room is known for its use of fresh herbs, vegetables, and fruit grown on the island, harvested just minutes away. The food is excellent, but some may consider the setting and service too over-the-top formal for little Lanai.

See map p. 295. In the Lodge at Koele. ☎ *808-565-4000.* www.fourseasons.com/ koele. *Reservations required. Collared shirts and long pants requested for men. Main courses: $42–$50. AE, DC, MC, V. Open: Fri–Tues 6–9 p.m.*

Hulopoe Court
$$$$ **Lanai City**   **HAWAII REGIONAL**

Hulopoe is more casual than the Manele Bay Hotel's fine dining room, Ihilani (see later), but more formal than the hotel's Ocean Grille. The 17th-century palanquin in the adjoining lower lobby, the Asian accents, the tropical murals by gifted Lanai artists, and the vaulted ceilings add up to an eclectic ambience, capped off by marvelous ocean views. The menu ventures throughout the Pacific Rim for inspiration, showcasing island ingredients such as Maui asparagus, hearts of palm, and locally caught fresh fish. The gourmet breakfast options include fresh-baked pastries, tropical fruit, Kona coffee, and an impressive buffet with omelets made to order. At dinner, the roast duck with *soba* noodles and a ginger-plum sauce and the crispy whole Pacific snapper with a chili-soy dipping sauce are excellent choices, but try to save room for the chocolate macadamia-nut cheesecake, drizzled with caramel sauce. Service is excellent, as you might expect.

See map p. 295. In the Four Seasons Resort Lanai at Manele Bay. ☎ *808-565-2290.* www.fourseasons.com/manelebay. *Reservations recommended. Main courses: $32–$44. AE, DC, MC, V. Open: Daily 7–11 a.m. and 6–9:30 p.m.*

Ihilani
$$$$$ **Lanai City**   **ITALIAN**

The most lavish and elegant dining venue at the Four Seasons at Manele Bay is a stunner, with rich wood paneling, sparking chandeliers, and ocean views. It's an ultraromantic setting for contemporary Italian cuisine that's complemented by a fine wine list. Local island ingredients often steal the show in traditional Italian recipes, as with the fresh-caught *onaga* in a zesty *puttanesca* sauce. You'll find homemade pastas (such as the spinach gnocchi) and hearty, intense dishes such as the slow-braised *osso buco* and the grilled rack of lamb, rubbed with garlic and oregano and served with your choice of steakhouse sides. Desserts feature an over-the-top Italian flair, from the selection of house-made gelatos to such creations as the warm almond soufflé topped with fresh Fuji apple compote.

See map p. 295. In the Four Seasons Resort Lanai at Manele Bay. ☎ *808-565-2296.* www.fourseasons.com/manelebay. *Reservations strongly recommended. Main courses: $34–$50. AE, DC, MC, V. Open: Tues–Sat 6–9:30 p.m.*

Lanai City Grille
$$$$ **Lanai City**   **HAWAII REGIONAL**

The new owners of the Hotel Lanai have done a great job reinventing the hotel's main dining room. Their boldest and most impactful stroke was choosing Hawaii Regional Cuisine champion chef Bev Gannon, of Maui's Haliimaile General Store and Joe's Bar and Grill, to design the menu. Expect a contemporary American menu with plenty of vibrant Pacific fusion accents, but not too much fuss. The barbecued ribs and slow-cooked rotisserie chicken suit the Upcountry vibe, while local-caught fish is well prepared for those who want a lighter choice. The restaurant is justifiably popular and always full; even Manele Bay resort guests regularly migrate up the hill for dinner, escaping the high prices and fanciful resort fare for heartier, down-home cooking. The décor has a pleasing, almost retro simplicity, with warm wood paneling and cozy fireplaces in both rooms; a renovation has lightened the ambience without losing its charm. A friendly bartender mans a fine full bar; ask for a Lanai Tai for a local twist on the mai tai. Service is friendly and accommodating to locals and visitors alike. You can count on live music with dinner on Fridays. All in all, it's my favorite place to dine on the island.

See map p. 295. In the Hotel Lanai, 828 Lanai Ave., Lanai City. ☎ *808-565-7211.* www.hotellanai.com. *Reservations highly recommended. Main courses: $20–$38. AE, MC, V. Open: Wed–Sun 5–9 p.m.*

Lanai Coffee Works
$ Lanai City COFFEEHOUSE

Oahu's popular Ward Warehouse coffeehouse has opened a branch in Lanai City, with a menu of espresso coffees and drinks, ice cream (from gelatos to local brands, such as Lapperts and Roselani), and a small selection of pastries. It's Lanai City's gathering place, a tiny cafe with tables and benches on a pleasing wooden deck surrounded by tall pines, and a stone's throw from Dole Park. Formerly a plantation house, the structure fits in with the surrounding plantation homes in the heart of Lanai City. Coffee Works also has some nice gift items available, including T-shirts, tea infusers, chai, teapots, cookies, and gourmet coffees.

See map p. 295. 604 Ilima Ave., Lanai City (across from Post Office). ☎ *808-565-6962.* www.coffeeworkshawaii.com. *Most items: under $6. MC, V. Open: Mon–Sat 6 a.m.–4 p.m.*

Ocean Grill
$$$–$$$$ Lanai City AMERICAN/STEAK AND SEAFOOD

At the most casual restaurant in the Four Seasons at Manele Bay, you'll dine poolside under the shade of a beach umbrella. Lunchtime brings satisfying choices that include chilled gazpacho, a hearty Cobb salad, a vegetarian wrap, a kalua pork and cheese quesadilla, fish and chips, or a thick, juicy burger. At dinner, begin with a tropical cocktail in the Pool Bar before sitting down to enjoy a grilled steak or a wide variety of seafood offerings. The day's fresh catch can be grilled, pan-sautéed, or wok-seared with your choice of sauce (lemon-gingergrass, pineapple-mango salsa, or a simple lemon butter). Desserts include such all-American favorites as a banana split or a chocolate brownie cake a la mode. Even nonguests drop by to enjoy one of Lanai's few alfresco beachfront dining spots.

See map p. 295. In the Four Seasons Resort Lanai at Manele Bay. ☎ *808-565-7700.* www.fourseasons.com/manelebay. *Main courses: Lunch $12–$20; dinner $24–$40. AE, DC, MC, V. Open: Thurs–Mon 11 a.m.–5 p.m. and 5:30–9 p.m.; Tues–Wed 11 a.m.–5 p.m.*

Pele's Other Garden
$–$$ Lanai City DELI/PIZZERIA/JUICE BAR

This popular Lanai City eatery, featuring a patio with umbrella tables outside, is a full-scale New York–style deli that also offers box lunches and picnic baskets to go — perfect for a day at the beach. (You can also buy deli meats, cheeses, and salads by the pound.) At lunch, the first-rate pizzas, sandwiches, and wraps are popular. Daily soup and menu specials, excellent pizza, fresh organic produce, fresh juices, and special touches, such as top-quality black-bean burritos, roasted red peppers, and stuffed grape leaves, are some of the features that make Pele's Other Garden a must. Sandwiches are made with whole-wheat, rye, sourdough, or French bread, baked on the island and delivered fresh daily; the turkey is free-range. In the evening, the place becomes a full-fledged bistro-style dining room where you can also order pastas (butterfly pasta with garlic shrimp, fettuccine with smoked salmon), a great chicken parmesan, and robust salads incorporating local-grown greens. Beer, wine, and specialty cocktails round out the evening experience. All in all, a terrific place to dine at any time of day. The bright yellow building is easy to spot along tree-shaded Dole Park.

See map p. 295. Dole Park, 811 Houston St., Lanai City. ☎ *888-764-3354 or 808-565-9628. Reservations recommended. Main courses: Lunch $7–$12; dinner $17–$22; family pizzas $14–$23. AE, DISC, MC, V. Open: Mon–Fri 10 a.m.–2:30 p.m.; Mon–Sat 5–8 p.m.*

The Terrace
$$$–$$$$ Lanai City AMERICAN

Located next to the Formal Dining Room in the Lodge at Koele, between the 35-foot-high Great Hall and a wall of glass looking out over manicured English gardens, the Terrace is far from your typical hotel dining room. The menu may be fancy for comfort food, but it does, indeed, comfort. Hearty breakfasts of waffles and cereals, fresh pineapple from the nearby Palawai Basin, poached eggs and lobster hash with chive hollandaise, and Kauai Shrimp Benedict (sautéed Kauai shrimp, grilled taro bread, and wilted spinach with poached eggs and blue crab hollandaise) are a grand start to the day. Dinner choices are the American classics such as roasted veal chop on herb mashed potatoes with fava beans and carrots; pepper roasted rib-eye steak with blue cheese mashed potatoes; and seared organic chicken breast accompanied by sautéed baby spinach, double-smoked bacon *lardoons,* and glazed pearl onions and leeks. I like this choice better than the more formal main dining room, and the food is equally fine.

See map p. 295. In the Lodge at Koele. ☎ *808-565-4580. Reservations recommended for dinner.* www.fourseasons.com/koele. *Main courses: Breakfast and lunch $12–$22; dinner $29–$46. AE, DC, MC, V. Open: Daily 7 a.m.–2 p.m. and 6–9:30 p.m.*

Having Fun on and off the Beach

If you like big, wide, empty, gold-sand beaches and crystal-clear, cobalt-blue water full of bright tropical fish — and who doesn't? — then go to Lanai. There is something for everyone and plenty to see and experience.

Relaxing on Lanai's best beach

With 18 miles of sandy shoreline, Lanai has some of Hawaii's least crowded and most interesting beaches. Lanai's best, bar none, is **Hulopoe Beach,** a perfect playground for spinner dolphins and human visitors alike. Black-lava fingers, protecting swimmers from the serious ocean currents that sweep around Lanai, border this big, palm-fringed, gold-sand beach. In summer, Hulopoe is perfect for swimming, snorkeling, or just lolling about; the water temperature is usually in the mid-70s. Swimming is usually safe, except when swells kick up in winter. This bay, located at the foot of the Four Seasons Resort Lanai at Manele Bay, is a protected marine preserve, and the schools of colorful fish know it. So do the spinner dolphins who show up almost daily to frolic in the surf, as well as the humpback whales that cruise by in winter. Hulopoe is also Lanai's premier beach park, with a grassy lawn, picnic tables, barbecue grills, restrooms, showers, and ample parking. Resort guests enjoy covered beach chairs and towel service.

You can find some of Hawaii's best **lava-rock tide pools** along Hulopoe Bay's south shore. These miniature underwater worlds are full of strange creatures, including *asteroids* (sea stars), *holothurians* (sea cucumbers), spaghetti worms, Barber Pole shrimp, and Hawaii's favorite local delicacy, the *opihi,* a tasty morsel also known as the limpet. Youngsters enjoy swimming in the enlarged tide pool at the bay's eastern edge.

When you explore tide pools, do so at low tide. Never turn your back on the waves. Wear tennis shoes or reef walkers because wet rocks are slippery. Collecting specimens in this marine preserve is forbidden, so don't remove anything from its natural habitat.

Enjoying the water

Lanai has Hawaii's best water clarity because it lacks major development and has low rainfall and runoff. Its coast is also washed clean daily by the sea current known as "The Way to Tahiti." But the strong currents pose a threat to swimmers, and the waters have few good surf breaks. Most of the aquatic adventures — swimming, snorkeling, and scuba diving — are centered on the somewhat-protected south shore, around Hulopoe Bay.

The main outfitter for watersports are **Adventure Lanai Ecocentre** (☎ **808-565-7373;** www.adventurelanai.com).

Body boarding, bodysurfing, and board surfing

When the surf's up on Lanai, catching the waves is a real treat. Under the right conditions, Hulopoe and Polihua are both great for catching waves. Body boards ($10 a day) are available through **Adventure Lanai Ecocentre** (☎ 808-565-7373; www.adventurelanai.com). The beach shack at Hulopoe Beach provides complimentary boogie boards for guests of the Four Seasons Resort at Manele Bay and the Lodge at Koele.

Ocean kayaking

The **Adventure Lanai Ecocentre** (☎ 808-565-7373; www.adventure lanai.com) offers half-day sea kayak/snorkel adventures (as well as kayak/scuba trips) aimed at introducing beginners to the world of ocean kayaking. The center provides state-of-the-art kayaks (with lightweight graphite paddles and full back-support seats), life vests, the latest in snorkel equipment, dry bags, towels, water, and snacks. After receiving instruction on how to kayak, your group will set off to explore the waters around Lanai, with stops for snorkeling, snacks, and beachcombing. The four-hour trip costs $129. Rental kayaks are also available, starting at $32 a day for a single kayak or $54 a day for a double kayak.

Catchin' a wave

Everyone, from small kids to grandparents, can learn to surf with the **Lanai Surf School & Surf Safari** (☎ 808-306-9837; www.lanaisurf safari.com), which offers two-hour, two-person private lessons for $185 per person, or group lessons for $155 per person. The lesson can be customized to your experience level. Lessons include guided four-wheel-drive transport to a great surfing beach. If you're an experienced surfer who'd rather set out on your own, you can rent long or short boards for $58 per day, body boards for $30, or stand-up board and paddles for $75. A range of sizes is available to suit different sized riders and styles.

Also contact **Adventure Lanai Ecocentre** (☎ 808-565-7373; www.adventurelanai.com). The four-hour Surf Safari is $129, and surfboard rental is $45 a day. It also offers lessons in surf kayaking, if you'd rather ride the waves sitting down.

You can find two of Hawaii's best-known dive spots in Lanai's clear waters, just off the south shore: **Cathedrals I** and **II,** so named because the sun lights up an underwater grotto like a magnificent church.

Trilogy Lanai Ocean Sports (☎ 888-MAUI-800 [888-628-4800]; www.visitlanai.com) offers several diving trips, some of which take in the Cathedrals. Call the Maui office for details on current offers.

The **Adventure Lanai Ecocentre** (☎ 808-565-7373; www.adventure lanai.com) is a PADI Adventure Dive Center. Its instructor can teach you to dive, or if you're already certified, you can join them on a variety of outings around Lanai.

Guests of the Four Seasons resorts can also arrange for group and private diving charters through the concierge.

Snorkeling

Hulopoe is Lanai's best snorkeling spot. Fish are abundant and friendly in the marine-life conservation area. Try the lava-rock points at either end of the beach and around the lava pools. The beach shack provides free snorkel gear to guests of the two Four Seasons resorts. You can also rent for $10 a day from the **Adventure Lanai Ecocentre** (☎ 808-565-7373; www.adventurelanai.com), which also offers ocean kayaking/snorkeling trips.

Sportfishing

Spinning Dolphin Charters of Lanai (☎ 808-565-7676; www.sport fishinglanai.com), owned and operated by longtime Lanai resident Captain Jeff Menze, will take you out on the *Fish-n-Chips* in search of marlin, *ono* (wahoo), *ahi,* spearfish and mahimahi. A four-hour charter for up to six people costs $700. Individuals can also join a regular Sunday- or Wednesday-morning charter for $150 (you'll be with other travelers, but there's still a maximum of only six people).

Hitting the links

The **Challenge at Manele,** next to the Four Seasons Resort Lanai at Manele Bay at Hulopoe Bay (☎ 808-565-2222; www.fourseasons.com/maneleleay; greens fees: $225, $210 for guests), is a target-style, desert-links course designed by Jack Nicklaus. Following a recent facelift, it's now one of the most challenging — and rewarding — courses in the state. Check out the local rules: "No retrieving golf balls from the 150-foot cliffs on the ocean holes 12, 13, or 17," and "All whales, axis deer, and other wild animals are considered immovable obstructions." If that doesn't give you a hint of the uniqueness of this course, maybe the fact that you must reserve tee times 90 days in advance will confirm it. Facilities include a clubhouse, a pro shop, rentals, a practice area, lockers, and showers.

The **Experience at Koele,** next to the Lodge at Koele in Lanai City (☎ 808-565-4653; greens fees: $225 for nonguests, $210 for guests) is a traditional par-72 course designed by Greg Norman with fairway architecture by Ted Robinson. The course has very different front and back 9 holes. All goes well until you hit the signature hole, no. 8, where you tee off from a 250-foot elevated tee to a fairway bordered by a lake on the right and trees and dense shrubs on the left. To level the playing field, you can choose from four different sets of tees. Facilities include a clubhouse, a pro shop, rentals, a practice area, lockers, and showers. Book tee times a minimum of 90 days in advance.

Bicycling around Lanai

Mountain bikes are available for rent through the **Adventure Lanai Ecocentre** (☎ **808-565-7373;** www.adventurelanai.com). They rent 24-speed aluminum-frame front-suspension bikes, and rentals come with helmet and an island bike trail map. Call for current rates.

The **Lodge at Koele** (☎ **808-565-7300**) also has mountain bikes to rent for $8 an hour, $35 for four hours, and $40 to $55 for eight hours.

Clay shooting

Experience Lanai's hunting culture at **Lanai Pine Sporting Clays and Archery** (☎ **808-559-4600**). Nestled in a 200-acre pine-wooded valley, this verdant complex offers a fresh challenge for beginners and experts alike. First-timers are fitted with a shotgun that minimizes recoil, and instructors provide clay shooting pointers and safety tips. Fourteen stations are available, simulating movement patterns of duck, quail, pheasant, and even rabbit. An archery range and an air rifle gallery broaden your target-practice options, but clay shooting is certainly the highlight. An introductory lesson is $80, including 25 cartridges and targets, and runs 45 minutes to an hour; a 50-cartridge package for experienced clay shooters is $110. A 45-minute introductory archery lesson is $50, while a 45-minute air-rifle session is $50. Advanced lessons are also available.

Seeing the Sights

You need a four-wheel-drive to reach all the sights that I list in this section. Renting one can be an expensive proposition on Lanai, so I suggest that you rent one just for the day (or days) you plan on sightseeing; otherwise, you can easily get to the beach and around Lanai City without your own wheels. For details, see the section "Getting around" earlier in this chapter.

For a guided four-wheel-drive tour, contact **Adventure Lanai Ecocentre** (☎ **808-565-7373;** www.adventurelanai.com), which offers four-hour off-road tours for $129 per person.

If you decide to rent a four-wheel-drive, be sure to visit some of the following sights.

Garden of the Gods (Keahi Kawelo)

This is Lanai's most compelling sightseeing stop. A dirt four-wheel-drive road leads out of Lanai City and the Lodge at Koele, through the now uncultivated pineapple fields, past the Kanepuu Preserve (a dry-land forest preserve teeming with rare plant and animal life), to the so-called Garden of the Gods, out on Lanai's North Shore. This place has little to do with gods, Hawaiian or otherwise. It is, however, the ultimate rock garden: a rugged, barren, beautiful place full of rocks strewn by volcanic forces and shaped by the elements into a variety of shapes and colors — brilliant reds, oranges, ochers, and yellows. Being out here in this barren, beautiful, otherworldly place will really bring home the truth that you're in the middle of nowhere. Don't be surprised if you see axis deer striding across the boulder-strewn landscape. Go early in the morning or just before sunset, when the light casts eerie shadows on the mysterious lava formations. Drive west from the Lodge on Polihua Road; in about 2 miles, you see a hand-painted sign that points you in the right direction — left, down a one-lane red-dirt road, through a kiawe forest, and past sisal and scrub to the site.

Kanepuu Preserve

This fragile ancient forest on the island's western plateau has 49 species of plants unique to Hawaii, and it survives under the Nature Conservancy's protective wing. Botanists say the 590-acre forest is the last dry lowland forest in Hawaii; the others have all vanished, trashed by axis deer, agriculture, or "progress." Among the botanical marvels of this dry forest are the remains of *olopua* (native olive), *lama* (native ebony), *mau hau hele* (a native hibiscus), and the rare *aiea* trees, which were used for canoe parts. The self-guided tour takes about 10 to 15 minutes to walk; the trail, open 9 a.m. to 4 p.m., is accessible from the Garden of the Gods. Guided hikes must be arranged in advance. Contact the **Nature Conservancy field office** at ☎ **808-572-4508** to reserve.

Shipwreck Beach

The remote, 8-mile-long, windswept Shipwreck Beach, located on Lanai's northeastern shore, is named for the rusty ship *Liberty* stuck on the coral reef — a sailor's nightmare and a beachcomber's dream. The strong currents yield all sorts of flotsam, from Japanese handblown-glass fish floats and rare pelagic paper nautilus shells to plenty of junk. This place is also great for spotting whales from December through April, when the Pacific humpbacks cruise in from Alaska to winter in the calm offshore waters. The road to the beach is paved most of the way, but you really need a four-wheel-drive to get to this deserted beach at the end of Polihua Road; the road ends at the turnaround about 1½ miles form the end of the pavement. It's a short hike from here to see the shipwreck from the old cement lighthouse foundation. An easy desert trail leads south from the foundation to some ancient Hawaiian petroglyphs.

Keomoku Village

Visiting Keomoku Village, on Lanai's east coast, is really getting away from it all. All that's in Keomoku, a ghost town since the mid-1950s, is a 1903 clapboard church in disrepair, an overgrown graveyard, an excellent view across the 9-mile Auau Channel to Maui's crowded Kaanapali Beach, and some very empty beaches that are perfect for a picnic or a snorkel. This former ranching and fishing village of 2,000 was the first non-Hawaiian settlement on Lanai, but it dried up after droughts killed off the Maunalei Sugar Company. The village is a great little escape from

Lanai City. Follow Keomoku Road for 8 miles to the coast, turn right on the sandy road, and keep going for 5¾ miles.

Luahiwa Petroglyph Field

With more than 450 known petroglyphs in Hawaii at 23 sites, Lanai is second only to the Big Island in its wealth of prehistoric rock art, but you have to search a little to find it. Some of the best examples are on the outskirts of Lanai City, on a hillside site known as Luahiwa Petroglyph Field. The characters you see incised on 13 boulders in this grassy 3-acre knoll include a running man, a deer, a turtle, a bird, a goat, and even a rare, curly-tailed Polynesian dog. To get there, take the road to Hulopoe Beach. About 2 miles out of Lanai City, look to the left, up on the slopes of the crater, for a cluster of reddish-tan boulders (believed to form a rain *heiau,* or shrine, where people called up the gods Ku and Hina to nourish their crops). A cluster of spiky century plants marks the spot. Look for the Norfolk pines on the left side of the highway, turn left on the dirt road that veers across the abandoned pineapple fields, and, after about a mile, take a sharp left by the water tanks. Drive for another half-mile and then veer to the right at the V in the road. Stay on this upper road for about a third of a mile until you come to a large cluster of boulders on the right side. Take a short walk up the cliffs (wear walking or hiking shoes) to the petroglyphs. Exit the same way you came. Go between 3 p.m. and sunset for ideal viewing and photo ops.

The Munro Trail

In the first golden rays of dawn, when lone owls swoop over abandoned pineapple fields, hop into a four-wheel-drive and head out on the two-lane blacktop toward Mount Lanaihale, the 3,370-foot summit of Lanai. Your destination is the Munro Trail, the narrow, winding ridge trail that runs across Lanai's razorback spine to the summit. From there, you may get a rare Hawaii treat: On a clear day, you can see all the main islands in the Hawaiian chain except Kauai. Note: The Munro Trail was inaccessible at press time, so you should call the visitors bureau before you set your heart on this trip.

Shopping the Local Stores

There's not much shopping on such a tiny island, but there are a handful of treasures you won't want to miss.

Central Bakery, 1311 Fraser Ave., Lanai City (☎ **808-565-3920**), is the mother lode of the island's baked delights. Although Central Bakery isn't your standard retail outlet, you can call in advance, place your order, and pick it up. The staff prefers as much notice as possible, and it's worth it. The guava chiffon and chocolate chantilly cakes are in great demand, and the breads are legendary. The bakery also sells a delectable assortment of cookies, brownies, muffins, and breakfast pastries.

Gifts with Aloha, Dole Park, 363 Seventh St., at Ilima Street (☎ 808-565-6589; www.giftswithaloha.com), sells fabulously stylish hats and hatbands, T-shirts, swimwear, quilts, dresses, children's books and toys, Hawaii-themed books, *pareus* (long, wrap-around skirts usually made from a colorful or decorative fabric), candles, aloha shirts, and much more. The fragrant soaps and bath products made on Maui make wonderful gifts to bring home. If you fall in love with a minigarden, fountains, or lamp, you can have it shipped back to the mainland.

The Local Gentry, 363 Seventh St., behind Gifts with Aloha, facing Ilima Street (☎ 808-565-9130), is a wonderful boutique with clothing and accessories that rise above the standard resort-shop fare. Everything has a relaxed island flair. Expect brands such as Tommy Bahama, Putumayo, and other casually sophisticated brands.

Also overlooking Dole Park, in the heart of Lanai City, is **Dis 'n Dat,** 418 Eighth St. (☎ 808-565-9170; www.suzieo.com), housed in a charming 1928 plantation cottage and specializing in its own fun and affordable island-themed jewelry, which has been featured in *Us Weekly, People, InStyle,* and *Teen Vogue* magazines.

The **Mike Carroll Gallery,** 443 Seventh St. (☎ 808-565-7122; www.mike carrollgallery.com), a working gallery and studio featuring the original island art of mainland transplant Carroll, who captures the spirit and beauty of Lanai and Maui in his gorgeous oils. The best shopping stop on the island, bar none.

Stop by the **International Food & Clothing Center,** 833 Ilima Ave. (☎ 808-565-6433), for groceries, housewares, T-shirts, fishing supplies, over-the-counter drugs, wine and liquor, paper goods, and hardware. There's even a takeout lunch counter.

A local landmark for two generations, **Pine Isle Market,** 356 Eighth St. (☎ 808-565-6488 or 808-565-6775), specializes in locally caught fresh fish, but you can also find fresh herbs and spices, canned goods, ice cream, toys, zoris, and other basic essentials of work and play. The fishing section is outstanding, with every lure imaginable.

Lanai Plantation Store (☎ 808-565-7227) tends to be the center of news and activity on the island, and a great stop for necessities and affordable souvenirs. The Dollar Rent A Car counter is attached, so this is a good place to pick up water and snacks for a day exploring the island in your four-wheel-drive. The Plantation Store is also the island's gas station.

At the **Lanai Marketplace** on Dole Square, farmers sell their dewy-fresh produce, home-baked breads, plate lunches, and handicrafts from 7 to 11 a.m. or noon on Saturday.

Enjoying Lanai after Dark

Except for special programs, such as the annual **Pineapple Festival** in May, when some of Hawaii's best musicians arrive to show their support for Lanai, the only regular nightlife venues are the **Lanai Theater** (☎ **808-565-7500**), which screens first-run movies in a charming setting at the corner of Seventh and Lanai avenues in Lanai City, and the two resorts, the Four Seasons Lodge at Koele and Four Seasons Resort Lanai at Manele Bay, where the **Hale Ahe Ahe Lounge** makes a great place to enjoy a convivial evening cocktail. And don't forget the friendly bar at the Lanai City Grille, open Wednesday through Sunday.

Fast Facts: Lanai

Banks

In Lanai City, there's a branch of the Bank of Hawaii at 460 Eighth St. (☎ 808-565-6426; www.boh.com), and a First Hawaiian Bank at 644 Lanai Ave. (☎ 808-565-6969; www.fhb.com). Both have ATMs.

Dentists

For emergency dental care, call Dr. James Sagawa, 730 Lanai Ave. (☎ **808-565-6418**).

Doctors/Hospitals

If you need a doctor, contact the Straub Lanai Family Health Center, 628-B Seventh St. (☎ 808-565-6423) or the Lanai Community Hospital, 628 Seventh St. (☎ 808-565-6411; www.lch.hhsc.org).

Emergencies

Call the police, fire department, or ambulance services at ☎ **911**, or the Poison Control Center at ☎ **800-362-3585**. For non-emergencies, call the County of Maui Lanai Police, 855 Fraser Ave. (☎ 808-565-8400 or 808-565-6428).

Weather

For a complete Maui County weather report, including Lanai, call the National Weather Service at ☎ 866-944-5025.

Part V
The Part of Tens

In this part . . .

*I*t wouldn't be a *For Dummies* book without some of these lists of ten! In the first of the three chapters, I'll introduce you to the wonderful world of dining, Maui style. Next, you'll find insider tips on how to ditch the tourist trappings and comfortably fit in like a local. In the final chapter, I'll share the secrets of maximizing your romantic experience on Maui.

Chapter 18

Ten Steps to Incredible Island Dining

. . . .

In This Chapter

▶ Knowing what you're eating
▶ Maximizing your dining experiences

. . . .

*E*ating well on Maui isn't a problem. Hawaii has lured some of the world's finest chefs to its kitchens and managed to cultivate some stars of its own in the process — and the largest and finest bunch of them has chosen the Valley Isle as muse. Anyone who loves quality seafood, fresh-grown veggies, sweet tropical fruits, and even artisan-crafted cheeses will think he's died and gone to heaven, because Maui is the bounteous breadbasket of the Hawaiian Islands.

But that's far from the end of the bounty. Maui's melting-pot society sets a global table. Although Asian flavors and cooking styles are most prevalent, island menus travel the globe, from old-world European culinary classics to good ol' (local) ranch-raised, fire-grilled steaks. Hawaii's cooks have even managed to put their own spin on some of the world's most revered foods — pizzas, burgers, and burritos — with rousing success.

However, you may want to know a few facts about island dining before you sit down to a meal — the first being that Hawaii has two brands of homegrown cuisine. Local food is the traditional everyday eats of the locals, while Hawaii Regional (or Hawaii Island) Cuisine is the gourmet version. But both are hybrid cuisines, informed by European and Asian influences. This chapter tells you more about island cuisine and what else to expect on the culinary front.

Savoring Maui's Freshest Foods

If you love seafood, you've come to the right place. In fact, Hawaii's **seafood** may be the best in the world — some of the world's finest chefs think so — and the selection is generally much more diverse than what you find in your average mainland supermarket. And Maui's chefs definitely know how to select, prepare, and serve the fruits of the sea. (For details on the variations you may find on island menus, see the section "Working Your Way around the Menu: A Translation List for Seafood Lovers," later in this chapter.)

But Maui's bounty isn't limited to the sea. A wealth of **fresh-grown vegetables** — including leafy lettuces, vine-ripened tomatoes, and sweet Maui onions — thrives in the lava-rich soil.

Maui's verdant Upcountry plays host to Surfing Goat Dairy, which crafts some of the finest **goat cheeses** in all the land. The hard and soft chèvres come in a range of creatively ripened and herbed varieties. If you spot one of these extraordinary chèvres on a local menu, don't pass it up. The charming goat farm has even developed into a tourist attraction in its own right, so you can also go right to the source (see Chapter 13).

Maui has also raised its profile in the **herbs** market. Upcountry's Alii Kula Lavender Farm has learned that Maui has just about perfect growing conditions for fragrant lavender. Alii Kula has also had the business sense to partner with some of Hawaii's premier food purveyors in order to generate some uniquely flavorful food products, such as aromatic lavender tea and flavorful lavender scones, which can be found at markets, on restaurant menus, and at the farm's own store (see Chapter 13).

And **fruits** are Maui's real forte. All you need to do is head to the local supermarket to discover a whole new world of citrus, more varieties of banana than you ever knew existed, and other colorful tropical treats. (See the section "Shopping at a Maui Supermarket," later in this chapter, for more details.)

Tropical fruit comes as no surprise, of course — but who knew that Hawaii offered so much **island-raised meat?** The Big Island is home to the largest privately owned cattle ranch in the United States: Parker Ranch, covering 225,000 acres, including more than 50,000 cattle, and serving as the heart of Hawaii's *paniolo* (cowboy) country. Ranch-raised beef and lamb appear on fine-dining menus all over the state. In fact, although Maui doesn't boast nearly the bounty of island-raised meat that the Big Island does, you may get lucky enough to find a Maui-raised steak on a menu or two when you're on the island.

Tasting Traditional Island Eats

Local food is a casual, catch-all affair. As evidenced by the list of food terms that appears later in this chapter (see the section "Mastering More Everyday Hawaiian Food Terms"), outsider influences on the local cuisine arrived in Hawaii from all over the map, from Portugal to Japan and just about everywhere in between.

Lomilomi salmon is the perfect example of local food as a hybrid cuisine. Islanders didn't have natural access to the cold-water fish, but they accepted it in trade from globetrotting explorers and traders.

Discovering how to prepare it seviche-style for short-term preservation, they quickly became accustomed to accepting it in trade and incorporated it into their diet as a staple.

Local food is generally starch heavy and high in calories, so don't expect it to have a positive impact on your waistline. Local food is most commonly served as a **plate lunch,** which usually consists of a main dish (anything from fried fish to teriyaki beef), "two scoops rice," an ice-cream-scoop serving of macaroni salad, and brown gravy, all served on a paper plate. Plate lunches are cheap and available at casual restaurants and beachside stands. An excellent place to indulge in this local tradition is Maui's **Aloha Mixed Plate,** located in a wonderful waterfront spot in Lahaina; if you're based elsewhere on the island, check out local favorite **Da' Kitchen,** with locations in Kahului and Kihei. **Gazebo Restaurant,** in Napili on Maui's west shore, is a great place to try breakfast with local flavor, such as Portuguese sausages. (See Chapter 11 for details on all three restaurants.)

Another great place to try local food is at a luau, a traditional feast that's not a tourist trap but a genuine part of island culture, thrown to celebrate everything from a baby's birth to a college graduation. (For more on luaus, see "Knowing What to Expect at a Luau," later in this chapter.)

Finding Maui's Gourmet Side

About a dozen or so years ago, Hawaii's kitchens underwent a culinary revolution: the birth of Hawaii Regional Cuisine (HRC). Island chefs were tired of preparing stodgy continental fare that was unsuited to Hawaii living, so they created a new standard of gourmet cuisine using fresh local ingredients in creative combinations and preparations.

Hawaii Regional Cuisine is often disguised under other names — Euro-Asian, Pacific Rim, Indo-Pacific, Pacific Edge, Euro-Pacific, Island Fusion, and so on — but it all falls under the jurisdiction of Hawaii Regional Cuisine. Although it has variations, you can expect the following keynotes: plenty of fresh island fish, Asian flavorings (ginger, soy, wasabi, seaweed, and so on) and cooking styles galore (searing, grilling, panko crust, and wok preparations), and fresh tropical fruit sauces (mango, papaya, and the like).

Hawaii Regional Cuisine has really matured in recent years, with the finest HRC chefs putting clever multicultural spins on the established canon, based on their training and heritage. You may already know of Roy Yamaguchi, who has installed outposts of his **Roy's Restaurant** chain not only on each island but also around the world, from New York to Guam. Maui stars include Beverly Gannon, of **Haliimaile General Store** and **Joe's Bar & Grill.** Even though David Paul is no longer at the helm, **Lahaina Grill** remains a faultless outpost of Hawaii Regional Cuisine.

In 1999, the next generation of island chefs banded together under the label Hawaiian Island Chefs, taking their craft to the next level — and they've succeeded in spades. Instead of emphasizing broad-based fusion in island cuisine, these upstarts generally start from an ethnic or thematic base, incorporating Hawaii ingredients and adding their own individual stamp. The stellar James McDonald works his magic at chic sister seafood restaurants **I'o** and **Pacific'o,** while D.K. Kodama, who reinvented sushi for adoring gourmands at Maui's **Sansei Seafood Restaurant and Sushi Bar,** has continued to expand his empire. Although eating at some of these restaurants may be a splurge, I encourage you to treat yourself to a gourmet island meal at least once during your trip. (See Chapter 11 for reviews of these establishments and more of Maui's top choices.)

Working Your Way around the Menu: A Translation List for Seafood Lovers

Even savvy seafood eaters can become confused when confronted with a Hawaiian menu. Although the mainland terms are sometimes included, many menus only use the Hawaiian names to tout their daily catches. Furthermore, some types of seafood that make regular appearances in Hawaii's kitchens simply don't show up on mainland menus.

You're likely to encounter many of the following types of seafood while you're in Maui:

- ✔ *Ahi:* This dense, ruby-red bigeye or yellowfin tuna is a Hawaiian favorite — and it may be one of yours, too, as popular as it has become on the mainland. *Ahi* is regularly served raw, as sushi and sashimi, or panko-crusted and seared in Hawaii Regional Cuisine. Yellowfin is the beefier of the two.

- ✔ *Aku:* This meaty, robust skipjack tuna is also known as *bonito* (which may be familiar to sushi fans). Aku is best as raw sushi, because it can get too dry if not expertly cooked.

- ✔ *Au* (ow): This firm-fleshed marlin or broadbill swordfish sometimes stands in for *ahi* in local dishes. Pacific blue marlin is sometimes called *kajiki,* while striped marlin often shows up as *nairagi.*

- ✔ *Hebi* (heh-bee): This mildly flavored, almost lemony, spearfish is sometimes the day's catch in upscale restaurants.

- ✔ *Mahimahi:* Like *ahi,* this white, sweet, moderately dense fish is likely to also be familiar to you; it's Hawaii's most popular fish and shows up regularly on mainland menus.

- ✔ *Monchong* (*mon*-chong): This exotic fish boasts a flaky, tender texture and a simple flavor. It's best served broiled, sautéed, or steamed.

- ✔ *Onaga* (o-*na*-ga): This mild, moist, and tender ruby-red snapper is served in many fine restaurants; sample it if it's available.

✔ **Ono** (*oh*-no): *Ono* means "good to eat" in Hawaiian, and this mackerel-like fish sure is. Also called *wahoo,* it's similar to snapper, but firmer and drier. You should have multiple opportunities to try this popular, distinctly flavored fish; it's often served grilled and in sandwiches.

✔ **Opah** (*oh*-pa): This rich, almost creamy moonfish is good served just about any way, from sashimi to baked.

✔ **Opakapaka** (oh-pa-ka-*pa*-ka): Either pink or crimson snapper, this light, flaky, elegant fish is very popular on fine-dining menus.

✔ **Shutome** (shuh-*toe*-me): This fish is what mainlanders call swordfish. It's a sweet and tender steaklike fish that is great grilled or broiled.

✔ **Tombo:** Tombo is albacore tuna, but this firm, flavorful whitefish surpasses the canned stuff by miles when prepared appropriately.

✔ **Uku** (*oo*-koo): This gray — pale pink, really — snapper is flaky, moist, and delicate.

✔ **Ulua** (oo-*loo*-ah): Ulua is large jack trevally, a firm-fleshed, flavorful fish also known as *pompano.*

Demand for fish has driven down the populations of certain fish species, such as Chilean sea bass and Hawaiian grouper *(hapuupuu),* to dangerously low levels. If you'd like to know which fish are relatively abundant and which ones are overfished before you make your menu choices, you may want to pack a copy of the **Monterey Bay Aquarium's Seafood Watch Pocket Guide.** The printable guide — available at http://montereybay aquarium.com/cr/SeafoodWatch/web/sfw_regional.aspx?region_ id=3 — makes it easy to make the environmentally correct choice at a glance. The color-coded card indicates which menu-common species are abundant and relatively well managed, which are not currently in danger but are under watch, and which are in danger of severe depletion.

Many of Maui's restaurants serve top-notch seafood from local waters, and I recommend a whole slew of them in Chapter 11. My absolute favorite place to enjoy the fruit of the island's waters is the splurge-worthy **Mama's Fish House** in Paia.

Mastering More Everyday Hawaiian Food Terms

All the following foods are common in plate lunches and at luaus. A number of them also pop up on gourmet menus — usually with expensive ingredients and prepared with a twist, of course:

✔ **Bento:** A Japanese box lunch.

✔ **Haupia** (how-*pee*-ah): Creamy coconut pudding, usually served in squares. A favorite luau dessert.

✔ **Kalua pork:** Pork slow-cooked in an *imu* (underground oven); listed on menus as luau pig on occasion. Sometimes it's served in a pulled kalua pork sandwich, much like barbecue pork in the Southeast or Texas.

✔ **Kiawe** (kee-*ah*-vay): An aromatic mesquite wood often used to fire the wood-burning ovens.

✔ **Laulau:** Pork, chicken, or fish wrapped in ti leaves and steamed.

✔ **Lilikoi** (lil-*ee*-koy): Passion fruit.

✔ **Lomilomi** (low-mee-*low*-mee) **salmon:** Salted salmon marinated, seviche-like, with tomatoes and green onions.

✔ **Lumpia** (lum-*pee*-ah): The Portuguese version of a spring roll, but spicier, doughier, and deep-fried (and usually stuffed with pork and veggies).

✔ **Malassada** (mah-lah-*sah*-da): The Portuguese version of a dough-nut, usually round, deep-fried, and generously sprinkled with pow-dered sugar.

✔ **Manapua** (man-ah-*poo*-ah): A bready, doughy bun with sweetened pork or sweet beans inside, like Chinese *bao*.

✔ **Ohelo** (oh-*hay*-low): A berry very similar to a cranberry that com-monly appears in Hawaii Regional Cuisine sauces.

✔ **Panko:** Japanese bread crumbs, most commonly used to prepare *katsu* (deep-fried pork or chicken cutlet). Creative chefs often use it for other purposes, most commonly as a tempura-like crust on sushi-grade *ahi* rolls.

✔ **Poi:** The root of the taro pounded into a purple, starchy paste; a staple of the island diet, but generally tasteless to most outsiders.

✔ **Poke** (*po*-kay): Cubed raw fish — usually *ahi* or marlin — seasoned with onions, soy, and seaweed.

✔ **Ponzu:** A soy-and-citrus dipping sauce popular with Hawaii Regional Cuisine chefs.

✔ **Pupus:** Appetizers or hors d'oeuvres.

✔ **Saimin** (*sai*-min): A brothy soup with ramenlike noodles, topped with bits of fish, chicken, pork, and/or vegetables. Saimin is served almost everywhere in Hawaii, from plate-lunch stands to museum cafes to McDonald's.

✔ **Shave ice:** The island version of a snow cone, best enjoyed with ice cream and sweet *azuki* (red) beans at the bottom.

✔ **Taro:** A green leafy vegetable grown in Hawaii; the root is used to make poi (see earlier in this list), while the leafy part of the veg-etable is often steamed like spinach.

Enjoying Other Local Favorites

Lest all this unfamiliar food talk makes you think otherwise, remember that the majority of Hawaii islanders are red-blooded, flag-waving Americans, and they love a good burger just as much as your average mainlander.

My favorite burgers on Maui are served at **Cheeseburger in Paradise/ Cheeseburger Island Style,** while the island's best pizza is served at Paia's colorful and creative **Flatbread Company.** (See Chapter 11 for all the juicy details.)

Hawaii has also co-opted Mexican cuisine and made the burrito its own, most successfully at Lahaina's **Cilantro Fresh Mexican Grill** and **Mañana Garage,** in Kahului, where island-grown ingredients and fresh-caught fish provide top-quality, surf-style filling. (Again, see Chapter 11 for details.)

Discovering Maui's Ethnic Eats

Thanks to its proximity to the Eastern Hemisphere and its large, multi-faceted Asian population, the Hawaiian Islands boast a wealth of fabulous Asian restaurants — Chinese, Thai, Vietnamese, Japanese, Indonesian, and so on. With the exception of Japanese, most Asian restaurants tend to be very affordable. Furthermore, because island palates are more accustomed to dining Asian style, you find that dishes aren't Americanized for a mainland population; flavors are bold and strong, ingredients fresh and crisp. While dining out on Maui, you may just find yourself enjoying the finest ethnic food you've ever eaten.

Maui's ethnic standout is **A Saigon Cafe** (see Chapter 11), whose piquant flavors and friendly service make it well worth seeking out in off-the-tourist-track Wailuku. I never miss it when I'm on the island. Also consider **WokStar,** in Kihei, for a fresh take on noodle dishes from Indonesia and around the world; and **Café des Amis,** in Paia, for savory Indian curries as well as well-prepared Mediterranean fare.

Shopping at a Maui Supermarket

Whenever I'm in a foreign country, I always take the time to visit the local supermarket. And even though Hawaii is part of the United States, its grocery stores are a world apart — a trip to the market is an entertaining culinary adventure. If you're staying in a condo or a vacation rental, you'll want to stock the pantry, but even if you're not, I highly recommend an excursion to your local Safeway, KTA, Star Market, or Foodland.

Hawaii supermarkets offer a number of treats that you don't find at your average mainland supermarket. **Poi** (taro root mixed with water and pounded into a paste — similar to polenta in consistency), for example, comes in instant, premade, and make-your-own forms; I defy you to find poi in *any* form in your hometown supermarket.

The bounty in the seafood case is much more diverse than what you see at your local Safeway back home. Hawaii refrigerator cases regularly contain such taste treats as sushi-grade tuna, fresh Pacific octopus, and whole squid (insert "yum!" or "yuck!" here, depending on your taste buds). If you have access to a barbecue at your hotel or condo complex, grilling up a fresh fish filet is a simple but magnificent dinner.

Just about any Hawaii supermarket has multiple aisles devoted to Asian foods, from noodles to bizarre candies. The juice refrigerator case is also a treat, so don't be afraid to try something new. My husband never misses an opportunity to chug **POG** (passion fruit–orange–guava juice) when he's in the islands.

Java lovers, rejoice. Maui's local brew is available in just about any average market. All Hawaii-grown coffees are delicious, but the world-famous **Kona coffee,** grown on the Big Island, is the top of the heap (and it makes a great, affordable gift to bring home to your favorite caffeine addict).

You can find the greatest bounty among the fresh fruits, where you uncover such tropical treats as mangoes, guava, star fruit, litchi, *lilikoi* (passion fruit), and much more. Whenever I go to Hawaii, I eat as much papaya as I can. (Mainland imports just don't equal the island-grown fruits.) Cut your papaya in half, dig out the seeds, and serve with a squirt of lime — island breakfast doesn't get any better than this. Pineapples are another Hawaii taste treat; the small white pineapples are sweetest, and you usually find them clearly labeled at the market. The Big Island's lava-rich soil produces extra-flavorful citrus fruits; Kau oranges, for example, are legendary for their sweetness. Even watermelon is an extra-special treat; Molokai-grown watermelons are the best in the world — full of seeds, but fabulous.

Among Hawaii-grown vegetables, Maui onions are the ultimate treat. They're very sweet, like Vidalias, but with a distinctive flavor all their own. Slice 'em thick and throw 'em right on the barbecue. Dense, purple, Molokai-grown sweet potatoes are another of my favorites.

Don't shy away from tropical fruits or other foods just because you're unfamiliar with them. Islanders are friendly and talkative folks. Supermarket attendants — or even your fellow shoppers — can advise you on how to cut or clean island fruits. Just ask, and you're likely to find yourself on the receiving end of some friendly conversation.

Hawaii shopping does have a downside — namely, high prices. Although you can save quite a few bucks by stocking up and cooking for yourself back at the condo instead of eating in restaurants for three meals a day, you still have to be prepared to pay more for staples than you would back home. The general rule is: Expect anything that has to wing its way across the Pacific to cost more than you usually pay.

Unfortunately, Maui's supermarket prices are high all across the board. Fish is about the same price as on the mainland, and the quality is generally better, but pick up some ground beef for burgers and expect to pay $3 a pound. Your average breakfast cereal goes for $5 or $7 a box. At first glance, you may think the prices of milk and bread are a joke: Expect to pay about $6 a gallon for milk, and around $4.50 or $5 for a loaf of bread.

Sipping a Tropical Cocktail

California entrepreneur Vic Bergeron — more popularly known as Trader Vic — may have been responsible for the birth of the mai tai, but it's practically the official state cocktail in Hawaii. The classic mai tai is a magical sweet-tart concoction of Jamaican rum, fresh lime juice, and chunky ice, generally served in a tumbler and topped with a fresh sprig of mint.

A mai tai is a simple blend, and any bar worth its salt in Hawaii can mix you a well-balanced drink. But score an out-of-sorts bartender on the wrong night, and you end up with either a sickly sweet syrup that couldn't do justice to a stack of flapjacks, or a thick, face-distorting blend strong enough to power up an SUV.

For the perfect blend of ideal mai tai–making and only-in-Maui ambience, the bar at any of the big resorts can satisfy your sunset cravings. In Lahaina, **Cheeseburger in Paradise** is the place to go for the top concoction (see Chapter 11).

Of course, mai tais may not be your drink of choice. If that's the case, don't worry, you can find plenty of other ways to toast your time in paradise. Personally, I'm a big fan of the piña colada — not a Hawaii cocktail, sure, but it never fails to put me in the tropical mood, especially when a colorful paper umbrella and a generous slice of pineapple are included. Again, Cheeseburger in Paradise makes the island's best, but you can't go wrong at most of the island's finer restaurants, either.

Microbrews are serious business on the islands. The finest wear the **Kona Brewing Company** label.

Knowing What to Expect at a Luau

A luau is the ideal place to experience island traditions — but only to a degree, of course. Any commercial luau (read: any luau you're likely to attend) will be tainted by its commercialism. But a few luaus do a great job of bringing genuine island culture into the mix.

The best luaus — offering the best mix of good food, amenities, setting, and authentic culture — are on Maui. The **Old Lahaina Luau** and the **Feast at Lele** are the best luaus Hawaii has to offer, hands down; Old Lahaina Luau now offers a morning fete complete with a local-style breakfast feast and entertainment two days a week, called Ho'omana'o. Be sure to reserve right away (see Chapter 11).

What should you plan for when attending a luau? Luckily, most luau feasts are self-sufficient, idiot-proof ventures, so after you make your reservations, all you need to bring is your appetite and aloha spirit. Dress for the festivities in bright, bold colors, even if you don't own any aloha wear — bright colors really suit the mood. Other than that, just wear what's comfortable for you, and bring a sweater if the weather is expected to cool down after dark. (All luaus take place outdoors, most in breezy oceanfront settings.)

When you make your reservations, you're usually told when the gates open and when you should plan to arrive. Come in plenty of time to wander the grounds because the best luaus feature authentic craft making, games, and the like in the hour before the festivities formally begin. The luau pig, which has been baking all day in its *imu* (under-ground oven), is also unearthed early in the program, and unless you're squeamish, you don't want to miss it.

Upon arrival, the Hawaiians typically greet you with a lei, made of either fresh flowers or shells, and a cocktail, often a mai tai (or fruit juice, if you're too young or a teetotaler). They lead you to your assigned seat, usually at a communal table with chairs (although the Old Lahaina Luau now features some traditional seating, on cushions facing low-slung tables).

Cocktails are usually included in the pay-one-price admission fee to a luau. Open bars are common, but some luaus limit you to a certain number or kind of drink. If it matters to you, be sure to ask when booking.

After the luau pig is unearthed from the *imu,* you'll be asked to take a seat and then invited to fill your plate from the buffet luau spread; the best luaus clearly mark the dishes so that you know what you're sam-pling. In addition to the kalua pork (shredded from the bone after the luau pig is unearthed), you can expect traditional dishes, such as poi, the tasteless purple paste that's the staple starch of Hawaii. Poi is worth trying for its iconic status, but you're unlikely to become a fan. People usually don't eat poi alone, but with other starches; ask an attendant what's best in the night's feast for poi dipping. You're likely to prefer such dishes as *lomilomi* salmon, *poke,* and *haupia* (see "Mastering More Everyday Hawaiian Food Terms," earlier in this chapter). If you're a less-than-adventurous diner, don't worry — you can find plenty of familiar dishes on hand, including chicken teriyaki, long rice, and salad. You can refill your plate as often as you like. After dinner, the evening's entertain-ment begins, usually a hula show that lasts an hour or so before the evening winds down.

Most luau food is satisfactory at best, so don't expect a gourmet feast (the exception being the Feast at Lele, which eschews the standard setting for intimate seating, food prepared by one of Hawaii's best chefs, and full table service). Top-notch luaus like the Old Lahaina Luau serve well-prepared fare, but remember that they're still cooking in bulk for hundreds. Come for the party and plan to have a first-rate dinner at a standard restaurant on another night.

The kind of luau that's right for you is your call; some luaus are more suited to couples, for example, while others are great for families with kids. Some luaus feature wholly authentic Hawaiian entertainment (primarily chanting and dancing), while others blow the wad on glitzy Vegas-style extravaganzas with glittering costumes. (Note: Any luau that calls itself authentically Hawaiian shouldn't have fire-knife dancers, which is a Samoan tradition.)

Luaus are pricey — usually $50 to $105 a head, depending on the fete — so choose carefully. Before you commit, see Chapter 11 and ask your reservations agent to make sure that you end up at the party that's right for you.

Chapter 19

Ten Ways to Lose the Tourist Trappings and Look Like a Local

*H*awaii may be the 50th state, but it's an ocean — and a world — apart from its 48 mainland brethren. In fact, because it didn't join the star-spangled party until 1959, Hawaii came into the Union as an adopted adult, complete with its own unique personality, fully formed (indeed, ancient) culture, and distinct worldview.

Maui sits closer to Tokyo than it does to Washington, D.C. — or even Chicago. The islands don't always share the Eurocentric perspective that many Americans have of the world.

Even the population is dramatically different. Unlike the rest of the United States, no one ethnic group forms a majority in Hawaii. Although Caucasian and Japanese are the two largest ethnic groups (each accounts for roughly 22 percent of the population), nearly 35 percent of islanders consider themselves of mixed ethnicity. Hawaii's residents, as a group, don't consider race a factor in marriage; they're just as likely to marry someone from a different race as not.

If you want to come across as an *akamai* (a-*kay*-my; smart) traveler instead of advertising your status as a *malihini* (ma-li-*hee*-nee; newcomer), read on.

Mastering the Three Most Important Phrases in the Hawaiian Language

Everyone in Hawaii speaks English, of course, but a few Hawaiian words and phrases have made their way into the common vernacular, and regularly pop up in everyday conversation.

You probably already know the Hawaiian word ***aloha*** (a-*lo*-ha), which serves as an all-purpose greeting — hello and welcome, goodbye as well. *Aloha* is a warm and wonderful word full of grace, compassion, and good feeling, so use it liberally. I can't think of a better way to get caught up in Hawaii's true spirit.

Islanders don't like "goodbye" to be so permanent. So to really sound like a local, part from others warmly with ***a hui hou*** (ah *hoo*-ee ho), which means "until we meet again."

Another word that every visitor needs to know is ***mahalo*** (ma-*ha*-low), which means "thank you" and is used extensively throughout Hawaii. If you want to say "Thanks very much!" or "Thank you so much," say *mahalo nui loa* (ma-*ha*-low *noo*-ee *low*-ah). You'll impress the locals with your efforts, and you'll flatter them with your graciousness, too.

Discovering More Hawaiian Words

Take a few minutes to study the following list. That way, when you're in a restaurant and the waiter offers your little ones a *keiki* menu, describes today's lunch special as particularly *ono,* or asks you if you're *pau* when he comes to clear your plate, you'll feel like a regular *kamaaina:*

- ✔ ***Alii*** (ah-*lee*-ee): Hawaiian royalty

- ✔ ***Halau*** (ha-*lau*): School

- ✔ ***Hale*** (*ha*-lay): House

- ✔ ***Haole*** (*how*-lee): Foreigner or Caucasian (literally "out of breath" — pale, or paleface); a common reference, not an insult (usually)

- ✔ ***Heiau*** (heh-*ee*-ow): Hawaiian temple

- ✔ ***Hui*** (*hoo*-ee): A club, collective, or assembly (for example, an artists' collective is an artists' *hui*)

- ✔ ***Hula*** (*hoo*-lah): Native dance

- ✔ ***Imu*** (*ee*-moo): Underground oven lined with hot rocks that's used for cooking the luau pig

- *Kahuna* (ka-*hoo*-nah): Priest or expert

- *Kamaaina* (ka-ma-*eye*-nah): Local person

- *Kane* (*ka*-nay): Man (you may see this word on a restroom door)

- *Kapu* (*ka*-poo): Anything that's taboo, forbidden

- *Keiki* (*keh*-kee): Child

- *Kupuna* (koo-*poo*-nah): An elder, leader, grandparent, or anyone who commands great respect

- *Lanai* (*lah*-nigh): Porch or veranda

- *Lei* (lay): Garland (usually of flowers, leaves, or shells)

- *Luau* (*loo*-ow): A celebratory feast

- *Malihini* (ma-li-*hee*-nee): Stranger or newcomer

- *Mana* (*ma*-na): Spirit, divine power

- *Muumuu* (moo-oo-*moo*-oo): A loose-fitting dress, usually in a tropical print

- *Ono* (*oh*-no): Delicious

- *Pau* (pow): Finished or done

- *Pali* (*pah*-lee): Cliff

- *Pupu* (*poo*-poo): Starter dish, appetizer

- *Wahine* (wa-*hee*-nay): Woman (you may see this word on a restroom door)

Pronouncing Those Pesky Hawaiian Words and Place Names

Because the Hawaiian language has only 12 characters to work with — the five vowels (*a, e, i, o,* and *u*), plus seven consonants (*h, k, l, m, n, p,* and *w*) — Hawaiian words and names tend to be long and difficult, with plenty of repetitive syllables that can really twist your tongue. Master just a few basic rules, however, and *Honoapiilani Highway* and *Haliimaile* will be rolling off your tongue like *Main Street* and *Anytown, USA,* in no time.

Half the letters in the Hawaiian language — *h, k, l, m, n,* and *p* — sound just as they do in English. The one consonant that sounds different in Hawaiian is *w. W* usually carries the *v* sound when it follows *i* or *e;* for example, the Oahu town of Haleiwa is Ha-lay-*ee*-vah. At the beginning of words and after *a, u,* and *o,* though, it's usually your standard *w* sound — hence Wailea (why-*lay*-ah) and Makawao (mah-*kah*-wow), two Maui destinations.

The vowels are pronounced like this:

a	*ah* (as in *father*) or *uh* (as in *above*)
e	*eh* (as in bed) or *ay* (as in *they*)
i	*ee* (as in *police*)
o	*oh* (as in *vote*)
u	*oo* (as in *too*)

You sound almost all vowels separately, although you do pronounce some together, as in the name of Waikiki's main thoroughfare, Kalakaua Avenue, which is pronounced kah-lah-*cow*-ah.

Remember this tip when trying to pronounce a Hawaiian word or name: Get into the habit of seeing long words or names as a collection of short syllables, and you'll find them much easier to say. (Accents almost always fall on the second-to-last syllable.)

The trick is to know where to put on the breaks. That leads me to important tip number two: All syllables end with vowels, so a consonant always indicates the start of a new syllable. An example: The tongue-twisting Kealakekua Bay (the famous marine preserve off the Big Island's Kona coast), which throws nearly everyone for a loop. Break the syllables down by reading the consonants as red flags, though, and see how easy it becomes: kay-ah-lah-keh-*koo*-ah.

Discovering more about the Hawaiian language

If the vocabulary list and pronunciation key in this chapter whet your appetite for the Hawaiian language, a few Web sites can help you discover more. Probably most comprehensive — and the best place to start — is the **Hawaiian Language** Web site (www.geocities.com/~olelo), which is great for beginners.

If you want to translate specific words or terms, use the searchable online dictionaries at the **Coconut Boyz' Hawaiian Dictionary** (www.hisurf.com/hawaiian/dictionary.html) and **Ulukau, the Hawaiian Electronic Library** (www.wehewehe.org).

If you prefer a hard-copy Hawaiian-language reference or dictionary, you can find several at online bookstores, including Arthur Schultz's pocket-size *All About Hawaiian,* and the comprehensive *New Pocket Hawaiian Dictionary,* published by the University of Hawaii and generally considered the standard; you can order it online at www.uhpress.hawaii.edu.

The Hawaiian language actually has a 13th character: the glottal stop, which looks exactly like a single opening quotation mark (') and is meant to indicate a pause. I've chosen not to use the glottal stop throughout this book; it's often left out in printed Hawaiian and on store and street signs. Although serious Hawaiian-language students study volumes about the glottal stop and its equal importance to its fellow consonants and vowels, you don't need to worry about it for your purposes; you can basically ignore it when you see it.

I lay out these basics so that you can understand how the language works, but don't expect to become an expert at pronouncing Hawaiian words anytime soon. Whenever I return to Hawaii, I always feel that it takes me a day or two to get my tongue back in working order — and I *know* this stuff. Still, I have fun practicing — and with these basic tools under your belt, you'll quickly get the hang of it. Practice with *aloha* and *mahalo* and you'll really impress the locals when you get to Maui.

Knowing How to Give and Take Directions

Leave your compass at home, because islanders have a different sense of direction than mainlanders do. Even though locals think of the islands as having north shores and south shores, west coasts and east coasts, seldom does anybody direct you using the most common directional terms.

Instead, they send you either **makai** (ma-*kai*), a directional meaning toward the sea, or **mauka** (*mow*-kah), meaning toward the mountains. Because each island is basically a volcano with a single coastal road circling it, those two terms are often all you need to know. When *makai* and *mauka* don't do the trick, locals are likely to invoke relative terms rather than *north, south, east,* or *west.*

Remembering That You're in the United States

Don't say "back home in the U.S." when you're talking to folks in Maui. This tip seems like a real no-brainer, but that long flight across the Pacific and the one-of-a-kind Hawaii ambience and culture can really play tricks with your mind. Islanders are, by and large, a patriotic bunch, so they don't take kindly to being left off the national map. Refer to the continental United States as the mainland, which is what they do.

Another very important point in the same vein: Locals are always called *islanders,* never *Hawaiians,* unless they're of native blood, which not that many islanders are. (*Hawaiian* is an ethnic label.) Many families who have made their homes in the islands for centuries are of Chinese, Japanese, South Pacific, or even Portuguese decent — or usually some rich generational combination of ethnicities.

Wearing Sunscreen

You don't need a trained eye to spot the newest arrivals — they're lobster-red from their excruciating sunburns. Way too many newcomers fry themselves on day one of their vacations in an overzealous quest to tan, putting a major damper on their trip — and, sometimes, their long-term health — in the process.

Hawaii's sun-loving population has achieved the dubious distinction of having the highest incidence of skin cancer in the United States, and as a result, has developed quite an attachment to sunscreen. Deep-tanning Coppertone days are a thing of the past, so islanders will merely look on in horror rather than admiration if you whip out a bottle of SPF 8 to spread on your just-flown-in virgin skin.

Most locals I know use SPF 25 or SPF 30 sunscreen on a daily basis; you should, too. Never go out in the sun, not even for ten minutes, wearing anything less than SPF 15. Stick with an SPF 30 or SPF 45 if you have a light complexion.

You don't need a high-ticket brand. In fact, I've had some of the best luck with garden-variety drugstore brands (although I do love the California Tan Heliotherapy line). Just find something that works for you and stick with it. Conversely, if you find that a certain sunscreen doesn't jibe with your skin's chemistry, don't lament the $8 you spent; simply toss the bottle and switch to something else before you find yourself burned.

Your best bet is to apply sunscreen — liberally — first thing in the morning, before you get dressed (to avoid missing those inch-below-the-cuff spots, which can result in nasty burns). Apply more sunscreen before you head to the beach, and do regular reapplications (every hour or two) as you sit on the sand, no matter how high the SPF. Don't throw on a T-shirt and consider yourself covered; the average white T-shirt only offers coverage equal to SPF 6 sunscreen. And ignore all claims of "waterproof" — always give yourself a fresh coat immediately after swimming.

Always make sure you apply sunscreen under bathing-suit straps, on the tops of your feet, on the back of your neck, and on your ears and lips — all spots that are the easiest to forget but the most sensitive to painful burns. To prevent sunscreen from dripping into your eyes, use a waxy sunscreen stick around your eyes and a high-SPF lip balm; both are available at just about any Hawaii convenience store.

Additionally, sunglasses and a hat are two more important weapons for fending off the island sun. Throw away those $5 shades and splurge on a decent pair with UV filters to protect your corneas from sunburn and to prevent cataracts. Wear a hat with a wide brim that goes all the way around because baseball caps leave some of your most vulnerable areas — your ears and neck — exposed to the sun's harsh rays.

Infants under 6 months should not be directly exposed to the harsh Hawaii sun. Older babies need zinc oxide to protect their fragile skin, and kids should be slathered with high-SPF sunscreen every hour. They also need shades, hats, and other protective gear.

Dressing the Part

You probably can't think of anything more tacky-touristy than a bold tropical-patterned aloha shirt, right? Wrong!

Invented by an enterprising Honolulu tailor looking for a new way to drum up business in 1936, the aloha shirt has spawned a whole wardrobe of bright, tropical-print clothing for men, women, and children, collectively known as *aloha wear.* In the process, aloha wear has developed into a way of life in the Hawaiian Islands. Spirited, beautiful, easy to wear, and comfortable, aloha wear is the embodiment of the Hawaii lifestyle.

Aloha wear is acceptable just about anywhere in Hawaii, from the beach to the boardroom to the best table at a four-star restaurant. Of course, the key to wearing aloha wear well is understanding the line that separates sublime from goofy — or, in plainer terms, how to tell good aloha wear from bad aloha wear.

You can find aloha wear in any shape, from traditional aloha shirts (wearable by men and women alike) to generous women's muumuus or sexy minidresses. Basically, the key is quality. Silk is top of the line, and great for evening, but skip it for daywear on warm days (when you may perspire). Quality rayon and cotton are terrific alternatives for day and evening.

Look for beautiful, well-designed prints with strong colors and no bleeding. Look for quality buttons (coconut or wood are best but not a must) and pattern matching at the seams and pockets. Excellent brands that offer consistently top-quality aloha wear include **Kahala Sportswear, Kamehameha Garment Co.,** and the **Paradise Found** and **Diamond Head** labels, all of which have revived vintage designs; **Reyn's,** which boasts beautiful patterns in a range of flattering styles, especially for women; **Tommy Bahama's,** whose top-quality clothing lines are generically tropical but suit the Hawaii mood perfectly; and, one of my all-time favorites, **Tori Richard,** which employs some of Hawaii's finest artists to design its patterns. **Sig Zane's** all-cotton aloha wear and accessories are the height of subdued sophistication and nature-inspired beauty. Hilo Hattie is the largest manufacturer and distributor of aloha wear (producing more than 300,000 shirts annually); although Hilo Hattie's stuff isn't the height of aloha fashion, its quality has increased substantially in recent years and it remains very affordable.

The cardinal rule of wearing aloha wear like a local rather than a tourist? No matching. No themed husband-and-wife shirts, no mother-and-daughter muumuus, no two garments on one person in the same pattern. Period.

At some of the high-end resorts or fancier restaurants — the big-money places, the kind that would require a jacket and tie if you were on the mainland — they request that you wear "resort attire." For women, resort attire generally means a long or short dress or coordinating pants and top — more dressy-casual than full dressy, if you know what I mean. For men, it generally translates to pants (not shorts) and a collared shirt. Neatly presented aloha wear always does the trick, of course. (A tiny handful of Maui's most expensive resort restaurants do require men to wear a jacket, but I don't recommend them. Go to Europe if you want to pack a blazer.)

 Don't let a flower lei outstay its welcome. Fresh-flower leis are a short-term treat, enjoyed at the height of their fragrance and beauty and disposed of after the moment has passed. So don't wear old, dying leis; nothing will peg you as a tourist with a capital *T* quite so blatantly. Most leis only last a day — which provides you with the perfect excuse to find a fresh one tomorrow!

Remembering Your Island-Style Manners

In many Eastern cultures, the common practice is to remove your shoes when you enter a private home. Hawaii homeowners follow the same practice — which is one reason why flip-flops and other slip-on-style shoes are so common in the islands. You find that this practice is almost always upheld in bed-and-breakfasts, and even condos may request that you leave your shoes at the door. No one is policing you, of course, but be sure to honor the request.

Islanders pride themselves on their laid-back manner and friendliness, and they really show it in their driving habits — so leave your need for speed at home. Take it easy, don't be in a hurry, and don't honk your horn to chastise other drivers, which islanders consider the height of rudeness. If the car in front of you isn't moving quickly enough or someone cuts you off, just let it slide. Use your car horn to greet friends in Hawaii.

Leaving Your Laptop at Home

Islanders tend to take life nice and easy. The clock doesn't rule them, and they don't like to rush. They call it "island time." Buy into it — lock, stock, and barrel — while you're there. Do as the locals do: Take life as it comes, don't stress if things don't happen with the utmost timeliness, and leave plenty of space in your day to do nothing but appreciate the beauty that surrounds you.

Smiling a Lot and Saying "Aloha" to Strangers

Who knows? You may even get yourself mistaken for a local.

Chapter 20

Ten Ways to Enjoy Maui's Romance

Maui is the place to leave it all behind. Relax and bask in the romance. In this chapter, I give you the ten best ways to forget it all and find Hawaiian happiness no matter how you define romance.

Luxuriating in the Lap of Luxury

Sometimes you just have to indulge yourself — especially if this trip is your honeymoon. Theoretically, you only do this once, so you may as well do it right. If staying in an oceanfront room that lets the sound of the waves lull you to sleep and the caress of the ocean breeze kiss you awake is important to you, or if you've found the luxury B&B of your dreams tucked away in a rain-forest hideaway, don't visit Maui on the cheap. Spend the extra money and make memories.

If you really want to splurge on that ultradeluxe beach resort or a zippy convertible sports car but you're worried about the cost, consider splurging for just *part* of your trip. Book the oceanfront suite or red convertible Mustang for a few days (cruising the road to Hana with the top down is the ultimate Hawaii vacation dream), and make more budget-friendly choices during the rest of your stay (perhaps by moving to a still-romantic but more affordable B&B in Upcountry Maui). You won't regret it, nor will you feel quite so guilty about it after you add up your total costs.

Making Maui Feel Like Paradise at Any Budget

But maybe your budget just doesn't allow for a big splurge. Don't despair — despite all those luxury resorts, Maui doesn't have to be a super-expensive destination.

To find true Hawaii happiness, follow this rule: The simpler, the better. You don't need a flat-screen TV, 24-hour butler service, or a telephone in the bathroom to be content. Some of my happiest times on Maui have been spent sitting on the lanai of a budget condo, watching the sunrise as I sipped home-brewed, Maui-grown coffee and nibbled on fresh papaya bought from a farm stand. Room service and Frette bed linens wouldn't have improved the moment one iota. So you don't have to overdo it — save the extra dough for having fun!

Planning Your Time before You Leave Home

After you've booked your airfare, accommodations, and rental car, you're set until you get to Maui — unless you're dying to partake in some specific activity after you arrive.

If you have your heart set on dining at a particular special-occasion restaurant, catching a highly recommended snorkel cruise, or attending a certain live performance, special event, or luau, make your reservations from home; otherwise, you may miss out, which would be a crying shame.

Certain popular activities, such as the terrific Old Lahaina Luau or Trilogy snorkel cruises, book up weeks in advance, as do tee times at the top golf courses and tables at in-demand restaurants. Make any can't-miss plans before you leave home. See Chapter 8 for more details.

Setting Aside Time for Relaxation

Work plenty of do-nothing time into your plans. Keep your time loose and go with the flow; don't plan your days in the same detailed way you'd map out your itinerary on a grand tour of Europe, with its myriad museums and historical sites.

A romantic getaway to Maui is less about seeing everything and more about leaving the conventions of regular life — including a hard-core commitment to time management — behind. Don't feel guilty that you're not doing or seeing enough. You do enough the other 50 weeks out of the year, don't you?

Enjoying a Heavenly Drive

No Hawaii road is more celebrated than the "heavenly" **Hana Highway** (Highway 36), the super-curvaceous road that winds along Maui's northeastern shore, offering some of the most stunning natural sightseeing in the entire state.

The Hana Highway winds for some 52 miles east from Kahului, crossing more than 50 one-lane bridges, passing greener-than-green taro patches, magnificent seascapes, waterfalls, botanical gardens, and rain forests before passing through the little town of Hana and ultimately ending up in one of Hawaii's most beautiful tropical places: the Kipahulu section of Haleakala National Park. Kipahulu is home to Oheo (oh-*hay*-oh) Gulch, a series of waterfall pools that tumble down to the ocean. Just past the town of Hana is romantic Hamoa Beach. (Learn more about Hamoa in the section "Spending a Day at Maui's Most Romantic Beach.")

Despite the draws at the end of the road, remember that this drive isn't so much about the destination as it is about the journey. The drive takes at least three hours, but allow all day to do it. If you race to arrive in Hana as quickly as you can, you'll be as perplexed as so many others who just don't understand the drive. Start out early, take it slow and easy, stop at scenic points along the way, and let the Hana Road work its magic on you. It will — I promise. In fact, for the ultimate romantic getaway, I suggest staying overnight in Hana (see Chapter 10 for recommendations).

See Chapter 13 for full coverage of the drive, including great stops along the way.

Making Mornings Your Ocean Time

Maui's beaches tend to be less crowded, and the surf and winds tend to be calmer, in the morning hours — particularly in winter. Always take the day's first snorkel and dive cruise, when conditions are calmest and clearest; outfitters don't offer discounts on their afternoon sails either.

Romancing a Day at the Beach

Off the Hana Highway (see earlier in this chapter), about 2½ miles past the town of Hana, **Hamoa Beach** is a remote, romantic spot. This half-moon-shaped beach at Maui's easternmost point is breathtakingly lovely, with surf the color of turquoise, golden-gray sand, and verdant hills providing a postcard-perfect backdrop. The Hotel Hana-Maui likes to maintain the beach as its own, but it has to share, so even if you're not staying at the hotel, feel free to make your way down the steps from the lava-rock lookout point and stake out your spot. If you are staying at the hotel, you'll enjoy a free shuttle ride down the hill and waveside service. The beach is generally good for swimming and wave-riding in the gentle seasons, but stick close to the shore because the ocean is open and unprotected. Stay out of the water entirely in winter, but come to enjoy the glorious setting anyway. The hotel maintains minimal facilities for nonguests, including a restroom.

Toasting the Sunset Every Evening

You can't get closer to the ocean than the alfresco tables at **I'o,** 505 Front St., Lahaina (☎ **808-661-8422;** www.iomaui.com; $$$). Overseen by the award-winning chef James McDonald, I'o is a multifaceted joy, with a winningly innovative, mostly seafood menu, first-rate service, and a top-notch wine list.

My favorite casual Kaanapali restaurant, the **Hula Grill Kaanapali,** in Whaler's Village, 2435 Kaanapali Pkwy. (☎ **808-667-6636;** www.hulapie. com; $$$), serves an excellent steak-and-seafood menu and overflows with quintessential Hawaii charm. The indoor/outdoor setting on the sand is ideal for sunset-watchers; tiki torches make the after-dark hours magical as well. Diners on a budget can stick to the bar menu ($) without losing out on ambience.

Despite the high prices, I just love **Mama's Fish House,** just off the Hana Highway, at 799 Poho Place, Paia (☎ **808-579-8488;** www.mamasfish house.com; $$$$$). The fresh fish is as fabulous as it can be, and the beachfront tiki-room setting is quintessential romantic Hawaii. The lengthy list of tropical drinks (with umbrellas!) puts you right in the mood. My favorite restaurant on the island, hands down.

Mala, an Ocean Tavern, 1307 Front St., Lahaina (☎ **808-667-9394;** www. malaoceantavern.com; $$$–$$$$), makes sunset a somewhat more affordable, but no less spectacular, celebration. The tiki torch–lit terrace is so close to the surf that you may just feel the sea spray kiss your cheek when the wind kicks up. This is such a marvelous spot that green sea turtles regularly hang out in the shallows here — apparently, they know how satisfying the food and ambience are, too.

Sarento's on the Beach, 2980 S. Kihei Rd., Kihei (☎ **808-875-7555;** www. tristarrestaurants.com; $$$$–$$$$$), seamlessly fuses white-linen elegance and white-sand romance, making this sophisticated Italian-Mediterranean outpost a wonderful place to celebrate the majesty of a Maui sunset every evening. If you don't want to splurge on dinner, take a seat in the sexy bar to revel in a pair of perfectly poured cocktails and stupendous sunset views.

Dining in Style

'   Dubbed "Maui's little French jewel" by *Bon Appétit,* **Gerard's,** in the Plantation Inn, 174 Lahainaluna Rd., Lahaina (☎ **808-661-8939;** www. gerardsmaui.com; $$$$$), is an excellent choice for couples in love. Gerard's may be the perfect special-occasion restaurant; the garden patio tables are the prime place to woo.

Lahaina Grill, 127 Lahainaluna Rd., Lahaina (☎ **808-667-5117;** www. lahainagrill.com; $$$$–$$$$$), is consistently voted "Best of Maui" for good reason; it repeatedly offers a faultless dining experience. (Last time I was here, a honeymooning couple sitting next to me reported that they loved Lahaina Grill so much that they dined here three times in the week they were on Maui.) Expect distinctive New American flavors that are bold without being overpowering. The dining room is stylish yet delightfully homey, and the expert service is a nice change of pace from the usual Maui surfer style.

Sonz Maui at Swan Court, at the Hyatt Regency Maui Resort & Spa, 200 Nohea Kai Dr., Kaanapali (☎ **808-667-4506;** www.sonzmaui.com; $$$$$), is a welcome recent addition to the West Maui dining scene, thanks to its warmly romantic setting, first-rate service, and genuinely innovative Hawaii Regional Cuisine that makes the most of Maui's local bounty. Classic European twists add both heartwarming comfort and delightful surprises. One of the island's finest wine lists is the cherry on this very pleasing cake.

Haliimaile General Store, 900 Haliimaile Rd., Haliimaile (☎ **808-572-2666;** www.bevgannonrestaurants.com; $$$$), continues to deliver one of Hawaii's finest all-around dining experiences. The top-quality, island-style cooking of Chef Bev Gannon, the queen bee of Hawaii Regional Cuisine, is joyfully presented in a refreshingly casual and pretension-free, plantation-style setting. A delight from start to finish, it's well worth the drive Upcountry for couples in search of a casually romantic experience. See Chapter 12.

Capische?, in the Diamond Hawaii Resort & Spa, 555 Kaukahi St., Wailea (☎ **808-879-2224.** www.capische.com; $$$$$), is my first choice for romance in South Maui. This top-quality Mediterranean-Italian spot is in a fabulous alfresco setting with dreamily panoramic views of the South Maui coast, plus a delightfully indulgent menu that will make you feel as though you've dined somewhere truly special.

Joe's Bar & Grill, at the Wailea Tennis Center, 131 Wailea Ike Dr., Wailea (☎ **808-875-**7767; www.bevgannonrestaurants.com; $$$$), is another wonderful South Maui choice. Joe's serves a pleasing menu of upscale American home cooking with island twists, and low lighting and well-spaced tables make for a surprisingly romantic ambience after dark.

For a complete listing of all the restaurants I recommend, see Chapter 11.

Mellowing Out Like a Local

Islanders tend to take life nice and easy. A clock doesn't rule them, and they don't like to rush. They call it "island time." While you're in Maui, do as the locals do: Take life as it comes. Don't stress if things don't happen with the utmost timeliness. And leave plenty of space in your day for you and your beloved to do nothing but appreciate the beauty that surrounds you.

You probably already know the Hawaiian word *aloha,* which serves as an all-purpose greeting — hello, welcome, or goodbye. But what it really means is "love" — and that's the whole purpose of your visit to Hawaii, isn't it? *Aloha* is a warm and wonderful word, full of grace, compassion, and good feeling, so use it liberally; I can't think of a better way to get caught up in Hawaii's true spirit.

Quick Concierge

● ●

Fast Facts

American Automobile Association (AAA)

Although roadside service is available on Maui, the only AAA office in Hawaii is on Oahu at 1130 Nimitz Hwy., Honolulu (☎ 800-736-2886 from Maui; www.aaa-hawaii.com). The office is open Monday through Friday from 9 a.m. to 5 p.m. and Saturday from 9 a.m. to 2 p.m.

For information on becoming a member before you leave home, call ☎ 800-AAA-HELP (800-222-4357) or point your Web browser to www.aaa.com, where you'll be linked to your regional club's home page by entering your zip code. See Chapter 4 for details on the many benefits of AAA membership.

American Express

The only American Express office on Maui is located in Kaanapali at the Westin Maui, 2365 Kaanapali Pkwy. (☎ 808-661-7155).

Cardholders and traveler's-check holders should call ☎ 800-528-4800 or 800-221-7282 for all money emergencies. To make inquiries with American Express Travel or to locate other branch offices, call ☎ 800-AXP-TRIP (800-297-8747). For more information, visit www.americanexpress.com.

Area Code

All the Hawaiian Islands are in the **808** area code. Note that if you're calling another island from Maui, you must dial 1-808 first, and you'll be billed at long-distance rates

(which can be more expensive than calling the mainland, so be sure to use a long-distance calling card if your cellphone package doesn't come with free long-distance). You can leave off the area code when you're on Maui and calling another Maui number.

ATMs

All the major resort areas on Maui have plenty of ATMs. Branches of Hawaii's most popular banks are plentiful, and all are connected to the major global ATM networks. Most supermarkets also have ATMs inside (though these may charge a higher fee). Do yourself a favor and don't set off for a remote area (say, Upcountry or Hana) without stocking up on cash first: I also recommend taking the same approach if you visit the islands of Molokai or Lanai. These areas do have ATMs, but why waste your precious vacation time tracking them down?

One of Hawaii's most popular banks, with branches throughout the state, is Bank of Hawaii, which is linked with all the major worldwide networks. To find the one nearest you, call ☎ 888-643-3888 or point your Web browser to www.boh.com and click Locations in the upper navigational bar. If you don't find one near you, try First Hawaiian Bank (www.fhb.com). You can also find ATMs on the MasterCard/Maestro/ Cirrus network by dialing ☎ 800-424-7787 or going online to www.mastercard.com;

to find a Visa/Plus ATM, call ☎ 800-843-7587 or visit www.visa.com and then click the ATM locator at the bottom of the start page.

Baby Sitters and Baby Stuff

Any hotel or condo can refer you to a reliable baby sitter with a proven track record. If yours can't, contact Happy Kids (☎ 888-669-1991 or 808-667-5437; www.happykidsmaui.com), The Nanny Connection (☎ 808-875-4777 or 808-667-5777; www.thenannyconnection.com), or Nana Enterprises (☎ 888-584-6262 or 808-879-6262; www.nanaenterprises.com). Baby's Away (☎ 800-942-9030 or 808-875-9030; www.babysaway.com) rents cribs, strollers, highchairs, playpens, infant seats, and the like; they deliver whatever you need to wherever you're staying, and pick it up when you're done.

Business Hours

Most offices are open from 8 a.m. to 5 p.m. The morning commute usually runs from 6 to 8 a.m., and the evening rush is from 4 to 6 p.m. Bank hours are Monday through Thursday 8:30 a.m. to 3 p.m. and Friday 8:30 a.m. to 6 p.m.; some banks are open on Saturday. Shopping centers are open Monday through Friday 10 a.m. to 9 p.m., Saturday 10 a.m. to 5:30 p.m., and Sunday noon to 5 or 6 p.m.

Credit Cards

If your Visa card is lost or stolen, call ☎ 800-847-2911 or 410-581-9994. MasterCard holders should call ☎ 800-307-7309 or 800-627-8372. American Express cardholders should call ☎ 800-268-9824 or 800-528-4800 (for cardholders) and ☎ 800-221-7282 (for traveler's check holders).

Dentists

Emergency dental care is available at Aloha Lahaina Dentists, 134 Luakini St., Lahaina (☎ 808-661-4405). If you're in South Maui, call Kihei Dental Center, 1847 S. Kihei Rd. (☎ 808-874-8401; www.hawaiifamilydental.com). In Central Maui, contact Hawaii Family Dental Center, Kahului Center, Lono Center, 95 Lono Ave., Suite 210 Kahului (☎ 808-877-5328; www.hawaiifamilydental.com).

Doctors

West Maui Healthcare Center, Whalers Village, 2435 Kaanapali Pkwy., 2nd Floor, behind Leilani's, Kaanapali (☎ 808-667-9721), takes walk-ins daily 8 a.m. to 9 p.m.; note that there is an additional charge for visits after 6 p.m. Doctors on Call (☎ 808-667-7676) takes appointments at the Hyatt Regency in Lahaina, at the Westin Maui in Kaanapali, and at the Ritz-Carlton in Kapalua.

In Kihei, call Urgent Care Maui, 1325 S. Kihei Rd., Suite 103 (at Lipoa Street, across the street from Star Market), Kihei (☎ 808-879-7781), open daily from 7 a.m. to 10 p.m.; doctors are also on call after hours.

If you need medical attention while you're out in Hana, contact the Hana Community Health Center, 4590 Hana Hwy. (☎ 808-248-8294).

Your hotel's concierge or front-desk staff should also be able to direct you to a reliable doctor in the immediate area, should you need one.

Emergencies

Dial ☎ 911 from any phone, just like back home.

Etiquette

Hawaii's customs are much like those on the mainland, but take notice of a few small differences.

In Hawaii, remove your shoes before entering anyone's home. Most bed-and-breakfasts are likely to make the same request of you.

Aloha wear is perfectly acceptable (and wonderfully festive) formal wear in the islands. There's no need to bring more formal wear to the islands. If you prefer something more subdued, resort casual (such as a polo shirt and trousers for men, warm-weather dresses or pants and top for women) is appropriate even in the finest resorts and restaurants.

When you're driving, don't honk your horn in frustration. Chill out like the locals; honking to hurry someone along or to express anger is considered rude. Islanders only honk to greet friends.

Don't say, "Back home in the U.S. . . ." Most folks refer to the lower 48 as the mainland.

Holidays

In addition to the same national holidays observed in the rest of the United States, Hawaii celebrates a few other special days: Prince Kuhio Day (Mar 26), King Kamehameha Day (June 11), and Statehood Day, sometimes called Admission Day (the third Fri in Aug). All government offices are closed, and some local businesses may close as well, so plan accordingly. See the calendar of events in Chapter 3 for a full rundown of Maui's special celebrations.

Hospitals

Around-the-clock emergency care is available from Maui Memorial Medical Center, 221 Mahalani St., Wailuku (☎ **808-244-9056;** www.mmmc.hhsc.org), in Central Maui. This is the island's only full-service hospital.

Information

The Maui Visitors Bureau is located in Central Maui at 1727 Wili Pa Loop, Wailuku, HI 96793 (☎ 800-525-6284 or 808-244-3530; www.visitmaui.com), but it's not really designed as a walk-in office. Call before you leave home to order your free Maui travel planner or check the Web site for a wealth of good information.

Some of Maui's resort areas have dedicated visitor associations that provide information, including the Kaanapali Beach Resort Association (☎ 808-661-3271; www.kaanapaliresort.com) and the Kapalua Resort (☎ 800-527-2482; www.kapaluamaui.com). For official national park information, contact Haleakala National Park (☎ 808-572-4400; www.nps.gov/hale).

After you land at Kahului Airport, stop over at the state-operated Visitor Information Center while you're waiting for your baggage and pick up a copy of *This Week Maui, 101 Things to Do on Maui,* and other free tourist publications, many with great maps of the island. If you forget, don't worry — you can find them at malls and shopping centers around the island.

In addition, all the big resort hotels are overflowing with printed info. Even if your hotel or condo doesn't have a dedicated concierge, the staff can point you in the right direction, make recommendations, and give advice.

For information on the island of Molokai, contact the Molokai Visitors Association, located at the Moore Center, 2 Kamoi St., Suite 200, Kaunakakai, HI 96748 (☎ 800-800-6367 or 808-553-3876; www.molokai-hawaii.com).

For information on the island of Lanai, contact Destination Lanai (☎ 800-947-4774; www.visitlanai.net).

Internet Access

Almost all hotels offer wireless or wired Internet access that you can connect to using your personal computer; the price of access can range from complimentary to $15 or $20 a day. Most bed-and-breakfasts and condos even offer Internet access these days. Check with your hotel in advance to see what your options are. Brand-name hotels usually have business centers where you can check your e-mail on one of their computers; often access is free unless you want to print, but call ahead to confirm if it matters, as a few still do charge.

Liquor Laws

The legal drinking age in Hawaii is 21. Beer, wine, and liquor are sold in grocery and convenience stores at any hour, seven days a week. It's technically illegal to have an open container on the beach. Bars stay open until 2 a.m.; places with cabaret licenses are able to keep the booze flowing until 4 a.m. Grocery and convenience stores are allowed to sell beer, wine, and liquor seven days a week.

Maps

AAA supplies excellent free maps of Hawaii to members only. For more information on becoming a member, see Chapter 4.

All rental-car companies hand out good free map booklets of Maui to navigate your way around, as do the free visitor publications available around the island.

If you want more complete topographic maps of each island, the best are printed by the University of Hawaii Press. They're available from just about any bookstore in the islands. If you want to order them before you leave home, contact Basically Books, 160 Kamehameha Ave., Hilo, HI 96720 (☎ 800-903-6277 or 808-961-0144; www.basicallybooks.com). Or go straight to the source and order them directly from the UH Press (www.uhpress.hawaii.edu).

Newspapers/Magazines

The *Maui News* (www.mauinews.com) is the island's daily paper; the Web site can provide you with a great source of information before you leave home. Additionally, a number of free newspaper weeklies, such as *Maui Time* and the *Maui Weekly*, are available from racks around town.

If you're interested in the performing arts, look for a copy of *Centerpiece,* the free bimonthly magazine published by the Maui Arts and Cultural Center. Hotel concierges usually have copies.

Hawaii magazine is a glossy monthly that's targeted to visitors; it offers a good introduction to the islands. You can usually find the current issue in the travel magazine section at your local branch of the big chain bookstores, such as Borders and Barnes & Noble.

The *Honolulu Advertiser* (www.honoluluadvertiser.com) and the *Honolulu Star-Bulletin* (www.starbulletin.com) are the two statewide daily newspapers.

Ocean Safety

Keep these snorkel tips in mind as you don your fins and head into the water:

Always snorkel with a friend and keep an eye on each other.

Look up every few minutes to get your bearings. Check your position in relation to the shoreline and check whether there's any boat traffic.

Don't touch anything. Not only can your fingers and feet damage coral, but it can give you nasty cuts. Moreover, camouflaged fish and spiny shells may surprise you.

Before you set out, check surf conditions by calling one of the local dive or snorkel shops, which can give you the latest on local conditions and recommend alternative spots if the prime ones are too rough for snorkeling.

Pharmacies

Longs Drugs (www.longs.com), Hawaii's biggest drugstore chain, has a branch in Central Maui at the Maui Mall, 70 Kaahumanu Ave. (between Puunene Avenue and the Hana Highway), Kahului (☎ 808-877-0041). If you're in West Maui, head to the branch at Lahaina Cannery Mall, 1221 Honoapiilani Hwy. (between Kapunkea and Kenui streets), Lahaina (☎ 808-667-4384). In South Maui, head to Longs Kihei Center, 1215 S. Kihei Rd. (just north of Lipoa Street), Kihei (☎ 808-879-2259).

Police

The main headquarters of the Maui Police Department is in Wailuku at 55 Mahalani St., near Maui Memorial Medical Center (☎ 808-244-6300). District stations are located next to the Lahaina Civic Center, 1760 Honoapiilani Hwy., on the mountain side of the highway, just north of Lahaina (☎ 808-661-4441), and in Hana on the Hana Highway, near Ua Kea Road (☎ 808-248-8311). Of course, if you have an emergency, dial ☎ 911 from any phone.

Post Offices

In West Maui, a big branch office is next to the Lahaina Civic Center at 1760 Honoapiilani Hwy. between Kaanapali and Lahaina (on the mountain side of the highway; it's easy to spot; ☎ 808-661-8227), and in downtown Lahaina adjacent to the Lahaina Shopping Center, 132 Papalaua St. (between Front and Wainee streets; ☎ 808-661-0904).

In South Maui, you find a post office at 1254 S. Kihei Rd., across the street from Longs Kihei Center (☎ 808-874-9143).

Satellite post offices are located around the island, as well as on Molokai and Lanai; to find the one nearest you, call ☎ 800-275-8777 or visit www.usps.com.

Safety

Although Hawaii is generally quite safe, visitors have been crime victims, so stay alert. The most common crime against tourists is rental-car break-ins. *Never* leave any valuables in your car, not even in your trunk. Thieves can be in and out of your trunk faster than you can open it with your own key.

Be especially careful at high-risk areas, such as beaches and remote areas. Never carry large amounts of cash with you. Stay in well-lighted areas after dark. Don't hike on deserted trails alone.

See Chapter 12 for tips on ocean safety and more. Chapter 8 has additional tips on staying healthy when you travel.

Smoking

In Hawaii, smoking is against the law in all enclosed public spaces, period, including bars and restaurants. In addition, no smoking is allowed within 20 feet of doorways, windows, or ventilation intakes. Hotels are allowed to reserve 20 percent of their rooms for smokers, as long as they're clustered on the same floor; notable exceptions include Westin and Marriott hotels, which are now 100 percent smoke free, as are most B&Bs. Car-rental agencies also have mostly smoke-free cars; if you want a car you can smoke in, it's best to note it when you make your reservation.

Taxes

Most purchases in Hawaii are taxed at roughly 4 percent; the exact amount will vary depending on the county you're in and may be embedded in the total purchase price or shown as an independent line item on your bill. Expect taxes of about 11.42 percent to be added to your hotel bill.

Taxis

Call Maui Airport Taxi (☎ 808-281-9533; www.nokaoitaxi.com), Kihei Taxi (☎ 808-879-3000), Wailea Taxi (☎ 808-874-5000), or Maui Taxi Service (☎ 808-276-9515; www.mauipleasanttaxi.com). The mandated fare on Maui is $3 per mile, accommodating up to six people.

Time

Hawaii standard time is in effect year-round. Hawaii is two hours behind Pacific standard time and five hours behind eastern standard time. In other words, when it's noon in Hawaii, it's 2 p.m. in California and 5 p.m. in New York during standard time on the mainland.

Hawaii doesn't observe daylight saving time, so when daylight saving time is in effect on the mainland, Hawaii is three hours behind the West Coast and six hours behind the East Coast — so in summer, when it's noon in Hawaii, it's 3 p.m. in California and 6 p.m. in New York.

Hawaii is east of the International Date Line, putting it on the same day as the U.S. mainland and Canada, and a day behind Australia, New Zealand, and Asia.

For the exact local time, call ☎ 808-643-8463.

Traffic Laws

Hawaii is a no-fault insurance state. If you drive without collision-damage insurance, you're required to pay for all damages before you leave the state, regardless of who is at fault. Your personal auto policy may provide rental-car coverage; read your policy or check with your insurer before you leave home and bring your insurance ID card if you decline the rental-car company's optional insurance. Some credit-card companies also provide collision damage insurance; check with yours.

Seatbelts are mandatory for everyone in the car, all the time, and children under 4 must be strapped into car seats.

You can turn right on red unless a posted sign specifies otherwise.

Pedestrians always have the right of way, even if they're not in a crosswalk

Weather and Surf Reports

For Maui's current weather and forecasts, call ☎ 866-944-5025, which also supplies sunrise and sunset times. For wind and surf reports, call ☎ 808-877-3611.

For statewide marine reports, call ☎ 808-973-4382. For statewide coastal wind reports, call ☎ 808-973-6114.

To check the weather forecasts online, log on to www.hawaiiweathertoday.com. I like to compare forecasts, so you might also check the Weather Channel's site at www.weather.com or CNN's weather page at www.cnn.com/weather, both of which offer multiday forecasts for hundreds of destinations around the globe. You can find the official National Weather Service forecast for the Hawaiian Islands online at www.prh.noaa.gov/pr/hnl.

Toll-Free Numbers and Web Sites

Airlines

Air Canada
☎ 888-247-2262
www.aircanada.com

Air New Zealand
☎ 800-262-1234 in the U.S.
☎ 800-663-5494 in Canada
☎ 0800-737-000 in New Zealand
www.airnewzealand.com

Alaska Airlines
☎ 800-252-7522
www.alaskaair.com

American Airlines
☎ 800-433-7300
www.aa.com

Continental Airlines
☎ 800-523-3273
www.continental.com

Delta Air Lines
☎ 800-221-1212
www.delta.com

go!
☎ 888-IFLYGO2 (888-435-9462)
www.iflygo.com

Hawaiian Airlines
☎ 800-367-5320
www.hawaiianair.com

Island Air
☎ 800-652-6541
www.islandair.com

Northwest Airlines
☎ 800-225-2525
www.nwa.com

Pacific Wings Airlines
☎ 888-575-4546
www.pacificwings.com

Qantas
☎ 800-227-4500 in the U.S.
☎ 13-13-13 in Australia
www.qantas.com

Southwest Airlines
☎ 800-435-9792
www.southwest.com

United Airlines
☎ 800-864-8331
www.united.com

US Airways
☎ 800-428-4322
www.usairways.com

WestJet
☎ 888-937-8538
www.westjet.com

Major hotel and motel chains

Best Western International
☎ 800-780-7234
www.bestwestern.com

Castle Resorts and Hotels
☎ 800-367-5004
www.castleresorts.com

Choice Hotels International
☎ 877-424-6423
www.hotelchoice.com

Classic Resorts
☎ 800-642-6284
www.classicresorts.com

Doubletree Hotels
☎ 800-222-8733
www.doubletree.com

Four Seasons Hotels and Resorts
☎ 800-819-5053
www.fourseasons.com

Hilton Hotels
☎ 800-HILTONS (800-445-8667)
www.hilton.com

Hyatt Hotels and Resorts
☎ 888-591-1234
www.hyatt.com

Marc Resorts Hawaii
☎ 800-535-0085
www.marcresorts.com

Marriott Hotels
☎ 888-236-2427
www.marriott.com

Ohana Hotels
☎ 800-462-6262
www.ohanahotels.com

Outrigger Hotels and Resorts
☎ 800-OUTRIGGER (800-688-7444)
www.outrigger.com

Premier Resorts
☎ 888-774-3533
www.premier-resorts.com

Prince Resorts Hawaii
☎ 888-9-PRINCE (888-977-4623)
www.princeresortshawaii.com

Radisson Hotels International
☎ 1-888-201-1718
www.radisson.com

Renaissance Hotels and Resorts
☎ 1-888-236-2427
www.renaissancehotels.com

ResortQuest
☎ 800-GO-RELAX (800-467-3529)
www.resortquest.com

Ritz-Carlton
☎ 800-542-8680
www.ritzcarlton.com

Sheraton Hotels and Resorts
☎ 866-716-8140
www.starwoodhotelshawaii.com

Starwood's Luxury Collection
☎ 800-325-3589
www.luxurycollection.com

W Hotels
☎ 877-946-8357
www.whotels.com

Westin Hotels
☎ 800-937-8461
www.westin.com

Car-rental agencies

Alamo
☎ 800 GO ALAMO (800-462-5266)
www.alamo.com

Avis
☎ 800-331-1212
www.avis.com

Budget
☎ 800-527-0700
www.budget.com

Dollar
☎ 800-800-4000
www.dollarcar.com

Enterprise
☎ 800-261-7331
www.enterprise.com

Hertz
☎ 800-654-3131
www.hertz.com

National
☎ 800-227-7368
www.nationalcar.com

Thrifty
☎ 800-847-4389
www.thrifty.com

Where to Get More Information

Destination Lanai
☎ 800-947-4774
www.visitlanai.net

Haleakala National Park
P.O. Box 369
Makawao, HI 96768
☎ 808-572-4400
www.nps.gov/hale

Hawaii Visitors and Convention Bureau (HVCB)
2270 Kalakaua Ave., Suite 801
Honolulu, HI 96815
☎ 800-464-2924
www.gohawaii.com

Kaanapali Beach Resort Association
222 Papalaua St, Ste 208
Lahaina, Maui, HI 96761
☎ 888-661-3271 or 808-661-3271
www.kaanapaliresort.com

Kapalua Resort
800 Kapalua Dr.
Kapalua, HI 96761
☎ 800-KAPALUA (800-527-2582)
www.kapaluamaui.com

Maui Visitors Bureau (also provides information on Molokai and Lanai)
1727 Wili Pa Loop
Wailuku, Maui, HI 96793
☎ 800-525-6284 or 808-244-3530
www.visitmaui.com

Maui.net
www.maui.net

Molokai Visitors Association
The Moore Center
2 Kamoi St., Suite 200
Kaunakakai, HI 96748
☎ 800-800-6367 or 808-553-3876
www.molokai-hawaii.com

Planet Hawaii
737 Bishop St., Suite 1900
Honolulu, HI 96813
☎ 877-91-ALOHA (877-912-5642) or 808-791-1000
www.planet-hawaii.com

Index

• *N* •

Accommodations Index

Restaurant Index

Notes

· ·

BUSINESS, CAREERS & PERSONAL FINANCE

Accounting For Dummies, 4th Edition* 978-0-470-24600-9	**E-Mail Marketing For Dummies** 978-0-470-19087-6	**Six Sigma For Dummies** 978-0-7645-6798-8
Bookkeeping Workbook For Dummies† 978-0-470-16983-4	**Job Interviews For Dummies, 3rd Edition*†** 978-0-470-17748-8	**Small Business Kit For Dummies, 2nd Edition*†** 978-0-7645-5984-6
Commodities For Dummies 978-0-470-04928-0	**Personal Finance Workbook For Dummies*†** 978-0-470-09933-9	**Telephone Sales For Dummies** 978-0-470-16836-3
Doing Business in China For Dummies 978-0-470-04929-7	**Real Estate License Exams For Dummies** 978-0-7645-7623-2	

BUSINESS PRODUCTIVITY & MICROSOFT OFFICE

Access 2007 For Dummies 978-0-470-03649-5	**PowerPoint 2007 For Dummies** 978-0-470-04059-1	**Quicken 2008 For Dummies** 978-0-470-17473-9
Excel 2007 For Dummies 978-0-470-03737-9	**Project 2007 For Dummies** 978-0-470-03651-8	**Salesforce.com For Dummies, 2nd Edition** 978-0-470-04893-1
Office 2007 For Dummies 978-0-470-00923-9	**QuickBooks 2008 For Dummies** 978-0-470-18470-7	**Word 2007 For Dummies** 978-0-470-03658-7
Outlook 2007 For Dummies 978-0-470-03830-7		

EDUCATION, HISTORY, REFERENCE & TEST PREPARATION

African American History For Dummies 978-0-7645-5469-8	**ASVAB For Dummies, 2nd Edition** 978-0-470-10671-6	**Geometry Workbook For Dummies** 978-0-471-79940-5
Algebra For Dummies 978-0-7645-5325-7	**British Military History For Dummies** 978-0-470-03213-8	**The SAT I For Dummies, 6th Edition** 978-0-7645-7193-0
Algebra Workbook For Dummies 978-0-7645-8467-1	**Calculus For Dummies** 978-0-7645-2498-1	**Series 7 Exam For Dummies** 978-0-470-09932-2
Art History For Dummies 978-0-470-09910-0	**Canadian History For Dummies, 2nd Edition** 978-0-470-83656-9	**World History For Dummies** 978-0-7645-5242-7

FOOD, GARDEN, HOBBIES & HOME

Bridge For Dummies, 2nd Edition 978-0-471-92426-5	**Drawing For Dummies** 978-0-7645-5476-6	**Knitting Patterns For Dummies** 978-0-470-04556-5
Coin Collecting For Dummies, 2nd Edition 978-0-470-22275-1	**Etiquette For Dummies, 2nd Edition** 978-0-470-10672-3	**Living Gluten-Free For Dummies†** 978-0-471-77383-2
Cooking Basics For Dummies, 3rd Edition 978-0-7645-7206-7	**Gardening Basics For Dummies*†** 978-0-470-03749-2	**Painting Do-It-Yourself For Dummies** 978-0-470-17533-0

HEALTH, SELF HELP, PARENTING & PETS

Anger Management For Dummies 978-0-470-03715-7	**Horseback Riding For Dummies** 978-0-470-09719-9	**Puppies For Dummies, 2nd Edition** 978-0-470-03717-1
Anxiety & Depression Workbook For Dummies 978-0-7645-9793-0	**Infertility For Dummies†** 978-0-470-11518-3	**Thyroid For Dummies, 2nd Edition†** 978-0-471-78755-6
Dieting For Dummies, 2nd Edition 978-0-7645-4149-0	**Meditation For Dummies with CD-ROM, 2nd Edition** 978-0-471-77774-8	**Type 1 Diabetes For Dummies*†** 978-0-470-17811-9
Dog Training For Dummies, 2nd Edition 978-0-7645-8418-3	**Post-Traumatic Stress Disorder For Dummies** 978-0-470-04922-8	

INTERNET & DIGITAL MEDIA

AdWords For Dummies
978-0-470-15252-2

Blogging For Dummies, 2nd Edition
978-0-470-23017-6

Digital Photography All-in-One
Desk Reference For Dummies, 3rd Edition
978-0-470-03743-0

Digital Photography For Dummies, 5th Edition
978-0-7645-9802-9

Digital SLR Cameras & Photography
For Dummies, 2nd Edition
978-0-470-14927-0

eBay Business All-in-One Desk Reference
For Dummies
978-0-7645-8438-1

eBay For Dummies, 5th Edition*
978-0-470-04529-9

eBay Listings That Sell For Dummies
978-0-471-78912-3

Facebook For Dummies
978-0-470-26273-3

The Internet For Dummies, 11th Edition
978-0-470-12174-0

Investing Online For Dummies, 5th Edition
978-0-7645-8456-5

iPod & iTunes For Dummies, 5th Edition
978-0-470-17474-6

MySpace For Dummies
978-0-470-09529-4

Podcasting For Dummies
978-0-471-74898-4

Search Engine Optimization
For Dummies, 2nd Edition
978-0-471-97998-2

Second Life For Dummies
978-0-470-18025-9

Starting an eBay Business For Dummies,
3rd Edition†
978-0-470-14924-9

GRAPHICS, DESIGN & WEB DEVELOPMENT

Adobe Creative Suite 3 Design Premium
All-in-One Desk Reference For Dummies
978-0-470-11724-8

Adobe Web Suite CS3 All-in-One Desk
Reference For Dummies
978-0-470-12099-6

AutoCAD 2008 For Dummies
978-0-470-11650-0

Building a Web Site For Dummies,
3rd Edition
978-0-470-14928-7

Creating Web Pages All-in-One Desk
Reference For Dummies, 3rd Edition
978-0-470-09629-1

Creating Web Pages For Dummies,
8th Edition
978-0-470-08030-6

Dreamweaver CS3 For Dummies
978-0-470-11490-2

Flash CS3 For Dummies
978-0-470-12100-9

Google SketchUp For Dummies
978-0-470-13744-4

InDesign CS3 For Dummies
978-0-470-11865-8

Photoshop CS3 All-in-One
Desk Reference For Dummies
978-0-470-11195-6

Photoshop CS3 For Dummies
978-0-470-11193-2

Photoshop Elements 5 For Dummies
978-0-470-09810-3

SolidWorks For Dummies
978-0-7645-9555-4

Visio 2007 For Dummies
978-0-470-08983-5

Web Design For Dummies, 2nd Edition
978-0-471-78117-2

Web Sites Do-It-Yourself For Dummies
978-0-470-16903-2

Web Stores Do-It-Yourself For Dummies
978-0-470-17443-2

LANGUAGES, RELIGION & SPIRITUALITY

Arabic For Dummies
978-0-471-77270-5

Chinese For Dummies, Audio Set
978-0-470-12766-7

French For Dummies
978-0-7645-5193-2

German For Dummies
978-0-7645-5195-6

Hebrew For Dummies
978-0-7645-5489-6

Ingles Para Dummies
978-0-7645-5427-8

Italian For Dummies, Audio Set
978-0-470-09586-7

Italian Verbs For Dummies
978-0-471-77389-4

Japanese For Dummies
978-0-7645-5429-2

Latin For Dummies
978-0-7645-5431-5

Portuguese For Dummies
978-0-471-78738-9

Russian For Dummies
978-0-471-78001-4

Spanish Phrases For Dummies
978-0-7645-7204-3

Spanish For Dummies
978-0-7645-5194-9

Spanish For Dummies, Audio Set
978-0-470-09585-0

The Bible For Dummies
978-0-7645-5296-0

Catholicism For Dummies
978-0-7645-5391-2

The Historical Jesus For Dummies
978-0-470-16785-4

Islam For Dummies
978-0-7645-5503-9

Spirituality For Dummies,
2nd Edition
978-0-470-19142-2

NETWORKING AND PROGRAMMING

ASP.NET 3.5 For Dummies
978-0-470-19592-5

C# 2008 For Dummies
978-0-470-19109-5

Hacking For Dummies, 2nd Edition
978-0-470-05235-8

Home Networking For Dummies, 4th Edition
978-0-470-11806-1

Java For Dummies, 4th Edition
978-0-470-08716-9

Microsoft® SQL Server™ 2008 All-in-One
Desk Reference For Dummies
978-0-470-17954-3

Networking All-in-One Desk Reference
For Dummies, 2nd Edition
978-0-7645-9939-2

Networking For Dummies,
8th Edition
978-0-470-05620-2

SharePoint 2007 For Dummies
978-0-470-09941-4

Wireless Home Networking
For Dummies, 2nd Edition
978-0-471-74940-0